MAKING PEACE

The role played by the Community of Sant'Egidio in the international arena

edited by Roberto Morozzo della Rocca

New City

Translated from the italian original *Fare Pace*
© 2010, Leonardo International s.r.l.

Translated by John Milfsud

First published in Great Britain by
New City
Unit 17, Sovereign Park, Coronation Road
London NW10 7QP
© 2013, New City, London

Cover design an graphics by Hildeberando Moguiê

British cataloguing in Publication Data: A catalogue reference
for this book is available from The British Library

ISBN: 978-1-905039-18-0

Typeset by New City
Printed in Malta by Gutenberg Press

MAKING PEACE

Contents

INTRODUCTION

Andrea Riccardi

This book brings together several anecdotes of peace and the quest for peace in situations of conflict. They are accounts of events from the last twenty years which show that, even in desperate and complicated conditions, peace is achieved through dialogue, the search for common ground, mediation and agreement. The thread that unites these stories – largely, though not exclusively, involving African countries – is the Community of Sant'Egidio. This book illustrates the role played by Sant'Egidio on the frontiers of war, whilst at the same time providing a closer look at various – often bloody – conflicts that have marked our times.

They are stories of war and peace that enable us to gain a more intimate understanding of the international panorama since the end of the Cold War. At that time, it was hoped that a great peace would emerge. This, however, did not happen. Instead, to use Huntington's terminology, clashes of civilizations and religions arose, whilst civil and ethnic conflicts continued – to say nothing of the outbreak of new ones. Against this backdrop, which did not match the expectations of 1989, peace nevertheless proved possible in various situations. So how did this happen? And in what ways did these stories of hope unfold? The answer lies in the story of the Community of Sant'Egidio since the end of the 1980s.

A unique international actor

Sant'Egidio is a very unique kind of "international actor". It is not an international organization, nor is it an NGO specializing in mediation; it is not a non-governmental agency, nor an offshoot of any government. It is a Christian community, established in Rome in 1968, known for its work among poorer people and those in situations of extreme poverty throughout the world. Over the years, it has become a fraternity (or, if you will, an international network) of communities firmly established in various countries around the world, in Europe to begin with, and then in the Americas, Asia, and particularly Africa. The question remains, however, how it is that a Christian community has managed to conduct peacemaking activities in various parts of the world between the late 20th century and the beginning of the 21st.

There are those who have construed Sant'Egidio's peacemaking role as a lay extension of the Holy See, acting unofficially where the authority of the Church could not and did not wish to act directly. Yet this is not the case, as Sant'Egidio has never intervened at the direction of the Vatican, which, incidentally, has rightfully sought to keep its way of operating distinct. In the 1990s, several Catholic bishops, especially in Africa, provided a strong impetus for the transition of their countries towards peace and democracy. Yet Sant'Egidio also differs from this case, as it is not an organization of Christians operating in their own country. Rather, it is an international actor that, over the course of time, has operated in different parts of the world.

The Italian origins of the Community could also suggest it acts in concert with the government in Rome. However, whilst there has been frequent interaction between the Community and Italian diplomacy (for instance, in the case of the Mozambique talks), Sant'Egidio has independently chosen its fields and modes of intervention. Indeed, the Community, in the various peacemaking operations described in this book, has shown itself to be an international actor capable of working with various governments and international organizations but freely making its own decisions and devising its own intervention proposals, having regard not to some national interest but rather to the interests of peace of a war-torn country.

For this reason, Sant'Egidio is distinct as an actor from Catholic Church associations or movements. Affectionately dubbed "the UN of Trastevere" by the famous Italian journalist Igor Man (so as to emphasize its international profile paradoxically linked to its convivial and Roman character), the Community not only engages in diplomatic and peacemaking operations, but performs and undertakes an elaborate range of roles and actions.

It is first and foremost a Christian community: faith and evangelical inspiration are at the heart of its existence and cohesion. It works for the poor in the affluent societies of the global North, just as it does for those in less-developed societies in the South. To this end, it has invested much in recent years in the care of AIDS patients in Africa, with 75,000 people receiving treatment (efforts which – as one of the chapters of this volume shows – have also necessitated working with governments in what could almost be viewed as a form of "health diplomacy").

The Community of Sant'Egidio has also been at the center of various initiatives aimed at fostering dialogue between religions and between believers and non-worshippers. In particular, since the World Day of Prayer for Peace at Assisi in 1986, convened by Pope John Paul II, the Community has held annual meetings in various countries around the world between leaders of different religions and Christian Churches, in the knowledge that religions can provide crucial support for peace efforts, but can also sanctify war. John Paul II firmly supported this process of dialogue "in the spirit of Assisi", as this inter-religious meeting held since 1986 has been described, maintaining an active and direct relationship with the Community.

Hence, dialogue is ingrained in the DNA of the Community. In the 1990s, and especially after September 11, 2001, this quest for dialogue might have come across as naive in a world that seemed headed for a clash of civilizations and religions. War – on the cultural front but also on the battlefield – seemed a painful necessity. Sant'Egidio, however, gave no credence to this axiom, which was presented as irrefutable. This did not stem from in-principle pacifism but from a realism shaped by the experience of peacemaking in various conflicts over the previous two decades. Indeed, the Community does not only bear "witness" to the – let's say, moral or religious – value of peace, but acts and intervenes tangibly to seek peace in situations of conflict. It would thus be more appropriate to speak of peacemakers rather than pacifists.

Sant'Egidio, despite having rather unique characteristics in the sphere of international relations, is a recognized actor on the world stage – so much so that political leaders and diplomats from various countries have visited and made contact with the Community. The meeting with George W. Bush, who during his visit to Rome felt the need to consult with the Community, made headlines. Many wondered why the American President would want to meet with Sant'Egidio after having seen Vatican and Italian authorities in Rome.

Yet it was a little known fact that, since the early 1990s, American diplomats had been in constant contact with the Community apropos of various conflict situations, including those in Mozambique, Algeria, Albania and Kosovo as well as others, especially in Africa. Secretary of State Madeleine Albright had already visited the Community, as had various UN Secretaries-General. French diplomatic representatives had also had ongoing contact with the Community, to discuss various crisis areas, including Ivory Coast in particular, as had diplomats from other European countries such as Great Britain, Germany, Switzerland and Belgium.

In addition, Sant'Egidio had entertained relations with Russia since the collapse of the Soviet Union, when the Community encouraged Gorbachev's efforts in certain circles in Rome to open up relations. Nor should Sant'Egidio's contact with several African leaders, together with those from Latin America, be overlooked. This is not intended as a roll-call of important names to draw attention to the role of Sant'Egidio, but rather as a way of demonstrating that this Community, made up of religiously-inspired women and men who are not professional diplomats, has credibility and, above all, an ability to intervene in fields usually reserved for politicians and diplomats. At the very least, it is considered by those professionally engaged in diplomacy as a group with whom it is worthwhile liaising and maintaining contact.

So where has this expertise and capacity to intervene come from? It was forged in the events recounted in this book, through contact with difficult situations of conflict. It grew out of a tight network of contacts, constantly nurtured, but also from the Community's ability to embrace dreams and hopes of peace from all over the world. It would be wrong to think of the Community as an unwieldy organization replete with human and financial resources. It has one great resource, namely: an interest in the plight of the world, and often in that of forgotten countries – an interest which it steadfastly maintains and acts upon through its diverse range of contacts.

Its capacity for action also derives from an evangelical spirituality that views war as an evil. During the First World War, Benedict XV spoke of a "useless massacre", whilst his distant successor John Paul II described the decision to go to war as an "adventure without return". This conviction is not just a matter of principle, but rather stems from the experience of many traumatic war-torn scenarios, and has become a very realistic and persistent hope, namely, that peace is possible.

It is crucial to find ways of achieving it, patiently, by healing divisions, creating a framework of guarantees for the future, demonstrating that there is nothing worse than war, and providing an outlet for the will for peace of peoples that are "hostage" to war. While this provides the human and spiritual foundation for the actions of the men and women of Sant'Egidio, the tools with which those actions are carried out are at once simple yet sophisticated.

Is it possible to talk of a Sant'Egidio method?

The simple tools in question are those of dialogue between warring parties, refined through a long process of human trial and error that has spanned different peoples and conflicts. Boutros Boutros-Ghali, commenting in the context of the Mozambique Peace Agreement (signed in Rome after two years of negotiations mediated by the Community and the Italian government), spoke of a "technique which was different than those of the professional peace-makers, but which was complementary to theirs. [... A] technique of informal discretion [which] converge[d] with the official work of governments and of intergovernmental organizations [... culminating in a] unique combination of government work and non-governmental peace efforts".

Cameron Hume, an American observer of Sant'Egidio's efforts, wrote: "Despite being conducted by non-professional diplomats, the Mozambique peace talks produced sophisticated technical tools – combining expertise in psychology, historical and legal culture, flexibility and political culture – that were extraordinary. Paradoxically, the very fact of coming to the process as outsiders, as essentially mediators *super partes* that were nevertheless seriously dedicated to the cause of peace without standing to gain any possible political or financial benefits or international prestige, proved to be one of the strengths of the entire process. [...] The keywords throughout appeared to be friendship, dialogue and flexibility".

The Community's tools of "diplomacy" are effective, adaptable and incisive, but do not rely on financial or military leverage. Indeed, the introduction of systems of payment for negotiating parties has, in certain conflicts, had a perverse effect, namely, that of prolonging talks. In any case, these simple dialogue tools are not in the service of spontaneity or *embrassons-nous*. This is evident from the peace agreements and documents that have come out of peace processes where the Community has played a role, which are multilayered, complex and well thrashed-out.

In this regard, developing a human relationship with those in dispute is crucial. Understanding the motives and sentiments of each party, building trust, and fostering a less hostile climate are important stages in any serious peace process. The "seriousness" of peace efforts depends on a negotiation process engendering a desire in the parties to reach an agreement. This requires time and patience. Often, the length of talks and the time it takes for them to bear fruit means, sadly, that war continues and human lives are consumed by it. This gives rise to a moral and strategic issue requiring a major balance to be struck between the need for peace to be achieved immediately (and for this reason, pressure must be brought to bear) and for peace efforts also to be in earnest and provide long-term guarantees for the future.

The "simple" tools of human contact, or of reasoned political debate, are rooted in a very strong moral legitimacy, which does not correspond solely to the personal legitimacy of those working for Sant'Egidio, but rather that of the affected populations who, in general, yearn for peace and want it quickly. The Community is strongly attuned to this desire for peace, which is often almost incapable of finding expression.

This was the case with Mozambique, a peace success story that brought Sant'Egidio to the attention of the international arena. The Mozambican people, tired of a war that had killed one million people and destroyed the country, wanted peace. This is demonstrated by the fact that, after the signing of the Peace Agreement in 1992, there were no reprisals carried out between the two conflicting parties or among the people, despite the accumulated suffering and grievances of sixteen years of conflict. Peace was also sought by Albanians who, after the madness of almost half a century of national-communist dictatorship, were struggling to find the road to democracy. Burundians, Liberians, Guatemalans and Algerians – to cite some of the cases covered in this book – were also in search of peace.

There are, however, obstacles that prevent this desire for peace from gaining ground, which stem from divided and embittered political classes, rifts and resentments forged by armed conflict, and real or supposed grievances built up over years or decades of hatred. In such situations, "external" intervention like that of Sant'Egidio can remove impediments and enable peace to prevail.

The stumbling block is clearly political in nature, but it is also often one of culture and perspective. Peace may not seem feasible because living with the other side is not considered possible, there being no reasons or guarantees on which to build any trust. It is here that a role can be played by human contact which leads to dialogue and even a new vision of one's future and that of the country, with the realization that peace is possible and that the other side must not be demonized. All armed conflicts are fueled by the demonization of the opponent: if those on the other side cannot be destroyed, they should at least be condemned and loathed! However, peace processes require a different approach: that of agreement, compromise and the decision to live together peacefully. This requires at least a partial change in how the other side is viewed.

It is not easy to make the transition from the mentality of a guerrilla fighter, whose goal is to strike the enemy (even in the knowledge that victory is not possible), to that of a politician who accepts peaceful coexistence. Nor is it easy to move away from the mindset of a government (which considers guerrillas criminals) towards acceptance of an adversary-in-arms as a political dialogue partner. Time is needed for attitudes to change. In this regard, negotiations also often act as a political training ground, marking the transition from armed conflict to political conflict or debate. However, in order for this to happen, there needs to be an awareness that victory is not possible, that the price of continued fighting will be pain and bloodshed, and that the future could be better for everyone.

Trust does not bloom spontaneously and immediately. It is not a question of reconciliation between enemies to begin with, but of opening up dialogue between parties who have loathed each other, and who have dreamt for years of their opponent's death and annihilation. Through dialogue, hatred is diminished and the parties get to know each other better. At the same time, there is a need to develop a compelling blueprint for a shared future.

It is thus necessary to build a political framework for the future which provides guarantees of continued survival and freedom. Such guarantees are crucial, also because combatants are always tempted to make peace whilst keeping the option of a renewed resort to arms open if they feel penalized by the process. International and national guarantees are a cornerstone of any peace accord. It is necessary to create mechanisms, institutions and processes that enable the agreement to be implemented and provide security for the weaker party. The guarantees are aimed at moving towards a proper democratic process, in which the opinions, freedom and lives of all are protected, keeping in mind, however, that democracy is not achieved in a few months – especially after years of war.

Parties to a conflict often cannot envisage the possibility of peace. Hence, it is not just a question of building trust between the parties, but of letting them be "won over" by a vision of peace. In short, if I may reiterate the point, it is a matter of letting them be convinced that peace is possible for their country, for their respective political factions, for their families and for themselves as individuals. When the parties begin to relish the prospect of peace, even hatred loses its edge. Peace has its own force of persuasion and reason as well as an emotional appeal.

The above observations should be read as a reflection on the particular "cases" examined in this book. They do not provide a basis for the distillation of a "Sant'Egidio method" or a recipe for reconciliation. A lesson drawn from many examples may sharpen sensibilities and forewarn of possible risks and opportunities. The processes of peaceful settlement vary and must be adapted to different circumstances. Even the role of the "mediator" – in this case, the Community – varies. Sometimes, the conflict in question is two-sided, as was the case in Mozambique. At other times, there are many divisions, as in Burundi. In some cases, conflicts are ideologically motivated (RENAMO waged war on a communist government, whilst Algerian fundamentalists fought in the name of their faith). Today, however, ideological motives for conflicts are less common. Hence, this book does not set out to illustrate a Sant'Egidio method, but rather simply to tell the story of the role played by the Community on the frontiers of peace.

A strength in weakness

Sant'Egidio does not act as a group of diplomats in competition with official diplomatic efforts. On the contrary, the Community is of the view that in a world where so much has been privatized, the role of the State in international action remains pivotal. Very often, conflicts arise precisely because of the inability of the State to take on board the security, participation and welfare demands of its people. In various peace initiatives, the Community has worked closely with governments. In Ivory Coast, as the only actor that was not exclusively African, it participated in the reconciliation process alongside African governments. It has also consistently called for government intervention in certain situations marked by tensions. However, whilst an actor like the Community may be capable of intervening on several fronts, this does not obviate the need for States to take responsibility in matters of peace and war.

Moreover, as already noted, the Community lacks certain "strengths" which more or less characterize government intervention; it lacks economic and military muscle. Indeed, one could talk in terms of the "weak nature" of Sant'Egidio's interventions, or better still, it could be said that the Community has its own moral, spiritual and human strength – a "weak strength" – aimed at fostering dialogue and transforming the individual through peaceful engagement. It is a different kind of strength to that wielded through weapons or by governments, and it is often useful and sometimes necessary. There is a human factor (contrary to Marxist interpretations of history) that is crucial in deciding between peace and war.

It is human beings who decide, often one person. It is therefore necessary to establish real human contact, and to broaden the cultural and political horizons of a leader or ruling group. The "weak strength" of dialogue, friendship and humanity is thus necessary. Furthermore, the inherent "potency" of this kind of strength lies in not having any interest – whether political (as it is not focused on safeguarding one's future in the country) or financial (as the "cost" of mediation is merely a "Thank you!") – other than the achievement of peace.

Accordingly, peace efforts must not involve any one player taking the limelight, but rather should create a synergy between the different actors, making the dialogue process compelling and providing guarantees for the future. In this process, there is a role for States and for international organizations. However, there is also room – and indeed, sometimes it is necessary – for actors like Sant'Egidio, for whom peace is a passion not a profession, to take an active role. At times, peace processes can become hostage to the workings of bureaucracies or the pursuit of personal interests, thus struggling to create a climate of trust and produce convincing outcomes. In contrast, selflessness and personal disinterest exert a persuasive force in the healing of divisions created by conflicts.

Often, the breakthrough in peace processes comes with the mutual recognition by the warring parties that they both form part of national life. The other side is no longer seen as merely an enemy to be destroyed, but as an element to be integrated into the future of the country. Much divides parties to a conflict, including real or alleged grievous actions, great bloodshed, mutual accusations, a climate of violence that has led to deplorable acts, hatred for the other side that has become a cohesive factor for one's own faction, political propaganda, an almost mystical sense of representing good against evil, and so on. It thus becomes necessary to bring about a realization of what the parties have in common in order to embark on the road to peace.

The dawning of such awareness is never easy – not within national contexts, even where there has been a shared history and where a shared future is unavoidable. There are also far more complex situations, like that in Kosovo, which is examined in this book. In that case, the Albanians aspired to independence, whilst the government in Belgrade viewed their territory as an integral part of the Yugoslav State, indeed, as the cradle of Serb civilization. Serbs and Albanians have suffered from the ill-effects of a divisive memory since time long past. Another case in point is the tragic history between Hutus and Tutsis in the Great Lakes region. In this case too, it is difficult for an awareness of what the parties have in common to emerge. Every guerilla movement has its own "memory".

Often, parties or peoples who have fought each other are prisoners of their memory, or rather, of the memory of grievances suffered. They feel like victims of history and this – if not calling for vengeance – dictates a continuation of hostilities. Situations differ greatly and sometimes are not comparable. The solution offered by the international justice system is different to that of mediation processes. Reconciliation between the parties is desirable, but this is very difficult to achieve. The approach that is most realistic and conducive to peace is that based on acceptance of a shared future together, whether as political parties in a national democratic system or as autonomous neighbors.

However, this transition is not possible unless all the parties involved recognize what they have in common and that which unites them – or rather, that what unites them is far greater than that which has divided them. Here, it is the long-established approach of a diplomat of the Church, Angelo Giuseppe Roncalli, who became Pope John XXIII, that I wish to evoke. He said that we should be concerned with "seeking that which unites us rather than that which divides us". That which unites may be a sense of belonging to a common national family, but often it is also the minor aspects of people's lives that are fought over.

What successfully brings the parties together is the belief that there is no future in the annihilation of the other side. In other words, it is necessary to recognize that both sides have a place in the future of the country. In the case of the Kosovo conflict (involving an attempt at secession by the Serbs, and an assertion of independence by the Albanians on the basis of being the ethnic majority), step-by-step negotiations were aimed at forging at least a common language between two parties that had absolutely irreconcilable perspectives. It was also necessary to avoid the outbreak of war, which would have radicalized their positions even further, to say nothing of the sacrifice of human lives that it would have entailed.

War is a declaration that the parties have nothing in common. It becomes a bloody manifestation of division at all levels. Often, compared with grueling negotiations, war seems like the fastest solution, almost like surgery that is undoubtedly painful but capable of restoring peace. Yet is this really the case? It is worth reflecting on this carefully, but not so as to derive some general historical theory, which would be inapplicable and have little foundation. Contemporary history is littered with wars that have become inveterate, of quick solutions that have become long drawn-out affairs, and of legacies of hate that have been handed down from generation to generation. War is never a case of a straightforward surgical strike, but rather produces consequences that are, on the contrary, uncontrollable. For this reason, Sant'Egidio has sought to prevent the outbreak of armed conflicts. This was the case with Kosovo and Burundi. It is imperative to raise awareness at every opportunity of what unites the parties and put to one side that which divides them, both so as to restore peace in countries at war and to prevent new conflicts arising.

A vigilant observer at the window of the world

This book does not tell the full story of Sant'Egidio's peacemaking efforts. There have been many "lower-key" instances of the Community's involvement in this area. This book only deals with those considered to be of wider importance, though these have not always been capped with success. Peace processes are often tortuous and complex, with unexpected outcomes. Nevertheless, the quest for peace has consistently engaged and inspired the Community, even when it has involved remote countries with a low international profile.

Sant'Egidio took its first steps in the international arena in the early 1980s, first becoming involved in the situation in Mozambique, then taking an interest in the civil war in El Salvador between Marxist guerrillas and the government, and later in the Lebanese crisis. In Central America, Sant'Egidio cultivated the legacy of peace left by the martyred San Salvadorian archbishop, Msgr. Oscar Romero, through numerous ties of friendship and humanitarian operations.

As regards Lebanon, in a dramatic moment of crisis for the Christians of that country during the occupation of the Chouf region by Walid Jumblatt's Druze militia and the destruction of Christian villages, Sant'Egidio hosted a meeting at its headquarters in Rome between the Patriarch Maximos V Hakim and Jumblatt, which led to the decision to allow the release of Christians from the area. Some of these, refugees without any belongings, were then given shelter in Rome by the Community. In 1986, Sant'Egidio endeavored to liberate hundreds of Iraqi Christians who, having taken refuge in the mountains on the border between their country and Turkey, were unable to obtain political asylum over the border and were left in an impossible situation, risking capture and sentencing to death by Saddam Hussein's regime. The Community received them in Rome after having secured their safe passage across Turkish territory and then worked to ensure their settlement in various host countries.

Even in these "lower-key" – if you will – initiatives, an interplay emerged between humanitarian action, solidarity with poorer people, diplomatic efforts, and a focus on individuals or groups that are victims of war and violence. This interplay informed the efforts undertaken, albeit without success, in respect of the fate of Israeli soldiers held prisoner in Lebanon; the freeing – after protracted mediation – of a group of tourists captured by Öcalan's armed PKK forces; the secured release of Russian pilots in Angola and Ethiopia, and that of missionaries kidnapped in Africa; efforts aimed at guaranteeing the respect of Christians' rights in Sudan; and the freeing of a group of Italians kidnapped in Colombia by the ELN.

It is the extreme plight of men or women that compels the Community to act. Also significant in this regard is the work of Sant'Egidio (not geared towards ending a conflict, but involving fully-fledged diplomatic activity) in calling for a UN General Assembly vote in favor of a moratorium on the death penalty. This was a case of diplomatic action by Sant'Egidio, taken in conjunction with governments and other organizations, which rank alongside its efforts in the field of health diplomacy with respect to the treatment of AIDS in Africa.

Disease, poverty and the threat to human life "drive" a range of Sant'Egidio initiatives. It is here that it becomes evident how efforts of a more diplomatic or peacemaking nature are linked, at least in terms of their motivations and objectives, with the work among the poor and the commitment to social empowerment of thousands of Community members in the different countries where they live. War thus emerges – as we are wont to say at Sant'Egidio – as "the mother of all poverty". In this regard, the Community acts as a vigilant observer in the international arena and on the frontiers of war, human poverty and violence, on the alert to gauge needs and explore possible avenues to address them.

The international and diplomatic role that this Christian community– progeny of the Church of Rome – has ended up playing is peculiar, an outcome which, however, makes sense in a globalized world, where the distant becomes near. The peacemaking efforts of the Community demonstrate, among other things, that globalization is not just about markets, and it is not just a phenomenon against which we have to defend ourselves because it facilitates encroachment by others. Globalization is a reality that makes us "citizens" of the world with a responsibility and an ability to act. This brings to fruition the ancient Christian wisdom that no people are strangers – especially not those experiencing suffering.

PEACE IN MOZAMBIQUE

Mozambique

Area (in sq km)	799,380
Population (millions)	19.400
Population density (inhabitants per sq km)	24
Percentage of population <15 years	43.6
Annual change in population (%)	+1.7
Infant mortality per 1,000 live births (<1 year/<5 years)	107.9/152
Life expectancy at birth (male/female)	45/49
Illiteracy rate (%)	49.6
Doctors (per 1,000 inhabitants)	0.02
Percentage of adult population living with HIV/AIDS (adult prevalence rate)	12.2
Human Development Index (HDI), expressed on a scale from 0 to 1, to three decimal places	0.379
HDI, world ranking	168
GDP per capita (USD)	346
GDP per capita, world ranking	171
Personal computers (per 1,000 inhabitants)	5.6

Peace in Mozambique

Leone Gianturco

The wind caresses our faces as an expanse of coconut palms unfolds before us. Passing through motley markets, where pineapples, mangoes, bananas, roasted cashews and all manner of goods are traded in implausible plastic bags, we are left mesmerized by the stream of people bent on reaching their intended destination: on bikes, in minibuses, but mostly on foot. Once back in town, a riot of traffic and music assails us, whilst the icons of globalization look down on us and reveal a dynamic and ever-changing world. Heading back up towards the mountains, we come across colorful caravans of South African tourists in shorts: birdwatchers. We stop for a break in the middle of the savanna and dozens of children turn up. Curious faces break into disarmed and disarming smiles.

We are left astonished and dazed by the dazzling light, the changing landscape, the colors, the smell of rain and dried fish, the savannas, the inselbergs[1], the great rivers, the endless coasts, the sky – in turn clear or laced with clouds, and a world of people that rise with the sun. We are struck by the meekness of the children who watch us with big eyes as young mothers – now done with pounding manioc – gracefully and firmly enfold them in their *capulanas* after placing them on their backs.

It is really difficult to imagine we are in a country where, recently, a bloody civil war raged. And yet, that is the case.

Twenty years ago, all that any visitor could see of Mozambique was a handful of cities linked solely by air. You only needed to go a few kilometers out of the capital, with its half-deserted streets and empty markets, for the roads to turn into deathtraps, where minibuses full of passengers were stopped and in minutes were set alight along with their human cargo. In the countryside, where survival had at that point become a gamble, farmers bereft of any hope of cultivating the land again wore sackcloth, ate roots, and

25

had got used to sleeping in trees or other hiding places to avoid being killed in their sleep. Hundreds of men, women and especially adolescents filed through the bush barefoot, plagued by hunger and thirst, and forced to serve as goods carriers after having survived the destruction of their homes and the murder of their loved ones.

Eventually, the Peace Agreement was signed, putting an end to a civil war that had steeped the country in blood for more than sixteen years and had cost a million lives, created four and a half million refugees, destroyed thousands of schools, hospitals and health centers, and brought the country to a complete standstill[2]. The date was October 4, 1992. The Agreement, negotiated over the course of more than two years of talks held at the headquarters of the Community of Sant'Egidio in Rome, has worked.

The three adrenaline-filled days leading up to that October 4 had been marked by dramatic twists and turns and perilous standoffs. While the African presidents invited to attend the signing ceremony grew impatient in their Roman hotel suites, in Mozambique the population had its ears glued to the radio to follow the latest developments in the negotiations. Finally, it was signed. It was the Mozambican people themselves who were the first and main intended audience of the speeches made by Afonso Dhlakama, head of the RENAMO guerrilla group, and Joaquim Chissano, President of Mozambique, on that October 4 morning, with the live radio broadcast elevating millions of people to the status of participants in an unscheduled and extraordinary teleconference.

Dhlakama, after calling his opponent "my dear and respected brother", recalled the many victims of the civil conflict, expressing the hope that this blood had not been spilt in vain and would serve as a stark reminder of the need for genuine reconciliation. Then, over the air, he ordered his men to lay down their arms. Chissano, for his part, stressed that the signing of the Peace Agreement was "a victory for all Mozambican people", with no room "for losers or winners", proclaiming in conclusion that the peace settlement was "irreversible". The ceremony broke into applause, making up for many sleepless and seemingly unproductive nights.

Meanwhile, in Mozambique, the celebrations began. Freedom from civil war, the tentative beginnings of democracy, and the disarmament of hands and minds became a reality. The fruits of this peace have been incalculable. Eighteen years of peace are no trifling matter for a country where half the population is under the age of fifteen. The summary table below provides a statistical comparison between Mozambique as it was on October 4, 1992 and the situation fifteen years later:

Index	1992	2008
GNI per capita	USD 60	USD 370
Economic growth	Before 1992, GDP growth was negative	From 1992 to 2008, GDP grew at an average yearly rate of 7%
Relative poverty	Poorest country in the world (ranking 207th out of 207 countries)	Mozambique ranked 199th out of 210 countries
Infant mortality (0-1 years)	162 per 1000 births	90 per 1000 births
Child mortality (1-5 years)	283 per 1000 births	130 per 1000 births
Life expectancy at birth	44 years	42 years (net of the AIDS factor, it would be more than 50 years)
Illiterate female population	79%	65%
Illiterate male population	67%	34%
Primary school net enrolment/attendance	43%	81%
Telephones/1000 people	2	15 (mobile phones not included)
Foreign Direct Investment	USD 25 million	USD 3.8 billion
Inflation	54%	7%
Refugees	1.7 million	None. Mozambique became a country with an influx of refugees
Displaced persons	4 million	None (apart from emergencies due to floods and other natural disasters)
Level of democratization	One-party State	Pluralistic parliamentary democracy
Decentralization	None	33 elected mayors, 11 provincial assemblies and other elected local authorities

Sources: World Bank, IMF, IPU, OECD, UNCTAD, UNDP, UNESCO, WHO

So what precipitated this great southern African nation into a war from which there seemed to be no going back? And how was it possible to bring the nightmare to an end?

An African war

The fight for freedom from Portuguese colonial rule launched in 1962 by FRELIMO (the *Frente de Libertação de Moçambique*) was long and bitter. The Carnation Revolution of 1974 in Portugal accelerated the process and, in 1975, the African freedom fighters led by the charismatic Samora Machel took on the role of governing an independent Mozambique.

The early years of independence were marked by euphoria, but it soon became apparent that FRELIMO's African brand of Marxism-Leninism was not suited to a rural, poor and 97%-illiterate country. Structural reforms imposed from on high vexed the population, which did not understand the insistence on the notion of *homem novo* (or "new man") of their new rulers, who, in turn, mistook the people's desire for independence as the will for revolution. In its modern opposition to racism and ethnic divisions (and the purported obscurantism of the Catholic Church), FRELIMO immediately began to shun the traditional tribal system, forcing peasants accustomed to living scattered across the savannah to cluster in "communal villages" (*aldeias comunais*), conceived as a cross between Soviet *kolkhozes* and Chinese-style communes.

Meanwhile, the "unproductive" urban unemployed were deported by air to the forests of distant Niassa, where what awaited them were lions and a harsh climate that decimated thousands. Hundreds of children and adolescents chosen from among the *continuadores* (a sort of communist scout organization along the lines of the Soviet Young Pioneers) were sent to Cuba to be "trained up", whilst entire generations of young people would later be temporarily transferred to the factories of a "brother" country, namely, East Germany. The imported ideological dogmatisms, which were translated into harsh models of government, as well as the moralizing campaigns of President Samora, provoked angry reactions. Older people still remember the *Operação*

Produção ("Operation Production"), a mass compulsory relocation from cities to re-education camps.

The response was not long in coming. In 1976, RENAMO (the *Resistência Nacional Moçambicana*) was formed, a guerrilla movement which immediately declared its anti-communist stance. At first, its members included former Portuguese colonists (who had been dispossessed of their landholdings), members of the Rhodesian secret services, South African mercenaries, and a few disgruntled FRELIMO soldiers, like Afonso Dhlakama, who was then little more than twenty years old.

Over time, RENAMO would come to be known for its increasing ability to muster the anger of people in the North or South of the country. In a few years, its operations spread throughout the country. Its tactic was to conduct a scorched-earth policy, with the systematic destruction of infrastructure being the chosen strategy to undermine the government in Maputo. The population became hostage both to guerilla fighters who killed, kidnapped and ravaged, and to government troops, who likewise killed in retaliation and devastated areas where there was reported RENAMO activity.

Mozambique, a country almost three times the size of Italy, became a vast no man's land, characterized by impassable roads, wrecked bridges, and particularly bloody massacres which drove home their message by cutting people's ears and lips off. RENAMO recruited many teenagers who were kidnapped from their families in the countryside. The government, in turn, forcibly recruited young people in the cities, plucking them off the streets. The government recruits were known as *tira camisa* (or "shirts off") because during the raids in which they were press-ganged they were tied up with their own shirtsleeves. It was a no-win situation.

Both the guerrillas and government soldiers terrorized the population, which was suspected of sympathizing with the other side. Military forces from friendly countries, such as Zimbabwe and Tanzania, guarded certain "corridors" (with varying degrees of success) to enable the movement of people and goods at great risk.

Millions of Mozambicans suffered from hunger, millions were dispersed to provincial capitals or medium-sized towns, and millions took refuge in neighboring countries. Mozambique, already previously poor, earned the distinction of being the poorest country in the world. Yet whilst the population fervently yearned for peace, the war perpetuated itself in defiance of the common will.

At that time, the events unfolding in the country were not well-understood. At first glance, it seemed easy to write off the Mozambican conflict as "externally-driven", with RENAMO labeled as a group of *bandidos armados* ("armed bandits") engaged by Rhodesia and South Africa for the sole purpose of destabilizing a dangerous neighbor – as a Marxist-led country might prove to be. In order to bolster this view, the acronym used to denominate RENAMO in English (MNR – the Mozambique National Resistance) was somewhat contemptuously adopted, with the precise aim of underlining its "foreign" links. In support of this take on the situation, FRELIMO sought and obtained the endorsement of the international community, thereby managing for many years to exclude and discredit RENAMO as a dialogue partner. The fact remains, however, that even after the fall of Rhodesia and the weakening of ties with the apartheid regime, the conflict continued. The external backers had ceased to be so. The wires that bound the puppeteer (Rhodesia and, after 1980, South Africa) to the puppet (RENAMO) had by now been severed. So why did the war continue?

The outside interference that certainly lay behind the origins of RENAMO should not be glossed over, but the motivations which fueled the conflict were now to be found in the reaction to FRELIMO and its "European-style" revolutionary ideologies. There was an increasingly dawning realization that the war was attributable to internal causes. This was not a proxy war, like that in Angola, where there was a typical Cold War scenario involving, on one side, the United States backed by South Africa supporting UNITA, and on the other, the Soviets supporting the MPLA government with the help of the Cubans. In Mozambique, the Americans, South Africans, Soviets and Cubans did not have the influence they exerted in the Angolan context.

For this reason, the hatred that divided the two rivals was not automatically overcome – as some had believed it might be – with the progressive spread of international détente, symbolized by the fall of the Berlin Wall (in 1989). A conflict like that in Mozambique would not come to a halt as a result of changes in the international situation. Hence, there was a need to address those internal elements that had led to and fueled a war which had now become endemic – a conflict with its own dynamics on which traditional diplomacy would have little impact.

The responsibility for the delay in understanding the historical origins of the conflict must be attributed to the international community, which was more concerned with increasing aid-related business (that saw thousands of foreign aid-workers stationed in Maputo, whilst 20 kilometers away from the city there was a risk of being killed in an ambush), than with tackling the real causes of a conflict that had reduced Mozambique to a country with limited sovereignty.

The real story was more complex than any preconceived models. On the one hand, FRELIMO had become increasingly politically and economically independent from the Soviet bloc, whilst RENAMO could hardly be said to represent Western interests. A US State Department report in 1988, had branded the latter's guerilla fighters as *"Khmer Noir"*, the comparison being with Cambodia's *Khmer Rouge*, stripping it of any political dignity. For its part, RENAMO saw the entire international community as an "accomplice to FRELIMO". So it was that the West had no reservations in sympathizing with the pragmatic government in Maputo rather than with an unknown movement hidden in the impenetrable forests of Gorongosa, the guerrillas' headquarters.

It was not easy to grasp the true nature of RENAMO. Indeed, opinions were confused and divided, both among Mozambicans and within the international community. It was observed that the guerrilla movement had expanded its activities – albeit not on a secure basis – in much of rural Mozambique, that it had the obedience and allegiance of large proportions of the civilian population, and that it had significant military capability, with its troops displaying a strong sense of self-sacrifice and unity. It seemed to be predominantly military in character. Yet, little by little, it became clear that RENAMO also had a political agenda which, though basic, was nevertheless effective, and which consisted of opposing the political agenda of FRELIMO.

31

In other words, RENAMO had evolved in stubborn opposition to everything FRELIMO had done since the day of independence, and, hence, appeared to be a reactive movement. This did not mean that it lacked a political identity, but it was isolated, and its military capability was growing in proportion to the degree of its isolation.

Whilst the comings and goings of aid agencies, multilateral organizations and nongovernmental organizations continued in Maputo and other cities, any efforts aimed at bringing about any development in the country were thwarted by the state of general war. This situation also led to a state of denial, so that despite the fact that transport and infrastructure conditions made it impossible to operate, organizations such as the World Bank and the IMF simply ignored the war factor in their documentation, as if they were referring to some other country. Aid inflated the economy in a scenario of artificial growth. Meanwhile, the real Mozambique remained cut off from aid delivery, and embarking on development cooperation initiatives that might be effective or have a lasting impact was not possible.

Peace seemed more remote than ever. It was in the context of this stalled situation that Sant'Egidio's bid to find a Mozambican road to peace began to take shape. The initial approach, which informed many meetings and discussions, was based on understanding what drove and motivated the Mozambicans. It was also necessary to find the right people to involve in negotiations.

Initial contact (1977-1987)

The Community of Sant'Egidio's first encounter with Mozambique, dating back to 1977, was through Msgr. Jaime Gonçalves, on the occasion of a visit by him to Rome shortly after his appointment as Bishop of Beira, the second largest city in the country. In the newly independent Mozambique, the Catholic Church was regarded by FRELIMO as a remnant of Portuguese colonialism. The Marxist-Leninist government's hostility towards the Church took the form – in addition to the nationalization of all Church-run facilities – of a series of restrictions imposed on the activities of members of the clergy. A large number of missions were closed down. In one way or another, there was a prospect looming that Catholicism would be completely wiped out by means of a crude antireligious and slur campaign. On occasions, President Samora Machel was not averse to publicly addressing Catholic bishops as "monkeys". It was in this pressured (and oppressive) climate that Sant'Egidio set about assisting Bishop Gonçalves by organizing meetings between him and leaders of the Italian Communist Party, a move which on the face of it seemed naive but would later prove effective.

Italy had in fact considerably increased aid to Mozambique, becoming its largest donor country, in some measure due to the efforts of Italian left-wing political forces. Thus, in 1982 and 1984, at the ancient Sant'Egidio monastery in Trastevere, Gonçalves twice met the Secretary of the Italian Communist Party (the PCI), Enrico Berlinguer, who, prompted by a simple phone call to his office, had willingly agreed to the meeting. Realizing that it would be unreasonable to conduct a campaign against religion in an animist country, Berlinguer listened carefully throughout. He appeared almost outraged to learn that in Mozambique, a country where practically no one had a watch, it was forbidden to ring church bells to call people to mass. Years later, it would emerge that the PCI's interest in religious freedom was genuine, and this was to have beneficial consequences.

In the meantime, a severe drought had briefly brought Mozambique into the headlines. It was 1983. Speaking in the Church of Sant'Egidio, Bishop Gonçalves launched an urgent aid appeal for famine victims and took the opportunity to speak of the war, the existence of which was at that time almost unspoken of in the West. The Community's initial response was to set up a "Friends of Mozambique Committee", to channel efforts and aid, and to simultaneously dispatch a first planeload of humanitarian aid. In August 1984, to coincide with the arrival of two further planeloads of aid, Andrea Riccardi and Fr. Matteo Zuppi – future mediators of the peace process – were received in Mozambique by three government ministers. The humanitarian aid assisted in alleviating suffering and saved lives in danger. It also helped open doors with the civil authorities. By visiting the country, Riccardi and Fr. Zuppi were also able to understand its problems better.

A personal relationship, both frank and without preconceptions, was established with FRELIMO leaders. Candid and open dialogue, in mutual recognition of each other's identity, was followed by development cooperation as well as cultural exchange initiatives, in the spirit of selfless friendship. This also served to foster flexibility among FRELIMO's Afro-Marxists, who thought in ideologically rigid terms. For instance, they were convinced of the unpatriotic nature of the Mozambican Church when, in fact, it too had suffered under colonialism, as can be inferred even from the mere fact that the first Mozambican priest was only ordained in 1950, after centuries of Portuguese rule. Several meetings with senior Vatican officials were also organized. But the real start of the normalization of relations between the Mozambican State and the Catholic Church was signaled by an unanticipated meeting between Samora Machel and John Paul II in September 1985 in Rome.

The audience, both sudden and unexpected, was organized by Sant'Egidio whilst the President of Mozambique was flying from New York to Rome. Samora Machel did not wish to visit the Pope unless invited to do so, and he refused to bow to Vatican protocol (which requires that a request for an audience be made). However, the idea of a face-to-face meeting "on an equal footing" appealed to him. A certain amount of imagination was needed to circumvent procedural difficulties. Any remaining reservations were dispelled when Samara Machel learned that he would not be obliged to kneel before the Pope but could stay standing and simply shake his hand. This was how the greatly symbolic and cordial meeting with Pope John Paul II came to take place, representing a further step towards *détente* between FRELIMO and Mozambican Catholics. Samora Machel was reportedly left with "a great impression of the Pope", who, among other things, had acknowledged him "as a true nationalist". The President would later proudly show off photos of the meeting.

There were, however, divergent views on the question of peace. In 1987, with less misgivings than in the past, the Mozambican Episcopal Conference, in its pastoral letter The

Peace that People Want, openly called for direct negotiations between the FRELIMO government and RENAMO. But the time was not yet right, and the proposal of the bishops met with numerous critiques and strong opposition from FRELIMO.

In the meantime, Sant'Egidio continued its solidarity efforts in support of the Mozambican people, stricken by drought and natural disasters. In 1986, a "ship of solidarity" set off loaded with foodstuffs, medicine and agricultural implements. In 1988, a second ship transported over 7,000 metric tons of food aid destined for different areas of the country, as well as carrying numerous containers prepared by missionary groups. The distribution of aid was coordinated and supervised by volunteers of the Community together with missionaries and Caritas Mozambique. Yet while the humanitarian aid saved many lives, the crisis persisted in the form of war. The aid enabled parts of the population to be assisted so as to prevent them succumbing, in the short term, to starvation and disease. However, the rest of the country remained cut off. Without peace, any real development was inconceivable. Sant'Egidio thus began to take a direct interest in the question of how peace might be achieved.

From the forest to Rome (1987-1990)

The Community set about finding a way to establish effective contact with RENAMO beyond the meager and rudimentary documentation leaked out of the forest and offering no chance of reply or dialogue, in an attempt to understand its *raisons d'être* and ideas. Only direct contact would enable a better understanding of these men and, in particular, of how it might be possible to work for peace in Mozambique. The idea of talking with certain dubious "representatives abroad", resident in the US, was immediately dismissed. Indeed, it was widely rumored that there were internal divisions within the overseas arm of RENAMO.

Finally, in the summer of 1987, on the terrace of a Mozambican artist living in Rome named Bertina Lopes, Fr. Zuppi met Juanito Bertuzzi, an Italian who had lost some properties in Mozambique following the wave of nationalizations and who had kept in contact with representatives of RENAMO. Thereafter, Bertuzzi put Fr. Zuppi in touch with a man who would prove to be one of the more reliable contacts in RENAMO's overseas network of representatives, Artur Da Fonseca, operating mainly in West Germany and who bore the title of Secretary for External Relations, amounting to RENAMO's Minister of Foreign Affairs.

First it was necessary, however, to put his credibility to the test. In order to obtain proof of Da Fonseca's credentials, Sant'Egidio requested the release of a 65-year-old Portuguese nun, Sr. Irma Lúcia, who had been kidnapped by RENAMO. She was indeed set free on the agreed date of April 25, 1988, at a prearranged location on the border between Mozambique and Malawi. It was a sign that we were on the right track.

Soon after, in May 1988, Sant'Egidio organized a secret meeting between the by then Archbishop Jaime Gonçalves and the leader of the guerrillas, Afonso Dhlakama. Having left in a private plane from an airport in Lesotho, along with two unidentified passengers, headed ostensibly for Zaire, the Archbishop of Beira landed instead in Gorongosa in the heart of Mozambique, on a runway lined with a row of torches that loomed up suddenly in the night. For the occasion of the visit, he had dressed solemnly in archbishop's robes. The conversation with Dhlakama lasted for around two hours and was cordial in tone. Gonçalves was welcomed as a distinguished guest due also to his well-known scant regard for FRELIMO. The archbishop – after some understandable initial fears, apparently attending confession twice before embarking on his journey – was satisfied with the meeting. Dhlakama had displayed an interest in peace talks, but on conditions that were all still up in the air.

Then, in September 1988, John Paul II visited Mozambique. By then, Samora Machel was no longer on the scene. Having died in a plane crash, he had been succeeded by Joaquim Chissano. The Pope's visit took place against a backdrop of full cooperation between Chissano and Catholic bishops. John Paul II recalled the need to seek out "paths of reconciliation and dialogue", expressing the hope that "all parties involved" in the war would unite in the same "profoundly humanitarian sentiment, a distinctive value of

African peoples"[3]. Without entering directly into the merits of the issues to be negotiated, he urged for a settlement of the conflict based on the "unity and harmony" of the Mozambican people, including dialogue. The visit was the culmination of Sant'Egidio's efforts to improve Church-State relations – a goal which at this point could be said to have been achieved.

The following year, in August 1989, Andrea Riccardi was officially invited to participate in the Fifth Congress of the FRELIMO party. In his speech, he stressed that peace is "as precious as bread for the people", reiterating that Mozambique had "the strength to win the battle for peace", and reaffirming the "modest yet steadfast" support of Sant'Egidio. He concluded with these words: "We believe that understanding is possible between Mozambicans, and that your government has the moral and political strength to achieve a generous peace".[4] The thunderous applause of the delegates conveyed to everyone the great desire for peace. To speak of peace at a time when the best that was being contemplated was the possibility of "granting an amnesty to bandits" represented a new approach.

In that same year, after first informing President Chissano, several Mozambican religious leaders (both Catholic and Protestant) attempted to launch peace talks in Nairobi with the support of the Kenyan Ministry of Foreign Affairs. However, the initiative failed. FRELIMO and RENAMO never met directly. Subsequently, President Chissano declared that the churches' initiative had run its course and requested assistance from the governments of Kenya and Zimbabwe. But the attempt to meet with RENAMO in Malawi, in June 1990, fell through. Thus it was that the brief phase of "regional" peacemaking efforts came to end.

It is not uncommon today for Western powers and the United Nations to entrust a regional framework with the role of monitoring and settling conflicts. However, the case of Mozambique should serve as a reminder that this is not an approach that can be applied across-the-board. Often, neighboring countries are directly or indirectly associated with longstanding and more recent causes of a conflict, or act in furtherance of their own interests. Hence, the "region" may lack the necessary impartiality to bring about a solution to the conflict. Whilst it might also represent a show of confidence in the African Union or certain African States, passing on responsibility to the "region" may, at times, constitute a pretext for the West's disengagement from African crises.

The regional initiatives described above were, at any rate, a sign that something was beginning to happen. What these efforts undoubtedly lacked was the key element of mutual trust. RENAMO leaders still had reservations. In February 1990, at the invitation of Sant'Egidio, Afonso Dhlakama – by then the acknowledged and undisputed leader of the anti-government guerrilla forces – made his first visit to Italy, which was shrouded in the utmost secrecy. Meeting those who would later serve as mediators, in person, represented a step forward in gaining the trust of the guerrilla movement – a step which was crucial if the latter was to risk taking the leap of faith that negotiations entailed. The need for dialogue was broached in these discussions.

Up till then, the diplomatic efforts of the major powers had failed to open up real channels of communication between RENAMO and FRELIMO. The involvement of Italy, however, undoubtedly presented certain advantages. Although Mozambique was a former Portuguese colony, there was a strong Italian presence in the country, especially in the field of cooperation. The PCI had been an important point of reference during the years of the struggle for independence. However, even Italian politicians of different persuasions – such as Giulio Andreotti – had always looked at Mozambique with interest, supporting, for instance, the Maputo government's pragmatic decision to align itself with the Western bloc without renouncing its socialist identity. Nevertheless, whilst these were important factors, they would not have been sufficient alone to justify settling on Italy. On the contrary, they could have given rise to suspicions on the part of RENAMO of a set-up, and to feelings of mistrust of a country perceived not as neutral but as too "friendly with FRELIMO".

Dhlakama's visit to Rome was followed by further contact with RENAMO, whilst the government began to drop its many preconditions to direct dialogue one after the other. Indirectly, RENAMO also dropped its request for "recognition". In March, on a visit to the then United States President George Bush Sr., Chissano declared himself open to negotiations. Meanwhile, the Church published yet another pastoral letter entitled Urging Dialogue for Peace.

In the spring of 1990, Sant'Egidio received two almost simultaneous requests: one, from the Mozambican government in the person of the then Labor Minister Aguiar Mazula at the behest of President Chissano (but not FRELIMO as a whole), called for a secret meeting to be held between a senior government representative and a RENAMO counterpart; the other, from Raul Domingos (then RENAMO's External Relations Secretary), officially requested the Community to host talks between RENAMO and the government. The two adversaries had, by different paths, come to respect the Community of Sant'Egidio. It was through this "divine coincidence"– as it would later lightheartedly be described – that the conditions were created for the launch of peace talks in Rome.

Seeking that which unites (1990)

Negotiations opened on July 8, 1990 in the sultry summer heat of Rome, with a cautious handshake under a big banana tree placed in the Community's garden, evoking an African setting. In a tense but hopeful atmosphere, Andrea Riccardi made a speech to the two delegations in which he spoke of "the great Mozambican family", noting that the parties were in agreement that the working method of the talks should be based on a phrase of Pope John XXIII, with a focus on "seeking that which unites rather than that which divides". Among other things, Riccardi went on to say:

That which unites is not little, rather there is a great deal. There is the great Mozambican family, with its very ancient history of suffering, both during the lamentable colonial period and during recent years. The unity of the Mozambican family has survived this history of suffering. We find ourselves today [...] before two brothers, truly part of the same family, who have had different experiences in these last years, who have fought each other. From family experience, we know that misunderstandings between brothers are often the most painful, the most profound even from a psychological point of view, because they call into question those things we hold most dear. Conflicts with outsiders pass, but between brothers it always seems more difficult. Nevertheless, brothers will always be brothers, notwithstanding all the painful experiences. Being Mozambican brothers, being part of the same great family, this is that which unites.[5]

Two days later, after the conclusion of the first round of negotiations, which were initially held behind closed doors, the parties wished to make public their commitment, leaving skeptics dumbstruck and filling their country with hope. The words of the Joint Communiqué, signed by the heads of delegation of the two warring parties, encapsulate the spirit that would lead to the Agreement of October 4, 1992:

The two delegations, acknowledging themselves to be compatriots and members of the great Mozambican family, expressed satisfaction and pleasure at this direct, open and frank meeting, the first to take place between the two parties. The two delegations expressed interest and willingness to do everything possible to conduct a constructive search for a lasting peace for their country and their people. Taking into account the higher interests of the Mozambican nation, the two parties agreed that they must set aside what divides them and focus, as a matter of priority, on what unites them, in order to establish a common working basis so that, in a spirit of mutual understanding, they can engage in a dialogue in which they discuss their different points of view [...] and create the necessary political, economic and social conditions for building a lasting peace and normalizing the life of all Mozambican citizens.[6]

The horseshoe table formation, specially set up for the occasion in what was to become the official negotiations room, enabled the delegations to be kept at a certain distance. In between them was a group of four observers who would later serve as mediators, comprising: Andrea Riccardi, founder of the Community of Sant'Egidio; Fr. Matteo Zuppi; the Honorable Mario Raffaelli, acting on behalf of the Italian government; and the Archbishop of Beira, Jaime Gonçalves. The composition of this small group, which – it is worth noting – worked on an entirely pro-bono basis, proved an invaluable resource, as will soon become apparent.

The involvement of diverse actors, who were not pursuing competing interests but rather acting as a beneficially and effectively complementary team, was a winning card. Indeed, it was evident that official diplomacy alone would not have succeeded in dealing with the complexities of a conflict, like that in Mozambique, which was not linked to international dynamics. On the two longer sides of the table sat the two delegations of the government and RENAMO, each facing the other. They were headed by Armando Guebuza and Raul Domingos. Guebuza, aged 47, was one of FRELIMO's highest-ranking officials and had a hard-line reputation. He was certainly a skillful politician and a polished speaker, educated at the Swiss Presbyterian mission in Maputo before becoming a Marxist and participating in the anti-colonial struggle (he would, as it happens, go on to succeed Chissano as President in 2005 in a peaceful Mozambique). Domingos, 33 and formerly a RENAMO military commander, was in charge of the movement's external relations. Whilst having had little political training, he was earnest, determined and tenacious. During the negotiations, he would gradually transform from the guerrilla he was into a considerably adept diplomat and politician.

The Roman mediation team immediately caused a stir because it was not made up of representatives of State powers or international institutions, but rather by a group of persons who could at best be described as people of good will. The fact that the group was "light on institutions" was a weakness but also represented an opportunity, as it allowed great freedom of action and lent the team a different kind of credibility than that attributed to States and major powers, namely: that of not having its own political or economic agenda to pursue.

The negotiations thus got underway. In Mozambique, popular reaction to the Joint Communiqué was intense. The people interpreted the statement as if it were a peace agreement. But in Rome, once the initial euphoria had died down, it seemed like an uphill struggle. It became immediately necessary to prevent the negotiations taking on the air of court proceedings, with the parties taking it in turns to level accusations at each other. The fact was that they had come to Rome with conflicting agendas. The Mozambican government urgently needed to normalize the situation in the country and sought an immediate ceasefire, which RENAMO, for its part, was not willing to grant because – in view of its isolation at an international level – the armed struggle was its only way of asserting its claims. The hope of quickly securing a cessation of hostilities was shared by the mediators, although they did not harbor the ill-advised aspiration of "imposing it".

The style of mediation adopted

Indeed, it was important to acknowledge that this was only the beginning. The parties to the dialogue had been fighting each other for 14 years. Given this situation, it was already a miracle that they had come together to talk. It is telling that, aside from drinking a quick toast together on the evening of July 10, 1990 after the signing of the Joint Communiqué, the only convivial encounter between the two heads of delegation in twenty-seven months of negotiations was a working breakfast between Guebuza and Domingos, held the following month. Only very rarely were there any informal meetings, and then always in the presence of the mediators. The parties felt more secure at the negotiating table, in a formal but still confidential setting that was closed to the press, or when communicating via the shuttle diplomacy of the mediators.

In a sense, the Sant'Egidio talks were sincere negotiations, between two parties at war.[7] A climate of trust cannot be produced out of thin air, and it is useless to pretend that it exists – even if the ultimate goal is to foster at least some measure of trust. Hence, there were no feigned expressions of familiarity, nor any aperitifs, drinks, or encounters in corridors. The only concession was a handshake before entering the negotiating room, which very soon became a tradition. In short, no climate of false friendship was fostered, but efforts were made to establish a common language and mutual respect. Any informality would have been unwarranted and insincere, given the tribulation that both sides were testament to and which all of Mozambique was experiencing.

It was for this reason too that it was decided to put the delegations up at separate hotels. There was also a tacit divvying-up of restaurants (although in this case it was also to do with differing tastes). The building of mutual trust would require great efforts on the part of the mediators, and could not be rushed without substantial progress being made on the matters under negotiation.

Ultimately, the dynamic of respectful meetings behind closed doors between "compatriots" (which was the term actually used) proved successful. No pleasantries or coffee breaks together. Clear rules were established: there would only be direct meetings, with no contact between the parties outside of these; any informal meetings would take place solely in the presence of the mediators; and there was to be no contact with the press, much to the disappointment and frustration of the latter (indeed, only in the final months was a spokesman for the negotiations appointed, in the person of Mario Marazziti).

Yet all this does not mean that these were cold negotiations. Cameron Hume, an observer to the negotiation process and at the time a diplomat at the US Embassy to the Holy See in Rome, wrote:

Despite being conducted by non-professional diplomats, the Mozambique peace talks produced sophisticated technical tools – combining expertise in psychology, historical and legal culture, flexibility and political culture – that were extraordinary. Paradoxically, the very fact of coming to the process as outsiders, as essentially mediators *super partes* that were nevertheless seriously dedicated to the cause of peace without standing to gain any possible political or financial benefits or international prestige, proved to be one of the strengths of the entire process. The very atmosphere created by the Community of Sant'Egidio – which is not just a former monastery ideal for important and private meetings, but also an entire group of people always at the ready to turn any human contact into an opportunity to iron out tensions and differences – played a not insignificant role, especially during the many grueling and critical stages of the talks.[8]

Many members of Sant'Egidio were involved in one form or another, not just the mediators and the few others functioning as a secretariat and dealing with external relations. There were many people who, also on a voluntary and unpaid basis, carried out a wide range of duties to ensure the negotiating machine ran smoothly. There were those who escorted the delegation, those who translated, those who acted as chauffeurs, those who oversaw relations with the press, those who prepared the rooms, those who looked after furnishings and fittings, and those who served drinks. Various areas of expertise came in handy, including computer skills (for preparation of text and documents), law (to deal with any legal issues), cooking (for obvious reasons), and languages (for interpreting in Portuguese, English and French), as well as photography, medicine, rehabilitation therapy and so on. Once the ultimate goal was clear, every detail was important. The delegations needed to be put at ease, allowing them to focus on what was more important, namely: peace.

The then Secretary General of the United Nations, Boutros Boutros-Ghali, reflecting – once peace was achieved – on the singular nature of the Mozambique negotiations, noted:

The Community of Sant'Egidio developed a technique which was different than those of the professional peace-makers, but which was complementary to theirs. For many years, the [Community] worked with utmost discretion in Mozambique in order to bring both parties in contact with each other. It did not keep those contacts for itself. It was very effective when it came to involving others who could contribute to a solution. The Community let her technique of informal discretion converge with the official work of governments and of intergovernmental organizations [... culminating in a] unique combination of government work and non-governmental peace efforts. Respect for both parties in conflict and for those who work in this area are indispensable for the success of similar initiatives.[9]

At Sant'Egidio's headquarters, each of the delegations had its own room, where they felt comfortable. Many rooms were used for the negotiations, so that sometimes only the church was free, where prayers were offered up for peace.

This brings us back to the strong religious inspiration that pervaded the peace effort. This spirit, without any coercion or denominational connotations, was conveyed to the delegations from Mozambique. The Sant'Egidio mediators would later, on several occasions, emphasize that peace had been the product of the "weak strength" of faith.[10]

Peace cannot be imposed

Although the four mediators did not have any military or economic resources at their disposal, they were able to grasp the complex terms of the issues involved, on a political and human level. They did not seek to buy peace by offering money, as has been attempted in some negotiation processes. Andrea Riccardi wrote that: "The strength of the mediators was that of representing the only way forward. Their strength also stemmed, paradoxically, from not having specific interests to protect in the country, other than securing rapid and lasting peace".[11] The mediators, in any case, had no funds with which to impose peace, aside from the money necessary to host the delegations in Rome and cover travel expenses, made available by various donors (including the Italian Ministry of Foreign Affairs, the Swiss government, international foundations and NGOs, parishes and others).

It is also widely-known that, in similar negotiation processes, it has been considered appropriate, even before talks begin, to set a time limit as a way of exerting psychological pressure. Beyond that date, delegates would probably be asked to leave their hotels or forced to settle their accounts, so as to pressure them into coming to an agreement. But the so-called deadline philosophy played no part in the Mozambique negotiations.

Not even the wording of documents was imposed. So how were they drawn up? Effectively, any proposal submitted by one party would, after a careful hearing of the reasons for which it was advanced, be considered in juxtaposition with the response of the other party. Subsequently, documents would be prepared on the basis of the wording provided by the two delegations, even when they had almost nothing in common. Sometimes, there was only one sentence or a paragraph that both sides could agree on. So be it! At least that was a starting point. And "step-by-step" (to use an expression dear to RENAMO), the page was eventually filled. The mediated text was the outcome of this process, which took into account the opposing viewpoints and was then honed and polished, until a final synthesis was achieved. Much time would be spent discussing one or two words or even a preposition, but then one of the parties would give in.

Peace was achieved in Mozambique because the parties were able, at least to some extent, to reconsider their positions. They believed that they themselves could do it, rather than waiting for solutions to come from who knows where. During the negotiations in Rome, a change took place among the members of both delegations, the kind of anthropological transformation that involves politically understanding the other side and its *raisons d'être* and of which Brazão Mazula has spoken at length.[12] The end result was an agreement that belonged to the parties. An Italian formula, for a Mozambican peace: an unwitting lesson in ownership, in a solution not imposed from on high, and in the definitive reappropriation of a negotiation process set up (of necessity) outside Mozambique by mediators who – other than Gonçalves – were non-Mozambican.

The country had no need of a peace settlement that was haggled over or rushed through under external pressure and in which the parties did not truly believe. What was needed was a settlement of which both parties were convinced, otherwise it would have led to an uneasy peace.

From violence to political struggle

Peace in Mozambique has also taken deep root because it was the fruit of a political coming-of-age. It is an apt example of how it is always possible to make the transition from armed struggle, seen as the only way of upholding one's views, to other ways of getting one's position across, particularly dialogue but also political disputation, which make democracy productive and guarantee pluralism. In order to achieve peace, there was no option other than to move the dispute between FRELIMO and RENAMO into the political – and then parliamentary –

sphere, since neither of the warring parties was able to restore peace to the country through a military victory that would eliminate their opponent.

The long and at times exhausting rounds of negotiations at Sant'Egidio's headquarters and in its garden enabled the mentality and culture of the delegations to evolve. It was no coincidence that the first of the seven protocols was only signed during the fifteenth month of negotiations, after a necessary period of acclimatization had enabled a common political language to be found.

RENAMO's so-called guerrilla psychology, developed over years of war and international isolation, had relegated its men to a closed and entirely self-referential way of thinking, with its own laws and atavistic mistrust. One initial hurdle was to convince RENAMO to recognize the government as such, in order that RENAMO in turn could then be recognized as a legitimate political entity. But how could recognition of RENAMO be assured? And how could it be made to accept a government against whom it was fighting? For RENAMO, the State did not exist because the State was FRELIMO, and it was this rigid association that needed to be overcome.

The draft Protocol of Basic Principles was an extra-agenda document through which the government and the guerrilla movement – having with great effort put behind them their obstinate political and mental reluctance to do so – finally accepted the need for mutual recognition of each party's right to exist. It provided for the acceptance by RENAMO of the legitimacy of the government – and, hence, the sovereignty of the State – which it had hitherto refuted, whilst for its part, the government accepted the existence of RENAMO as an opposition political movement, thereby effectively recognizing its right to participate in national and international political life. After the draft Protocol of Basic Principles, RENAMO requested and – not without resistance from the government – obtained an undertaking to have all laws, including the Constitution, interpreted in light of the agreement that was to be signed, which would be conferred the status of constitutional law.

The efforts to transform RENAMO into a political movement, encouraged by the mediators, met with a certain degree of approval among its leaders. It must be said that a contributing factor to the achievement of peace was the unity of the guerrilla movement. Unlike similar groups, RENAMO managed to retain a strong and united leadership, which facilitated the resolution of the conflict. Often in Africa, political and military groups break down into various factions, precisely at the point when negotiations are entered into. The case of Darfur, with its proliferation of armed groups, parties and movements, epitomizes the ease with which guerrilla movements can often split along ethnic lines, or into military and political wings.

Finally, attention should also be drawn to the efforts made by the FRELIMO government, which was more "advanced" than the RENAMO *bandidos* but also held back by ancestral fears and mistrust. Its ability to evolve and open itself up to change, with the transition from the single-party system that had marked the first fifteen years of independence to democratic political pluralism in all its forms, must definitely be acknowledged. It was, however, a slow change. While courageous decisions were being taken in Rome, many of FRELIMO's cadres, who were not so involved in the negotiation process, remained unconvinced of the feasibility of a diplomatic solution to the conflict because they did not view RENAMO as a legitimate dialogue partner, but still and exclusively as a puppet in the hands of South Africa and international reactionary forces.

Synchronization problems

It took time to get to the point of signing the Peace Agreement, in part because it seemed that the delegations were operating on different timetables and time zones. It was a question of bringing together two different worlds that ran according to their own logic and dynamics. First and foremost, their clocks needed to be synchronized. This meant months of preliminary work. In fact, the majority of the agreed positions, translated into documents signed by both parties, emerged during the latter half of the negotiations, after the Protocol of Basic Principles had clarified the mutual identity of the parties and brought their different approaches and ways of thinking into sync.

One factor which contributed to the length of the negotiations was the relationship between what was happening in Rome and what was happening in Mozambique. One of the major difficulties, which dampened RENAMO's enthusiasm, related to the very democratic changes that the guerrillas prided themselves on having fought for. So what was going on? Basically, changes that RENAMO had for years demanded – including democratization, political pluralism, economic liberalization, and so on – were granted by the government in Maputo before they were discussed at the negotiating table. For example, three weeks after the first meeting in Rome, on July 31, 1990, Chissano had announced the introduction of a multiparty political system. FRELIMO then unilaterally adopted a new Constitution and, in 1991, a law relating to political parties.

The problem was not the content of these measures, with which RENAMO agreed, but rather the unilateral process by means of which they were introduced. Thus, the changes RENAMO had fought for became a source of irritation. In the implementation of these reforms, it saw a final underhanded attempt by the government to de-legitimize its struggle – in short, a tactic to deprive it of room to negotiate. Paradoxically, all this slowed down the peace process. The situation in Mozambique required the government to perform a difficult balancing act, with one eye on RENAMO, so as not to heighten its sensitivities, and the other on the rest of the country, which was demanding reform.

Bringing the parties into sync was by no means a secondary consideration in the peace talks and demanded infinite patience on the part of the mediators. It was important not to forget that the negotiations had started from scratch with the first direct meeting between the two sides after years of war and violence. In short, the time required for mutual acceptance and for the parties to acclimatize also had to be observed in order to proceed towards peace. Mistrust and misgivings ran deep on both sides. It is true that Le Monde spoke of a negotiation process that was "dragging on", and that more than one diplomat expressed skepticism, but in

Rome it was clear that the negotiations would require time if a serious and definitive agreement were to be reached.

In the meantime, people were dying in Mozambique. The mediators were not unaware of this, and the knowledge of it weighed heavily on them. They urged the parties to declare ceasefires, set up demilitarized zones, and allow the passage of humanitarian convoys. But a hastily-reached peace agreement, with no guarantees of stability and, above all, of which the two parties were not convinced, could have cost the country even more misery in the form of a resumption of hostilities without any further prospects for peace.

Stable peace would have to be achieved through hard work and patience, built as it is on memory, friendship, selflessness, care, sensitivity, a willingness to understand, a love of history and complexity, and last but not least, steadfastness and patience. It was these elements that enabled a successful conclusion to the negotiations. Moreover, it must also be said that the negotiations in Rome were a truly African dialogue between Africans, even though they were held far from Africa – a distance which, incidentally, played its own positive part, as it allowed the delegations of both parties to work in safe conditions, free from the emotions and pressures that fighting necessarily gives rise to, and away from interference of any kind. Despite taking place within the perimeter of the walls of Sant'Egidio, this was genuinely a meeting between Mozambicans, where it was possible to address the reasons for the dispute head-on and, above all, for "members of the same family" to find a solution.

Naturally, the changes taking place in southern Africa, with the independence of Namibia, the peace talks and agreements in Angola, and the De Klerk era in South Africa, represented a further boost to peace in Mozambique. Even in Zimbabwe, there was weariness and discontent with the prolonged war that was tying up thousands of Harare's troops. These were factors that contributed to an easing of tensions. But none of this would have been enough to bring about peace in Mozambique. There was a need for a concerted effort, an ability to involve different actors (including African countries, Western governments and civil society) so that they interacted constructively, in the belief that no one alone held the answer.

The USA, UK, France, Portugal, the UN, military experts, lawyers, as well as governments of the region (notably Zimbabwe), were all present in Rome as observers. For its part, the Holy See maintained a benevolent attitude, which reassured the parties and was rewarded with respect. However, at the negotiating table, it was the two parties alone – as Mozambicans – who made the decisions, taking into account all that was said to them by the observers and experts present. Meanwhile, the four mediators ensured that the negotiations were kept on track, by coordinating the various interactions instrumental in the success of the negotiations.

Another important factor that contributed to the peace settlement was the pressure brought to bear by civil society. A case in point was the ceremony where 100,000 signatures collected in Mozambican parishes – urging the delegations to bring the talks to a speedy conclusion – were presented. The negotiating table, which was usually well-ordered, was buried under an avalanche of pages with signatures for peace. Raul Domingos, head of the RENAMO delegation, was taken aback when, by chance among the many signatures, he stumbled across that of his father, whom he had not seen for over ten years.

Towards the signing of the Peace Agreement

In mid-1992, a new factor intervened in the peace process: drought and famine hit Mozambique hard, particularly in the hinterland areas controlled by RENAMO which were inaccessible to international aid. Late on the night of July 16, 1992, an agreement was reached to create "humanitarian corridors" through which international aid could be delivered. Yet whilst the famine was a factor that stepped up the pace of the negotiations, the very functioning of these humanitarian corridors depended on the outcome of political negotiations. Indeed, the relief convoys would only start moving once the Peace Agreement was signed.

From August 5-7, 1992, with the help of the Presidents of Zimbabwe and Botswana, the first personal meeting between Chissano and Dhlakama took place in Rome. On a torrid evening, the two leaders, in the presence of the President of Zimbabwe, Robert Mugabe, finally managed to allay RENAMO's fears. Dhlakama had surprised everyone by openly revealing his misgivings, one of which was that Chissano would grant Mozambican citizenship to "millions of Zimbabweans" so that they would vote for FRELIMO, "as had happened many times before". After checking quickly with his colleagues, Chissano ascertained that, in fifteen years of independence, Mozambican citizenship had been granted to only eight people. The tension dissolved into relieved laughter. After a brief further consultation with his delegation, Dhlakama returned to the table at midnight declaring that he wished to continue negotiating and committed to signing a peace agreement by October 1. In the weeks that followed, the two delegations continued to talk, putting the finishing touches to the last documents which dealt with military questions and the reciprocal guarantees that would come into play upon the cessation of hostilities.

The date for the signing of the Peace Agreement was now approaching. However, on September 28, a letter from RENAMO's leader, who was still having qualms, called on the four mediators to postpone the deadline. The mediators, showing both flexibility and firmness, nevertheless succeeded in getting Dhlakama to come to Rome on the evening of October 1, whilst accepting de facto that the date for the signing would be postponed. There followed three days and three nights of relentless work, with the unexpected emergence of a new issue that had not been previously raised but was now considered crucial by RENAMO. It involved the question of the administration, during the transition period to elections, of the territories controlled by RENAMO. Meanwhile, the international guests were waiting in their hotels, with their bags ready to leave Rome should the negotiations come to a grinding halt. On the evening of October 3, the mediators managed to resolve the outstanding issues, thanks also to the flexibility shown by Chissano.

On October 4, 1992, in the presence of several African heads of State and representatives of numerous governments, Chissano and Dhlakama sealed the General Peace Agreement for Mozambique in a solemn ceremony. It consisted of seven protocols together with several annexes. The Agreement provided that: there would be an immediate cessation of hostilities; the troops of both parties would then focus on proceeding with partial demobilization, together with the redeployment of 15,000 men from each side into a single unified army; and war zones were to be demilitarized and political prisoners set free. The goal of lasting peace would then be pursued through free elections to be held within one year and, to that end, the Agreement set out in detail the key components of the legislative program to be adopted, including, in particular, a Political Parties Act and an Electoral Act.

The Agreement also contained guarantees for its proper implementation, including the timetable agreed with the UN and the required composition of the various joint commissions during the transition phase. It also provided for a Donors' conference, in which the international community would determine how to financially support the reconstruction of the country. The annexes included an agreement on the withdrawal of Zimbabwean troops with the establishment of ceasefire corridors and a Joint Verification Commission, as well as a declaration on guiding principles for humanitarian assistance in consequence of the 1992 drought.[13]

The effects of peace were immediately perceivable. Within weeks, it was already possible for everyone to move around the country freely. The Christmas and New Year festivities brought home this new-found freedom, to general amazement. The fact that the Agreement held surprised international observers and the Mozambicans themselves. There was dancing all over the country. Mozambican refugees in neighboring countries later recounted how euphoria prevailed over prudence when it was decided to release food supplies – up till then rationed out – to be consumed during large festivities, a sign of how strong confidence in the future had become. In Rome's Basilica of Santa Maria in Trastevere, at the end of a thanksgiving celebration, the Archbishop of Beira danced with his eyes closed, almost enraptured.

Memory, reconciliation, and justice

The Mozambique Peace Agreement brought with it an amnesty for acts committed in the course of war. Was this peace without justice? This goes to the heart of one of the most difficult issues to resolve to ensure lasting peace in countries emerging from armed conflict, the repercussions of which, as is well-known, can last for decades.[14] There are many possible solutions, including truth and reconciliation commissions, international tribunals, ordinary judicial proceedings, as well as other options. In the Balkans, inquiries into the atrocities of the recent past have triggered a vicious cycle of accusations and counter-accusations, political exploitation and designs of revenge. In other cases, such as in South Africa, choosing to base the entire process of reconciliation on memory and forgiveness ("there is no future without forgiveness") has given rise to a positive cathartic process.

For their part, the Mozambicans, in giving priority to "that which unites" and putting aside "that which divides", had indicated their chosen approach from the outset of the negotiations: to turn the page once and for all by granting a general amnesty, which would be backed up by reconciliation ceremonies and initiatives involving the population. This was a difficult – and far from inevitable – choice, which allowed the closing of the long and painful chapter of the war and the opening of a new one, transforming the former warring parties into political opponents within a parliamentary and institutional arena. It has to be said that Mozambique was spared ethnic hatred, which has unfortunately left a dramatic mark on other situations. But it was not easy to forget a million deaths. The courage to turn the page perhaps carried a risk of not working through the grieving process.

However, it did have the advantage of bringing the country together again much more rapidly.[15] Mozambique wanted to overcome the tragedy of the civil war in a single leap. The fact that today over half the population was born after the end of the military hostilities symbolizes the desire not to dwell vainly on divisive memories and resentments. What surprised many is that there were no reprisals carried out in Mozambique after October 4, 1992. Everyone immediately went back to living their lives without looking back to settle scores. Everyone knew that the war had produced cruelty, and that the war had spread death. In one sense, the war was responsible for the deaths, not people. Peace, having ousted war, was the new ruler. It would be unfair to say that this was an imposed removal or oblivion. Rather, it was the solution chosen by the Mozambicans. History, in bringing them peace, has done them justice.

A legacy of peace

Fr. Matteo Zuppi, in drawing some useful lessons for the pacification of conflicts from the case of Mozambique, listed the following key success factors:

The identification and recognition of the "real" parties to the negotiation. The mediation efforts for peace in Mozambique showed that a cultural and anthropological understanding of the parties to the conflict is crucial;

the establishment of clear mechanisms in negotiation texts, setting out all details in order to avoid any "elastic" or potentially divergent interpretations; for this to be achieved, it is essential that proposals come from the parties to the dispute and are not imposed by the mediators;

the fixing of a precise timetable, but also the establishment of clear mechanisms that enable it to be modified;

the transformation of a guerilla movement into a party (moving from armed to political struggle);

the provision of an economic underpinning for the political agreement reached (incentives are needed – including those of a material nature – for peace to work);

the choice, by the parties to the conflict, of mediators perceived as honest brokers, and not mediators imposed in pursuance of partisan, domestic or regional interests, or those of international entities;

the furnishing of national and international guarantees which protect the party who feels they are the loser.[16]

The case of Mozambique is one of the few examples of successful negotiations that have produced a lasting peace in Africa. Scholars and experts in conflict resolution have attempted to understand the reasons for this.

After 1992, quite a few Mozambicans have found themselves involved in the peace processes of other African countries. In the 1990s, Armando Guebuza, the head of the Mozambican government's delegation to the negotiations in Rome and today the country's president, was called on to chair a committee in the Arusha negotiations for peace in Burundi. Another protagonist of the Rome negotiations, Francisco Madeira, also helped negotiate a settlement of an internal conflict on the Comoros Islands in the Indian Ocean. These are just two examples.

Visiting Mozambique today, after eighteen years of peace, it is clear that its stable democracy is a model for Africa. The alphabet of Rome made it possible to combine the vocabulary of democracy with the grammar of dialogue. The very existence of the parliament, which functions relatively well despite difficulties, is the embodiment of a democracy at peace. Divisive factors – such as regional differences and disparities which, if unresolved, could be a source of instability in the long term – may undermine the future. Fortunately, in Mozambique there is no tribal issue. But the temptation of violence is always lurking in the background, as demonstrated by the February 2008 riots in Maputo following a rise in fuel prices. The reports of lynchings of real or alleged thieves, which sadly fill the pages of newspapers (in Beira, the country's second largest city, 27 people were lynched in 2007 alone), are now accepted with a sense of powerlessness by the population as the price to be paid in blood for the absence of a credible judicial system.

In this regard, the lesson that history teaches is more relevant today than ever: peace is a dynamic process, it should not just be preserved but must also grow, becoming a safeguard of human rights, economic development, the stability of life and of democratic institutions, security and the rule of law. Today, as in the past, there is a need to seek out "that which unites".

[1] Isolated sugarloaf-shaped hills and mountains devoid of vegetation, found amid plains or plateaus.

[2] For a complete account of the events that led to peace in Mozambique, cf. R. Morozzo della Rocca, *Mozambico una pace per l'Africa*, Milan 2002.

[3] Cf. Moçambique. Maputo. 18. IX. 1988. *Encontro com os Bispos de Moçambique*, Portuguese text of the speech issued by the Holy See Press Office,

and A. Purgatori, *Il Papa in Mozambico rilancia il ruolo mediatore della Chiesa*, "Corriere della Sera", September 17, 1988.

[4] Cf. FRELIMO, *Actas do Quinto Congresso*, August 1989.

[5] Cf. *Verbal oficial do encontro das Delegações do Governo da República Popular de Moçambique e da RENAMO*, no. 1 – July 8, 1990.

[6] *Annex to the text of the Acordo Geral de Paz de Moçambique*, Rome, October 4, 1992.

[7] For a complete account by one of the mediators, cf. A. Riccardi, *Paz 15 Anos: O porquê da memória*, "Notícias", Maputo, October 4, 2007.

[8] C. Hume, *Il processo di pace in Mozambico*, p. 34, typewritten manuscript held in the Community of Sant'Egidio Archive (hereinafter referred to as "ACSE"), Mozambique collection.

[9] B. Ghali, *"Message from the Secretary-General to the Seventh International Meeting for Peace of the Sant'Egidio Community"*, September 19-22, 1993.

[10] By "weak strength" of faith, what is meant is a spiritual conviction that, despite apparent powerlessness and a lack of potent material means, one can be effective by drawing strength from one's own character of altruistic selflessness and detachment from partisan interests.

[11] Cf. A. Riccardi, *La pace preventiva*, Cinisello Balsamo 2004, p. 134.

[12] Cf. B. Mazula (ed.), *Moçambique: 10 Anos de Paz*, CEDE (Centro de Estudos de Democracia e Desenvolvimento), Maputo 2002.

[13] For a complete version of the Agreement translated into English, cf. *General Peace Agreement for Mozambique, in The Mozambican peace process in perspective*, "Accord", Issue 3, London 1998.

[14] Cf. M. Zuppi, *La lezione del Mozambico: la pace è possibile*, "Limes", 3, 2006, p. 272.

[15] Cf. A. Bartoli, *Forgiveness and Reconciliation in the Mozambique Peace Process*, Radnor 2001.

[16] Cf. M. Zuppi, *La formula italiana in Mozambico*, "Aspenia", no. 29, 2005, p. 276.

The Platform of Rome for Algeria

Algeria

Area (in sq km)	2,381,741
Population (millions)	32.900
Population density (inhabitants per sq km)	14
Percentage of population <15 years	29
Annual change in population (%)	+1.5
Infant mortality per 1,000 live births (<1 year/<5 years	30.4/40
Life expectancy at birth (male/female)	74/76
Fertility rate (average no. of children per woman)	2.5
Illiteracy rate (%)	27.9
Doctors (per 1,000 inhabitants)	0.8
Percentage of adult population living with HIV/AIDS (adult prevalence rate)	0.1
Human Development Index (HDI), expressed on a scale from 0 to 1, to three decimal places	0.722
HDI, world ranking	103
GDP per capita (USD)	85
Personal computers (per 1,000 inhabitants)	9.0

The Platform of Rome for Algeria

Marco Impagliazzo

A country divided in two

Algeria achieved independence in 1962, after a long war of national liberation fought against France with no holds barred. For France, this last colonial war was also the bloodiest, with nearly one million people killed in eight years of clashes.[1] French colonial rule ended after 132 years, during which Algeria had been accorded the privileged status of a French "metropolitan territory". As soon as it obtained independence, the North African country lost its European-descended population, the so-called *pieds-noirs*, with some 800,000 people leaving the country within weeks. The majority of them were French, which included 140,000 Jews naturalized under the Crémieux Decree of 1870, but there were also groups of Spaniards, Italians and Maltese.

Independence brought an end to the coexistence of communities of Christians of European descent, Jews, and Muslims of Arab and Berber origins. The massive exodus of *pieds-noirs* from Algeria in 1962 was characteristic of the process of religious segregation and homogenization that took place in many Mediterranean countries during the twentieth century, marking the end of cohabitation between diverse religious and national communities.

The turmoil in Algeria during the 1990s had its roots in these events. The country underwent one of the longest colonization drives ever undertaken in Africa. Unlike other French dominions, Algeria was a settler colony. An entire generation of young French people fought a war in Algeria that left deep wounds in both countries, a case in point being the great controversy over the use of torture by the French army against Algerian insurgents. The presence in France of many descendants of *pieds-noirs* from Algeria marked, amongst other things, the first real wave of mass immigration from Africa to Europe.

In Algeria, the war had painful repercussions. For many years, the country was rocked by terrible vendettas and purges. Political leaders opted to establish a one-party regime which, from 1962, governed the country without any legal opposition being permitted until 1991, the year of the first multiparty parliamentary elections.[2] The army, guarantor of the regime's stability, played a predominant role in managing a national economy based on an industrial system linked to oil production and export of hydrocarbons.

Since the early years of independence, the country's development had been conceived in terms of a strategy that distinguished between two Algerias: a "useful" one, which included the cities, the coast and the desert with huge deposits of gas and oil, and a "useless" one, which took in the remainder of the national territory, including the countryside and villages. Fields remained abandoned because agriculture did not number among the priorities of leaders in Algiers who favored industry, in line with the model of socialist economies. Despite these imbalances, the country gained a reputation abroad for its original take on economic development, based on the concept of "industrializing industry" – the "useful" Algeria under another guise. Revenue from the oil industry did nothing but increase during the years of the presidency of Houari Boumedienne (1965-1979), one of the military leaders of the liberation struggle and responsible for the coup d'état that ousted the first President Ahmed Ben Bella.

This wealth enabled massive prestige spending. The management of revenues remained firmly in the hands of the President and a small governing group made up of military leaders and high-ranking civil servants who were members of the single party, the National Liberation Front (the FLN). Meanwhile, the "useless" Algeria expanded until it reached the outskirts of the cities, which were surrounded by belts of unproductive villages entirely dependent on urban centers. Huge *bidonvilles* (or shantytowns) grew up around the capital.

After the death of Boumedienne, the economy began to display worrying symptoms. The "useful" Algeria – that of industry, urban centers and oil – faltered, whilst life in the Algeria of the countryside, villages and *bidonvilles* was reduced to a struggle for survival. The crisis rapidly spread to the social and political spheres. At the end of the 1980s, the country's macroeconomic performance almost bore no relation to the real living conditions of the majority of the population. Prices rose notably, and although oil revenues remained high with profits growing, unemployment reached more than 50% of the working-age population. Deprivation and shortage of food affected broad swaths of the urban population. The social malaise was accompanied by a decline in moral standards and the emergence of widespread petty crime. People lived by their wits and *trabendo* – the Algerian term for contraband – flourished.

From political crisis to violence

The deterioration of the social situation saw the spread of propaganda by Islamist groups, who would later band together as the Islamic Salvation Front (the FIS) and who sought to tap into the despair of the younger generations, representing over 70% of the total population. In October 1988, the so-called "Couscous Revolt" broke out. In a manifestation of the depth of the social crisis, thousands of young people flooded into the center of Algiers, destroying all symbols of the regime. The bloody crackdown by the army increased the sense of alienation of young Algerians from their political and military leaders. The historical legitimacy of the regime, based on the victory in the war of independence against France, was no longer sufficiently compelling for a population that was mostly born after 1962.

The Islamist propaganda was simple and well-placed to tap into feelings of discontent. It advocated protest against the contempt (known as *hogra*) shown to citizens by State officials, and the need to overthrow a corrupt regime that was no longer capable of feeding the population. The wealth exhibited by a few – the inner circle of FLN and military leaders – was viewed as an insult to the great majority of Algerians, who watched as their living standards rapidly deteriorated. Even sections of the middle class, who were alarmed at how the economy was faring, joined the protest. As a consequence, the first free multiparty elections in independent Algeria saw a victory for the FIS[3] and the emergence, albeit with lesser impact, of political formations critical of the regime, such as Hocine Aït Ahmed's Socialist Forces Front (the FFS).

The electoral strength of the FIS was largely concentrated in those very parts of Algeria deemed "useless". In the countryside, in villages in agricultural areas, and in the vast outlying suburbs of Algiers, Constantine, Oran and other cities, the Islamists had been active for some time providing various forms of charity and support. The Islamic party also garnered support among sections of the conservative middle classes who subscribed to the religious values that the party cadres began to personify. The success of Islamism caused a split down the middle of the educated and Frenchified secular class, between those who – concerned by the radicalism of the FIS – saw the military as the lesser evil, and those – like the FFS leadership – who preferred to safeguard the newly-emerged democratic process and deal with the phenomenon politically.

In this climate, a resolve formed in leading army circles to wrest back power, culminating in the cancellation of the electoral process in January 1992 and the dissolution of the Islamic party two months later. High-ranking military officials, supported by sections of the secular bourgeoisie opposed to the FIS, clamped down on the protest movement and imposed a state of emergency. This triggered a profound crisis. Armed fundamentalist groups with violence as their creed sprang into existence, ushering in a civil war that would become a sort of "war with no name".

The "useful" Algeria once more became the focal point of the regime's interest and prevailed over those parts of the country deemed "useless", again relegated to the margins of political and social life. The war deepened the divide between the two Algerias. The cities became a refuge for thousands of peasants and poor people fleeing from areas of conflict. In Algiers, the first tent cities sprang up, some of which were not far from the center. The regime concentrated on defending oil fields, business districts, protected neighborhoods and communications infrastructure. At the same time, it showed no interest in most of the rest of the country and population. In rural areas, the presence of the State was confined to the appearance every so often of troops. The social crisis grew deeper, with the lives of Algerians becoming increasingly more difficult and the distribution of essential supplies either held up or partially blocked. The public health system was unable to meet the most basic of needs, and in central districts of Algiers there was frequently no water supply. On the ground, the conflict descended into deadly chaos. After an initial campaign of attacks against specific targets (including soldiers, police, intellectuals, journalists, and women) and following several efforts to adopt some form of unified front, the period between 1995 and 1996 saw terrorist operations become fragmented. Given the impossibility of defeating or destabilizing the regime, the armed groups engaged in a brutal scorched-earth policy of blind acts of violence and massacres of civilians, even in rural areas sympathetic to the now-dissolved FIS. In response, the military authorities limited their engagement to discrete and sporadic interventions, arming civilians so that they could defend themselves. The result of these contrasting strategies, both of which had contempt for the civilian population in common, was that of transforming the war into a bloody fratricidal conflict between gangs, which seemed to follow more of a mafia-feud logic than any military strategy.

At the end of 1996, the Algerian Prime Minister Ahmed Ouyahia asserted that the terrorism was a "residual" phenomenon. The international community expressed bewilderment. Estimates at that point put the figure at 80,000 lives lost in the violence, which had reached fever-pitch levels. The Algerian Prime Minister's statements were to be read from a "useful" Algeria perspective, implying that efforts to protect hydrocarbon fields and urban centers had proved successful, whilst the army had disengaged from many of the interior regions that were difficult to control, leaving patrolling and suppression to civilian militias which thereby reduced military losses. Moreover, the country's macroeconomic performance was favorable. The rising price of oil had dispensed with the need to renegotiate the expiring agreement with the International Monetary Fund, and inflation was slowing. The main and most ruthless armed group, the GIA, seemed to be following a contrary yet parallel logic, instigating devastating attacks on poor villages inhabited by destitute families, natural hotbeds of Islamist voters, thereby demonstrating that they were not seeking to carve out areas of influence within "useless" Algeria, nor to establish a fledgling Islamic State. This was a war of vested interests, where the stakes were land redistribution, land rents, and the control of transport and the import and export of goods. In these circumstances, the bulk of the population, particularly those living in rural areas, became easy hostages to the violence.

The tragic events in Algeria escalated in intensity, and in a certain sense became unfathomable. Each day brought news of attacks and violence against the civilian population, yet little was known about the situation on the ground, with few images and scant testimony emerging. It was a war with no name and no witnesses.

Understanding what was going on, the motives for such barbaric violence, and the reasons behind this seemingly insurmountable critical impasse, was becoming more and more difficult. Caught up in a tide of violence, Algeria, though part of the Mediterranean, was day by day drifting further away from the region's shared cultural commonalities.

On December 31, 1997, in his end-of-year televised address, the President of the Italian Republic, Oscar Luigi Scalfaro, while not explicitly mentioning Algeria, reminded Italians of the tragedy the North African country was experiencing, remarking that: "Europe cannot stand by and watch as thousands of people are massacred". A few days later, in the wake of a shocking series of massacres perpetrated against Algerian civilians, a request was made at the international level for outside intervention to enable the North African country to emerge from the crisis that had gripped it for the past six years.

Given the ferocity of the attacks against defenseless Algerian citizens, several European Union countries and the United States wondered at the inaction of the government in Algiers. Indeed, the government had for years continued to insist that there was no war in the country, but merely acts of terrorism that were "residual" in nature. Of the European Union countries, Italy expressed particular concern. Romano Prodi declared that Italy should play an appropriate role in the matter. On the following January 7, the Deputy Prime

Minister Walter Veltroni stated: "We have taken a step towards Europe undertaking a joint initiative in respect of Algeria. I do not think it is conceivable for European and international civil society to witness this slaughter without lifting a finger to do anything, which would be the same mistake made with Sarajevo". The Algerian authorities responded scathingly, accusing Italy and other European countries of meddling in the internal affairs of a sovereign country.

Protestations of interference became the *leitmotif* of Algiers' reactions against all those claiming any form of intervention was required in Algeria. They were leveled at the UN Secretary-General, Kofi Annan, when in October 1997 he declared that "the Algerian crisis is not solely an internal problem". Shortly after, the former President of Ireland Mary Robinson, then the UN High Commissioner for Human Rights, was met with a similar response when she requested information from the Algerian government regarding the events surrounding the massacres. Accusations of interference were meted out to the French, the Germans, the British and the Spanish, as well as to Bill Clinton when he supported the idea of an international inquiry into the massacres, proposed by the world's major humanitarian organisations.[4] Even the latter were not spared, with the Algerian government in particular denouncing Amnesty International in November 1997. As far as the Algerian military regime was concerned, only one stance from abroad was acceptable, namely, the condemnation of Islamic terrorism. Everything else fell into the category of interference and was considered direct (or presumed) support for the GIA. The military wanted a free hand to be able to carry out its task of eradicating terrorism. Algiers repeatedly insisted on this eradication approach, even as the death toll continued to mount and the military solution revealed itself as disastrous.

The Sant'Egidio initiative

One of the targets that has most frequently found itself in the sights of the Algerian regime is the Community of Sant'Egidio. Indeed, Egidio [Italian for Giles] would become a very familiar saint's name in the North African country, where, until a few years previously, only St. Augustine had been heard of. The Algerian authorities have attacked Sant'Egidio since November 1994, when, at the Community's headquarters in Rome, a peace initiative involving dialogue between the main Algerian political actors got underway. This meeting in Rome brought together Algerians of all political persuasions, ranging from the secular FLN to the Islamists of the FIS, to discuss a political solution to the national crisis.

These same Algerian parties would meet again in Rome in January, when, after a week of intense negotiations, they signed a joint proposal to the Algerian military government known as the Platform of Rome. This was a unique political document in the history of the Algerian conflict in that it represented the only non-military solution proposed to the Algerian crisis. Even today, Western governments, the international press, and experts in Algerian affairs continue to refer back to the Platform. Yet it is the government in Algiers that has spoken of it most insistently. In his final campaign rally for the parliamentary elections of June 5, 1997, Prime Minister Ahmed Ouyahia concluded his speech with the catch-cry: "Yes to peace, no to Sant'Egidio". Immediately after the signing of the Platform of Rome, unknown persons had scrawled "Long live Rome, long live Sant'Egidio, long live peace" on walls in Algiers as a challenge to the Algerian security forces. The words of the country's Prime Minister seemed to be aimed at blotting out those anonymous graffiti.

But what happened in Rome? And how did a Catholic organization come to be involved in a matter concerning an Arab-Islamic country?

On November 21-22, 1994, the *Colloque sur l'Algérie* was held in Rome. It saw the participation of key Algerian political leaders who had not met each other for some time. 250 accredited journalists from all over the world were also in attendance. At last, Algeria was not just making headlines for the number of deaths and attacks taking place. The initiative was proposed by the Community of Sant'Egidio, well-known for its mediation of the Mozambique peace talks. Initially, the sponsors of the *Colloque* had no intention of establishing a negotiating table, but of providing a forum in which "Algerian leaders of varying persuasions from the major political parties may present their views on the direction the country should take and contribute to possible solutions".[5] The letter of invitation to participants explained the nature of the meeting: "This will therefore not constitute a dialogue, which should in any case take place among Algerians in Algeria, but rather a free and genuine debate in which each participant can express his or her political viewpoint"[6].

The invitation was extended to the parties that had received significant numbers of votes in the first round of the 1991 parliamentary elections that were subsequently annulled. They included the National Liberation Front (FLN), the Socialist Forces Front (FFS), the Islamic Salvation Front (FIS), the moderate Islamist parties Ennahda and Hamas, the Rally for Culture and Democracy (RCD), the Party of Algerian Renewal (PRA), and the Movement for Democracy in Algeria (MDA). Also invited were the Workers' Party (PT), the Ettahadi Party and the Contemporary Muslim Algeria movement (JMC), which had not taken part in elections. The government was invited in the person of Foreign Affairs Minister Dembri, who was also afforded the opportunity to send a representative "to provide official input, considered crucial given the crisis".

In addition to the government and the parties, participation was also requested of trade unions (the General Union of Algerian Workers – UGTA), the National Union of Algerian Women (UNFA) and certain key figures, including Ahmed Taleb Ibrahimi, former Foreign Affairs Minister under President Chadli, Abdelaziz Belkhadem, the last President of the dissolved National Assembly and a member of the FLN's Political Bureau, and the lawyer Abdennour Ali-Yahia, President of the Algerian League for the Defense of Human Rights (LADDH). The invited guests further included a representative of the Supreme Islamic Council, the government authority responsible for the training of imams and the control of State mosques.

So how did the Sant'Egidio initiative take shape? The seeds were sown in September 1994, in Assisi, during the eighth International Meeting of Prayer for Peace[7] involving leaders from the major world religions. Andrea Riccardi, when questioned by journalists on the possibility of a Community of Sant'Egidio initiative in respect of Algeria, expressed his interest but did not conceal the difficulties inherent in any such undertaking. Riccardi would later explain that: "Some Algerian Muslim friends repeatedly asked us: 'Why do Christians, who often act to defend human rights, stop short when a Muslim country is involved?' It seemed to me a challenge that we urgently needed to take up". At that time, Sant'Egidio had been devastated by the assassinations of Fr. Henri Vergès[8] and Sr. Paule-Hélène Saint-Raymond, who had both worked in the diocesan library in the Kasbah of Algiers[9].

The Community had strong ties with the Church in Algeria. Since 1984, groups from Sant'Egidio had frequently visited the Maghrebi country in the context of interreligious encounters and exchanges and collaborative interaction between young people on both sides of the Mediterranean. The Algerian war of liberation had left its mark on the Algerian Church, but thanks to the leadership of its archbishop, Cardinal Léon Etienne Duval[10], it nurtured the idea that coexistence between Muslims, Christians and Jews was possible. Throughout the entire conflict, the Church had never come out in favor of an *Algérie française*. Its archbishop was the first to condemn the French army's use of torture against members of the FLN. As a result of taking these stances, Duval had attracted the hostility of a large proportion of the *pied-noir* community. Controversially dubbed "Mohammed" by some of his faithful, Duval was convinced of the need to maintain relations with the overwhelming majority Muslim population.

In the years following independence, Duval had been able to remain in Algeria and had gained a unique insight into fostering dialogue between Christians and Muslims in the context of the workings of the "Church within the realm of Islam". There was a close bond of friendship between Duval and the Community of Sant'Egidio. Indeed, the Rome-based Community was at home with the entire Algerian Church, including the appointed successor to the elderly Duval, Msgr. Teissier, as well as numerous priests and other religious brethren, such as the community of Trappist monks at the Notre Dame de l'Atlas monastery that would tragically be left shattered in May 1996 by the actions of the GIA.[11]

These were years of great turmoil in the Islamic world. In Algeria, the 1980s saw a crisis develop in traditional Islam, which was unable to fill the void left by the nationalist and socialist ideologies that had raised great hopes at the time the country had gained its independence. In its place, fueled without question by examples from abroad whilst also having its own homegrown characteristics and peculiarities, a new form of political Islam emerged which would later coalesce into the FIS. In Algeria, as in other Arab countries, a radical and political Islam developed among younger generations as an outlet for disillusion with the economic situation, anger at social injustice, and rejection of models imported from the West that were unattainable by the majority. With their hopes dashed, the younger generations found in the Islamic heritage a renewed sense of identity and of purpose in their struggle against the State, viewed as "all-consuming and corrupt". The religious radicalization of young Algerians was also facilitated by a process of "re-Islamization" that began in the latter period of Boumedienne's rule.

More particularly, as noted by Gilles Kepel[12], this involved a re-Islamization from the ground up, in the outlying suburbs of Algiers, among unemployed youth living in a vacuum of values and in contact with the big city. Islamism thus found itself performing the same function as had a certain brand of Marxism – anti-capitalist yet also anti-Soviet – among the West's younger generations in the 1960s and 1970s. It was more of a climate than an ideology, more of a hope and a protest than a clear political agenda. In the West, there began to be talk of "international Islamic extremists" who were credited with having a terrorist strategy against Western democracies. September 11, 2001 was still some way off, but after 1989 there was no lack of those in the West who foreshadowed that Islamism would take the place of communism as the new enemy: *islamisme nouvel communisme*, as Jean Daniel succinctly put it.

The case of Algeria was cause for concern. The West was not sorry to see the democratic electoral process in the North African country disrupted after the first round of voting had raised the prospect of an Islamist victory. It would seem that when faced with Islamism, the sole conceivable option is to adopt a *sécuritaire* – or repressive – strategy, so as to ensure the security of the West and protect civilization from barbarism. Yet the greatest risk to the West itself is that "Somalified" uncontrollable areas might be created at its very doorstep, against which no security policy can provide an effective defense. Algeria was poised to become just such an instance.

After the statements made in Assisi, a working group was set up at the Community of Sant'Egidio to consider whether it would be opportune to embark on a peace initiative for Algeria. The group, comprised of Fr. Matteo Zuppi, Marco Impagliazzo, Mario Marazziti and Mario Giro, initiated contact with representatives of the government, the different political parties and Algerian civil society. Establishing contact was not easy. Often the persons involved were in exile, in prison, or fearful of contact with the outside world. Nevertheless, reactions to the idea of a *Colloque sur l'Algérie* were, on the whole, positive.

In effect, the time was right. Between August and October, the last attempt at national dialogue in Algiers failed and the parties were considering how to break the negotiating impasse. Sant'Egidio's approach stressed the impossibility of an armed solution to the internal conflict and the need for the various parties to the crisis to come to an agreement. This was well-received. But would it be possible for them to meet around the same table and accomplish what had not proved possible in Algiers? The mistrust between the various political players in Algeria had deep historical roots. Even the word "dialogue" posed a problem. It might have seemed easier to organize bilateral meetings. The idea of the *Colloque sur l'Algérie* arose from the need to find a form of joint meeting that did not represent negotiations but provided a forum for a "free and genuine" debate of the real problems facing the country.

From the very earliest contact with the parties, the Sant'Egidio team was aware of their desire to express themselves free of the continuous scrutiny to which political forces in Algeria were subjected. The team also noted the fear of incurring criticism from the regime and from the media it controlled. Gradually, the possibility of devising an agreed common framework and of the parties accepting each other as dialogue partners began to emerge. The most delicate issue was that of the FIS. The Islamist party, whilst being the virtual winner of the first round of parliamentary elections held on December 26, 1996, had been dissolved. It was no longer active as a party, and it had no political contacts with other forces. Some of the FIS militants had merged into the confused jumble of armed groups, whilst others had concealed the fact of their previous party membership. As it was decided to invite the major leaders of parties and organizations representative of Algerian society to Rome, the invitation was also extended to the FIS.

The *Colloque sur l'Algérie* took place in a climate of growing trust between the Algerian interlocutors and culminated in a final Communiqué signed by all parties present, consisting of a concise seven-point declaration which affirmed the urgent need for a free and continuous flow of information on the crisis, reiterated the necessity of pursuing dialogue, and formalized a request to the Community of Sant'Egidio to provide "the forum and opportunity for further Colloques where conditions permit".[13]

The Platform of Rome: a peace offering

Less than two months after the *Colloque*, the Algerians were back at Sant'Egidio in an effort to give new impetus to the search for a solution to the crisis. As the country sank into an ever bloodier civil war, the hope was to present the government with a detailed peace offer. Following a series of intense talks, the Platform for a peaceful political solution to the crisis in Algeria[14] was signed on January 13, 1995 at the Community of Sant'Egidio's headquarters. At the foot of the document were the signatures of the seven most representative Algerian parties (who together had gained around 80% of the votes cast in the parliamentary elections of December 1991). They were: the FIS, the FLN, the FFS, the Movement for Democracy in Algeria (MDA), the Workers' Party (PT), and two moderate Islamist parties, with the addition of the Algerian League for the Defense of Human Rights. For the first time since the crisis erupted in January 1992, following the annulment of the first parliamentary elections in the history of the country's independence, Algerian political forces of all leanings had agreed on a political proposal. After three and a half years of war, which by then had already cost around 35,000 lives, the Platform of Rome represented the first genuine attempt to bring the protagonists of the crisis to a negotiating table.

This was a peace initiative, in the form of an agreement already at a very advanced stage, which was offered to the military government in order for the latter to appropriate it and use it to reconcile the divided country. With the Platform of Rome (also known as a "National Contract" in Algeria), the government in Algiers was given a significant opportunity to lead the country out of civil war by opting for democracy.

Up until January 1995, the various attempts at initiating a national dialogue to resolve the crisis had foundered due to a lack of coordination between the various political forces, as well as the systematic exclusion of the Islamic party, the FIS, winner of the first round of elections. In Rome, the main Algerian political leaders had come to a joint agreement. Faced with mounting public pressure, they had agreed to embark on a realistic peace process. One of the reasons for the success of the Platform of Rome was the inclusion of the FIS as a signatory. Critics of the initiative, in Algeria and elsewhere, chose instead to see the participation of FIS as undermining the meeting in Rome, as if it amounted to giving in to the initiators of the civil war, or even collusion with the perpetrators of the violence.

In effect, the FIS had its roots in the climate that prevailed between 1989-1991 when it became impossible to avoid taking a political stance, and during which the Front had triumphalistically touted itself as the only force conducive to the revitalization of Algeria, immune from the corruption that characterized the regime. The Islamic party viewed the other parties, both secular and nationalist, as having been rendered obsolete by the course of events. In those years, some of the leaders and militants of the FIS took extremist positions. After the dissolution of the party in March 1992, many of its members, feeling robbed of their victory in the first round of the December 1991 parliamentary elections, saw armed struggle as their only option. Consequently, they became guerrillas and terrorists.

However, by the end of 1994, given the radicalization of the conflict, the exclusion of the Islamist political wing from any dialogue would have made any negotiations futile and deprived them of any chance of halting the violence.[15] At the same time, the leadership of the FIS was by then convinced that no military solution of the conflict was possible and seemed intent on finding a way out. A window of opportunity therefore presented itself to engage the Islamist party in a peace initiative and to force it to make crucial democratic and human rights concessions.

The Platform of Rome was aimed at avoiding the risk of a "pact between hawks" being reached in Algeria, which would see the hardliners of the military regime and the extremists of the armed groups agree on a power sharing deal. Moves in this direction were underway at the initiative of certain Arab countries. A "pact between hawks" had for a long time had its supporters within one clan of the army, thought to be pragmatically sympathetic to the views of the extremists, or perhaps simply concerned with retaining power. Such an alliance would have entailed the exclusion of all democratic and secular forces (and indeed, civil society) as well as the ushering in of a military-Islamist dictatorship.

In contrast, the Platform of Rome envisaged a negotiated, comprehensive, and democratic solution, without the exclusion of any representative political group. Set alongside the secular parties (the FLN and FFS in particular), the FIS participated as another stakeholder and not as the outright protagonist. The Islamist party thus opted for the path of dialogue and abandoned the military struggle. In terms of the recent history of Islamic radicalism, this is the first case of an Islamist movement undertaking to accept a political framework for negotiating with other parties, based, in this case, on a Platform that contains all the necessary building blocks for democracy, such that it was described by the British weekly The Economist as "exemplarily democratic". It must also be said that, to date, the FIS has never gone back on the agreement signed in Rome.

The Platform was universally well-received. The US State Department, the French government, the EU Presidency, the European Parliament, Spain and Italy all expressed their approval of the document, its content, and the peace process set in motion in Rome. Yet it was especially the Algerian people who showed the greatest support for it. Letters, messages, and phone calls testified to the great hopes raised in Algeria by the agreements reached in Rome. It was at this time that the many "Long live Rome, long live peace" slogans began to appear on walls in Algiers. The regime's response, however, was negative. The spokesman of the government in Algiers, the same Ahmed Attaf who would later be appointed Foreign Affairs Minister, stated that the document was rejected "in its entirety and in every detail". Moreover, as far as the government was concerned, the meetings in Rome had been a *non événement*, or non-event – one which, however, it seemed everyone in Algeria was talking about. The Government organized demonstrations against the *non événement*, invoking the right to freedom from interference in internal affairs.

Yet the Platform had been drawn up and signed solely by Algerian leaders, who were forced to meet abroad due to the state of civil war and insecurity besetting the country. In 1995 in Rome, the silence regarding "Algeria's second war" was broken, and Italy found itself on the front line of a crisis on its very doorstep. Despite the lack of cultural interest shown towards Algeria, Italy was bound to the country by many interests, particularly of a commercial nature.

During the years of the Algerian crisis, the question arose as to whether Italy might have a political-diplomatic role to play. The initiative of the Community of Sant'Egidio called specifically on Italy to take a leading role in the matter. Unlike France, Italy did not have the kind of historical and visceral ties with Algeria that could raise suspicions of it harboring renewed colonial ambitions. Italy had always been considered a friendly country by Algeria, not only at a governmental level but also in the public's perception.

So how had Italy availed itself of this accumulated political and diplomatic goodwill? The fear of a possible energy blackmail had prevented any weighty initiatives being proposed which might have annoyed the authorities in Algiers, who were contrary to any outside intervention in the affairs of the country. Given that a third of Italy's annual gas demand was met by imports from Algeria, the specter of "the tap being turned off" – so to speak – loomed large. Nevertheless, there was no shortage of critics who maintained that Italy was too dependent on Algeria for its energy, and that the contracts entered into for the supply of gas were the product of corrupt procurement practices by Italian political leaders in the 1980s. The economic and trade links with the Maghrebi country were therefore seen as up for renegotiation, and one of the conditions that should be set in exchange for purchasing such large volumes of gas was that Algiers adopt a more determined approach towards resolving the crisis.

There had been no proper debate in Italy regarding the Algerian predicament and the possible role that Italy might play in relation to it. Only occasionally and in response to the most heinous attacks against the civilian population, had Italian political leaders taken any stance. Their statements took a broadly consistent line, and ranged from the views of the then Foreign Affairs Minister, Lamberto Dini, and those of the Foreign Undersecretary for European Affairs, Piero Fassino, to those of the Prime Minister, Romano Prodi, and in some cases, the Deputy Prime Minister, Walter Veltroni. In contrast, the Foreign Undersecretary for African Affairs, Rino Serri, continued to repose confidence in the line taken by the Algerian government.

The international reaction

As it was, January 1997 saw a deterioration in Italo-Algerian relations. On January 22, there was a meeting at Palazzo Chigi between Walter Veltroni and Hocine Aït Ahmed, the legendary figure of the Algerian war of independence and Secretary-General of the FFS, one of the parties that had signed the Platform of Rome. The announcement of the meeting resulted in an immediate formal protest being lodged against Italy by the Algerian ambassador in Rome, and condemnation of the Algerian socialist leader, who, during a press conference, made a dramatic appeal to Bill Clinton to appoint a mediator for the crisis. In an address to the nation on January 24, President Liamine Zéroual denounced the existence of an alleged foreign conspiracy against the nation's sovereignty.

In particular, the Algerian President once again decried the Platform in the following terms: "The Rome meeting was a political ploy that in reality used the terrorist movement to undermine the will of the sovereign Algerian people and keep the country in a spiral of destruction". In response to these statements, Piero Fassino, interviewed on January 26 by L'Unità, stated that Italy was in favor of a European political initiative to resolve the Algerian crisis. Fassino cited the Platform of Rome and the efforts of the Community of Sant'Egidio as an example of the Italian will to find a solution, adding: "I believe that international pressure should seek to achieve two outcomes: an agreement between all political forces aimed at completely isolating all acts of terrorism, whether perpetrated by the GIA or by hijacked elements of the State apparatus; and the immediate establishment of a genuine negotiating table between the government and the opposition in order to map out the steps required for a return to democratic normality".

From January 27 onwards, the Algerian press scathingly attacked Italy and its government, reiterating the accusations of interference. The Italian ambassador in Algiers was summoned to the Algerian Foreign Affairs Ministry, as had happened in the days following the signing of the Platform in 1995. Relations between Italy and Algeria became cold and strained.

Meanwhile, in France, the Socialist Party Secretary Lionel Jospin took up where Fassino had left off, criticizing Chirac for his inaction in Libération. The French politician cited the Platform of Rome and stated that there was a need for a European initiative: "France must break its silence. It must not give the impression of unconditionally supporting the Algerian authorities. The presidential elections in Algeria turned out to be a missed opportunity. You cannot commandeer an election to legitimize your own power". Jospin's words reflected a widespread disappointment among those in European political circles who had hoped Algeria's return to the polls would bring an end to the crisis.

On January 30, the Italian Foreign Affairs Minister, Lamberto Dini, responded to the Algerian accusations and tried a softer approach, without however yielding on the main thrust of Italy's position. "Italy", he said, "does not intend to submit a proposal for mediation, but to take steps in the international arena to ensure that the two opposing parties can find an even balance and thus come to an agreement to put an end to this extremely grave situation". After the stance taken by the French Socialists, with whom former President Valéry Giscard d'Estaing had in the meantime joined forces to suggest the involvement of the FIS in any negotiations, the Algerian response became even sterner, with the rejection of any European interference. The reply of the Algerian Foreign Minister Attaf was unequivocal: "It would be best for France to stay out of our affairs".

The wrangling between Europe and Algeria went on as the war in the North African country worsened. In early February 1997, there was news of a massacre that wiped out an entire village in the vicinity of Médéa, with 31 victims. Murderous campaigns that destroyed whole villages and slaughtered women and children began to take place on a scale not seen before.[16] On April 24, the Algerian government launched its campaign for the parliamentary elections. The validity of a poll held in such a tense climate would at the very least be debatable. On June 4, the eve of the election, the Chairman of the Italian Senate Committee on Foreign Affairs, Giangiacomo Migone, issued a statement which read: "It would be a mistake for the international community to ignore or downplay the serious limitations that, a priori, raise doubts regarding – if not make a foregone conclusion of – the outcome of this election, regardless of the tallied result".

The final result was as expected: the newly-formed government grouping – the Rassemblement National Démocratique (RND) – won by a large majority, taking 155 seats.[17] Voter turnout was low, as vouched for even by the official figures, which showed that 43% of eligible voters in the capital had cast their ballot. The United Nations, which sent an observer mission, criticized the conduct of the election.[18] All parties except for the RND complained of electoral fraud, whilst the international press remained skeptical of what it called a "sham election".

The elections did not thaw Euro-Algerian relations as the regime had hoped. European governments, including that of Italy, refrained from commenting on the results, and confined themselves to merely taking note of them. Negotiations over an Association Treaty between the EU and Algeria were having difficulty making any headway. June saw the beginning in France of the cohabitation between President Chirac and the socialist Jospin, who was appointed prime minister. Between June and August, despite the release by the authorities of the FIS leaders Abassi Madani and Abdelkader Hachani, the massacres took on an unprecedented scale, with hundreds killed every day.

As if to demonstrate that nothing could stand in the way of the military course chosen by the regime, Madani was quickly rearrested in late August after writing a letter to the UN Secretary-General declaring himself "ready to launch an appeal for an immediate halt to the bloodshed, as a preliminary step towards opening a serious dialogue". Despite the escalation of deaths[19], the military leadership refused to allow anyone to cooperate in peace-building efforts, least of all the head of a dissolved party who had dared approach a UN chief himself the object of scant regard in Algiers. Indeed, during a visit to Venice, Kofi Annan had only recently declared that "the Algerian crisis can no longer be considered – as has happened so far – an internal affair of the country". The responses from Algiers, which took the form of the usual charges of interference, were aimed not only at Annan but also at the Italian Foreign Minister Dini, according to whom "neither the government nor fundamentalist opposition forces in Algeria desire mediation".

In early September, the Algerian government called for local elections to be held on October 23. In Italian and European political circles, there was a growing conviction that a political initiative was needed. The inertia of the Algerian armed forces and security forces in the face of the recent massacres seemed appalling. Despite being stationed a few kilometers – sometimes even a few hundred meters – from where the massacres took place, military units did nothing as the carnage went on for hours. There was speculation as to the meaning of this behavior. On September 21, the AIS, the armed wing of the FIS, declared a unilateral ceasefire, which the government ignored. At the end of September, there was a further exchange between Attaf and Mary Robinson on violations of human rights in Algeria. At the beginning of

October, during a Franco-Italian summit, Chirac and Prodi raised the question of the Algerian crisis.

After the meetings, Chirac told the press that France supported Italy's proposal of an initiative to restore peace. Hints that there were moves afoot began to filter out of the various European governments. Requested to comment on the Algerian local elections of October 23[20], Italian Foreign Ministry sources issued the following statement to news agencies: "Although the experiment of the Sant'Egidio Platform in essence failed, it could prove a useful model in terms of method. The question is whether it can be replicated. The issue could be discussed at the meeting in Luxembourg".

Yet the increasing calls for action came more from the general public than from political circles, on the back of disturbing new revelations. In November, several British and French newspapers had published accounts by former agents of the Algerian security services, who accused the *Sécurité Militaire* of being responsible for many attacks hitherto attributed to the GIA. These bloody acts also included bombings in Paris and the murder of seven Italian sailors in 1994.[21] The Italian government requested an explanation from Algiers, which the latter refused to provide. A public demonstration under the banner of *Un jour pour l'Algérie* was called for November 10 in Paris[22], in memory of the victims of the crisis and to urge for a negotiated solution. A large crowd, including many North Africans, marched through the streets of Paris demanding peace. In New York, on November 18, Amnesty International presented its report on the situation in Algeria. It accused the regime of inaction and of failing to defend the population from violence, and proposed an international commission of inquiry into the massacres.

According to Amnesty, the death toll had reached the 80,000 mark.[23] A few days later, the European Parliament, at the instigation of humanitarian organizations, held a series of hearings into the violations of human rights, in which unnamed Algerian witnesses also took part. In responding to questions from Euro-parliamentarians, Foreign Minister Attaf lost his temper and stated: "Amnesty International now thinks it is incumbent upon itself to speak on behalf of terrorists". He also rejected the suggestion that the army was in any way responsible and denied claims that 12,000 people had vanished into thin air.[24]

1998 saw a continuation of efforts to find alternatives to the disastrous policy of eradication. Algiers found itself further isolated in the international arena by an American statement of January 6. The United States expressed its support for Amnesty International's request that a commission of inquiry be established. Around the same time, the German Foreign Affairs Minister, Kinkel, called for the EU partners to adopt a political initiative on Algeria. Jospin made it known that France was in agreement. In recent months, the French position had somewhat shifted in the direction of seeking a negotiated settlement. After the massacres in early January, the French Foreign Ministry spokesman had repeatedly urged Algiers "to ensure the legitimate right of the Algerian people to be protected".

Pressure on Algiers continued to mount[25] and the European Council decided unanimously to send a delegation to the North African country to explore possible solutions to the crisis. The regime, after an initial refusal, accepted the mission, provided that it was conducted "on the basis of the fight against terrorism". For the European Union, this was a tentative yet concrete step forward, signaling in any case that the "interference complex" – which until then inhibited any European political initiative – had been overcome.

At the same time, Sant'Egidio proposed that an international conference be held which would bring together all Algerian political parties – whether secular or Islamic, governmental or otherwise – including the dissolved FIS, in an attempt to isolate terrorism as much as possible and restore peace. This conference of Algerians, under international auspices, presupposed a willingness for dialogue on the part of the Algerian government which at that stage it did not harbor, but which might be thrust upon it by a lack of political prospects and the weariness of a country worn down by violence. In effect, something had started to stir in Algiers. On April 15, 1999, Abdelaziz Bouteflika, former Foreign Affairs Minister during the Boumedienne years and an old member of the National Liberation Front, was elected President of Algeria.

The election campaign was different to previous ones, with open debate and candidates intent on challenging each other over the major issues of the day, including terrorism, peace and the economic crisis. Algerians witnessed a never-before-seen phenomenon and a new atmosphere began to pervade the country. Up till then, terms such as "peace", "dialogue" and "reconciliation" had been taboo words in the political parlance of Algeria. With the presidential race, they became the words on every candidate's lips. It was like watching Algeria come out of a long hibernation – one that had been punctuated solely by proclamations of war on the now defeated "residual terrorism" and by complaints of "interference" and "treachery".

A new president and the "concorde nationale" initiative

Bouteflika, despite being considered close to the clans in power and thus termed the "consensus candidate", avoided the language used by the regime's elite and addressed the people in a direct and sometimes surprising manner. He spoke of a "strong and worthy" Algeria, criticizing the national vices and the resignation of Algerians. During election rallies, he did not hide a certain bitterness nor did he attempt to sweet-talk the crowds: "You fatten your sheep on this our land and then you go sell them as contraband in Morocco! You humiliate yourselves for the sake of getting a visa! Drugs, *trabendo*, the black market, racketeering ... what a disgrace! And what about you young people? What are you doing? You buy everything from overseas... even your toothpaste!". And when the room would burst into applause, he bid them: "Don't clap when I say these things! They're an embarrassment for Algeria!".

The words of the former "youngest Foreign Affairs Minister in the world" – who had taken office at the age of 26 and remained in the post for 16 years running – certainly conveyed a nostalgia for the past, for a time when the State and the people appeared united and when Algeria, a "beacon of the Third World", was respected internationally. Tapping into the pride and nationalism of Algerians, but without seeking to conceal the difficulties inherent in a crisis that was "multidimensional" (as it is customary to say in that part of the Mediterranean), Bouteflika also managed to broach the topic of peace. He broke with the official line and admitted the existence of the conflict and its terrible consequences, stating that he wanted to see "Algeria reconciled with itself".

All the other candidates (Taleb Ibrahimi, Aït Ahmed, Jaballah, Hamrouche, and Khatib), other than the former Prime Minister Sifi, were on the same wavelength as Bouteflika, acknowledging the need to put an end to the war through dialogue and negotiation. The parties that advocated the eradication approach, staunch champions of intransigence and war, were caught on the back foot. They had not presented candidates and had not foreseen that the election campaign would be infused with such a mood or raise such issues. Indeed, Said Saadi and Khalida Messaoudi's RCD party, finding itself wrong-footed, paradoxically called for a boycott of the election. The decision to oppose the holding of the ballot politically marginalized the extremist elements of the pro-eradication camp.

The election took place on April 15 amid a tense atmosphere. Bouteflika was the sole candidate running. In the end, the other six candidates in the presidential elections had all withdrawn from the contest, accusing the powers that be and the military of preparing to rig the vote in favor of the "consensus candidate". The springtime of Algiers seemed quickly to fade and the press spoke of "virtual elections", "hopes betrayed", and a "farce". Left alone in the running, Bouteflika won easily, receiving more than 70% of the votes cast. The voter turnout figure was disputed, with the government claiming it was 60%, whilst the opposition parties – united in a "coalition of six" – maintained it was just over 20%. Experts viewed the election results with caution. According to some, they represented yet another "vindication for the generals", while others, such as the historian Mohammed Harbi and the sociologist Laouhari Addi, felt that "Algeria's new President is beyond manipulation" and the "regime is now on the defensive". In Paris, the Foreign Ministry expressed its "concern", immediately sparking a dispute with France.

Nevertheless, Bouteflika continued to pursue the line taken during the election campaign. On April 27, the day of his inauguration into office, he gave his first speech as President and declared that "the priority of priorities is a return to civil peace, on which everything else hangs". He appealed to the political forces, including those who had criticized the manner in which he had been elected, stating "we are all called to join in the effort to put an end to the causes of the rifts and hostilities", and that "if dialogue can help eliminate the causes of the violence and restore civil harmony, then we need to revive it". "The army", he went on to say, "is not extrinsic to the nation – it may be consulted where necessary, but it will not have the power to make decisions on these matters". Bouteflika drew strength from being the first non-military President elected (except for the interlude of the High Committee of State and Boudiaf, who, however, had not been elected). At the same time, he knew the Algerian power system well from having moved in its circles and been one of its key figures during the country's better years.

Throughout the twenty years of his self-imposed exile and silence, he had maintained his contacts. Despite the "one-horse race" of the election, the watchwords of reconciliation and peace retained their currency. Bouteflika allowed himself to opine favorably on the Sant'Egidio Platform of January 1995: "The Rome agreement is not the Koran – there are passages that could be added or removed. But it's a bit like if I was feeling ill, and there was a pharmacy run by a Jew further ahead, I would keep walking until I got to the pharmacy with the medicine I need – regardless of who the pharmacist is". It was now possible to talk openly of an episode that the Algerian press wasted no time in dubbing "the hushed-up prelude" to the journey towards a peaceful settlement.

The first step of the President-elect was to take in hand the matter of the "AIS". The Islamic Salvation Army, some several thousand men strong, had been operating under a temporary truce since 1997. Bouteflika arranged for contact to be resumed with the leaders of the armed wing of the FIS with a view to transforming the truce into a permanent cessation of hostilities. In exchange, he launched a "concorde nationale" [or national concord] program by which former guerrillas would be gradually reintegrated into society. This was a complicated move, requiring talks with the political leaders of the FIS, Madani and Belhadj, but most of all, the backing of military leaders who, up till then, had preferred to keep the AIS in a state of suspension.

The response of Mezrag, leader of the AIS, was not long in coming. In a letter to the President made public by the press in Algiers, he conveyed his support for the "concorde nationale" initiative, whilst stipulating the usual conditions of the recognition and legal reinstatement (in whatever shape or form that might now take) of the Islamist party. Even Abassi Madani, from his home where he was under house arrest, expressed his "approval and support for Mezrag's decision to lay down arms for good". A legal solution of the thorny issue of the AIS was beginning to draw nearer. It was in any case well-known that the men of the armed wing of the FIS had for at least a year been working alongside the army in operations against GIA diehards, who were responsible for the worst of the atrocities played out in Algeria since 1991.

The reaction of the pro-eradication secular parties and the groups aligned with them was one of strong protest. Bouteflika declared that in the event of a 'no' vote in the National Assembly, he would submit his proposal to the people in a referendum, in the certainty that "the majority of the people are in favor of national reconciliation". With these initiatives, the new head of State caught Algerian political actors on the back foot. Some of his supporters, traditionally inclined towards intransigence, were certainly thrust into an embarrassing situation. At the same time, however, he also stole the thunder of the pro-dialogue opposition forces and of nearly all the former candidates in the April 15 elections. Bemusement and hope mingled in the observations of Algerian commentators. The most frequently asked question was whether Bouteflika would be able to hold firm in his position vis-à-vis the military regime, which continued in its silence.

The only vocal resistance to the President's proposals came from members of victims of terrorism family associations, though they were opposed by groups representing relatives of those that had been "made to disappear", who were in favor of reconciliation. Meanwhile, the President changed neither the government nor the Prime Minister appointed by his predecessor. He also made it clear that he had no intention of dissolving the parliament. Among his supporting majority were fierce opponents of dialogue as well as members of the FLN (out of whose ranks Bouteflika himself had emerged) and moderate Islamists. A cloud hung over the future of the RND, the party founded by Zéroual, which had already undergone a split during the election campaign.

The Algerian press reported rumors crediting the pro-dialogue arm of the FLN, silenced since 1996, with exerting a strong influence over the President. Abdelhamid Mehri, the former FLN Secretary-General who had signed the Sant'Egidio Platform, reemerged on the scene. Speaking to an Arab television network, the politician stated: "Our brother Bouteflika has made some decisions that are certainly a first step towards national *entente*; this is in keeping with the spirit of the Rome agreement, which continues to be relevant and the broad principles of which could be developed further".

In late June 1999, another step was taken towards the goal of "concorde nationale". From Switzerland, where he was attending the Crans Montana Forum, the President announced an amnesty for thousands of jailed Islamists, starting with those who had not committed any acts of bloodshed. On the same occasion, the official toll (of approximately 26,000 victims) for the crisis that had gripped Algeria since 1992 was contradicted by Bouteflika, who said: "There have been a million victims... and one hundred thousand deaths". He went on to add: "I will do everything I can to achieve peace. The halting of the electoral process in 1992 was an act of violence". In Algiers, the impact of these statements was momentous. The entire political approach of the preceding years seemed to be under fire. In a piece entitled "Sant'Egidio Bouteflika-style", Le Matin, one of the newspapers most hostile to dialogue, observed: "By adopting the arguments of the advocates of the Platform of Rome, Bouteflika has officially signaled the application within the country of the Sant'Egidio approach. Algeria has altered course within the space of two months".

On July 5, a national holiday in Algeria, 3,000 prisoners were released. Addressing the Military Chief of Staff, Bouteflika asked the army "for candid and sincere assistance, in the name of the Constitution and the laws of the Republic, to bring about what today we call civil concord". Also in early July, the National Assembly was called on to vote on the draft "concorde nationale" law. The debate was confused, with the government majority supporting a law it did not see as its own, whilst the pro-dialogue opposition sought to raise the stakes so as not to be left out of the fray. In the end, there was an almost unanimous vote in favor, with the sole abstention of Aït Ahmed's FFS and Louisa Hanoune's PT, who nevertheless issued positive statements lamenting solely the failure of the Charter to declare an end to the "state of emergency" in the country. The RCD, isolated in its pro-eradication stance, walked out of the Assembly refusing to vote.

Having achieved this result, the President could focus his attentions on the summit of the Organization of African Unity (OAU), which was scheduled to commence in Algiers on July 12. This was Bouteflika's opportunity to launch the country's comeback on the international stage, something the President was well-placed to pull off given his sixteen-year tenure as Foreign Affairs Minister, his intimate knowledge of African affairs, and his relationship with many African leaders that had been personal friends for decades. During the summit, Bouteflika excelled himself, even securing a peace agreement between Eritrea and Ethiopia. This was the Algeria the President wanted: a linchpin of African politics that was highly-regarded abroad. Confirmations of this were quick to arrive, with Alitalia, Air France and Lufthansa announcing the resumption of flights to Algiers, which had been suspended since the December 1994 hijacking of a French Airbus.

On July 28, the Spanish Foreign Affairs Minister was in Algiers, with his French counterpart Hubert Védrine arriving hot on his heels on the 29th. There was talk of Franco-Algerian *retrouvailles*. Chirac made it known that he was ready to visit Algiers. The pro-dialogue opposition forces chose this moment to relaunch their proposal for a "national conference on peace" to reach a "comprehensive solution". Bouteflika responded by calling the referendum he had long contemplated. On September 16, Algerians were asked to vote for or against the "concorde nationale" law.

A sort of scramble for the same patch took place between the President's supporters and the pro-dialogue opposition, with each side intent on proving that it best represented the people's desire for peace.

On July 12, responding to questions from international press representatives attending the OAU summit, Bouteflika spoke again of the Sant'Egidio Platform whilst telling of a meeting he had had in 1995 with Zéroual. The latter had asked for his opinion on the Platform. He repeated the story of the Jewish-run pharmacy and added:

Regarding the speculation at the time about who knows what kind of foreign manipulation was going on behind Sant'Egidio, I say that Algeria at that stage was going through an extremely difficult time. Even if there had been foreign manipulation, to the extent there were proposals which were positive from my perspective and that of my party, I was ready to defend them and consider them. Zéroual said to me: 'But we've already proposed the first section in consultations with the parties and they didn't accept it". I replied: 'When you proposed it and they rejected it, they showed their immaturity. That doesn't mean they don't have the right to grow up and come to you now saying that you were right... So I can't see why you wouldn't accept what you yourselves have already previously proposed'. Zéroual added: 'The second part would involve the State giving in'. I asked him: 'What do you mean by the State giving in?'. He responded: 'The unconditional release of the *chouyoukh* [the leaders of the FIS], the release of prisoners'. I said, 'Come on, it's not the Koran. It's a working document. You just need to make a few changes around the edges to say that the prisoners will be freed as soon as such and such conditions are met. That way the dialogue continues'. But it seems I wasn't convincing enough.

On July 16 and 23, Bouteflika first visited Constantine and then Oran. In the eastern capital, he observed: "This is a fine state of affairs. The toll already stands at 100,000 people killed, counting both sides. Every drop of Algerian blood is precious to me; it matters to me. And every Algerian who falls is a loss for the whole country, regardless of the side they were on. We are not at war with some foreign enemy [...] Even if there were such a thing as clean wars, this would still be a dirty one. It couldn't be dirtier than this because we're killing each other [...] Would peace perhaps seem more appropriate if we anticipated 300,000 deaths? I believe that common sense, simple common sense, tells us that we need to stop this fight to annihilation now".

In Oran, he maintained that he had "never made any secret of my unshakeable belief in reconciliation". He spoke once more of the Sant'Egidio Platform, again in the same terms. On this occasion too, the impact of his statements on Algerian public opinion was considerable. "It's the first time since the signing of the Platform", noted one newspaper in Algiers, "that an Algerian official, in the line of duty, who moreover happens to be the head of State, has publicly tackled the issue of the Sant'Egidio meeting in front of television cameras without any hang-ups, and without having to apologize to his audience. It's also the first time that millions of television viewers have heard the President himself say that this "National Contract" could serve as a foundation for a solution to the Algerian crisis.[26] The French paper Le Monde ran the headline: "Bouteflika harks back to Sant'Egidio plea and breaks taboo".

In a speech summoning the electorate to a September 16 referendum, Bouteflika focused heavily on peace: "I cannot stress this enough. Neither one side nor the other has a homeland that can be exchanged for another. Whatever comfort asylum might provide, the only paradise on earth for Algerians is Algeria itself. With this in mind, no opportunity should be dismissed out of hand. Any course of action that could set in train a peaceful dynamic should be encouraged, embarked upon and carried through to completion". Meanwhile, the death of King Hassan II of Morocco provided another opportunity for the Algerian leader to consolidate his country's international influence. Whilst in Rabat, he had many meetings.

The international community noted with pleasure the decided improvement in Algerian-Moroccan relations. The meeting between Bouteflika and Barak also caused a stir. Conveying Europe's interest in the political initiatives undertaken by the Algerian President, Romano Prodi, President-elect of the European Commission, wrote to Bouteflika stating: "Europe strongly supports your commitment towards national reconciliation".

In the September referendum, over 90% of votes cast were in favor of the "concorde nationale" initiative. There was, however, no shortage of difficulties for the Algerian President. The hard-line wing of the pro-eradication camp opposed the referendum. The former communists of the MDS [Mouvement Démocratique et Social] and their allies called for a boycott. The army continued to remain officially silent, leaving it uncertain as to what its actual position might be. But every now and again, the grapevine would let slip that the hard-liners among the generals were opposed. The majority was divided. Opposition lay in wait for Bouteflika's implementation of the government program. The President's problems would become evident when forming a new government.

It must also be said that violence had not yet lost its appeal. During those months, attacks and bombings, murders of children, and strikes on military convoys filled the news. Abdelkader Hachani, the number three man in the FIS who was negotiating on its behalf with the authorities, was also killed. The murder remained a mystery, like all "high-profile" assassinations in Algeria. But while the peace process suffered as a result of these events, it continued to move forward.

Notwithstanding the controversies that continued to stir up public opinion in Algeria, the new President decided it was necessary to sideline the *éradicateurs*, who were bent on waging war to the bitter end. He chose to pursue a national path to reconciliation, which took the form of various amnesty and other conciliatory laws. At first, the public was uncertain. Should those who had soiled their hands with so many foul deeds be forgiven? There was also a feeling that light ought to be shed on the many incidents that had remained unexplained, and which it was suspected had involved the complicity of the security forces in massacres and disappearances.[27] Bouteflika, however, would not permit such points of contention to stand in the way of Algeria's rebirth. He took the economy in hand and restored the luster to Algeria's international profile by making numerous trips and visits abroad. He relaunched diplomatic efforts on all fronts, his vision harking back to the country's golden age when Algiers was consulted to help resolve international crises, as had happened in a case involving Westerners kidnapped in Beirut during the Lebanon war.

The concorde process slowly moved ahead and Bouteflika's gamble succeeded, aided and abetted by a boom in oil prices[28] which lent a hand to the country's economic recovery. The old school of Algerian diplomacy got back into international gear, the economy improved and the violence decreased without, however, disappearing entirely. Thus it was that Algeria also managed to get through the difficult situation created by the Al Qaeda attacks of September 2001, which for several months bolstered the position of the pro-eradication extremist wing opposed to the President.

2004 saw Bouteflika easily reelected for a second term. Nevertheless, the crisis in the social fabric of the country has not yet been entirely overcome. Poverty has increased despite the State's coffers being full of petrodollars – a sign that the system of wealth distribution inherited from previous governments has not changed. The pro-eradication opposition remains aloof from the President, who has been accused of leniency towards former terrorists and Islamists. For its part, the pro-reconciliation camp has acknowledged his merits whilst doubting his democratic conviction and denouncing the persistence of murky links between political authorities and the army. Whilst moderate Islamists have spoken the praises of the President, he has been careful not to involve them too heavily. In 2003, the now long-banned FIS held, outside the country, what was effectively the first congress of its paradoxical political history. In 2004, amid controversy, the two leaders of the FIS in the 1990s, Ali Belhadj and Abassi Madani, were released.

President Bouteflika has effectively sought to lead the country out of a decade of bloodshed. However, he has failed to rid Algerian politics of its old vices, including impositions from on-high, undisclosed links between political and military leaders, and the intimidation of opponents. The fight against corruption has not made any headway and the Algerian economy is still held back by the usual ills. During his second term, Bouteflika has devoted much of his attentions to economic reform, with a view to stabilizing the country and transforming the successes achieved in the international arena and in the field of national reconciliation into benefits for Algerian society. Nevertheless, the situation remains desperate for at least seven million Algerians still living below the poverty line, representing a potential hotbed for new waves of terrorism and violence.

Appendix

Platform for a peaceful political solution to the crisis in Algeria

On this day, January 13, 1995, the Algerian opposition parties gathered here in Rome at the headquarters of the Community of Sant'Egidio, declare that:

Algeria is currently experiencing a tragic ordeal of unparalleled proportions.

Since achieving their hard-won independence more than thirty years ago, the Algerian people have not been able to see the principles and all the objectives of November 1, 1954 brought to fruition, and have watched all the hopes raised after October 1988 gradually fade.

Today, the Algerian people live in a climate of fear never before seen, oppressed by intolerable social and economic conditions. In this visually undocumented war, abductions, kidnappings, killings, systematic torture, mutilations and reprisals have become a daily reality in the lives of all Algerians.

The consequences of the events of June 1991 and the coup d'état of January 11, 1992, the cancellation of the electoral process, the banning of political activities, the dissolution of the FIS, the establishment of a state of emergency, together with the adoption of repressive measures and reactions to them, have created a dynamic of conflict.

Since then, the violence has continued to escalate and spread. Attempts by the authorities to organize civilians into militias have marked a new low in politics of the lowest order. There is a real risk of civil war, which threatens the physical wellbeing of the population, the country's unity and national sovereignty.

There is an urgent need for a comprehensive, political and fair solution in order for new prospects to emerge for a population that aspires to peace and popular legitimacy.

The authorities have only initiated a sham dialogue, which has served as a front for unilateral decision-making and *fait accompli* politics.

Genuine negotiations remain the only means by which to achieve a peaceful and democratic solution.

A – *Framework of values and principles*

The participants give their undertakings on the basis of a national contract, the principles of which are as follows and the acceptance of which is a necessary precondition for the validity of any negotiations:

article 1 of the declaration of November 1, 1954: "The restoration of the democratic and social sovereign Algerian State within the framework of the principles of Islam";

the rejection of violence as a means of gaining or remaining in power;

the rejection of dictatorship of any form or nature whatsoever and the people's right to defend their freely-elected institutions;

the respect and furtherance of human rights as enunciated by the Universal Declaration on Human Rights, the International Covenants on Human Rights, and the International Convention against Torture, as per the attached legal instruments;

the handover of political power between parties through universal suffrage;

the respect of popular legitimacy. Freely-elected institutions may only be impugned by popular will;

the supremacy of legitimate law;

the guarantee of fundamental freedoms, both individual and collective, regardless of race, sex, religion and language;

the consecration of a multiparty system;

the non-interference of the army in political affairs. The return of the army to its institutional role of safeguarding the unity and territorial integrity of the country;

the constituent elements of the Algerian national character, namely: Islam, Arabism and Amazighism. The culture and the two languages that have contributed to the formation of this national character must be institutionally accommodated and fostered within this unifying framework, without any exclusion or marginalization;

the separation of legislative, executive and judicial powers; and freedom of religion and respect for religious beliefs.

B - *Measures that need to precede negotiations*

The effective release of FIS leaders and all political prisoners.

The provision to FIS leaders of all the requisite means and assurances to enable them to assemble freely and meet with those whose opinion is deemed necessary for making decisions.

The liberalization of the political system and the media. The annulment of the dissolution of the FIS. The full restoration of the rights of all political parties to conduct their activities.

The lifting of bans and suspensions on the publication of newspapers, writings and books imposed pursuant to extraordinary powers.

The immediate, effective and verifiable cessation of the practice of torture.

Desistance from carrying out death sentences, extrajudicial executions and reprisals against the civilian population.

The condemnation of and the call for an end to the persecution of and attacks against civilians and foreigners and the destruction of public property.

The establishment of an independent commission of inquiry into acts of violence and serious violations of human rights.

C – *The restoration of peace*

A new dynamic for peace entails a gradual, parallel and negotiated process, including:

on the one side, the adoption of measures aimed at achieving real *détente*: the closure of prison camps, the lifting of the state of emergency and the repeal of extraordinary powers; and

on the other side, an urgent and unequivocal call for an end to the violence. All Algerians aspire to the restoration of civil peace. The methods to be used to achieve this goal shall be agreed by the two parties to the conflict with the active participation of other representative parties.

This dynamic for peace requires the comprehensive involvement of representative and peaceful political forces that are able to contribute to the success of the process and ensure public support.

D - *The return to constitutional legality*
The parties undertake to abide by the Constitution of February 23, 1989, which may be amended solely by constitutional means.

E - *The return to popular sovereignty*
The parties involved in the negotiations shall establish a transitional legal framework for the implementation of the matters herein agreed and the monitoring thereof. To this end, they shall establish a National Conference vested with substantive powers, comprising members from the authorities in power and from other representative political forces.
The Conference shall:
determine the necessary institutions, procedures and duration of the transitional period, which shall be as short as possible in view of the need to proceed to the holding of free multiparty elections enabling the people to exercise their sovereignty to the fullest;
ensure freedom of information, free access to the media and conditions conducive to the exercise of the people's freedom of choice; and ensure that the outcome of the election is respected.

F - *Assurances*
All the parties involved in the negotiations shall be entitled to obtain mutual assurances. Without derogating from their right to make independent decisions, the parties hereby:
oppose any interference in the internal affairs of Algeria;
denounce the *de facto* internationalization of the situation resulting from the confrontational policy conducted by the authorities;
express their continued belief that the crisis can only be resolved by Algerians and within Algeria;
undertake to conduct an awareness-raising campaign within

the international community in order to publicize this Platform and ensure that the initiative receives support;
agree to launch an international appeal in support of the need for a peaceful political settlement in Algeria;
call on the international community to show active solidarity with the people of Algeria;
and agree to maintain contact with each other and ongoing consultation and coordination.

Signed:
On behalf of the LADDH: Abdennour Ali-Yahia
On behalf of the FLN: Abdelhamid Mehri
On behalf of the FFS: Hocine Aït Ahmed; Ahmed Djeddai
On behalf of the FIS: Rabah Kebir; Anwar Haddam
On behalf of the PT: Louisa Hanoune
On behalf of the MDA: Ahmed Ben Bella; Khaled Bensmain
On behalf of Ennahda: Abdallah Jaballah
On behalf of the JMC: Ahmed Ben Mouhammed

---

[1] There is a quite a vast body of literature dealing with the war in Algeria, with studies and memoirs still being published in France and Algeria to this day. For a broad overview of the war as well as some more detailed accounts, see, inter alia: Y. Courrière, La guerre d'Algérie, Paris 1968-1971, 4 vols.; A. Horne, A Savage War of Peace. Algeria 1954-1962, London 1977; E. Behr, The Algerian Problem, London 1961; and P. Tripier, Autopsie de la guerre d'Algérie, Paris 1972.

[2] Following the municipal elections of 1990.

[3] In the first round of the parliamentary elections of December 1991.

[4] Namely: Amnesty International, Human Rights Watch, the International Federation for Human Rights (FIDH), and Reporters without borders.

[5] Letter of invitation to the Colloque, November 3, 1994, author's own personal collection of documents pertaining to the Colloque sur l'Algérie.

[6] Ibid.

[7] The title of the eighth "People and Religions" International Meeting of Prayer for Peace, organized by the Community of Sant'Egidio, was Friends of God, witnesses of peace, Assisi, November 11-13, 1994.

[8] In respect of Henri Vergès, cf. H. Vergès, A. Delorme & Frères maristes des écoles, Du Capcir à la Casbah: Henri Vergès, petit frère de Marie, témoin de l'amour au service des jeunes Algériens, Broché 1996.

[9] Henri Vergès and Paule-Hélène Saint-Raymond were murdered on May 8, 1994. On October 23, 1994 in Algiers, two Augustinian missionary sisters of Spanish nationality, Esther Paniagua and Caridad Alvarez, were also killed on their way to attend mass in the working-class neighborhood of Bab-el-Oued. The GIA claimed responsibility for both these attacks.

[10] As regards Cardinal Léon Etienne Duval, cf. M. Impagliazzo, *Duval d'Algeria. Una Chiesa tra Europa e mondo arabo (1946-1988)*, Rome 1994.

[11] For an account of the incident involving the death of monks from the Notre-Dame de l'Atlas monastery, cf. M. Duteil, *Les Martyrs de Tibhirine*, Éditions Brepols, Paris, 1996; and *Sept vies pour Dieu et pour l'Algérie*, B. Chenu (ed.), Bayard Éditions-Centurion, Paris 1996.

[12] G. Kepel, *La Revanche de Dieu, chrétiens, juifs et musulmans à la reconquête du monde*, Éditions du Seuil, Paris 1991.

[13] The final Communiqué of November 22, 1994 read as follows:
"The participants of the *Colloque sur l'Algérie*, gathered here in Rome on November 21-22, 1994, pay tribute to the Community of Sant'Egidio for the initiative it has taken in convening in Rome the *Colloque sur l'Algérie*, which has enabled a fruitful exchange of information and communication;
reaffirm the need to provide the Western world with a free, complete and continuous flow of information;
acknowledge that the *Colloque sur l'Algérie* has represented a first step in that direction;
express their hope that this *Colloque* marks the first in a series of contacts that will assist in resolving the impasse, with a view to opening up proper negotiations;
reiterate their opposition to any foreign interference and, furthermore, deny that there has been any interference by any foreign government;
express their hope that this step forward has paved the way for further such initiatives; and
call on the Community of Sant'Egidio to lead the way – as a source of constant information and by raising awareness of the complexity of the crisis in Algeria – in countering simplistic and dualistic interpretations of the situation, and to provide the forum and opportunity for further *Colloques* where conditions permit."
Signed:
Ahmed Ben Bella, Hocine Aït Ahmed, Abdelhamid Mehri, Anwar Haddam, Louisa Hanoune, Ahmed Ben Mouhammed, Abdallah Jaballah, Abdennour Ali-Yahia.

[14] For a detailed account of the various stages of the meetings in Rome which led to the signing of the Platform cf. M. Impagliazzo & M. Giro, *Algeria in ostaggio. Tra esercito e fondamentalismo, storia di una pace difficile*, Guerini e Associati, Milan, 1997. An English translation of the Platform [originally in French] is provided in the Appendix to this chapter.

[15] In October 1994, the last attempt at dialogue undertaken by the Algerian President Zéroual had failed.

[16] Human Rights Watch conducted its mission in Algeria between March 30 and April 13. Its report, published in June, was also very critical of the regime. On April 21, the worst massacre up till then took place, with 93 people – including many women and children – killed in a village 25 km south of Algiers. The episode became known as the "guillotine on the truck" incident. From April 26 to early May, the FIDH carried out its mission in Algeria. Its report, issued in early June, shed new light on the violence perpetrated by the GIA, but also on human rights violations committed by the regime.

[17] Then came the MSP (the former Hamas) with 69 seats, the FLN with 64, Ennahda with 34, the FFS with 20, the RCD with 19, and the PT with 4.

[18] On June 8, the UN Observer Mission issued a statement in Algiers heavily criticizing the conduct of the election, and went as far as refusing to hold a scheduled joint press conference with the government.

[19] On August 29, the worst massacre took place, with 300 people killed in Sidi Rais, south of Algiers.

[20] Elections which, as was foreseeable, were won by the RND.

[21] Reported in The Observer. This was followed by articles containing similar accounts in Le Monde. The Independent published other testimonials by lawyers and former security agents who spoke of 12,000 people having disappeared in Algeria.

[22] Organized by Reporters without borders, the FIDH, SOS Racisme and other French groups.

[23] The figure proposed by Amnesty International was backed up by Human Rights Watch and the FIDH.

[24] Attaf was in Brussels to meet with the then President of the European Council, the Luxembourgian Poos, who had invited him with a view to negotiating the dispatch of a Council delegation to Algiers. On that occasion, Attaf categorically refused.

[25] In Italy, the Secretary of the then Democratic Party of the Left (PDS), Massimo D'Alema, after a series of statements by the party's Foreign Affairs Spokesman, Umberto Ranieri, came out in favor of peace negotiations for Algeria. In an interview with Il Messaggero, the Secretary of the PDS stated that "a mistaken view has prevailed on Algeria, especially in French – and consequently in American – political circles. The view holds that in order to fight Islamic terrorism, it is necessary to uncritically support a military regime, when in reality, by so doing, Islamic terrorism and the military regime have become mutually supportive. The only way out of this situation is to reestablish a national dialogue that is also capable of bringing to light moderate Islamic forces" (December 21, 1997). D'Alema's views came very close to those of Lionel Jospin, and reflected the influence of the common approach towards the Algerian question adopted by the Socialist International – of which the parties of both were members.

[26] It may be worth noting that on August 3, "Boutef" – as young people in Algiers informally call him – broke another taboo, relating to calls for the increased Arabization of education and the State bureaucracy. Responding to criticisms from within his own majority, notably from the moderate Islamists of Nahnah's MSP party, who complained of the continuing use of the French language, the President stated: "Algeria is neither more Arab nor more intelligent than other Arab countries, and should not needlessly shut itself off". Nahnah initially responded with a scathing attack, accusing Bouteflika of "having betrayed the Constitution", but immediately calmed down in the face of the resolve shown by the head of State, who had no intention of backing down.

[27] The bloody events included a series of bombings of the Paris Metro and the murder of seven Italian sailors in 1994, as well as other large-scale massacres within Algeria. Cf. L. Aggoun & J.-B. Rivoire, *Françalgérie. Crimes et mensonges d'État*, La Découverte, Paris 2004; H. Souaidia, *La sale guerre*, La Découverte, Paris 2001; and N. Yous, *Qui a tué à Bentalha? Algérie: Chronique d'un massacre annoncé*, La Découverte, Paris 2000.

[28] In general terms, Algeria's largest trading partner is France, accounting for 25% of total imports to Algeria, followed by Spain with 12%, the US with 11% and Italy with 8%. Algeria is self-sufficient only as regards energy products. As far as the hydrocarbons sector is concerned, France is not as dependent on Algeria as other European countries, particularly Italy. Algeria has a dense network of oil and gas pipelines. The most important of these is the Transmed pipeline, built by the Italians, which connects the country to Italy and Slovenia via Tunisia. The capacity of Transmed is 24 billion m3 of gas a year. By way of comparison, in western Algeria at the end of 1996, the American company Bechtel completed a major new gas pipeline, the GME (Maghreb-Europe), linking Algeria, Morocco, Spain and Portugal. When working to full potential, the GME can reach capacities of 8-9 billion m3 per year.

The Case of Guatemala

Guatemala

Area (in sq km)	108,889
Population (millions)	12.152
Population density (inhabitants per sq km)	112
Percentage of population <15 years	41.7
Annual change in population (%)	+2.6
Infant mortality per 1,000 live births (<1 year/<5 years)	29.4/45
Life expectancy at birth (male/female)	64/71
Fertility rate (average no. of children per woman)	4.5
Illiteracy rate (%)	28.2
Doctors (per 1,000 inhabitants)	0.9
Percentage of adult population living with HIV/AIDS (adult prevalence rate)	1.1
Human Development Index (HDI), expressed on a scale from 0 to 1, to three decimal places	0.663
HDI, world ranking	117
GDP per capita (USD)	1,995
GDP per capita, world ranking	109
Personal computers (per 1,000 inhabitants)	18.0

The Case of Guatemala

Roberto Morozzo della Rocca

Guatemala's "internal armed conflict" lasted thirty-four years – from 1962 to 1996. This was the bloodiest civil war in Latin America in the 20th century, resulting in 200,000 deaths, 10% of which were due to clashes between the regular army and guerrillas and 90% to massacres of civilians. It was also the longest-running internal conflict on the Bolivarian continent after that in Colombia, which is still raging.[1] Warlike violence developed in Guatemala through the sweeping exercise of absolute power by individuals, groups and institutions. Since colonial days, wielding power in Guatemala had traditionally meant perpetrating violence on the weak.

This was the case in every milieu, from the government to the military, from the haciendas to the judicial system, and from public institutions to the intimacy of the family circle. Given the semi-feudal nature of this society, it is not surprising that the 20th century saw a radicalization of political conflict which led to the emergence at the beginning of the 1960s of a Marxist guerrilla movement, made up of former officers from the armed forces. Successive governments were to respond with particularly brutal counterinsurgency strategies, especially during the rule of General Ríos Montt (1982-1983), a proponent of the *tierra arrasada* (or scorched-earth) policy that destroyed hundreds of villages and militarized civil society.

The first stage of the peace negotiations

By the end of 1980s, Guatemala was worn-out. The *comandancia*, the general command of the various guerrilla groups, kept its battle-weary units in defensive positions. But the government was not able to force the guerrillas to surrender. A purely military solution did not seem possible.

103

In addition, the government was isolated internationally because of the acts of brutality inflicted on the civilian population as part of the counterinsurgency strategy. The ruling generals were succeeded by civilian presidents of Christian-democratic and liberal leanings.

Attempts were made to launch peace negotiations. Talks in Madrid sponsored by the Spanish Prime Minister Felipe Gonzales failed. More productive were the efforts of Msgr. Quezada Toruño, appointed by the Guatemalan Episcopal Conference to head the National Reconciliation Commission (CNR) established pursuant to the Esquipulas Peace Accords between Latin American governments, who in 1987 undertook to resolve their "internal armed conflicts" by peaceful means. Full-blown peace negotiations got underway in 1990 in Oslo, where the guerrilla *comandancia* and Quezada Toruño, along with other members of the CNR, were guests of the Norwegian government. The Bishop emerged from the meeting having been appointed *conciliador*, whilst the UN was designated an "observer" to the fledgling peace process, which in its early stages would involve meetings between the *comandancia* and various sectors of Guatemalan society (including representatives from political parties, the private sector, trade unions, Churches and the academic community). 1991 saw the commencement of talks at a purely political level to discuss the "democratization" of the country.

The negotiations proceeded tentatively. In January 1993, President Serrano demanded, as an ultimatum, that a peace agreement be signed within ninety days, placing a ceasefire and the demobilization of the guerrillas at the top of his negotiating agenda. This unrealistic proposal was rejected by the *comandancia*, whose priorities were to discuss democracy, human rights, the protection of indigenous peoples, socio-economic reforms, and the role of the army. The peace process was stalling. Beyond the cut and thrust of the negotiations, neither the government nor the guerrillas had any serious intention of reaching the compromises necessary for restoring peace. As far as the executive was concerned, the guerrilla movement had been defeated on the ground and must accept the prevailing political and economic reality of the country, confining its negotiations to the social reintegration of its troops. For the guerrillas, the talks were – for the time being – a tactical non-strategic maneuver, useful for regathering its ranks and weakening the position of the government and the military.

A bungled attempt in May 1993 by Serrano to impose a kind of personal dictatorship modeled on Alberto Fujimori's regime in Peru led to a backlash, with the election as President of Ramiro de León Carpio, a Human Rights Ombudsman with democratic leanings. He attempted to revive the peace process by modifying its framework. Disillusioned by the government's actions, Quezada Toruño stepped down from his role as *conciliador*, with the UN becoming the sole mediator under the designation of "moderator". In January 1994, the government accepted the negotiating agenda sought by the guerrillas, pushing ceasefire discussions down to the last item on the agenda.

Over the course of 1994, agreements were signed dealing with human rights, the resettlement of uprooted population groups to their places of origin or places of their choice, and the establishment of an inquiry into human rights violations and acts of violence committed during the civil war. Nevertheless, the peace talks once again came to a halt due to disputes at the negotiating table between the two sides – just as the final leg of the process seemed imminent. There was deep mutual mistrust. The parties accused each other of holding up the negotiations and not following through on the agreements reached. The UN seemed powerless in the face of this impasse and there was no mutual recognition between the parties. The government refused to acknowledge the guerrilla movement as a political dialogue partner, formally deeming it a criminal organization, and for their part, the guerrillas maintained that the government was not representative of the country. The government negotiating team sought to have the guerrilla movement dissolved, whilst the latter claimed that President de León Carpio and his executive were token figures of authority, held to ransom by hardliners and intransigent elements within the military and private enterprise.[2]

Breaking the impasse: meetings in Rome and Paris

The Community of Sant'Egidio first had contact with the *comandancia* in 1993. Active in Guatemala both in indigenous rural areas and in the capital, the Community had earned an international reputation for mediating peace in Mozambique. The guerrillas initially contacted Sant'Egidio hoping for political support, then realized that the Community could not align itself with the movement's ideological agenda, being an independent organization concerned if anything with the common good of Guatemala and, above all, with peace. However, Sant'Egidio observed that the *comandancia*, although Marxist-oriented, no longer spoke in terms of revolution and was open to the possibility of a "bourgeois democracy" provided it was not socially unjust. The circumstances seemed favorable for the Community to facilitate the peace process and the Guatemalan Episcopal Conference encouraged its efforts to do so.[3]

Roberto Bonini, an Italian member of Sant'Egidio involved in international cooperation activities in Central America, entertained cordial relations with President de León Carpio. The latter was scheduled to make a State visit to Italy in March 1995. Sant'Egidio invited him to meet with the *comandancia* in Rome in secret, so as to avoid possible criminal charges for abuse of office and the risk of being accused of complicity with the enemy by those opposing the peace process. Ramiro de León Carpio accepted without hesitation. "Rome is Rome, after all", he remarked, keen to reach a peace agreement by the end of his presidential term. The *comandancia* was less enthusiastic regarding the scheduled meeting but still willing to meet with the President.

On March 4, 1995, de León Carpio made his way to the Sant'Egidio monastery in Trastevere, ostensibly to visit the Community. The presidential retinue was distracted by abundant refreshments and a demonstration of the activities carried out by Sant'Egidio, while de León Carpio, proceeding through a maze of the internal passageways within the ancient convent, withdrew to a private room with the founder of the Community, Andrea Riccardi. Here he was met by Pablo Monsanto and Rodrigo Asturias, members of the *comandancia*, who had arrived much earlier with Roberto Bonini and Riccardo Cannelli, also of Sant'Egidio. It was a cordial and mutually respectful meeting lasting ninety minutes. It was mostly the President, who appeared enthused, that took the initiative. He expressed his utmost willingness to negotiate, moving beyond the inflexibility shown by the government delegation at the negotiating table, with a view to concluding a peace deal before the expiration of his term at the end of 1995. To the *comandancia* leaders, Ramiro de León Carpio came across as a dialogue partner with a genuine interest in progressing the negotiations, capable of understanding (whilst not endorsing) some of the underlying reasons that had led the URNG[4] to go down the path of armed struggle – a course that he described as "illegal but not unfounded". De León Carpio wanted to convey that neither he nor his government regarded the guerrillas as enemies, and that many areas of fair compromise and agreement could be found in the negotiations in progress, but that there were obstacles and constraints, stemming from the prevailing balances of power within the country, which prevented him from going beyond certain limits in the negotiations at the risk of his own personal safety:

This is a unique window of opportunity. You should take advantage of my term in office. You know I'm willing to negotiate, but that won't necessarily be the case with the next President you end up dealing with. We can meet each other halfway or come to an agreement on many issues, but as you know, the real problem is with certain sections of CACIF[5], and even more so the army. Currently, the army is more receptive, to the extent that the Minister of Defense met with you in Oslo two weeks ago after consulting with me and obtaining my approval. But you know very well that I have limits. On some issues, I can't go beyond a certain point or concede too much, otherwise they'll kill me.[6]

It was shocking to hear a President admit to the existence of such constraints on his will and ability to maneuver. Perhaps in that moment de León Carpio was thinking of the assassination of Jorge Carpio Nicolle, his cousin and a former presidential candidate, who was killed a few weeks after the election of Ramiro as President. The murder, which was never solved, had probably been intended to send out a blanket message.

Another issue broached during the meeting was the presidential elections to be held at the end of the year. At the time of the meeting in March 1995, the field of possible candidates and forces at play was rather fluid. The former coup leader, General Ríos Montt, was attempting to run as a candidate, despite the legal obstacle posed by the Guatemalan Constitution, which expressly prohibited the election of persons who had previously come to power by means of a coup d'état. Many in Guatemala were trying to gauge the intentions of Ramiro de León Carpio, who, on the strength of support from certain sections of the public, was in a position to stand as a candidate subject to resigning from office by the end of May.

Finally, there was also the possibility that the Left might take part in the presidential elections with one or more candidates. De León Carpio wished to be clear with Monsanto and Asturias and stated that he would not be standing for the presidency again. It was then that Pablo Monsanto announced, rather solemnly, that for the first time the URNG would not boycott the elections, but would participate in the poll in a manner yet to be decided, so as not to make it easier for Ríos Montt and to give the peace process a chance. The Guatemalan President seemed pleased to hear this and summed up how he saw the overall political scenario playing out in the lead-up to the elections as follows:

Ríos Montt is trying to run for office, but he cannot and must not stand for election. The Constitution forbids it and the army, which is changing, would also be against it. The army is thinking about the future, and with Ríos Montt, the clock would be turned back. I myself am not thinking of standing, both because I've already served a purpose, and because I don't want to give Ríos Montt any excuse to have the Constitution changed in his favor. There are other possible candidates, such as Arzú with PAN (the National Advancement Party), who might stand a good chance. But there's also an opening on the Center-Left of the Guatemalan political spectrum that needs to be taken up. You could fill that vacancy...[7]

As regards the peace negotiations, the two guerrilla leaders reaffirmed the URNG's position that it could not submit to any preset deadlines for final signature, which would hamstring the process. "Our position on the negotiations", they explained, "is determined by the need to discuss the key points thoroughly, taking the time needed to do so, to ease the way for the changes required for the democratization of Guatemalan society".[8]

In response, Ramiro de León Carpio proposed that a channel of communication could be kept open to facilitate dialogue in the event the formal negotiations ran into difficulty, noting that: "Being able to make direct contact is crucial, so that when controversial issues or problems arise in the talks, I can let you know 'this is how far we can go, this is a point that can be conceded, but regarding that other matter, don't insist on it because you'd be going too far'. It would be very useful to find ways of keeping the line of communication we've established today open".[9]

The parties left the meeting having agreed they would maintain close contact through confidential channels. Roberto Bonini would act as a "go-between" between the *comandancia* based in Mexico City and President de León Carpio, passing on their messages. The meeting was regarded by both sides as largely successful. The *comandancia* felt that dealing with the President would help break the impasse and move the peace process forward. This was despite the fact that it remained skeptical regarding the extent of the influence of the President, who did not have a strong party behind him, and who risked – as he himself had admitted – being assassinated if he conceded too much to the guerrillas.

In point of fact, March 31 saw the signing by the government and the guerrillas of the landmark Agreement on the Identity and Rights of Indigenous Peoples. Bonini put his role as "go-between" to the test, speaking in turns with the guerrilla commanders in Mexico City and the President in Guatemala City. Sant'Egidio was seen as a "facilitator" by the parties, without anyone else, including the UN's official mediator Jean Arnoult, being aware of it. Secrecy was a *condicio sine qua non*. One might even say that the discretion observed by Bonini, but which also characterized the overall *modus operandi* employed, was the key to the effectiveness of these informal talks and to the parties being on the same wavelength. The meeting in Rome also led to progress in the mutual recognition of the parties, which up till then had not been accorded at the negotiating table. The *comandancia* showed respect for the President and the Guatemalan institutions, whilst de León Carpio acknowledged the guerrillas' right to take their place in society as a legitimate political movement. These attitudes were not put on public display, yet they infused the dialogue with a sense of trust that had previously been lacking.

Time was working against the Guatemalan President's plan. Not having any illusions in this regard, Sant'Egidio sought to help the peace process along by fostering greater confidence between the parties. To this end, Bonini and Cannelli organized a further secret meeting between the *comandancia* and de León Carpio during an official visit by the latter to Paris. On June 23, the scenario in Rome was played out again at the headquarters of the Catholic magazine La Vie. The President set off there on the pretext of an interview with the editor of the magazine, Jean-Claude Petit, then went off with the guerrilla leaders, skillfully eluding observation by French intelligence operatives and prying Guatemalan officials who were overly curious regarding the President's movements.

The meeting was amicable like the previous encounter, but the *comandancia* did not intend to follow up on the President's proposals regarding the sensitive area of socio-economic issues, due to a political crisis within the guerrilla movement which meant it was forced to take a break from the negotiations. De León Carpio nevertheless informed the *comandancia* how far the government could go in terms of making concessions. This would later help the *comandancia* to make realistic proposals at the negotiating table, gaining as much ground as it could without causing a breakdown in talks with the government delegation, which knew nothing of the President's indiscretions.

As it was, the negotiations plodded along till the end of the year. The slightest concession on socio-economic issues faced opposition from Guatemalan industrialists and landholders. In addition, there were occasionally fresh outbreaks of military activity that weighed heavily on public opinion and the prevailing atmosphere of the official talks. Some political forces in Guatemala questioned the validity of the agreements negotiated in the peace process, claiming that they were "government" rather than "State" agreements, so that future presidents and governments would not be bound by them. Bonini and other members of Sant'Egidio continued shuttling back and forth between the *comandancia* and the President, ironing out tensions and misunderstandings. In order to avoid bringing the negotiations to a halt, the guerrillas gave up their pursuit of radical agrarian reform and simply accepted rural modernization as the priority. By then, however, de León Carpio had reached the end of his term.

Arzú and the comandancia in San Salvador

Two strong candidates ran in the presidential elections of January 1996: Álvaro Arzú, a pragmatic businessman who supported the continuation of the peace process, and Alfonso Portillo, a protégé of Ríos Montt, who felt it was unnecessary to negotiate with the guerrillas as he considered them underdogs in terms of military might. On November[7], Bonini spoke with Arzú and informed him of the secret meetings that had taken place between the *comandancia* and de León Carpio. At the time, Arzú's attentions were focused on a rather uncertain election campaign and not on peace, but he was interested in what he called "the Roman way". Ten days later, however, he asked Bonini to organize a meeting with the full *comandancia*, undoubtedly hoping to secure the electoral support of the guerrilla movement against Portillo.

A meeting was thus arranged which took place on December 5, 1995 at the headquarters of the Community of Sant'Egidio in the nearby capital of El Salvador, amid very tight secrecy to avoid compromising Arzú's electoral bid. The latter talked for seven hours with the guerrillas, who were initially ill-disposed towards him. A relationship of trust was nevertheless established, thanks in part to the presence – alongside the soon-to-be President – of Gustavo Porras, who would soon prove to be pivotal to the peace negotiations.

Porras, a moderate progressive with an upper class background, was a childhood friend of Arzú and his political adviser. More importantly, he had been a member of the guerrilla movement before dissociating himself from the

111

armed struggle and the political vision that went with it. Porras had had longstanding relations with the four guerrilla leaders of the *comandancia*, all present at the meeting in San Salvador, and in particular, he knew the most influential figure among them, Rolando Morán, quite well.[10]

Arzú and the *comandancia* discussed the elections first, for which Arzú did not meet with the support he would have wished for from the guerrilla representatives. They then moved on to speak of many issues that formed part of the peace talks (such as economic reforms, the role of the army, the reorganization of the police and intelligence services, the role of the private sector and so on). The guerrillas were pleased with Arzú's approach to the peace negotiations, which was not simply defensive as if the challenge were to concede as little as possible. Arzú asked the guerrillas to join with him in the process of changing the country, acknowledging their movement's status as a political dialogue partner in its own right.

The members of the *comandancia* were astonished, not to mention caught on the back foot when Arzú asked them directly: "If I win the election, what do you think are the most important things that will need to be dealt with in the first few months?". Having grown accustomed to being treated like criminals by previous governments, that question marked a turning point in the meeting for the guerrilla leaders. Two months later, Commander Rolando Morán would say to Porras: "Arzú treated us with respect, just as one politician should treat another".

At this point, it is worthwhile quoting some excerpts from the lengthy minutes of the meeting in order to give an idea of the tone that prevailed:

Arzú: This meeting is important because it allows us to get to know each other and lay the foundations for understanding each other better in the long term, so I hope this is just the first of a number of meetings. I realize that we must reach a peace agreement; the country needs it. Maybe the public does not see this as the biggest issue at the moment, but those with political responsibilities cannot fail to appreciate that in order to embark on all the necessary reforms and to attract foreign investment, the country needs peace. Guatemala needs to get out of its current situation, it needs to modernize, the economy needs stability, and the mindset of the past that has paralyzed the country for many years needs to be put behind us. Everybody needs to contribute so that we can come up with a governance plan. You represent a significant political force and I need your help and support. I never believed the surveys that said you only accounted for 1% of the votes. I knew that you could fill a political void that was opening up. Sure the electorate is fickle – I know that only too well. I'm not sure I'll win the election. Portillo can count on the vote of the evangelical sects, who have rallied strongly behind him [...] It is important to overcome ingrained preconceptions, that are often deliberately engendered by the press. For instance, I am portrayed as some madcap privatizer, as someone who wants to sell off all the State's assets. But it isn't true. If we meet and get to know each other, we can overcome many prejudices.

Morán: This meeting is very important for us too, whatever the outcome of the elections, because this channel of communication could represent a huge breakthrough for the country's political framework. For some time now, the URNG *comandancia* has accepted the need and sought to establish direct personal contact with political leaders. This could help to overcome many mutual prejudices. We have often been depicted as criminals and terrorists. This suits those who oppose change, those who do not want to see a process of modernization get underway in Guatemala. For years they said we were in the service of Moscow or Havana.

The military leaders we spoke with during the negotiations told us they were protecting US interests in Guatemala that were under attack from the Soviet Union. But we have taken up arms as Guatemalans who wanted a fairer and more democratic country. We don't want to labor under these prejudices. It's good to talk, even to have heated discussions, so that we can pinpoint our differences. But you can rest assured that if you're elected and your government moves in the right direction, we can guarantee you the support of the people [...]

Monsanto: We're willing to cooperate with all forces who want to set change in motion. We certainly can't agree to publicly support you in the election, because that would be like the old way of doing politics, with all the parties doing secret deals. We're interested in keeping this line of communication open, regardless of the outcome of the elections. If you win the election and your government does the right thing, at that point we can promise you the backing of the people.

Arzú: In your opinion, what are some of the important issues that the government should deal with in its first three months, and how do you think I can demonstrate my good faith? I realize that the first three or four months will be fundamental for any process of change. During that period, it'll be necessary to act decisively, otherwise it'll all be more difficult later.

Morán: That's a really difficult question to answer!

Monsanto: The problem of public housing, for example, is one of the most urgent issues. Or the occupation of land by refugees. There are areas in towns and in the countryside that have been occupied by groups of refugees [...]

Asturias: Another pressing issue is non-productive land – those huge tracts of land intentionally kept uncultivated by large landholders. These could be taxed or be put on the market. It's one of the items on the agenda in the negotiations, but we've encountered great resistance from landowners.

Arzú: This is clearly one of the issues that involves key interests of landowners. They come up with all sorts of reasons to justify the fact that they keep these lands uncultivated. Their latest brainwave is forest conservation, using the excuse of protecting Guatemala's ecosystem. But the important and difficult thing is deciding on the criteria to use for assessing land.

Porras: Any plan to modernize the economy will undoubtedly come up against powerful economic interests, such as those of landholders and some sections of the military. It is crucial not to give in. These guys need to understand that they can't go on enjoying such blatant privileges without being subject to taxes. The amount of wealth they've accumulated over the years is staggering. The State needs to take a stronger stand... [11]

The comment of the guerrilla leaders the day after the meeting spoke volumes: "That was an incredibly good meeting. We thank God and we thank Sant'Egidio. We've changed our mind about Arzú [...] He opens up some very important political prospects for us [...] We thought that we would be faced with [...] someone arrogant and overbearing. But he was very accommodating and his views were quite interesting".[12] In similar fashion, Arzú observed that it had been "a very important meeting, although I understand why they can't publicly support me [...] They're people you can talk to. Even Monsanto, whom I'd been told was a real hardliner, is reasonable. And I was really struck by the fact that they're united. If I'm elected, I want to solve the peace issue in the first five to eight months of my term".[13]

Viewed with hindsight, the meeting in San Salvador proved to be decisive for the peace process. Arzú gained the trust of the commanders. Porras, after some initial embarrassment, reestablished a rapport with his old comrades-in-arms, grounded in a shared language even if their political views now differed. The commanders were convinced that it was possible to dialogue seriously with Arzú. A sort of metamorphosis took place in the relationship between the guerrillas and the government (for although Arzú was not yet President, he already headed a political majority in parliament). There was a shift from cold objective negotiations to a greater personal subjective involvement. Ten years later, Pablo Monsanto would remark that:

The meeting in San Salvador marked a crucial dividing line in the whole process. Without any shadow of a doubt, the periods before and after the meeting in San Salvador can be seen as two quite distinct stages. It marked a turning point for all the members of the *comandancia* general. We felt on that occasion that we had the opportunity to speak with total clarity [...] The encounter left us with a different feeling than previous meetings we had had with the other Presidents, such as Ramiro de León Carpio and Serrano.[14]

Speaking for the other side, Porras similarly recalled that:
The meeting in San Salvador kicked off the peace process proper [...] In my opinion, both this meeting and the other four secret – or rather, discreet – meetings facilitated by Sant'Egidio were crucial. It was these that really laid the foundations for the process of building peace, from the subjective point of view of the actors

involved [...] In terms of what the fundamental outcomes of these meetings were, I would point first and foremost to the fact that the *comandancia* got to meet the man who would become the future President, Álvaro Arzú, and conversely, he was able to make contact with the commanders. Neither had met the other before, and, as often happens, both had certain preconceptions and prejudices – in the literal sense of having pre-judged each other.[15]

Some have observed there was a "change of chemistry" between the parties in San Salvador, which saw two enemies become mere rivals who, moreover, were keen to reach an agreement in the greater interests of the country.[16] The *comandancia* wished to reform the country, whilst Arzú wanted to modernize it. These goals were not the same, but an understanding could be reached. A relationship of trust was established that would lead Arzú, who became President a few weeks later, to prohibit government forces from mounting ideological attacks on the guerrillas, and the latter to meet the government halfway, declaring a ceasefire even before military issues were discussed at the negotiating table. Sant'Egidio's gambit of direct dialogue, with no preset agenda and away from the strictures of ideology and officialdom, had paid off. On January 7, 1996, Arzú won the presidential elections, albeit with no more than a 3% margin over Portillo. Just prior to the election, he asked Sant'Egidio to organize another meeting with the guerrillas, where he would be represented by a team of negotiators led by Porras.

It might be going a little overboard to describe the meeting, which took place in Mexico City on January 3-4, as resembling a honeymoon between the guerrillas and Arzú's men, but it wouldn't be too much of an exaggeration. Contrary to their previously-stated position, the *comandancia* leaders now declared they would tacitly support Arzú in the elections. They foreshadowed agreement with Arzú's proposed government platform, and submitted a document outlining a moderate position on socio-economic issues, which were the main focus of negotiations yet to take place. Overall, their attitude was very flexible.

Now that there was trust between them, the two sides felt surer they would come to an agreement. They spoke evocatively of the end of the negotiations and of "dialogue between compatriots". Yet following Arzú's inauguration into office, fears emerged among the guerrillas. Jean Arnoult, the UN mediator, had not been informed of the secret meetings. How would he react to finding out that there had been parallel talks alongside the formal negotiations? The involvement of the UN, not just in the negotiations but also via its physical presence within the country in the form of the MINUGUA mission, was the guerrillas' best guarantee of future compliance with the agreements reached. The *comandancia* seemed to be suddenly wracked with guilt at having somehow cheated on the UN.

It was also keenly aware for the first time of being at the point of no return between war and peace, after many years of armed struggle. It was a sea change for the guerrillas. How would they adjust to normal life? What would they do after demobilization? Faced with the real possibility of peace, there was a sense of disorientation, as often happens with guerrillas and armed movements in such cases. There were concerns that militants on the ground might not be ready for peace. The *comandancia* thus declared it was prepared to "make significant steps forward with the government but without rushing things", which was perhaps simply a sign of nervousness at the idea of peace after decades of war.

Towards peace

On January 21, there was another meeting at the headquarters of Sant'Egidio in San Salvador, with the same measures taken to ensure it remained secret. Representing the government were Porras and the new Interior Minister Rodolfo Mendoza. They were met with the members of the *comandancia*. The talks were frank. The guerrilla leaders were informed of purges that were about to take place in the armed forces and the police, as well as other measures aimed at strengthening the country's democratic framework. The *comandancia*, for its part, took the call for a ceasefire seriously. The climate was very collaborative. As regards the UN, it was agreed that the existence of direct contact between the parties should be disclosed, without however making too much of it. In order to avoid offending the sensibilities of UN chiefs, it was decided to reaffirm the UN's role as the sole recognized mediator in the peace process. On going public regarding the role played by Sant'Egidio, the Community would be described as having acted as a "facilitator".

On January 28, the parties met again, this time in Mexico City. The government reported on the progress of the purges and its meetings with the UN, whose representatives had approved the informal talks between the parties that had taken place outside the official negotiations. The guerrillas revealed the internal difficulties they were experiencing. Monsanto stated: "Each step we take has to be explained to our militants [...] Some of these people have been fighting a war for thirty years, and they need in-depth political explanations, otherwise there is a risk of everything coming unstuck, or worse still, of insubordination. I also say this so that you can understand why, at times, things move slowly".[17] The *comandancia* was by then in favor of the ceasefire (due to take effect from March), but it had to be justified to its fighters.

The parties left having agreed to meet again at Sant'Egidio's headquarters in Rome, where, on February 11-12, 1996, the last secret meeting between the government and the guerrillas took place. Gustavo Porras arrived with the news that he had been appointed by Arzú as the head of the government delegation to the official negotiations. The composition of the new government delegation, along with the national reform program that it would push for in the peace talks, were carefully examined during the meeting. The fact that Porras was now head of the official negotiating delegation made it unnecessary to continue with the parallel talks facilitated by Sant'Egidio. It was thus decided to publicly disclose the talks facilitated by the Community of Sant'Egidio via a Joint Communiqué signed by the government and the guerrillas. This was done by means of two press conferences, one held in Rome and the other in Guatemala City. The Communiqué read as follows:

In view of the approaching formal resumption of peace negotiations between the Government of Guatemala and the General Command of the URNG, the parties have agreed to publicly disclose the following:

1.   In December 1995, under the auspices of the Community of Sant'Egidio, direct and personal contact was made between the then presidential candidate Álvaro Arzú and certain members of his political team on the one hand, and the General Command of the URNG on the other. This contact has been maintained over time. The Community of Sant'Egidio, a Catholic organization, known internationally for its contribution to peace processes in different areas of the world, and particularly for resolving the armed conflict in Mozambique, encouraged the parties to meet with the aim of supporting the peace process in Guatemala.

2.   The parties, by mutual agreement, decided that their dialogue should take place secretly, a decision from which the dialogue has unquestionably benefited. In due course, both the Government of the Republic of Guatemala and the General Command of the URNG informed the United Nations of this dialogue, in the persons of Mr Marrack Goulding, Under-Secretary-General of the UN, and the UN moderator Jean Arnoult, who expressed their satisfaction at the development of this initiative.

3.   From the outset, these meetings were conceived with the aim of creating conditions conducive to furthering the peace talks, whatever the outcome of the elections. After the elections, the meetings continued in the spirit of frank and open political dialogue, without any pre-established conditions, targets or agendas, in order to allow a broad exchange of respective views, thoughts and assessments of the national situation.

4.   This political dialogue was a complementary initiative to the official negotiations, and the pursuance thereof was in keeping with the provisions of the Framework Agreement of January 1994, in which the parties recognized 'the desirability of resorting to all measures that will be conducive to rapprochements and agreements between them'.

5.   Five meetings have been held to date within the ambit of this dialogue, and the parties are pleased to advise that these have made a positive contribution to the establishment of a climate of trust and goodwill that will need to prevail at the negotiating table, thus ensuring more rapid progress towards agreements which lay the foundations for a firm and lasting peace, reconciliation, and the participation of all Guatemalans in the massive and constructive task of advancing the country.

6. In disclosing this information to the national and international community, the Government of the Republic of Guatemala and the General Command of the URNG wish to convey their political willingness to maintain their dialogue on the terms already established, with the good offices and invaluable support of the countries who make up the group of 'friends' to the peace process, and to express their appreciation and gratitude to the Community of Sant'Egidio for its facilitation and guidance.[18]

For Sant'Egidio, it was now time to step aside. The goal of giving new impetus to the negotiations, based on mutual trust, had been achieved. The impasse in the talks had been lifted and the parties had been placed in a position to understand each other.[19] The final stages of the negotiations between the government and the guerrillas was led by the United Nations. In the last few months before the peace agreement was signed, both the government and the guerrillas played a double game. On the one hand, they negotiated with each other in order to reach agreements that were satisfactory to both sides, exchanging tokens of mutual recognition, whilst on the other, they reassured their more radical or ideologically-minded members of where they fitted in with the decisions being made and the terms of the agreements being discussed and signed.

The socio-economic issues under discussion and the legitimization of the guerrillas as a political movement alarmed some sections of Guatemalan society. It was observed that "the Right was obsessed with the URNG's legitimization and its legal integration into the country's civil and political life [...] The possibility that the peace process might open up the political system, which till then had been exclusive, became a source of tension within the army and the private sector. Constant pressure was applied to put an end to the peace process and thereby shut the door on the opportunities that had begun to open up".[20]

Nevertheless, all the obstacles were overcome. On December 29, 1996, after an eleventh-hour rush of signings of the last outstanding agreements in Oslo (Agreement on a Definitive Ceasefire), Stockholm (Agreement on Constitutional Reforms), Madrid (Agreement on the Basis for the Legal Integration of the URNG), and Guatemala

City (Agreement on the Implementation Timetable), the Agreement on a Firm and Lasting Peace was able to be signed in Guatemala City, putting an official end to the armed conflict in Guatemala.[21]

Twelve years have passed since the signing of the Guatemala peace accords. Whilst security issues and socio-economic difficulties persist in all their chronic severity, there is no denying that Guatemala has changed for the better in recent years, thanks to peace and to a certain degree of political stability that has been achieved. It is true that there has been strong resistance to change in certain sectors of society, which came to the fore in 1998 during the referendum on constitutional reforms. Likewise, it cannot be said that the very high expectations of Guatemalans – who pinned their hopes of an immediate improvement in their material living conditions on the peace agreements – have been completely fulfilled.

However, the cessation of the internal armed conflict has meant the end of a nightmare for Guatemala and made it a country with very serious problems which are, however, in certain respects within the ordinary realm of social injustice that has existed throughout its history. Efforts are currently in progress to redress this situation. In any event, on the evening of December 29, 1996, in Guatemala City, rhetorical gestures did not seem out of place. At the end of the official signing ceremony for the peace agreements, which was attended by UN Secretary-General Boutros-Ghali and various heads of State and government, Álvaro Arzú and Rolando Morán walked out together to light a peace torch. Many of the people who filled the square could not believe their eyes. The highest representative of the State and of the Guatemalan armed forces together with the leader of the oldest Central American guerrilla movement were formally putting an end to a brutal conflict – one that had lasted for decades and claimed hundreds of thousands of victims, mostly civilians from indigenous Mayan communities.

[1] For more on the Guatemalan civil war, cf. D. Pompejano, *Storia e conflitti del*

centroamerica. Gli Stati dell'allerta (1860-1990), Florence 1991; A. Rouquié, *Guerres et paix en Amérique central*, Paris 1992; and E. Torres-Rivas & G. Aguilera Peralta, *Desde el Autoritarismo a la Paz*, FLACSO, Guatemala 1998.

[2] In respect of the peace process in Guatemala, cf. G. Aguilera Peralta, R. Bran & C. Ogaldes, *Buscando la paz, el bienio 1994-1995*, Guatemala 1996; E. Torres-Rivas, *Negociando el futuro: la paz en una sociedad violenta. La negociación de paz en 1996*, Guatemala 1997; Torres-Rivas & Aguilera Peralta, *Desde el Autoritarismo a la Paz*, cit.; S. Jonas, *De Centauros y Palomas: el proceso de paz guatemalteco*, Guatemala 2000; and J. Hernàndez Pico, *Terminar la guerra, traicionar la paz*, Guatemala 2005.

[3] Cf. the report on Msgr. Avila's visit to Sant'Egidio in Rome on February 22, 1995, held in Roberto Bonini's own personal collection of documents pertaining to the case of Guatemala (hereinafter referred to as the RBC).

[4] Unidad Revolucionaria Nacional Guatemalteca, that is, the guerrilla movement.

[5] Guatemala's peak business association.

[6] Cf. The report on the Meeting between Ramiro de León Carpio and the URNG in Rome on March 4, 1995, RBC.

[7] Ibid.

[8] Ibid.

[9] Ibid.

[10] Rolando Morán was the *nom de guerre* of Ricardo Ramírez de León, commander of the largest guerrilla formation in Guatemala, the Guerrilla Army of the Poor (EGP).

[11] Cf. The report on the Meeting between Álvaro Arzú, Gustavo Porras, Rodolfo Mendoza, and the URNG *comandancia* in San Salvador on December 5, 1995, RBC.

[12] Cf. The report on the Meeting with the URNG *comandancia* in San Salvador on December 6, 1995, RBC.

[13] Cf. The report on the Meeting with Álvaro Arzú in Guatemala City on December 7, 1995, RBC.

[14] Pablo Monsanto in Foro: *La Comunidad de San Egidio y el proceso de paz en Guatemala*, Guatemala 2005, p. 60.

[15] Gustavo Porras in Foro: *La Comunidad de San Egidio y el proceso de paz en Guatemala*, cit., pp. 40-41.

[16] Cf. Jonas, op. cit., pp. 108-109.

[17] Cf. The report on the Meeting between representatives of the Guatemalan government and the URNG *comandancia* in Mexico City on January 28, 1996, RBC.

[18] *Joint Government-URNG Communiqué*, Rome and Guatemala City, February 12, 1996.

[19] For more on the role played by the Community of Sant'Egidio in the Guatemalan peace process, cf. R. Bonini, *Dar una mano a la paz. Crónica de la facilitación de la Comunidad de San Egidio en el proceso de paz de Guatemala (1995-1996)*, Guatemala City 2007.

[20] Jonas, op. cit., p. 200.

[21] In addition to the Community of Sant'Egidio, the many people and organizations that had each contributed, according to their capacity, to the achievement of peace and to bringing an end to the bloody conflict were expressly thanked during the ceremony, including: the various Guatemalan governments and their respective Peace Commissions, composed of civilian and military representatives; the *comandancia* of the URNG and its Political and Diplomatic Commission; the

various social sectors involved in the Assembly of Civil Society; the Catholic Church and the "conciliator" Msgr. Quezada Toruño; the United Nations and its "moderator" Jean Arnoult; and the international community and the countries comprising the group of "friends" to the peace process.

Peace in Burundi

Burundi

Area (in sq km)	27,834
Population (millions)	7.216
Population density (inhabitants per sq km)	259
Percentage of population <15 years	46.4
Annual change in population (%)	+2.1
Infant mortality per 1,000 live births (<1 year/<5 years)	65.6/190
Life expectancy at birth (male/female)	43/45
Fertility rate (average no. of children per woman)	6.7
Illiteracy rate (%)	46.1
Doctors (per 1,000 inhabitants)	0.1
Percentage of adult population living with HIV/AIDS (adult prevalence rate	6.0
Human Development Index (HDI), expressed on a scale from 0 to 1, to three decimal places	0.378
HDI, world ranking	169
GDP per capita (USD)	107
GDP per capita, world ranking	189
Personal computers (per 1,000 inhabitants)	-

Peace in Burundi

Angelo Romano

In the spring of 1995, Burundi was at a major crisis point. The coalition government, made up of quite disparate parties, was unable to stem the escalating ethnic and political violence. It was just under a year since the genocide in Rwanda. Many foreshadowed there would be another in its twin Burundi – a country with a similar ethnic composition. In the midst of this worrying situation, the President of Burundi Sylvestre Ntibantunganya, together with a large government delegation, went to Rome. There, on May 14, he visited the Community of Sant'Egidio, whom he knew had mediated the Mozambique peace talks. He was in fact received in the very room where the Mozambique peace negotiations had been conducted.

The President was very tense. As a Hutu with a mostly Tutsi army, his life was in danger. In October 1993, Ntibantunganya had miraculously escaped death in the putsch that had plunged Burundi into crisis and during which his wife was brutally murdered. Andrea Riccardi and Fr. Matteo Zuppi informed him that Sant'Egidio was prepared to do all it could to assist Burundi in finding the road to peace. The President welcomed this willingness to help, and scheduled a meeting for the following day with the Burundian Foreign Minister, Jean-Marie Ngendahayo.

The next morning, accompanied by the Burundian Ambassador to Italy[1], the Minister spoke plainly: it was imperative that contact be established with the Hutu guerrilla movement, the National Council for the Defense of Democracy (CNDD). The government wished to begin peace talks, to be conducted entirely in secrecy, and sought Sant'Egidio's assistance to this end. The request was very direct and the Ambassador was clearly surprised. Fr. Zuppi offered to help line up the necessary meetings.[2]

Shortly thereafter, this request also received a further boost from the former President of Burundi, Pierre Buyoya, with whom Fr. Zuppi and Andrea Riccardi met to gauge what leeway there might be for possible mediation efforts. The former President was a Tutsi who hailed from the army and from the clan that had always ruled the country. He wanted his country to move towards democracy, and had accepted the people's verdict when they voted him out of office. Buyoya hoped that Sant'Egidio would act as a mediator and offered his diplomatic support to facilitate contact with political and military figures linked to the former single party, the Union for National Progress (UPRONA).

Thus, Sant'Egidio received a sort of two-tiered request to make contact with the CNDD guerrillas, the first coming through President Ntibantunganya, a Hutu, with a mandate to negotiate on behalf of the ruling government, and the other through Buyoya, a Tutsi, which to a certain extent manifested a desire for dialogue – albeit yet to be put to the test – on the part of the ruling elite linked to UPRONA and its traditional support base. It could be said that the approval of these two representatives – one of whom came from the realm of "formal" power, recognized internationally though undermined within the country, and the other from the sphere of those wielding "real" power, namely, the army and the Tutsi ruling elite – brought about a convergence in their positions.

But what had happened in Burundi and what had led to this crisis? Unfortunately, the predicament in Burundi, like that in Rwanda, can all-too-easily be attributed to ethnic divisions. The ethnic composition of the country is 84% Hutu, 15% Tutsi and 1% Twa pygmy.[3] According to currently accepted wisdom, the problem in Burundi can be summed up as follows: power has always been in the hands of the Tutsis who control the army, the Hutus have always sought to solve this problem by violent means, and the military has always responded to Hutu rebellions by suppressing them. However, the reality is more complicated – and more interesting – than any such reductive interpretations. As has rightly been observed: "Conflicts in Africa are often depicted as wars between one tribe that dominates the government and another that feels left out. In reality, like anywhere else, conflicts in Africa are complex and can even prove incomprehensible to the uninitiated".[4]

A crisis with ancient roots

The paradox of Burundi is that it is one of the few African countries with a pre-colonial past characterized by a history of national unity, with a common language and common traditions found throughout the country. Hutus and Tutsis are not ethnic groups that were thrown together within arbitrary borders drawn by European powers. The Kingdom of Burundi was one of an array of States that – certainly by the 17th century – dotted the landscape of the Great Lakes region. Like Rwanda, Burundi had a complex monarchic structure, with a feudal society and system of government.

The division between Hutus and Tutsis was based on the complementary roles of the two groups: the Hutus were farmers, while the Tutsis were cattle breeders. These different roles also corresponded to different lifestyles and even completely different diets, which is probably the origin of the distinct physical traits that are often – though not always – found. The Tutsis, of above-average height, had a high-protein diet (almost solely comprised of milk and dairy products). The Hutu diet, on the other hand, consisted mainly of starchy foods and legumes. The Tutsis also had a particular military tradition, linked to rituals and dances that to this day still form part of the culture and history of Burundi.

However, unlike the more polarized Rwanda, power in Burundi was in the hands of a third ethnic group, the Ganwa, a form of noble elite considered to be neither Tutsi nor Hutu, with a complex clan system that determined the balance between the various groups. The Burundian royal court was a lavish tribal affair, with photographs of the Ganwa nobility that came into contact with the first European explorers providing a striking visual record. Burundian Queens wore garments decorated with abstract motifs that would look quite modern by today's standards. The nobles were proud, dressed in leopard skins, surrounded by a very formal court and steeped in very strict protocol. Before the evangelization of the country, the King also had priestly duties. The most important ceremony in Burundi was the blessing of the seeds, which people traveled from every corner of the country to participate in as a show of national unity and loyalty to the monarchy.[5]

Initially under German and later Belgian control, Burundi – merged with Rwanda under colonial rule – became the object of ethnographic studies that were typical of the preoccupation of European administrators with the acquisition of knowledge and classification. It was at this point that a poisonous seed was sown that would lead to a devastating cultural shift for the country. Hutus and Tutsis, the embodiment of different social roles and functions, became ethnic and racial categories in the "scientific" studies of the time. The Tutsis, claimed experts, were different from the Hutus, with a distinct physical appearance, culture, character, and psychological make-up. Thus, their racial identity must also be different. The Tutsis, it was argued, were not Bantus but "Hamites" (from Ham, who, along with Shem and Japheth, was one of Noah's sons in the Book of Genesis) that had migrated to the country following the course of the Nile. They were a type of "false Negro", similar to Europeans, and were born politicians, practiced dissimulation, had a political culture with a capacity for long-term planning, and were the natural leaders of their country. The Hutus, on the other hand, were classed as Bantus, with all the defects of "Negroids", including a simpler psychology, an inability to conceal anger or joy, and an outlook that was characteristically short-sighted.

The ethnology of the time pared down and equated the complex histories of Rwanda and Burundi on the basis of racist ethnic concepts. It would take too long to list here the discrepancies inherent in this view, such as the existence of Hutu clans linked to the monarchy or local chiefdoms, or the extremely poor living conditions of the vast majority of Tutsis, far removed from the court and the political games of the Ganwa chiefs. In any event, the damage was done. The history of Burundi was no longer the story of a single nation but rather one of separate ethnic groups, immutable because they were defined by race, and all the country's problems could be traced back to the relationships between them.

Many Tutsis saw their caste prejudices as vindicated by the colonizers, who justified the Tutsis' social role as a product of racial superiority. Conversely, many Hutus saw the source of all their problems as stemming from the underhanded tyranny of the Tutsis, who were "interlopers from Ethiopia or

Egypt". These ideas became deeply ingrained in the psyche of Burundians. To quote a senior official of one radical Hutu movement: "The Hutus arrived in Burundi in around 2000 BC, the Tutsis only got here in 1700 AD. We were here first, then they tricked us and took over!".[6]

Two groups of people united by centuries of shared history and by a common tradition, religion and language were suddenly considered distinct. Belgian colonial policy laid the groundwork for ideological prejudices, as the Tutsis were preferred for positions in the administration and the armed forces. Another intervening factor also fueled the confusion and misunderstanding: Belgium (where the Flemish and the Walloons were starting to oppose each other politically) viewed the Hutus and Tutsis in Rwanda and Burundi through the lens of its own internal strife, drawing simplistic correlations and parallels.

After the Second World War, the winds of independence swept through the region. The Tutsi elite, in both Rwanda and Burundi, began to form pro-independence political groups. The Belgian administration considered this behavior as tantamount to a betrayal and effected a sudden change of policy – preferring Hutus over Tutsis – with dramatic consequences. It was felt that the situation warranted a drastic reduction in the political hegemony of the Tutsis, pursued by supporting Hutu revolutionary movements it was hoped would spawn a class of leaders more compliant in their dealings with Brussels.

In Rwanda, the monarchy and the feudal system were brought down in 1959 with the support of Belgian military forces, through what was termed a "social revolution". A republic was declared and the Hutus, who had assembled their own leadership, were able to take power. The violence against the hated Tutsi feudal overlords began immediately. Soon, the vendettas intensified, and although the country was still under Belgian military control, thousands of Tutsis who were members of the nobility and the ruling elite fled to Tanzania and Uganda. They would subsequently mount several armed raids as a means to returning to the country as conquerors. These proved unsuccessful, and indeed resulted in harsh indiscriminate reprisals against Tutsis still living in Rwanda.[7] The legitimacy of the Republic of Rwanda was founded on the supposed victory of the *peuple majoritaire*, that is, the Hutus. There was a misguided belief that the plight of Tutsi refugees abroad could be ignored and that a State could be built on the basis of "ethnic quotas", with citizens' ethnicity even specified in identity cards.

As it was, the ethnic problem spread from Rwanda to Burundi. Here the struggle for independence had been conducted jointly by Hutus and Tutsis through the same political movement: UPRONA. Massacres of Tutsis in Rwanda increased the fears of their Burundian counterparts, who began to see their Hutu compatriots in a new light. Hutu plots met with tough retaliatory measures from the Tutsis, culminating in the end of the monarchy and the establishment of a Tutsi-led military dictatorship in 1965. UPRONA, in which both Hutus and Tutsis participated alongside each other, became the single party of a new political system, in which ethnicity officially had no relevance and Hutus and Tutsis had equal rights. However, this seemingly moderate facade served to conceal what was really a discriminatory regime, in which Tutsi ethnicity and close ties to the Tutsi clans who controlled the army were central.

The establishment of an authoritarian regime did not bring any measure of tranquility to the country. In 1972, the military, which was increasingly fearful of how events were playing out in Rwanda, decided to carry out a "surgical strike" to eliminate the possibility of any Hutu leadership emerging. In response to several armed attacks carried out by Burundian Hutus from neighboring countries, Tutsi military forces set about exterminating almost all educated Hutus, who were potential leadership material. Within a few weeks, there were more than 100,000 people killed across the country, with teachers, students, trade unionists, politicians and priests consigned to mass graves. No one was ever prosecuted for this crime, which remained a taboo topic in the country until the late 1980s, weighing heavily as a result on the prospects for coexistence between the different constituent peoples of the country.[8] As at least one commentator has observed, in the Great Lakes region ethnic massacres might seem to provide the best explanation for ethno-racist ideologies, but in fact they are just a tragic consequence of them.[9]

In the years that followed, there would be a succession of military regimes in Burundi headed by Tutsis from the same sub-clan, up until the beginning of the democratization process, which got underway in 1990 under the presidency of Major Pierre Buyoya. The democratization was sparked by a changing world order. After the collapse of the Soviet empire, the West became much less tolerant of Western-aligned dictatorships. France in particular adopted this stance, as emerged from the famous speech made by President Mitterrand in La Baule in 1990, where he stated that French economic aid to African governments would be conditional on the existence of – or the initiation of transition towards – democratic political systems.[10]

Burundi thus began to lay the foundations for its move towards democracy. However, the democratic process was hampered by a past that was unmentionable, by crimes that had gone unpunished, and by seemingly inescapable ethnic preconceptions. Melchior Ndadaye was the leading figure in the push for change. Of Hutu origins, he established a party, the Front for Democracy in Burundi (FRODEBU), with an agenda of freeing the country from its ethnic predicament. He won a crushing victory in the elections held in June 1993, receiving around 65% of the vote, whilst the former single party, UPRONA, was heavily defeated. However, the parties were not simply divided along ethnic lines. Buyoya, the presidential candidate for UPRONA who received approximately 34% of the vote, was not endorsed solely by Tutsis, and even Ndadaye, FRODEBU's candidate, was not just supported by Hutus.

The new President was critical of those professing tribalism, and appointed as Prime Minister Sylvie Kinigi, a member of UPRONA, which was now in opposition. There was an air of optimism. But those sections of the Tutsi establishment that had always pegged their fortunes on maintaining close links with those in power and the financial resources at their disposal, did not wish to step aside and feared legal consequences for their past transgressions.

This gave rise to the coup which took place on October 21, 1993. Military troops attacked the presidential palace and the private homes of Ministers, killing the President, many members of the government, the Speaker of the National

Assembly, elected Governors, and representatives of the FRODEBU party. It was never revealed who was responsible for the coup, although it was clear that many soldiers had acted in support of the coup while others had refrained, and others again were opposed to it but not to the point of taking up arms against the putschists.[11] The attempted coup d'état was also followed by ethnic clashes. The Hutus reacted to the death of "their" President by killing Tutsis by the thousands in almost every part of the country. The army responded, adding massacre to massacre. Within a few weeks, the number of victims had risen to around 50,000.

The surviving members of the legitimate government, having taken refuge under French military protection in a hotel in the capital, Bujumbura, opened up negotiations with officers of the Army General Staff. The "partial" coup created an extremely complex situation for three years. The Hutu-majority FRODEBU, winner of the elections, trusted neither the military nor UPRONA (both Tutsi-controlled), which it believed were involved in the coup, but was forced by circumstances to negotiate. The military and UPRONA, for their part, did not trust FRODEBU's leaders, whom they saw as linked to the ethnic violence carried out against Tutsis, but they were forced by international pressure and by an inability to control the internal situation to come to an agreement.

By a series of complicated compromises and power-sharing arrangements, an initial government was formed under the presidency of Cyprien Ntaryamira (a Hutu member of FRODEBU), which was however to be short-lived. Ntaryamira himself died on April 7, 1994, killed along with the President of Rwanda, Juvénal Habyarimana. In Rwanda, the death of the latter triggered the systematic massacre of Tutsis, without distinction, and certain Hutu members of opposition movements. Those responsible for the massacres were the Presidential Guard and a militia known as Interahamwe, formed especially and trained by Hutu extremists. The Presidential Guard struck at political leaders, whilst Interahamwe targeted the general Tutsi population.[12] Faced with an unresponsive UN peacekeeping force, the massacres increased and spread quickly throughout the country, thanks also to an effective propaganda campaign.[13]

134

According to more reliable accounts, around 800,000 people were killed in three months. In effect, Tutsis living in Rwanda were nearly completely wiped out. The few that survived owed their lives to the successful push of the Tutsi-led Rwandan Patriotic Front (RPF), whose troops descended on Kigali after a rapid offensive launched from the Ugandan camps where Tutsis in exile had regrouped to regain power in Rwanda. The victory of the RPF, led by the current Rwandan President Paul Kagame, resulted in the displacement of approximately 1,200,000 Rwandan Hutus, who settled in the refugee camps in Kivu, spurred on by what was left of the army and the Interahamwe militias, who wished to transform eastern Zaire (today the Democratic Republic of the Congo) into a base for their bid, in turn, to reconquer Rwanda.

In Burundi, partly as a result of the shockwaves generated by the genocide, the so-called Convention of Government was signed in September 1994, consisting of a complex agreement between FRODEBU, UPRONA and other political parties aimed at creating a national unity government. The United Nations strongly endorsed this initiative. The underlying goal was to isolate the extremists in both ethnic groups. Sylvestre Ntibantunganya, one of the few Hutu FRODEBU leaders who had survived the coup, was elected President. The Prime Minister was Antoine Nduwayo, a Tutsi member of UPRONA.

The search for peace

In May 1995, little more than a year after the Rwandan genocide, Burundi had a UN-sponsored national unity government, whose Ministers accused each other of appalling crimes; it had an army led by a Colonel whose behavior during the coup of 1993 had been described by a United Nations inquiry as ambiguous to say the least; it had armed Tutsi gangs operating in Bujumbura, carrying out ongoing assassinations of leading Hutu figures; and it had an anti-government guerrilla movement, the CNDD, whom many claimed to be directly linked to the Interahamwe Hutu extremists, tainted by their role in the Rwandan genocide.

The Tutsis were also convinced that the Hutus from the FRODEBU party who were members of the government were in fact secret supporters of the CNDD guerrillas. All these factors made for a volatile situation.

As mentioned previously, at the request of President Ntibantunganya and his predecessor Buyoya, the Community of Sant'Egidio decided to work towards bringing peace to Burundi. It established contact with the CNDD rebels. Representatives from the Burundian political scene were invited to Sant'Egidio, including Jean Minani (the leader of FRODEBU)[14] and Charles Mukasi (the Chairman of UPRONA), in an attempt to gain an understanding of the complexity of the situation in Burundi. Particularly useful was the visit of the Speaker of the National Assembly, Léonce Ngendakumana, a Hutu member of FRODEBU, accompanied by a large delegation of Burundian parliamentarians.[15] There were also meetings with military delegations.[16]

These initial contacts took place over two years between 1995-1996, and involved a wide range of meetings and visits. Liaison with the Church in Burundi was also significant in gaining an insight into the country's crisis and the possible ways out of it. In particular, Sant'Egidio established a working relationship with the Archbishop of Bujumbura, Msgr. Simon Ntamwana (now in Gitega), and the then Bishop of Bururi, Msgr. Bernard Bududira. These two Bishops, one Hutu and the other Tutsi, having maintained a united stand throughout the conflict, had ensured the impartiality of the Burundi Church in the midst of the civil war. Over the course of the conflict, many Christians who refused to fall in line with crude ethno-racist ideology would be struck down by extremists on both sides.[17]

Burundian and European bishops, missionaries, priests and other religious brethren visited Sant'Egidio and told of their experiences of Burundi. They were people who had lived in the villages, were no strangers to the *rugos* (the Burundian peasants' huts), and vividly recalled the stories told by the elders. Many European members of clergy maintained they supported the emancipation of the oppressed masses of Hutus who were subjected to brutal military authority, but most of all they strongly condemned the horrors of the civil war.

Initial contact with the CNDD, the anti-government guerrilla movement, took the form of meetings with various representatives in Italy and Europe. Then, after a few months, there were meetings with Léonce Ndarubagiye, the Chief of Staff to the CNDD's Chairman, and finally with the Chairman of the movement himself, Léonard Nyangoma. At that time, the CNDD stood accused of being a Burundian version of the Interahamwe militias, perpetrators of the Rwandan genocide. From the earliest conversations with members of the CNDD, they were at pains to stress their right not to be judged in the light of the situation in Rwanda. Ndarubagiye stated:

We are not Hutu extremists. We chose to establish a liberation and resistance movement because the people of Burundi were at the end of their tether, because everything that had been settled was completely betrayed. The problem with Burundi is ethnic politics. You can't fend off someone who's pointing a rifle at you with the Declaration of Human Rights [...] We're fighting an army that is still commanded by officers who went on radio to say that they'd toppled the Ndadaye government. I'm a Tutsi, so I can't support a movement that wants to kill all Tutsis. It's a system we want to destroy.[18]

The movement, which appeared to be a composite of varied groups, revealed internal contradictions, yet it held a certain appeal. Many parliamentarians from the FRODEBU party, who notwithstanding the threats and violence had remained in Bujumbura, had close links to the movement. Léonard Nyangoma, the founder of the CNDD, was a prominent figure in the Burundi political landscape, having been a trade union leader during the military regime, one of the founders of FRODEBU, and later the Minister of Labor in Ndadaye's government. During the 1993 coup, he narrowly escaped being caught by soldiers sent out in search of him. A few months later he chose to take up armed resistance. In a paradox typical of Burundi, he found himself waging war against his former colleague, President Ntibantunganya, who in fact was also a founding member of FRODEBU. For Nyangoma, however, Ntibantunganya was a traitor, having formed a coalition government with what he called the UPRONA putschists.

137

After these initial contacts, Fr. Zuppi established a direct line of communication with Nyangoma and suggested the option of opening up negotiations with the incumbent government, which would also involve representatives of the other actual belligerent – the army. The approach proposed was accepted, though it looked to be fraught with difficulty. The parties aligned with the Tutsis in the Convention of Government spoke of the CNDD members as genocidaires – criminals not to be bargained with. It is worth noting that certain parties that were signatories to the Convention, who did not even have seats in the National Assembly, represented a very small but extremely aggressive minority.[19]

Publicly announcing negotiations with the CNDD would have meant the end of the coalition government, and would probably have brought an already serious situation to a head. Around this time, there were dozens of murders in Bujumbura, mainly of politicians with links to FRODEBU, the party that had won the elections. Armed gangs of youths controlled different areas of the city, with the Hutus concentrated in Kamenge, and the Tutsis prevailing over the university and the city center. Any negotiations between the government and the CNDD would need be preceded by some informal preliminary meetings, to give the parties an opportunity to take stock of each other.

The idea was discussed at Sant'Egidio with delegations sent by Nyangoma[20]. This gave rise to a preliminary question, namely: who were the parties? For the government, the answer was straightforward: the CNDD was the other side. But for the guerrillas, there was a clear rejection of the compromise that had – with the backing of the entire international community – made the Convention of Government power-sharing coalition possible. As one CNDD representative stated:

The Convention is an out-and-out rejection of democracy by the military and certain politicians, including Sylvestre [A.N.: Ntibantunganya, the President]. There are some who say that democracy is not possible in Burundi because the majority of the population is illiterate, so the last elections meant nothing and should be seen as just some sort of ethnic census. It's this humiliation of the people that the Convention symbolizes.[21]

As far as the CNDD was concerned, President Ntibantunganya was a hostage or an accomplice to the military. The real negotiating party could therefore only be the army. The army was the be-all and end-all – it held the real political power in the country.[22] But how could the guerrillas negotiate directly with the army if there was an internationally recognized – albeit weak – government? The Burundian military publicly professed obedience to the coalition government, even if on a practical level they displayed considerable autonomy and political influence. What might be described as the "Tutsi front" was a complex and divided group, whose internal balances of power were prone to change. Moreover, many members of the military and leading figures from Tutsi circles identified with Pierre Buyoya's views.

Then again, however, the worsening situation had also leant credence to other positions and movements. The former Burundian President Jean-Baptiste Bagaza, deposed by Buyoya in a bloodless coup in 1987, had returned to Burundi in the early 1990s, and had founded an extremist movement, PARENA, which had some followers in the lower cadres of the army. It was the desire for revenge against Buyoya that motivated Bagaza's political schemes.[23] As it happens, there was no shortage of people in the army who were aware that the ongoing war could not be won, and that it was necessary to negotiate. During an event in Rome organized by Sant'Egidio, the Minister of Defense Firmin Sinzoyiheba, a Tutsi, stated: "Sure, we only have 15,000 men, but that's not the problem. We could put together an army of 100,000 men without any major problems, but even that would not resolve anything if 80% of the population [that is, the Hutus] were against us. The real problem is a political one: finding a way out of all of this, with proper safeguards in place for everyone".[24]

Secret meetings

In 1995, Sant'Egidio organized a series of meetings between CNDD emissaries and informal government envoys. The backdrop to these meetings was very complex. The national unity government – formed, that is, pursuant to

139

the Convention of Government – was under tremendous pressure. UPRONA officially viewed the CNDD as a Burundian version of the Interahamwe militia, made up of criminals who wanted another genocide of Tutsis, and who were not to be negotiated with. According to this logic, anyone proposing dialogue with the CNDD became an accomplice to their extermination plan.

In reality, however, this official position belied a range of different views. The former President Buyoya believed that only negotiations could bring the country out of civil war, and though he was not a member of the government, he had great influence over it. The problem was that talks could only take place secretly. For Buyoya himself, urging for public negotiations would have meant exposing himself to attacks from his longstanding rival, the former President he had deposed, Bagaza, whom many pointed to as the instigator of a number of the violent incidents in the capital.

Nor were matters any simpler for the members of FRODEBU. The President of Burundi, Ntibantunganya, had asked Sant'Egidio to mediate talks with the rebels. But even he had to maintain total secrecy, in order to avoid being accused by Tutsi extremists of complicity with the genocidaires. It was therefore impossible to send an official delegation to negotiate with the CNDD. In any case, in confidential face-to-face meetings, everyone agreed that secret talks were the only feasible option.

After repeated discussions with Ntibantunganya and with Buyoya, a solution of sorts was arrived at. In close consultation with the President, Buyoya would recommend the names of certain members of the government considered trustworthy. In this way, a satisfactory balance would be struck, with a group of envoys who enjoyed the trust of the former Tutsi President whilst also having the backing of the current Hutu President.

The first meetings of a "government" envoy with CNDD representatives proved very problematic.[25] Indeed, the encounter was like an unfruitful preliminary skirmish. In terms of the guerrillas, it became apparent that they needed to see a clear mandate to negotiate on the part of the authorities in power. But how was it possible to obtain such a mandate without putting paid to the negotiations before they even got off the ground? In reality, the meeting was a sort of warm-up exercise. Nobody was ready for the main event yet. After more than two years of civil war and atrocities, the Rwandan genocide and mutual demonization, dialogue between the parties was not easy at all.

Meetings between the informal envoys of the government and the CNDD continued in 1995 and into the first half of 1996. The list of participants in these pre-negotiation talks was varied, but it must be said that from the outset the Burundians displayed a very good grounding in politics, not without a tendency towards nit-picking and squabbling. The delegations met in rooms within the Sant'Egidio monastery in Rome. The CNDD envoys were formal though hostile in manner, tending to keep any informal contact with the other side to a minimum. They had received instructions from Nyangoma not to fall for any patriotic *embrassons-nous*, and not to trust their opposing counterparts. Both delegations read hidden messages and threats into the words of the other side, even in innocent or casual remarks.

The positions of the parties were poles apart. The approach of the government envoys towards the guerrillas alternated between making promises and concessions to them in the hope of securing a ceasefire, and threatening to have them permanently politically outlawed on the basis of allegations of crimes against humanity. For their part, the guerrillas initially insisted: "Give back the power you stole! Only then will we negotiate". This provocative attitude defied all negotiating logic, for how could a government negotiate if it agreed to step down as a precondition to talks. But the CNDD saw everyone as a putschist: the military, for obvious reasons; the United Nations, because it had not defended a legitimate government; the French, for supporting Buyoya; and the Tanzanians, because they had always been considered hostile to the Hutu cause. Viewed from this perspective, the negotiations became a kind of cathartic arena in which "to tell it like it was", breaking with the farce that the Convention of Government epitomized, with a government whose President, when asked by a journalist if the army took orders from him, had replied: "Theoretically, yes".

The prevailing international situation also had an impact on the situation in Burundi. With the end of the Cold War, Africa was no longer a prize contested between the two blocs. Eastern Europe absorbed the attentions of European governments, whilst Africa, previously a strategically-disputed territory, became peripheral. Conflicts in the former Yugoslavia once again brought the reality of war to Europe after half a century of peace, and became the focus of the international community. The United States reviewed its role in Africa, and sought – though not always successfully – new key political partners.

Yet the 1990s had begun quite differently. The dramatic crisis in Somalia, which followed the collapse of the Siad Barre regime in 1991, had seen significant international mobilization to restore minimum living standards and security in the country. The role of the United States as a "global policeman", after the apparent success of the First Gulf War, looked like it could prove useful in other settings, and Somalia did not seem too difficult a case. Operation Restore Hope, with its massive US commitment, was intended to set the mold for intervention in the new world order. Yet the ignominious outcome of this mission, with the Americans withdrawing after clashes in Mogadishu and a futile manhunt for Aidid, the ill-fated UN intervention, and finally, the total international withdrawal from the country, are now common knowledge.

The Somali episode was not examined in any great depth, perhaps because it was an embarrassment for many. Instead, it would prove to have significant consequences in subsequent years. It was thought a lesson could be drawn from the Restore Hope experience, namely: never again intervene militarily in African interethnic conflicts, and never again assume that it was feasible to impose politically correct solutions on peoples accustomed to tribal and clan-based models of social organization.[26] This might explain – though it is only one of the possible reasons – why, at the beginning of the Rwandan genocide, the UN military contingent essentially failed to respond to the situation, and then left the country following the murder of a group of Belgian soldiers who were part of the mission.[27]

During the genocide, no country wanted to intervene militarily in Rwanda or even threaten to do so (which would probably have had a deterrent effect, especially when the massacres first started). Only France deployed a belated military mission, Operation Turquoise, which was itself the subject of some controversy. Moreover, the Organization of African Unity (OAU) played no noteworthy role during the Rwandan crisis, nor did any neighboring country.

It is also worth mentioning some other destabilizing factors. The dissolution of the Soviet Union came at a cost for numerous African countries. The various forms of aid received by many African States aligned with the Eastern bloc represented a major component of national budgets. The sudden demise of Soviet aid had serious consequences. The vacuum created was soon filled by other partners and forces that were not always readily identifiable. There was, for instance, a remarkable increase in the trafficking of small arms from the armories of former Warsaw Pact members. The costs of financing a conflict thus came down considerably in the early 1990s. Affordable weapons of all kinds were available on the African market, transported even to the Great Lakes area via very inexpensive freighter aircraft, loaded for their return journey with rare minerals found in abundance in the region.[28] In short, it became a simple matter to start a war in Africa.

The crisis in Burundi also emerged during a political period in which the limitations of the UN and other key players on the international scene became evident. Many Burundians believed that what they loosely thought of as the "international community" would come to the rescue of their fledgling democracy endangered by the military coup: that the UN, the United States and particularly France, which as previously mentioned had been an advocate of democratic transition since 1990, would never permit a coup like that staged in October 1993 without taking action. Yet as one witness recalled: "I was hiding and the soldiers were looking for me. I heard the sound of armored vehicles on the streets and I thought: 'Run all you like! The French paratroopers will be here soon anyway!' But time passed and finally, sadly,

I realized that nobody would be coming".[29] The surviving members of the Burundian government, having evaded the soldiers and taken shelter in a hotel under French protection, spent days making radio requests for the UN to intervene – all to no avail. Instead, it was decided to support the holding of negotiations which would lead to the formation of the Convention of Government power-sharing coalition, amidst a climate of continuing insecurity. Many repeatedly called for an international conference on the Great Lakes region, which the UN only succeeded in organizing in 2004.[30]

The United States, after the unfortunate Somali experience, reshaped its power relations and alliances in Africa. Their priority shifted towards new leaders: Nelson Mandela certainly, but also Yoweri Museveni in Uganda, Paul Kagame in Rwanda, Meles Zenawi in Ethiopia, and Isaias Afewerki in Eritrea. American popularity in Africa was growing. The Great Lakes region was placed under careful observation by the United States, which soon felt the need – as did the European Union – to post a "special envoy", a diplomat with responsibility for the area and in direct communication with the President's office, who could closely monitor the evolution of a crisis that had deep roots and long-term ramifications. The American appointment fell to Howard Wolpe, whilst the European role had gone to Aldo Ajello.[31] The increasingly more structured US presence in Africa did not, at any rate, envisage direct military intervention as an option, preferring instead to provide forms of military cooperation, economic aid, and support to leaders considered trustworthy.

The Rwandan crisis certainly did nothing to ease Franco-American relations. The "Fashoda syndrome" was evoked to describe French resentment towards American encroachment in an area considered to be within its own sphere of influence.[32] The French political and diplomatic world was in uproar, and did not conceal its frustration in the face of growing US influence in Africa, particularly in the Great Lakes region. Kagame, the new leader of Rwanda, was described in French circles as a vehicle for American penetration in the region. The system of pragmatically-motivated economic and military cooperation with African countries, managed directly by the French political elite (without any great deal of explanation to the public), went into meltdown with the Rwandan catastrophe. It was the end of *Françafrique* as conceived by Jacques Foccart, the *éminence grise* of French African policy.[33] The genocide in Rwanda raised many questions that were difficult to answer for the French leadership, which under Lionel Jospin would choose to adopt a more cautious and detached approach.[34]

The lack of Western political initiative was matched by a certain proactiveness on the part of the former Tanzanian President Julius Nyerere. In 1995, the latter had discussions in Cairo with another retired President, Jimmy Carter, regarding the crisis in the Great Lakes region. Subsequently, the leaders of countries bordering Burundi – in diplomatic parlance, the countries of the "region" – entrusted Nyerere with the task of establishing talks between the political parties in Burundi. So how did this initiative come about?

In the 1990s, Mwalimu Julius Nyerere was a former President with an illustrious track record but whose full potential, in some respects, had not yet been fulfilled. He had built up his country, Tanzania, by creating a strong national identity and a sound leadership team. He had developed an impressive network of international relationships, also by providing support to the various African liberation movements over the course of thirty years.[35] He put in place a democratic system, even if in practice it was firmly controlled by his party. He did, however, pursue economic policies that were disastrous, turning his country in the early 1990s into a glaring example of flawed State planning. In short, Tanzania did not have the financial wherewithal to be a key player on the international political stage.

Nyerere, having left the presidency, dreamed of being a founding father of the emerging African Union, and a peacemaker in the conflicts that plagued the continent. He surmised that he could carve himself a role in what was a weak political and diplomatic landscape, and proposed the involvement of the countries in the "region" to resolve the crisis in Burundi. Nyerere had already sought to play a role during the crisis in Rwanda. Indeed, the previously mentioned fatal attack on the Rwandan Hutu President Habyarimana, had taken place while the latter was returning from Arusha, in Tanzania, where he had signed a peace agreement with the Tutsi RPF guerrillas led by Kagame.

Nyerere conceived a vision that wove together both nationalism and Pan-Africanism. He realized that the Americans, French, Russians and Cubans no longer wished to intervene directly to resolve political and military crises in Africa. There was a political vacuum on the question of Africa and Nyerere wanted to fill the breach, with Tanzania leading the way both at a regional level and within the OAU. But Tanzania did not have the military and economic means to do so, now that the system of international aid it had been able to count on before 1989 had disappeared. Consequently, Nyerere worked hard to develop an African mechanism for resolving conflicts – not without reliance, however, on financial and political support from the United States and the European Union.

Thus a practice or method emerged which was later followed in other African crises, with mixed success. The countries of each "region" would take responsibility for the crises in their area with a view to finding an African solution for them, whilst looking to the international community to finance peace mediation efforts. Returning to the case in point, Nyerere obtained the approval of the countries in the "region", which he then used to lend international legitimacy to his role as facilitator in the Burundi crisis. From this moment on, the case of Burundi would exemplify a new way of dealing with crises in Africa, in line with the motto "African solutions for African problems".[36]

Having secured the endorsement of the countries in the region and the OAU, Nyerere organized a series of meetings in Tanzania with representatives from the Burundian political parties. He met with favor among Burundians linked to FRODEBU, who were mostly Hutus, and conversely, with a certain amount of suspicion from those affiliated with UPRONA, especially Tutsis from the establishment and the army. Despite his involvement being seen by critics as a hegemonic bid by Tanzania, the meetings eventually went ahead, bringing to light the profound rift in Burundi's political landscape. FRODEBU, the winner of the last elections, sought Tanzanian military intervention to restore the legitimate government, thereby putting an end to the humiliating experience of the Convention of Government, punishing disloyal troops and reestablishing order. UPRONA was strongly opposed to these requests, accusing FRODEBU's leaders of complicity in acts of genocide against Tutsis. Added to this were the attacks carried out by the CNDD. Operating from Zaire, thanks to the support given to the movement by Mobutu, the guerrillas attacked Burundi, crippling communications and inflicting losses on the army. Nyerere did not know how to approach the guerrillas, who viewed him with a degree of mistrust due to certain longstanding resentments.[37] It was at this point that he decided to get in touch with Sant'Egidio.

Rome and Arusha

Nyerere went to Rome and had a series of meetings with Sant'Egidio. He wanted to gauge the level of the Community's involvement with the Burundian crisis. The former President was a very vibrant man of great personal charm, a quick political thinker, convinced of the crucial importance of resolving the crisis in Burundi. Through his close relations with the Mozambican leadership, he knew of the role the Community had played in mediating the Mozambique peace talks. He valued the network of contacts established by the Community with the guerrillas, and its capacity for dialogue.

In the end, Nyerere agreed to pursue a joint strategy with Sant'Egidio. This involved a kind of two-track negotiation process, whereby talks between the warring parties would be entrusted to Sant'Egidio, and dialogue between the recognized political movements with seats in the National Assembly would be overseen by the former Tanzanian President.

This would satisfy the representatives of the political parties who warned against according legitimacy to perpetrators of violence. Charles Mukasi, Chairman of UPRONA, stated: "The day it's accepted that throwing a bomb gives you political credibility, I'll throw a couple myself!.[38] The truth of the matter was that the conflict was creating an elaborate farce, in which the official facade almost never corresponded to what was really going on. Almost all the political actors were more or less directly linked to the parties involved in the armed conflict.

The need to maintain a forum for political dialogue irrespective of the armed clashes seemed obvious to all, albeit difficult to achieve in practice. Nyerere had organized meetings between the parties in Mwanza, Tanzania, which descended into mutual finger-pointing, with the Tutsis accusing the Hutus of being genocidaires, and the Hutus responding with accusations that the Tutsis were putschistes. There was a clear need to negotiate an end to the civil war, but the question was how and with whom.

In 1996, the situation on the ground seemed fairly straightforward. On one side, there were the CNDD guerrillas, and on the other, the regular army. In reality, however, there was a proliferation of worrying movements. An assortment of Tutsi and pro-Tutsi militia groups operating unimpeded, particularly in Bujumbura, were behind the assassinations of leading figures from FRODEBU. Additionally, a manifestation of Hutu extremism, the Party for the Liberation of the Hutu People (or PALIPEHUTU), which had been on the scene in Burundi since 1980, would periodically resurface. Part armed wing, part phantom reappearing on and off in the story of Burundi, PALIPEHUTU to this day remains difficult to fathom or make sense of. It seems to have served as a handy label for nebulous Hutu fringe groups, often devoid of leadership or political vision. However, all these movements were certainly outnumbered by the two main belligerents.

Nyerere and Sant'Egidio thus divided up the roles. The former Tanzanian President would focus on the dialogue between the political parties, finding common ground between them which would enable an agreement to be reached with the guerrillas that would resolve the country's security problems. It was necessary, however, to convince the CNDD not to view the talks between the parties as a hostile act – as a preliminary step towards convergence between the parties which would exclude the CNDD from the political life of the country. Léonard Nyangoma was wary of the representatives of the Burundian political parties. He feared that a climate of compromise between the parties would cloud what he saw as a straightforward situation, involving the CNDD as democrats fighting to restore the Constitution on one side, and the military as putschists on the other.

There was no room, in Nyangoma's view, for the parliament, the political parties and the complications they brought with them. They must all be forced to fall in with one side or another. Moreover, Nyangoma, one of the founders of the FRODEBU party, was contemptuous of the party's leadership, which, when faced with the army's offensive, had chosen the humiliating road of compromise rather than taking the decisive step of armed resistance as he had.

In consultation with Nyerere, Sant'Egidio redoubled its efforts to convince Nyangoma and his colleagues to participate in talks with the government, and at the same time to accept the dialogue between the political parties as an important part of the process of bringing peace to the country. The meeting in Rome at the headquarters of Sant'Egidio on May 14, 1996, between Nyangoma and the former Tanzanian President, represented a major turning point in this regard. The dialogue was productive and much mistrust was allayed. Nyerere viewed Nyangoma with interest, but was also concerned that the head of the guerrillas saw himself as being the exclusive dialogue partner for any talks on the future of the country.

Buyoya's return to power

Nyerere had in the meantime initiated meetings with the Burundian political parties, insisting on two points: the deployment of an armed international force in Burundi (which everyone assumed would be Tanzanian or South African) and the need for dialogue with the rebels. But the emphasis placed on these issues inevitably raised the hackles of members of the Burundian political elite, who to varying degrees were linked with the army. The prospect of an international force was viewed as akin to having a Trojan horse within the country, and in this regard, the role played by the Tanzanian army during the crisis in Uganda between 1978-1979 was recalled.[39]

Tensions grew further after a meeting between the countries of the "region" in Arusha in June 1996. President

Ntibantunganya, along with Prime Minister Nduwayo, called for military intervention by the countries of the region in order to guarantee security in Burundi. The request elicited a chorus of adverse reactions in Burundian army circles and raised suspicions of an anti-Tutsi plot, whilst Hutu members of FRODEBU were jubilant. A massacre brought the situation to a head when a Tutsi refugee camp in Bugendana was attacked by CNDD rebels on July 19, 1996, leaving around 350 dead, all of whom were civilians. It was a brutal act, to which there was quite a strong response. President Ntibantunganya was attacked whilst visiting the victims, and the army would no longer guarantee his safety. In the end, he took refuge in the US embassy, where he remained for over a year. It was the end of the Convention of Government. Ministers and members of FRODEBU left the country, taking sanctuary in Tanzania. A few days later, the Minister for Defense, Firmin Sinzoyiheba, announced the name of the new President: Pierre Buyoya.

The change of government forced Sant'Egidio to reassess its involvement. However, after initial enquiries, it emerged that both Buyoya and Nyangoma wished to continue the secret meetings between the delegations of both sides. The CNDD took satisfaction in Buyoya's bloodless coup because it made matters clear: now it was truly possible to negotiate with the army.[40] Sant'Egidio thus stepped up its efforts to bring together the two parties. The level of cooperation with Nyerere and those assisting him also intensified, as did consultation with the international diplomatic representatives involved in the peacemaking efforts.[41]

Negotiations between belligerents

The next round of negotiations was held in absolute secrecy. The Burundian government delegates were forced to come up with elaborate stories to tell their families in order to justify their long trips abroad. This time, however, the delegations came with a clear mandate. The government and the CNDD had direct responsibility over their respective heads of delegation, and they made this unequivocally clear from the outset of the talks. The experience of the informal meetings had in any case created a climate of confidence, because nothing during those meetings had leaked to the press or to the political scene back in Burundi. This contributed greatly to a belief that it was possible to negotiate and to do so successfully using the same approach as before.

The negotiations took place at Sant'Egidio's headquarters, solely in the presence of members of the Community. No international representatives were allowed by the two parties to participate in the meetings. Only the opening ceremony of the negotiations was attended by representatives of the UN, the OAU, the US, South Africa, the Italian government, and a special envoy of Nyerere.[42] The CNDD's position in Rome was clear: the negotiations had to be comprehensive. Everything was up for discussion, including the Constitution, the judiciary, the composition of the army, and the education system[43]. For the representatives of Buyoya's government, the agenda was different: a cessation of hostilities needed to be negotiated, underpinned by a series of "technical" agreements, before moving on to the political dialogue mediated by Nyerere, which would involve representatives from all Burundian parties.

Within the CNDD, not everything was cut-and-dry. Wide sections of the movement were in favor of an all-out armed solution without any compromises. Be that as it may, the guerrilla representatives initially took a tough line and questioned the legitimacy of the government, demanding the "restoration of institutional and constitutional order". Things were still at the point-scoring stage, where for each party everything the other side did was "unconstitutional", as opposed – naturally – to their own actions. The dialogue between the parties was problematic, peppered with veiled threats. But it was a case of the tragedy of the civil war in Burundi permeating the halls of the Sant'Egidio monastery. There was not a single member of the two delegations who had not lost family members in the civil war, some of them killed during the talks. The negotiations would subsequently progress beyond this initial period of adjustment and became more constructive.

The government delegation included high-level politicians, involved in turns in the successive stages of the negotiations. The military representatives were competent and pragmatic, all trusted men of Buyoya. They were cynical regarding what the United Nations or other countries could do for Burundi, after the lessons learned from the genocide in Rwanda. On one occasion, whilst discussing the future balances to be struck within the country, the two delegations lingered on the issue of possible international guarantees to ensure the maintenance of peace and security in the country. One of the military representatives bitterly remarked: "What guarantees? The guarantee is war. Unfortunately, that's it". For the military, it was maintaining a relative position of strength that mattered, which needed to be such as to pose a real threat to the prospect of any breach of future agreements. In other words, in the event that the Tutsi minority did not have political power, it should have an armed force at its disposal that would deter any attempts at genocide.

The CNDD saw things in a similar vein, but from the opposite point of view. They felt that the army only understood the language of military might, and that only force could make it accept the necessary democratic changes (which would give power to the overwhelming Hutu majority). Nyangoma, however, was a politician not a soldier, and followed the unfolding situation on the ground from a certain distance. Whilst the CNDD had an armed wing, the Forces for the Defense of Democracy (FDD), which had its own military hierarchy in which senior officers were often former noncommissioned officers in Burundi's regular army, Nyangoma firmly believed that the political arm should prevail over the military wing.

The talks finally produced an important result in March 1997. A Framework Agreement was signed between the government "in power"[44] and the CNDD, which was intended to give the negotiations some form of overall structure, by outlining an agenda of items to be discussed. This was the first step in a negotiation process that was completely unprecedented for Burundi. The document signed at Sant'Egidio on March 10, 1997 read as follows:

The Government of Burundi and the National Council for the Defense of Democracy (CNDD), mindful of the seriousness of the crisis that has torn the country apart since October 21, 1993; convinced that the best means of resolving the dispute that has set

Burundians against each other is negotiation; and, eager to end the cycle of violence that afflicts the people of Burundi, hereby resolve to resort to direct negotiations.[45]

The Agreement provided for the dialogue to take place "in the presence and with the mediation of the Community of Sant'Egidio".[46] It was envisaged that the two sides would discuss each item on the agreed agenda, and that once debate on all points had concluded a specific protocol would be adopted, which would set out the basic principles and how they were to be implemented. The agenda listed the following items: a) the restoration of constitutional and institutional order; b) the issue of the army and police forces; c) the suspension of hostilities; d) the issue of the administration of justice; the establishment of an international criminal tribunal to adjudicate on acts of genocide and other political crimes committed in Burundi since the country gained independence; and identifying and banning genocidal ideologies, and mechanisms for their suppression; e) identifying other parties and ways of involving them in the negotiations; and f) the terms and guarantees for a permanent ceasefire.[47] The Agreement marked a turning point. It was the first time the belligerents had engaged in constructive talks after many years of mutual demonization.

The parties gave reciprocal undertakings that the Agreement would be kept secret, as the conditions were still not right to make the process public. However, this necessary assurance was subjected to intense external pressure. Indeed, immediately after Buyoya came to power, the countries of the region authorized Nyerere to apply pressure on the Burundian government by imposing heavy economic sanctions on Burundi, which the former Tanzanian President could maintain or lift as he deemed appropriate. Along with the stick came the carrot of future economic aid to Burundi as a reward to the government if it chose to cooperate. This too was left for Nyerere to decide.

In order for the sanctions to be lifted, the Burundian government needed to meet certain conditions, and more particularly, to open up negotiations for a ceasefire – something Buyoya had just done by signing the Framework Agreement of Rome. The Burundian President found himself in a paradoxical position: he was incurring sanctions for not negotiating with the guerrillas, when, effectively, he was already in talks with them. Buyoya considered Nyerere's conduct to be openly hostile to the government and favorable to the FRODEBU party, the winner of the elections and a great supporter of Tanzania's peace initiative. Since Buyoya's coup d'état, FRODEBU was almost entirely dependent on assistance from Tanzania, where most of its leaders now lived. FRODEBU insisted not only on the need to maintain economic sanctions, but that they should be made even tougher. Many of the party's leaders longed for Tanzania to come to their military aid. One senior FRODEBU official said on several occasions that "if Tanzania gives me five thousand men, I'll solve everything".[48]

Hemmed in by the difficult economic situation, at a meeting of the heads of State of the region Buyoya revealed the document signed in Rome to the leaders. The sanctions were partially lifted but rumors of what had taken place in Italy spread. Without fully understanding the reasons for Buyoya's actions, the CNDD leaked the entire Agreement to the Burundi press, leading to outraged reactions in the Tutsi camp. Charles Mukasi, the Chairman of UPRONA, disavowed what had been done by the government. The complex power balances within the government camp were upset. The tensions made it impossible to continue with the negotiations commenced in Rome. For several weeks, there were fears that a coup would take place in Burundi.

The CNDD had made an error leaking the document, thereby jeopardizing the future of the negotiations. It was a time when the guerrilla movement considered itself to be in a very strong position. It had forced Buyoya and the army to negotiate. FRODEBU was undermined, and the positions of some sections of its members almost coincided with those of the guerrillas. Moreover, the CNDD was no longer internationally disregarded. Nyangoma believed that the CNDD's military pressure exerted substantial influence over the government in Bujumbura, which was considered weak. The guerrilla movement was confident that a military solution would be effective and launched an offensive in the South of the country. It was believed that the offensive would in any event resolve matters: either by achieving a complete military victory, which would render the negotiations superfluous, or by resulting in a major tactical gain, which would force the government to resume negotiations notwithstanding the fact that they were no longer secret.

However, things turned out differently. The military offensive failed, resulting in heavy losses for the guerrillas and unexpected political consequences within the CNDD itself. Indeed, the military fiasco brought to light latent tensions between the military and political wings of the movement, with the FDD's military hierarchy feeling that it was marginalized by the political leaders of the CNDD.

All-parties talks

In August 1997, Nyerere unsuccessfully attempted to convene a meeting in Arusha of representatives of the various Burundian political parties. Buyoya, already on bad terms with Nyerere over the economic sanctions episode, decided not to take part, fearing a possible Tanzanian-backed coup in his absence. The meeting in Arusha was only attended by Burundian parties and factions based outside the country. The CNDD participated and accepted the political dialogue process. Nyerere attributed the opposition movement's willingness to negotiate to the warm-up talks that had taken place in Rome.[49] Be that as it may, the negotiations were in deep crisis. Nyerere and Buyoya argued with each other from a distance, and there was talk of making radical changes to the structure of the negotiations. But the countries of the region renewed Nyerere's appointment as facilitator, and reinstated the economic sanctions on Burundi that had previously been eased following the signing of the Framework Agreement of Rome.

In effect, the Burundian conflict had a facilitator who was not chosen by the parties but imposed, who was vested by the countries of the "region" with discrete means of applying pressure, and who had American and European financial backing. Nyerere's *modus operandi* gave the impression not so much of a classic negotiator and facilitator but of an international political actor. In other words, Nyerere proceeded according to his own overall political agenda, which certainly had its merits, but which placed him in a position that was substantially different to that of a neutral mediator.[50]

In the meantime, another crisis erupted. Indeed, an unpredictable chain of events began to unfold which led to the long war in eastern Zaire, the fall of Mobutu, and the Rwandan and Ugandan occupation of the mining areas in Kivu. Without going into the details of the complex Congolese question, it is simply worth noting that Zaire served as a rear base for the CNDD guerrillas. CNDD leaders would talk on Burundian cellphones from Uvira in Zaire with their activists in Burundi, but now they had lost their most secure bases after having suffered a heavy defeat in the offensive in southern Burundi. The Congolese conflict had a favorable outcome from the point of view of Burundian Tutsi interests, and the CNDD lost logistical bases and political backers.

It was at this stage that the divisions within the CNDD came to a head. The FDD commander Jean-Bosco Ndayigenkurukiye distanced himself from the movement, arguing with Nyangoma and the leadership, which was accused of living comfortably whilst sending the soldiers off to the slaughter. Nyangoma, albeit secretly, accused Tanzania and Nyerere of fuelling the split. In reality, the CNDD was suffering the consequences of the dispersal of its leadership across at least four African countries, the blows it had been dealt on the military and organizational fronts, and its tendency to believe its own propagandistic hype.[51] The split, for a long time played down by the CNDD leadership, in reality involved most of the fighters, whose loyalty was to a military leader at the front rather than a political leader who lived between Nairobi and Dar es Salaam.

However, Nyerere did not give up. Having received the renewed endorsement of the countries in the region and of the OAU, and bolstered by Western financial backing, he carried on with his plan for negotiations involving all the Burundian political factions, with the inclusion of the armed movements. Negotiations finally recommenced in June 1998 in Arusha. The government agreed to participate, preferring negotiations it felt were not particularly neutral as opposed to risking open Tanzanian support for the CNDD-FDD guerrilla splinter group. The new leader of the Hutu guerrillas, Jean-Bosco Ndayigenkurukiye, was looking for new political backers and was more easily exploited than Nyangoma. The government in Bujumbura feared Nyerere would make Ndayigenkurukiye a pawn in his game. Buyoya viewed the Arusha negotiations as a lesser evil than the risk of a rupture with Tanzania, which could clear the way for open support of the CNDD-FDD guerrillas.[52]

Sant'Egidio was officially present at the talks, attending meetings of the organizing team and those with Ambassadors and Special Envoys. The negotiations had a clear but complex structure. All the players were there, including representatives of the legally-recognized political parties, even those with negligible numbers. Also in attendance were the armed movements, including the CNDD, in crisis with its FDD offshoot, PALIPEHUTU, and a forgotten group, FROLINA, making a reappearance. Initially, it was not clear if any guerrillas belonging to the latter two movements were present. In total, there were 17 movements and parties represented in the negotiations. Additionally, there was a delegation from Buyoya's government and one from the National Assembly.[53]

The Arusha meetings got underway solemnly but several issues soon surfaced. Nyerere firmly insisted that, as a precondition to political dialogue, the armed movements agree to a suspension of hostilities. In long meetings, Fr. Matteo Zuppi tried to explain to him that this approach, which might seem sound in theory, would in reality cause further complications, as in order to agree to a ceasefire the guerrilla movements would need to show their militants that they had gained something and, if possible, tell them that they had won. Buyoya might also have to demonstrate some concrete outcome of a ceasefire, which could otherwise discredit him in the eyes of the military. Under pressure from Nyerere, the armed movements agreed. A declaration calling for the suspension of hostilities was signed which, however, was not reflected in actions on the ground.

The war continued as before. In addition, the three armed movements were beset by internal tensions and splits partly as a result of the declaration signed in Arusha. Their fighters did not understand what they had gained after years of sacrifice to justify agreeing, on paper, to lay down their arms.

Overall, the structure of the negotiations in Arusha was very unusual for peace talks. The number of participants was quite high, with over a hundred delegates. Fragmentation was the order of the day, and the working method was parliamentary in style. Weeks would be spent haggling over rules of procedure, which would then have to be laid down by authority of Nyerere due to a lack of agreement. However, the parties did talk – and their talks were comprehensive. Various parallel committees, established after exasperating disputes, considered the following major issues: the nature of the conflict in Burundi; democracy and good governance; peace and security; the reconstruction of the country; and the guarantees necessary for the implementation of the eventual agreement. Fr. Matteo Zuppi was entrusted by Nyerere to chair the committee on peace and security, which was to discuss the cessation of hostilities and the integration of the armed groups into a new national army.

The Arusha negotiations, characterized by much contention, were protracted. The *per diem* allowance paid to each participant from the negotiation funds Nyerere had at his disposal, encouraged many to drag their heels. Every extra day in Arusha meant more income for the individuals concerned, and the representatives of the smaller groups, in particular, willingly availed themselves of this material gain.[54] Over the course of the negotiations, the numerous participants became polarized around two main groupings, the so-called "G7" and "G10", the former being pro-Hutu and the latter pro-Tutsi. This reduced fragmentation, but did not contribute, as such, to agreed solutions being found for the issues under discussion.

Nyerere died suddenly in October 1999, leaving the negotiations in a delicate and confused state. However, the "region" soon appointed a highly prestigious figure as his successor, in the person of Nelson Mandela. Under his stewardship, the negotiations quickly produced a series of results. Mandela was firm in his resolve not to fall for any of the thousand Burundian legalistic traps devised by the plethora of players involved. His single-minded purposefulness became proverbial. He would often intervene personally to put paid to the many captious proposals advanced by the more contentious parties. He visited Burundi, where, drawing on the South African experience, he steadfastly insisted on the need for reconciliation between former enemies.[55] The upshot was positive, even if Tutsis felt they were being compared to the Boers and made protestations to that effect: "We're Africans, we didn't come here from Holland!"

Mandela too called on the assistance of Sant'Egidio. In addition to chairing the committee on peace and security, the Community was asked to work together with the South African Deputy President, Jacob Zuma, to resolve the question of the armed movements not present in Arusha. This was no secondary issue as, in confirmation of the fragmentation that characterized the entire Burundi peace process, further splits occurred during the negotiations.

In August 2000, the Arusha Accord for Peace and Reconciliation in Burundi was signed. The signing was a solemn affair which took place in the presence of Mandela, with his fabled aura, the heads of State of the region, and Bill Clinton, who came to give his support. The Accord provided for various stages of transition, with one key aspect being the establishment of ethnic quotas at all levels of political life: in parliament, the political parties, government, and the military. In some Tutsi quarters, the quotas were viewed as a guarantee, albeit one which would permanently enshrine their minority status.

The army was to be composed half-and-half of Hutus and Tutsis. It seemed that the logic of negotiation had triumphed. Yet the war continued, as the political leaders who had signed the agreements were no longer heeded by their armed militants. Nyangoma may have signed, but the CNDD-FDD was now under different leadership. And as if that were not enough, the government in Bujumbura signed the Accord adding the proviso "without prejudice", thereby indicating that it was generally disposed to comply selectively with the terms of the agreement.

Notwithstanding this, the peace process moved forward and progress was made in reassembling at least some of the pieces of the Burundi puzzle.

The Arusha Accord established various milestones with a view to restoring normality to Burundi. In October 2001, a transitional government was installed in Bujumbura with the mediation of Mandela, which saw a handover of power from Pierre Buyoya to Domitien Ndayizeye, a Hutu member of FRODEBU. In the months that followed, there were further negotiations to secure a cessation of hostilities from the remaining armed groups, after the failed attempts of the previous months once again led by Buyoya. Hope began to grow among Burundian refugees of finally being able to return home.[56]

The CNDD-FDD and PALIPEHUTU-FNL, who had not signed the Arusha Accord, were still fighting. Both wanted to start again from scratch, seeking to achieve gains in direct negotiations with the government. To complicate matters further, there was yet another split within the CNDD-FDD. Internal tensions between leaders "outside" and "within" Burundi led Jean-Bosco Ndayigenkurukiye to exclude the latter from the higher echelons of the movement. The result was that precisely whilst Jean-Bosco Ndayigenkurukiye was participating in a meeting with Mandela in Pretoria in October 2001, the head of the leaders "within" the country, Hussein Radjabu, led a split that saw Pierre Nkurunziza – who would go on to become the current democratically-elected President of the country – confirmed as the leader of the majority of the combatants.

Given that this was the third movement claiming to use the CNDD nomenclature, to avoid confusion his movement was commonly referred to as the CNDD-FDD (Nkurunziza). For two years, the two CNDD-FDD armed movements, one led by Jean-Bosco Ndayigenkurukiye and the other headed by Pierre Nkurunziza, aside from waging war against the government fought each other, each of them stipulating to negotiators the exclusion of their rival group as a precondition to the start of peace talks. It would take too long to run through all the various stages of these negotiations, which saw the involvement of Gabon, South Africa and Tanzania, and with a key role played by the South African Deputy President Zuma. Suffice to say that the episode served to further highlight the dangers of the unleashing of divisive forces within the armed movements.

After several rounds of talks in Libreville, Pretoria, Dar es Salaam and elsewhere, in November 2003 a ceasefire agreement was signed with Pierre Nkurunziza's CNDD-FDD[57],

160

which had emerged as by far the largest group of fighters. The time elapsed had made it possible to gauge the by then negligible size of the Jean-Bosco Ndayigenkurukiye-led CNDD-FDD faction. Quotas were also set for the integration of the combatants into the Burundian army, which underwent a historic transformation, bringing together former enemies under the banner of a different approach to security and a new vision of the country. Only PALIPEHUTU-FNL persisted in hostilities.

Conclusion?

In August 2005, a delegation from Sant'Egidio was invited to attend the inauguration of the new democratically-elected President, Pierre Nkurunziza of the CNDD-FDD, which two years before had ceased hostilities. It was clear that the country wished to turn over a new leaf and embark boldly on a peaceful trajectory. The political landscape had changed significantly. The CNDD-FDD had overwhelmingly won the presidential and parliamentary elections. The traditional parties, UPRONA and FRODEBU, had come away from the polls with a much reduced support base. The small parties, once the bane of the negotiators in Arusha, had disappeared almost entirely.[58]

The country desperately wanted to start afresh. The Tutsis in the army were particularly pleased: "The guerrillas came and we took them in. Just before the peace agreements, everyone went on a recruitment drive to build up their numbers. All-in-all, the CNDD-FDD had 30,000 men. But it was easy. We already had the quotas so it was just a case of doing the math. It was the human aspect we had to work on. They came along and who knows what they thought they'd find. Instead, they saw the misery of the Burundian army. They understood we were fighting for our families, not for some privilege system. We were poor like them. We've made friends with many of them now".[59] There were those who explained that the peace accords were often preceded by local arrangements: "It has to be said that even before the final signing of the agreements, there were small local truces, like between one hill occupied by the army and another by the CNDD-FDD. The thinking was: why kill each other now when there's talk of peace? Others made deals like: no shooting anyone carrying water to soldiers at their posts!".[60]

For the former guerrillas of the CNDD-FDD, it was a moment of political triumph. The Sant'Egidio delegation met with the President-elect the night before his inauguration. Nkurunziza, surrounded by his associates, of whom many had taken part in the meetings in Rome in 1996-1997, thanked the Community for its help in achieving peace.[61] During the long ceremony the day after, Nkurunziza gave a speech on peace and reconciliation. The people around him – though the same could well be said of people across the country – listened with solemn gravity, contrite and unmoving yet moved. There was a palpable sense of great expectation and hope. Since 1993, around 300,000 people had been killed. The country was shattered and no family in Burundi had been left untouched by grief.

Burundi, thanks to the coordinated efforts of many, was now on track for peace – a goal which it seems to have recently achieved. After a series of attacks on Bujumbura carried out in April 2008, the last active rebel group, PALIPEHUTU-FNL, signed a final ceasefire agreement.[62] Tensions nevertheless remain very high in the political sphere, in part due to a worrying tendency towards internal fragmentation within the government party.[63] The story of Burundi itself shows that the roots of the conflict run deep and that painstaking efforts will be necessary to rebuild a peaceful civil and political coexistence – efforts which whilst entailing a burden also represent a shouldering of responsibility for the common good. For as Marguerite Barankitse – a Burundian woman who has dedicated her life to housing and caring for children made orphans by the civil war – has observed (in the words of Albert Camus): "Peace is the only battle worth waging".[64]

---

[1] The Ambassador was Colonel Jean-Baptiste Mbonyingingo.
[2] Cf. the report on the Breakfast meeting with the Foreign Minister of Burundi on May 15, 1995, at Sant'Egidio in Rome; document held in the Community of Sant'Egidio Archive (hereinafter referred to as "ACSE"), Burundi collection.

[3] Statistics and censuses are a minefield in countries experiencing ethnic conflicts. The figures specified here are more or less accepted by most experts. For more background on Rwanda and Burundi, see R. Lemarchand, *Rwanda and Burundi*, London 1970; J.P. Chrétien, *Burundi. L'Histoire retrouvée*, Paris 1993; F. Reyntjens, *L'Afrique des Grand Lacs en crise. Rwanda, Burundi: 1988-1994*, Paris 1994; Id., *Burundi: Breaking the Cycle of Violence*, London 1995; A. Guichaoua (ed.) *Les crises politiques au Burundi et au Rwanda (1993-1994)*, Paris 1995; C. Braeckmann, *Rwanda: Histoire d'un génocide*, Paris 1994; Id., *Terreur africaine. Burundi, Rwanda, Zaïre: les racines de la violence*, Paris 1996; and G. Prunier, *Rwanda: History of a Genocide*, New York 1997; see also F. Reyntjens & S. Marysse (eds.), *L'Afrique des Grands Lacs. Annuaire 1998-1999*, Paris 1999; and J.P. Chrétien, *L'Afrique des Grands Lacs. Deux mille ans d'histoire*, Paris 2000.

[4] L. Reychler, *Les crises et leurs fondements. La prévention des conflits violents in Fondation Roi Baudoin & Médecin sans Frontières, Conflit en Afrique. Analyse des crises et pistes pour une prévention*, Brussels 1997, p. 49.

[5] See the observations made on the Rwandan and Burundian monarchies in J. Ziegler, *Le pouvoir africain*, Paris 1979, pp. 50-112.

[6] Statement made to the author in July 1998 by D. Nyabenda, a representative of the armed movement PALIPEHUTU.

[7] The current Rwandan President, Paul Kagame, fled his country as a child when bands of armed Hutus attacked his home: cf. F. Misser, *Vers un nouveau Rwanda? Entretiens avec Paul Kagamé*, Brussels 1995, p. 32.

[8] Cf. R. Lemarchand & D. Martin, *Génocide sélectif au Burundi*, London 1974.

[9] Cf. Y. Ternon, *Lo Stato criminale. I genocidi del XX secolo*, Milan 1997, pp. 302-316 [*L' Etat criminel, les génocides au XXe siècle*, Paris 1995].

[10] See the observations on the role played by France during this period in M. Roussin, *Afrique Majeure*, Paris 1997, pp. 141-162.

[11] The report of the UN Commission on the coup d'état of October 21, 1993 and on the ethnic massacres which ensued stated: "Fully aware of the impending danger, the military commanders in fact did nothing to reinforce the palace guard, to prevent the "rebellious soldiers" from reaching the palace, or to take the President to a safe place. An armed confrontation is reported to have taken place between "attackers" and "defenders" for about six hours, with fire from cannon, rockets and small arms, yet no one was killed, no armored car damaged" (United Nations Security Council, S/1996/682, August 22, 1996). One of the few soldiers who opposed the putsch, to the point of being arrested and mistreated by the rebel soldiers, was the future Minister of Defense for the Ntibantunganya and Buyoya governments, Colonel Firmin Sinzoyiheba.

[12] See M. Huband, *The skull beneath the skin. Africa after the Cold War*, Boulder, CO/Oxford 2001, p. 179.

[13] Cf. the account given in J.P. Chrétien, *Rwanda: les médias du génocide*, Paris 1995.

[14] Cf. the report on the Visit of Jean Minani on September 20, 1995, ACSE, Burundi collection. In many respects, this visit was indicative of the rift within the country: Minani, a Hutu, did not announce his visit to Rome to the Burundian Ambassador to Italy, who was a Tutsi, only advising the First Counselor, Anselme Bankambona, also a Hutu. Cf. the report on the Meeting with Anselme Bamkambona on September 24, 1995, ACSE, Burundi collection.

[15] The Speaker of the National Assembly arrived in Italy on a State visit, which was characterized by certain unexpected incidents during his official

engagements. The then Speaker of the Italian Chamber of Deputies, the Hon. Irene Pivetti, put an end to a meeting with her Burundian counterpart after 18 minutes of conversation, creating a certain level of discomfiture. See the documentation pertaining to the visit of the Speaker of the National Assembly, Léonce Ngendakumana, of February 5-11, 1996, ACSE, Burundi collection. It must be said that, in general, Burundi did not arouse much interest in Italian political circles. One Burundian diplomat observed in 1995 that relations between Italy and Burundi were "nonexistent". Cf. the report on the Conversation with Anselme Bankambona on December 5, 1995, ACSE, Burundi collection.

[16] Cf. the report on the Dinner meeting with the Army Chief of Staff, Colonel Jean Bikomagu on September 14, 1995, ACSE, Burundi collection.

[17] Among those killed in Burundi were: the Archbishop of Gitega, Joaquim Ruhuna, a Tutsi who sheltered Hutus in peril after the putsch of 1993 at the Bishop's residence, and who was murdered by Hutu extremists in 1996; two Italian missionaries, Aldo Marchiol and Severino Maule, and a lay volunteer, Katina Gubert, killed in 1995 probably by the military; and forty-four seminarians, killed by the CNDD in Buta after refusing to split up into two groups – one for Hutus and one for Tutsis. Cf. A. Riccardi, *Il secolo del martirio*, Milan 2000, pp. 385-392.

[18] Cf. the minutes of the Meeting with the CNDD delegation on July 19, 1995, ACSE, Burundi collection.

[19] Almost all of these parties, who persistently tested the patience of the negotiators and were frequently a hindrance to the achievement of a peace deal, disappeared after the first democratic elections in 2005. In some cases, the amount of votes they received was lower than the number of candidates they had running.

[20] See the documents pertaining to the series of meetings held between September 21-23, 1995, ACSE, Burundi collection.

[21] Ibid.

[22] For a better understanding of the political ideology and mentality of the CNDD militants, see: L. Nyangoma, *Pour mieux connaitre le Conseil National pour la Défense de la Démocratie. Le Président Nyangoma fait le point sur sa politique Nationale et Internationale*, (booklet) s.l. March 15, 1995; and L. Ndarubagiye, *Burundi. The Origins of the Hutu-Tutsi conflict*, Nairobi 1995.

[23] An important key to understanding the existing power relations within the army and the antagonism between Buyoya and Bagaza was provided by the Burundian Ambassador to Italy, Colonel Jean-Baptiste Mbonyingingo, who, having got over his initial misgivings, became of invaluable assistance to Sant'Egidio in its negotiation efforts, as did the Defense Minister, Colonel Firmin Sinzoyiheba, who would later die in a helicopter crash before the conflict in his country had come to an end.

[24] Cf. the report on the Conference given by Burundi's Defense Minister Firmin Sinzoyiheba at the Centro Alti Studi della Difesa, in Rome, October 1995, ACSE, Burundi collection.

[25] Cf. the minutes of the Meetings between Marora, Idi and Ntahuga, October 31 to November 2, 1995, ACSE, Burundi collection.

[26] Cf. F. Mini, *Le (non) lezioni della Somalia*, "Aspenia", no. 29, 2005, pp. 236-244. It should be noted that the withdrawal of the American contingent in Somalia took place in March 1994, a month before the start of the Rwandan genocide. See also the observations in this regard in M. Huband, op. cit., pp. 277-306.

[27] Cf. C. Braeckmann, op. cit., pp. 122-147, and particularly the account given by the former commander of the UN peacekeepers in Rwanda in R. Dallaire (with B. Beardsley), *Shake hands with the devil: the failure of humanity in Rwanda*, New York 2004. See also the observations on weak international crisis-response mechanisms in A.C. Helton, *The Price of Indifference. Refugees and Humanitarian Action in the New Century*, New York 2002.

[28] The recent arrest of one of the most notorious arms dealers, the Tajik-born Russian Viktor Bout, has once again highlighted the extent of a phenomenon that was allowed to expand for more than a decade without any countermeasures being taken by the international community. According to some reports of the activities carried out by Bout, who had also been operating in the Great Lakes region, around 32 billion dollars worth of arms and ammunition "disappeared" from Ukraine between 1992 and 1998: cf. P. Landesman, *Arms and the Man*, "The New York Times", August 17, 2003; and G. Olimpio, Il *"Signore delle armi" prigioniero conteso*, "Corriere della Sera", March 9, 2008.

[29] As recounted to the author by Léonce Ndarubagiye, then Governor of Muramvya province.

[30] A delegation from Sant'Egidio attended the Conference: cf. *the report on the Great Lakes Peace Conference*, Dar Es Salaam, November 19-20, 2004, ACSE, Burundi collection.

[31] Cf. *the report on the Meeting with Ambassadors R. Bogosian, H. Wolpe and L. Nigro at Sant'Egidio on June 28, 1996*, ACSE, Burundi collection.

[32] Events in 1898 in Fashoda, Sudan came close to sparking an Anglo-French war due to colonial rivalries.

[33] Cf. J. Foccart, *Foccart parle: entretiens avec Philippe Gaillart*, Paris 1995, 2 vols.

[34] A series of articles in "Le Figaro" in January 1998 written by Patrick de Saint-Exupéry, concerning French complicity with the perpetrators of the Rwandan genocide, triggered a debate within France that turned the spotlight on how French cooperation with Africa was conducted. See M. Sitbon, *Un génocide sur la conscience,* Paris 1998; and F.X. Verschave, *La Françafrique: le plus long scandale de la république*, Paris 1998.

[35] Between 1974 and 1994, a Tanzanian had chaired the OAU's African Liberation Committee, which was dissolved once apartheid ended. The person in question was General Hashim Mbita, later involved by Nyerere in the Burundian peace talks in Arusha.

[36] This fresh approach to managing crises in Africa was the product of the new world order post-1989 and new ambitions on the part of Africans themselves. It also stemmed from a convergence of different interests, including those of African countries, such as Tanzania, intent on playing a greater international role, and those of the United States and European countries, who wished to disengage from African crises whilst maintaining external – mainly financial – support for local peace initiatives, so as not to fall foul of public opinion. In any case, advocating "African solutions for African problems" did not necessarily entail negotiated solutions, but could also include military options. Yoweri Museveni, the President of Uganda, and Paul Kagame, the President of Rwanda, for instance, are both supporters of African solutions to African crises involving the use of armed military intervention in neighboring countries.

[37] Nyerere was blamed for the death – viewed as "suspicious" – of the leading politician Rémi Gahutu, which occurred in a Tanzanian prison in 1990. Rémi Gahutu was seen as the first Burundian Hutu who openly called for armed

struggle for the liberation of Hutus. For an exploration of the "mythico-history" of Hutu exile communities, see L. Mallki, *Purity and exile: violence, memory and national cosmology among Hutu refugees in Tanzania*, Chicago 1995.

[38] Stated in conversation with the author in 1995. From the outset, Charles Mukasi, a Hutu member of the UPRONA party, represented the faction that rejected any suggestion of negotiating with the CNDD. In effect, UPRONA had never had an entirely Tutsi membership.

[39] In 1978, following the Ugandan attempt to annex the Kagera region of Tanzania, the Tanzanian army responded by occupying Uganda, putting an end to Idi Amin's government and installing Yusufu Lule as President. On that occasion, in a meeting with Giulio Andreotti, Nyerere had called for international financial backing for the Tanzanian military intervention: cf. G. Andreotti, *Diari 1976-2979. Gli anni della solidarietà*, Milan 1981, p. 347.

[40] This had been the CNDD's position right from the earliest meetings with its representatives, who saw Buyoya as the "real" dialogue partner given that he was the *de facto* head of the army and the person whom they believed had really been behind the failed putsch of October 1993. Cf. the report on the Meeting with Jerome Ndiho on June 10, 1995, ACSE, Burundi collection. Also pivotal in encouraging the movement to go down the road of dialogue was the meeting between a large CNDD delegation, headed by Nyangoma, and the US Special Envoy, Howard Wolpe, in May 1996.

[41] On November 8, 1996, a meeting was held at Sant'Egidio which was attended by, among others: Howard Wolpe, the US Special Envoy to the Great Lakes Region, Felix Mosha, the envoy from Julius Nyerere, and Welile Nhlapo, the South African Ambassador to Ethiopia, who was tasked with monitoring the situation in Burundi.

[42] "The opening ceremony of the negotiations, led by Andrea Riccardi, President of the Community of Sant'Egidio, and Fr. Matteo Zuppi, also of the Community of Sant'Egidio, was bolstered by the presence of Senator Rino Serri, the Italian Undersecretary of State for Foreign Affairs; Mr. Mohammed Sahnoun, Special Envoy of the UN and the OAU; Mr. Felix Mosha, Representative of President Nyerere; Mr Aldo Ajello, Special Envoy of the European Union; Mr. Howard Wolpe, Special Envoy of President Clinton and of Mr. Richard W. Bogosian of the US State Department; and Mr. W.A.W. Nhlapo, Special Envoy of the Republic of South Africa" (Procès-verbal, Rome, March 10, 1997, p. II, ACSE, Burundi collection). Many of those present at the opening ceremony would go on to have meetings on the sidelines of the negotiations with the two delegations, who had however mutually agreed that they would not disclose the content of the agreement being negotiated.

[43] The CNDD representatives arrived in Rome with thick reams of proposals regarding the future set-up of the country.

[44] This was the wording finally accepted by the CNDD, which rejected any other way of describing the government delegation.

[45] Agreement between the Government of Burundi and the National Council for the Defense of Democracy (CNDD), Rome, March 10, 1997, ACSE, Burundi collection.

[46] The Agreement provided that the two parties "may also agree to the presence of observers". It must be said that one of the aspects most appreciated by both parties was the neutrality of the negotiating framework offered by Sant'Egidio.

[47] Ibid.

[48] Remark made by P.C. Nahimana to the author in 1998.

[49] Cf. the report on the Visit to Tanzania and Burundi of August 23 – September 4, 1997, ACSE, Burundi collection.

[50] The issue of the confusion of mediation roles and mechanisms in the resolution of conflicts has been incisively and systematically analyzed in L. Nathan, *"When Push Comes to Shove". The failure of international mediation in African civil wars*, "Track Two" 8 (2) November 1999, pp. 1-23. Nathan, who also examines the case of Burundi, lists the following six basic mediation principles which have often been paid scant regard in negotiations to resolve civil wars in Africa:

" – mediators should not be partisan
the parties must consent to mediation and the choice of the mediator
conflict cannot be solved quickly and easily
the parties must own the settlement
mediators should not apply punitive measures
mediation is a specialized activity".

[51] The standard propaganda employed by the CNDD heavily stressed the reluctance of the Burundian army to fight and, conversely, the invincibility of its own guerrilla fighters. See, for instance, the Intagoheka propaganda video, a copy of which is held by the author. The defeat in the South of the country caused a reassessment of such hyperbole, as Tutsi soldiers – many of whom were originally from the South – fought with great determination, in part because of the proximity of their homes and families.

[52] The government in Bujumbura frequently accused Tanzania of supporting the rebels, yet the rebels themselves accused Tanzania of not helping them and of secretly supporting Buyoya. What cannot be denied is that the Burundian refugee camps in Tanzania, situated – unfortunately for the refugees – on the border with Burundi, reluctantly served as a rear base for the CNDD-FDD. It would seem that, in actual fact, there was never more than a threat to provide Tanzanian assistance to the rebels, used as a further means of applying pressure on Buyoya's government.

[53] The parties that attended were: UPRONA (Union pour le Progrés National), FRODEBU (Front pour la Démocratie au Burundi), PARENA (Parti pour le Redressement National), ABASA (Alliance Burundo-Africaine pour le Salut), ANADDE (Alliance Nationale pour le Droit et le Développement Économique), AV-Intwari (Alliance des Vaillants), Inkinzo (Le Bouclier), PIT (Parti Indépendant pour les Travailleurs), the Parti Libéral, the Parti du Peuple, the Parti pour la Réconciliation du Peuple, the Parti pour la Socio-Démocratie, RADDES (Rassemblement pour la Démocratie, le Développement Économique et Social), and RPB (Rassemblement pour le Peuple du Burundi). Then there were the armed movements: the CNDD (Conseil National pour la Défense de la Démocratie), PALIPEHUTU (Parti pour la Libération du Peuple Hutu), and FROLINA (Front pour la Libération Nationale). In addition, there was a delegation from the Burundian government, as well as one from the National Assembly. During the negotiations, divisions emerged not just within the armed movements but also within the political parties, as besides receiving a per diem allowance, delegates in Arusha stood a good chance of becoming ministers or deputy ministers in the future transitional government. Within the ranks of the Parti Libéral, the Chairman Gaëtan Nikobamye's driver led a split and declared himself the leader of the new party. This example was soon followed by others. Nyerere rejected these maneuvers. During the session in Arusha in July 1998, by way of refusal to countenance leadership bids within the parties,

167

Tanzanian security personnel physically intervened to stop a fight for seats in the negotiating room.

[54] As regards the *per diem* (which in Arusha was $US150 a day per delegate) and the negotiating methodology used, see the critiques made in International Crisis Group, *The Mandela Effect: Prospects for Peace in Burundi, "Central Africa Report" No. 13*, April 18, 2000, pp. 11-12.

[55] See the documentary by Nico di Biase, Sant'Egidio. *Les artisans de la paix*, (ADR Productions, Ventura Film, Arte & TS1), 2001, which largely deals with the case of Burundi.

[56] According to the United Nations, in 2001 there were approximately 412,000 Burundian refugees in neighboring countries, in addition to 375,000 internally displaced persons, out of a total population of 6,849,000: United Nations, Office for the Coordination of Humanitarian Affairs (OCHA), Humanitarian Briefing Pack: Burundi, April 2002.

[57] During this period of time, delegations from Pierre Nkurunziza's CNDD-FDD visited Rome for several meetings at Sant'Egidio to reflect on the negotiating process.

[58] Léonard Nyangoma's political formation did manage to secure a representation – albeit very small – in parliament.

[59] Cf. the report on the Visit to Burundi of August 23-26, 2005, ACSE, Burundi collection.

[60] Ibid.

[61] Ibid.

[62] The Ngozi Declaration, between the President of Burundi, Pierre Nkurunziza, and the leader of PALIPEHUTU-FNL, Agathon Rwasa, was signed on August 29, 2008.

[63] In February 2007, Hussein Radjabu, the number two in the CNDD-FDD and *éminence grise* of the government, was accused of attempting to stage a coup and was imprisoned. Similar proceedings were also brought against the former President of Burundi, Domitien Ndayizeye. Currently, tensions are running high within the CNDD-FDD between those loyal to the President and followers of Hussein Radjabu.

[64] C. Martin, *Madre di diecimila figli*, Casale Monferrato 2007, p. 17 [*La haine n'aura pas le dernier mot. Maggy, la femme aux 10 000 enfants*, Paris 2005].

Albania in Transition

Albania

Area (in sq km)	28,748
Population (millions)	3.135
Population density (inhabitants per sq km)	109
Percentage of population <15 years	26.5
Annual change in population (%)	+0.2
Infant mortality per 1,000 live births (<1 year/<5 years)	17/19
Life expectancy at birth (male/female)	71/77
Fertility rate (average no. of children per woman)	2.2
Illiteracy rate (%)	1.0
Doctors (per 1,000 inhabitants)	1.4
Percentage of adult population living with HIV/AIDS (adult prevalence rate	-
Human Development Index (HDI), expressed on a scale from 0 to 1, to three decimal places	0.780
HDI, world ranking	72
GDP per capita (USD)	2,461
GDP per capita, world ranking	97
Personal computers (per 1,000 inhabitants)	12.0

Albania in Transition

Roberto Morozzo della Rocca

The Pact for the future of Albania

The Pact for the future of Albania – as it was dubbed by those involved and by the international press – was signed in Rome on June 23, 1997 at the headquarters of the Community of Sant'Egidio in Trastevere. The main signatories were Tritan Shehu and Fatos Nano[1], the Chairmen of the two principal Albanian parties, the Democratic Party and the Socialist Party respectively. The agreement concerned the upcoming Albanian elections of June 29, and the policies to be pursued subsequently in order to revive the fortunes of a country plunged into a deep crisis after the collapse of certain financial investment schemes. Having promised high rates of interest on deposits, these schemes became insolvent as soon as the flow of fresh funds dwindled and some customers began asking for their money back. The crash affected 70% of Albanian households and involved the loss of substantial amounts of savings, leading to an armed uprising and the ransacking of military arsenals for weapons by the bulk of the population.[2]

The key provisions of the Pact for the future of Albania set out the conditions that would guarantee the validity of the elections and acceptance of the outcome by the losing parties, as well as undertakings for ensuring the governability of the country after the polls. It was an extremely delicate moment, with fears that the country would descend into civil war, bloody reprisals and anarchy. Albania was a nation that had emerged from an iron-fisted dictatorship only a few years before, was barely acquainted with democracy, had a clan-based cultural mindset, lacked State traditions, and its people had always been accustomed to the use of arms (indeed, every family had its own gun, and now, a Kalashnikov stolen from the arsenals as well).

Albanian society was politically divided between supporters of Sali Berisha and his Democratic Party, in power since 1992, and Fatos Nano and the Socialist Party, the modern-day successor to the communist Workers' Party that had ruled the country from 1945 until the transition to democracy.[3] The North of the country primarily supported Berisha whilst the South predominantly backed Nano. The antagonism between these two main Albanian political figures reflected old regional divisions, but also heralded a major rift in the country at local level, despite the fact that Albanians were used to successive incoming leaders ensconcing people and clans from their own areas of origin in positions of power in Tirana.

Hence, the aim of the Pact for the future of Albania was to prevent unrest during the elections, putting in place vehicles for political dialogue in advance that would avert a feared resort to arms, and, at a later stage, supporting the workings of a peaceful democracy in which even the opposition would have an important institutional role to play. In the Pact for the future of Albania, the signatories acknowledged that the OSCE and the international community had laid the groundwork for a "sound electoral process", undertook to conduct a fair and non-violent election campaign, avowed the pivotal importance of the elections – and thereby implicitly rejected any recourse to arms – as a means to resolving the crisis, and agreed to accept the international community's verdict on the validity of the ballot. With respect to the period following the elections, the parties undertook to ensure the governability of the country through the formation of coalition rather than single-party governments, so as to facilitate political reconciliation. In addition, they agreed that the opposition, that is, the party defeated in the upcoming elections, would be granted key institutional positions such as the chairmanship of parliamentary committees, the office of Deputy Parliamentary Speaker, and the post of Chairman of the State Control Commission.

The agreement was signed during a solemn ceremony, attended by members of the diplomatic corps and the international press. The Italian government was represented by the Minister for Defense, Beniamino Andreatta, who had taken an active interest in this initiative. After the

172

signing, the Speaker of the Italian Chamber of Deputies, Luciano Violante, met with Fatos Nano, Tritan Shehu and other Albanian politicians present. Andrea Riccardi opened the proceedings of the meeting on behalf of Sant'Egidio, stressing, among other things, the need for Albanians to recognize the State as an instrument for the common good that did not belong to one or other of the embattled parties:

The difficulties and conflicts that have characterized recent events in Albania can be attributed to a desire to build a truly representative democracy that gives voice to the majority, provides guarantees for minorities and, above all, makes Albanians feel at home with the State and makes them realize that it is in the State that their future lies.

The intended scope of the agreement proposed here today, which has already been discussed among the representatives of the major parties, goes beyond the elections, whatever their outcome. The political parties have different visions for the future of Albania and different interpretations of its recent past, but this agreement shows that whilst much – naturally, given that they are political parties – divides them, there are matters on which they are profoundly united, including: the acknowledgement of the forthcoming elections as a pivotal moment for Albanian democracy and of the need to respect the will of the people, the desire for transparency, and the assurances to be accorded to the opposition. In short, there is a resolve to fully embrace democracy, with the State belonging not just to one party but to all Albanians. It is as if each of the parties, with all their differences, have solemnly committed themselves to achieving this goal, in the knowledge that in order for their differences to have any significance, what unites them – namely, a democratic State in Albania – must be guaranteed.[4]

The terms of the Pact were as follows:

We, the representatives of the political parties of Albania, in view of the grave situation facing the country and of the impending elections of June 29, 1997, agree as follows:

   1. We acknowledge that the efforts undertaken and the further

measures that will need to be taken by the government of national reconciliation, by the Electoral Commissions at all levels, as well as by the OSCE and the international community, throughout the country (in every constituency), constitute a necessary prerequisite for the conduct on June 29, 1997 of a sound electoral process.

2. We shall continue to strive to ensure that our parties conduct an election campaign, including during its final stages, that is in keeping with the rules of proper political dialogue, avoiding any violence that hinders freedom of movement and expression of political ideas.

3. The solution of the serious crisis facing Albania, as well as the establishment of an ongoing and lasting process of democratic evolution and the consolidation of a stable democracy, depend on free and fair elections being held on June 29, 1997. Only on this condition will the election results, as confirmed by the international community, be beyond dispute and respected not only by our political parties, but, above all, by all Albanian people throughout the country.

4. We undertake to ensure the governability of the country, in the knowledge that its welfare and development must absolutely constitute the fundamental plank of the platforms, as well as the driving inspiration, of each party. To that end, the grave situation in which the country finds itself necessitates the contribution of all the parties within the framework of a joint political partnership.

We therefore acknowledge the priority need for a real coalition government in which the majority party is supported by other parties that are thoroughly committed to the institutional and economic reconstruction of the country.

The opposition shall be entitled, *inter alia*, to hold positions of institutional responsibility, including, for instance, the chair of a significant number of parliamentary committees, one of the Deputy Parliamentary Speaker positions, and the post of Chairman of the State Control Commission.[5]

Affixed alongside the signatures of Nano and Shehu was that of Skënder Gjinushi, Chairman of the Social Democratic Party, a smaller party that was running on the same ticket as the Socialists. Shehu considered that his own signature

174

implicitly counted for the small parties allied with his party, including the Legality Movement Party (Legaliteti), which sought the restoration of the monarchy. Nano likewise believed that his signature ensured the endorsement of the Pact by the Unity for Human Rights Party of the Greek minority in the South of the country, and the Democratic Alliance Party, another small left-wing group.[6]

The Pact for the future of Albania was very well received in Albania. The people saw it as a guarantee of future peaceful coexistence, after months of gloom, turmoil and violence. Up till that point, the election campaign had been marked, as anticipated, by bitter rivalry between the Socialists and the Democrats. In the North, the Democratic stronghold, the Socialists had not been able to campaign freely, and in the South, the Socialists' heartland, the Democrats had encountered the same problem. The weeks leading up to the elections were interspersed with several violent incidents. Given that hundreds of thousands of Kalashnikovs and other weapons were in the hands of the population, the poll took place in conditions characterized as an emerging threat by the international community.

As far as Italy and the other European countries most actively involved were concerned, the deployment of a multinational military force (known as Operation Alba), as well as OSCE civilian personnel, served to ensure the existence of the minimum acceptable standards for the elections to be declared valid. To the astonishment of international observers, the elections held on Sunday, June 29 were conducted in an orderly and responsible manner. With unexpected patience and calm, Albanians lined up en masse to vote. "The vote on June 29th", reported "The Economist", "was not the catastrophe many had feared".[7]

Sant'Egidio: a part of Albania's history (1986-1996)

So how did Sant'Egidio pave the way politically for the agreement signed in Rome? The answer to this question was given by one of the two main signatories to the Pact, Tritan Shehu: "The Community of Sant'Egidio has become a part of our history over the last ten years, acting as a bridge not just between Albania and Europe. Sant'Egidio helped forge a connection between us Albanians, whilst we were endeavoring to break with the old logic of conflict and master the art of peaceful coexistence and cooperation [...] For us Albanians, the Community has played a major role in reducing tensions and conflict".[8]

Having emerged from communism in December 1990 as the very last of the Eastern European countries to do so, the Community had supported Albania through its humanitarian activities since 1991. During the transition years of 1991-1993, when people struggled to get hold of enough food to survive, when the trees lining the avenues were cut down for cooking and heating, when the only lights at night were stars, and when the landscape – almost as if to confirm Albania's fabled uniqueness – bore no signs of car ownership or other modern technology, Sant'Egidio distributed material aid without distinguishing between Christians and Muslims, between those persecuted by and those nostalgic for the old regime, or between city people and mountain folk. They were all in need. Even government ministers turned to the Community for medical care or a simple pair of eyeglasses, because everything was in short supply in Albania. In Tirana and elsewhere in the country, members of Sant'Egidio were engaged in health and welfare support activities, such as disease prevention, combating child malnutrition, training physiotherapists, providing care in psychiatric hospitals and prisons, getting clinical wards up and running again, offering eye care, twinning underprivileged Albanian elementary and high schools with overseas schools, distributing clothing, and providing basic necessities and school equipment and materials. But they also shored up river banks after floods and refurbished old water mains.

There were schools with no glass in their windows, where children studied in the cold sitting on stone instead of benches, which had been taken away to be used as firewood. Sant'Egidio put glass panes back in and replaced the benches. In Albania, a small country with a population of little more than three million, material life was rudimentary, the people were friendly, welcoming and bound to traditional values. Everyone knew all there was to know about everybody else. There was a sense of being able to do much to help, drawing on the great desire of Albanian society for emancipation and progress after half a century of isolation. Sant'Egidio acted on its own initiative but also channeled aid to Albania from international organizations (including UNICEF and the World Bank), from Caritas agencies around the world, from banks, schools and hospitals in Western countries, and from volunteer associations.[9]

The Rome-founded Community was therefore well-known in Albania. It had dealt with representatives from both sides of the political fence, having assisted the country in 1991-1992, when the Socialists were in government, as well as in subsequent years during the presidency of Sali Berisha. Its work was appreciated by politicians from across the political spectrum. In Albania, personal relationships were crucial; institutions and rules counted for relatively little, and only family, clan and friendship ties galvanized society. On various occasions, Sant'Egidio had helped ease relations between the Albanian and Italian governments. It had mediated disputes, suggested ways of dealing with corruption and smuggling, assisted in securing the release of seized fishing vessels, and facilitated development cooperation.

A relationship of trust had been established with Berisha, the then President of Albania, who was aware that the members of the Community in Albania acted not out of personal interest but for the common good of the country, and it did not bother him that they also maintained good relations with representatives of the Socialist Party. Berisha clearly decided on a case-by-case basis whether to accept the advice of Sant'Egidio. He chose not to when, in the interests of a transition to democracy that was in many respects incredibly peaceful, it was suggested that he show clemency towards Ramiz Alia[10] and Fatos Nano, who ended up being put on trial. He did, however, heed the request for the suspension of the death penalty in Albania.[11] From an Albanian cultural perspective, in which honor and the nation are prized above all, the members of Sant'Egidio had come to enjoy a level of respect reserved for a highly-esteemed and select category of people: those considered "friends of Albania". It was in these terms that Andrea Riccardi, for instance, was described in Albanian State documents of the late 1980s[12], when the founder of Sant'Egidio made several visits to Albania and established various personal contacts with a view to facilitating the resumption of ties between Tirana and the Vatican and the improvement of relations with Italy.

Riccardi began forging relationships with the Albanian authorities in 1986. In that year, he took part in a conference held in Bari on Luigj Gurakuqi, a political opponent of Ahmet Zogu, better known later as King Zog of Albania. Having escaped to Italy, Gurakuqi was killed in Bari in 1925 by assassins sent by the same said Zogu. The conference was attended by intellectuals and diplomats of the regime in Tirana, who viewed Gurakuqi as a hero and martyr. The contacts made in Bari gradually led to Riccardi establishing friendly relations with Albanian representatives in Italy, at a time when Albania was still hermetically sealed off from the rest of the world, with very few having access to key figures in the regime.

Thanks to the efforts of Ambassador Bashkim Dino, Albania's diplomatic relations with Italy were slowly regaining significance after decades of being practically nonexistent. There were no diplomatic ties, however, with the Holy See. Albania, having declared itself an atheist State and having constitutionally banned religion in 1967, had set about destroying or closing down all churches and mosques. In June 1988, Riccardi visited Albania. He was part of an official delegation from the University of Bari consisting of four people including the University's Rector, all of whom had in one way or another passed the test of "loyalty" to Albania. The trip had been allowed to go ahead by the regime, which was taking its first steps towards opening up to the outside world (indeed, as is well-known, Albania was closed to tourism, and could only be visited by those deemed politically acceptable after a long wait for visas). Riccardi had a thick beard and people wondered if he was a "baba", a dervish or some other kind of religious man, a point which aroused their curiosity because no clerics of any kind had been seen thereabouts for over twenty years.

Having established new relationships and strengthened existing ones with various leading Albanian figures in Tirana, Riccardi arranged secret meetings in Rome between

Albanian and Vatican diplomats, including Nuncio Francesco Colasuonno. The issues discussed included rapprochement between Albania and the Holy See, Mother Teresa (who was granted permission to return to Albania for the first time), and freedom of religion. John Paul II followed the progress of these meetings with interest, having on several occasions expressed his benevolence towards the Albanian people and called for freedom of religion to be restored, also at the suggestion of Riccardi himself, as had happened in the case of the Pope's visit to Taranto on October 29, 1989.[13]

The meetings between Albanian and Vatican diplomats were also followed every step of the way by Ramiz Alia, to whom Bashkim Dino (the Albanian Ambassador until 1988), then Chargé d'Affaires Qazim Tepshi, and subsequently the new Ambassador Dashnor Dervisci, reported directly from Rome.[14] This was how Dino described the situation: "Ramiz – much more so than Enver [Hoxha] – was particularly in favor of establishing official relations with the Holy See, and hence viewed the contact with Andrea Riccardi in a very positive light. Later, when Andrea explained that he was the founder of the Community of Sant'Egidio, far from ceasing to be favorably-disposed towards him, Ramiz also began to hold the Community in high regard, despite not understanding exactly where it fitted in to the Church. In fact, the impression he had was that of a religious organization that was serious, respectable and discreet, and certainly very well in with the Vatican".[15]

Slowly, conditions conducive to an easing of relations emerged. In 1990, Riccardi conveyed a message for Ramiz Alia to Ambassador Dervisci from the new Vatican Secretary of State, Archbishop Angelo Sodano[16], which expressed approval at the political developments in Albania and the hope that further steps would be taken towards the democratization of the country. The letter struck somewhat of a chord with Ramiz Alia, who was cautiously in favor of reforms, but was held back by the Enverist old guard. Sodano asked Riccardi to act as an intermediary to secure the Albanian government's acceptance of a letter to be delivered to Msgr. Nikolla Troshani, the last surviving Catholic bishop in Albania, prevented from performing his duties and confined to a remote village since the persecutions of the 1960s, from which time the Holy See had lost contact with him. Through the good offices of Riccardi, the letter was accepted by the Albanian diplomatic service and was delivered to the recipient, who was still under close surveillance.[17]

On the first three Sundays of November 1990, unlawful Catholic religious services were held in the cemetery of Shkodër, attended by thousands of Christians as well as Muslims. They were the first religious acts performed in public since 1967 and caused a stir in the country. Whilst the authorities did seek to create obstacles for these illegal gatherings, they stopped short of clamping down on them. It was a sign that the regime was nearing its end. A few weeks later, in December, student protests forced Ramiz Alia to introduce a multiparty political system. The first opposition party, the Democratic Party, was established under the leadership of Berisha. On December 20, the statue of Stalin in the center of Tirana was pulled down by crowds, a prelude to the toppling – in yet another public demonstration on February 20, 1991 – of the giant statue of Enver Hoxha in Skanderbeg Square, thus sealing the end of an era. Turning back for the moment to the events of November 1990, the Community of Sant'Egidio received requests for help from Shkodër for the few surviving elderly clerics as well as emotional and touching letters from worshippers who had attended the gatherings at the cemetery, so that these could be forwarded directly to John Paul II.

The designation of "friend of Albania" conferred on Riccardi would also be earned by Msgr. Vincenzo Paglia, who in 1991 was entrusted by John Paul II with the initially confidential but later official task of negotiating with the Albanian government on the issue of religious freedom. When he arrived for the first time in Albania, bringing with him 45 metric tons of foodstuffs for a starving country, Paglia was wearing the collar of a Catholic priest. Airport staff were so astonished to see a clergyman arriving in the country that they let him through without checking his passport, almost as if he were a Martian. As the only self-declared atheist State in the world, it was 24 years since a priest dressed as such had been seen in Albania.

Paglia met with Ramiz Alia several times. At first he was required to visit him in the evening, wearing a tie. Then, as he gained the confidence of the Albanian President, he was allowed to visit him during the day dressed as a clergyman – a public sign that relations were thawing. Paglia's mission was a success. From the very first meeting, on March 13, 1991, Paglia secured the restitution of the cathedral and seminary in Shkodër, a historically important city for Albanian Catholicism. The restoration work on the cathedral and seminary, which began immediately, was the first to take place in post-communist Albania. In the prevailing climate of transition, this was seen as a sign of great hope that the outside world was finally filtering through to Albania.

Ramiz Alia decided to meet the request conveyed by Paglia for the reinstatement of religious freedom. Religious practice gradually became legal again. The few churches and mosques not razed to the ground and which had been turned into cinemas, gymnasiums or warehouses, were returned to religious communities. In Tirana, only a bronze bell had survived. At first, it was put back to use by being suspended from a tree. The bell belonged to the Catholics, who also lent it out for use by the Orthodox community. During the years of persecution, a Muslim had illegally held on to it for safekeeping.

Having been apprised of the initial positive results of Paglia's missions, John Paul II entrusted him with the further task of restoring diplomatic relations between the Vatican and Albania, drawing on the goodwill established with Ramiz Alia and other Albanian leaders, such as Spiro Dede, Secretary of the Workers' Party Central Committee. The government finally agreed to resume full diplomatic relations with the Holy See, with the specification that the Nuncio should be made the doyen of the diplomatic corps. At the same time, Ramiz Alia asked Paglia to arrange for the submission to him of a proposal to amend the Albanian Constitution (which still proclaimed Albania an atheist State) with a view to reinstating religious freedom.[18]

Paglia would subsequently continue to work towards reviving religious life in Albania with the Socialist governments of Fatos Nano, Ylli Bufi and Vilson Ahmeti, and from March 1992 onwards, with the governments appointed by Sali Berisha, who had become the President and strongman of the country. Despite hailing from the old communist world of Enver Hoxha, Prime Minister Bufi confided, among other things, the following to Paglia: "Although I'm not a believer, as head of the government, I think the biggest mistake Enver Hoxha made was abolishing religious beliefs, because now, without that religious element in place, I don't know how to go about asking the people to rebuild the country on the basis of an appeal to a sense of solidarity. Banning religion was a monumental mistake, because it uprooted the foundation of ethical values that every society should be built on".

Paglia also liaised with the Nano and Bufi governments, and later with those appointed by Berisha, on matters concerning the Orthodox Christian community, which accounted for 20% of the population. The leaders in Tirana were aware of the existence of Albanian Orthodox Christians but it made them somewhat uneasy, as it did not fit in with their preconceived notions of the relationship between countries and religions in the Balkans. As far as they were concerned, the Greeks, Serbs and Bulgarians were Orthodox, not Albanians. Hence, they were not favorably disposed to the reestablishment of an Orthodox Church hierarchy in Albania, as would naturally have followed once religious freedom was reinstated if the situation prevailing prior to the persecution – that is, an autocephalous Albanian Orthodox Church – were to be restored. But was it a good idea to have Orthodox bishops in the country?

A widely-held perception that associated particular religious beliefs with certain nationalities saw the bishops as a potential vehicle for Greek nationalism. Over an extended period of time, Paglia mediated a solution between successive governments in Tirana and the Ecumenical Patriarchate of Costantinople[19], facilitating, in the end, the granting of permission for Archbishop Anastasios to enter Albania and establish himself in Tirana as Primate of the country's Orthodox community. This episode must be attributed to the cultural difficulties experienced by Albanian leaders in understanding religious issues after decades of not having engaged with them under an antireligious regime. By way of example, Berisha insisted that any Orthodox bishop should be an Albanian priest of his choosing, and that it would not matter if he was married. He did not want a bishop appointed from outside the country, and particularly not one with a Greek background. He had already rejected three bishops proposed by Istanbul because they were "Greeks". Similarly, Berisha refused to recognize the need for Orthodox Albanians to have at least one monastery. In particular, this issue concerned the ancient coenobitic monastery of Ardenica, which had been converted into an inn. Anastasios sought the restitution of the monastery in order to establish a monastic community there, from among which would be chosen future new bishops (who, as a rule in Orthodoxy, come from the ranks of celibate monks, and not married priests).

Of course, the assistance given to the Orthodox community was just one of many cases which saw Paglia negotiating with Nano, Bufi and Berisha in respect of various matters that facilitated humanitarian operations in Albania, and concerned the resumption of good relations between Albania and its surrounding countries, particularly Italy. Through these efforts, Msgr. Paglia and the members of Sant'Egidio working in Albania in the early 1990s came to be regarded in Tirana as Albania's "friends in the West".

The crisis of 1996-1997

When the collapse of "pyramid" investment schemes resulted in a major crisis within Albania, culminating in armed revolt, the Community of Sant'Egidio – having ascertained the seriousness of the situation – initiated efforts to mediate politically between the Democrats and the Socialists, in order to prevent the country from sliding into a state of endemic and unchecked violence. First and foremost, it was suggested to President Berisha in various confidential meetings that he form a coalition government or at least one with broad support from the opposition. This would happen – belatedly, and hence, in worse conditions than would have been the case had Berisha immediately acted on the suggestion – with the formation of the Bashkim Fino government.

Sant'Egidio was in constant contact with senior officials in the Italian government, who sought the Community's advice as the Albanian turmoil was threatening the very future of Prodi's prime ministership. Bitter political controversy was sparked in Italy by the arrival of some 9,000 Albanian refugees, with the number of temporary stay permits issued being no higher than this, despite figures circulated in March 1997 that were much greater and talk of an invasion of millions of Albanians from across the Adriatic. The country's participation in the multinational military contingent, aimed at restoring law and order in Albania, provoked heated debate among the majority forces underpinning the Prodi government. In Rome, Albania became a pressing issue.

The Italian political parties suddenly discovered they were all experts in Albanian affairs, only to then make choices revealing limited insight. Instead of pursuing a strategy geared towards placating the situation, both the Italian right and left became embroiled in the Albanian melee by backing the political parties they saw as their counterparts, almost as if a victory for Berisha was one for the Italian center-right and a triumph for Nano was one for the Italian center-left. Nevertheless, Prodi and Andreatta, the Minister for Defense who effectively headed Operation Alba, allowed themselves to be guided by Sant'Egidio's advice to maintain relations on both sides of the Albanian political divide.

It was imperative that national reconciliation, or at least some form of appeasement, be achieved in Albania. The Albanian political scene had become embittered, especially since November 1994, when President Berisha's draft Constitution failed to gain approval in a referendum. Criminal proceedings were brought against members of the Socialist party, with Fatos Nano receiving a severe custodial sentence. The polls held in May-June 1996 were marked by incidents of electoral abuse and fraud to the detriment of the Socialist opposition. Finally, there was the collapse of the financial investment schemes that had promised extremely high interest rates in order to attract deposits from savers, only to go inevitably bust.

It was estimated that the majority of Albanian households had entrusted savings to these schemes, and government officials had also endorsed them. From this stemmed the widespread anger and popular revolt of March 1997, with the Socialists urging the exasperated population in the South to take weapons from the army's arsenals, and the Democrats ransacking the arsenals in the North in response. A miscellany of armed gangs and groups formed, ranging from the politically-motivated to bands of brigands. Following the revolt, all penal institutions ceased to function and Berisha was forced to pardon his adversary, Nano, who would not leave his prison without due process, despite being the only inmate left there. In these circumstances, Sant'Egidio believed that in order to heal the various divisions within the country – which existed at a political and parliamentary level (between the Democrats and the Socialists), a geographic level (between the anticommunist North and the pro-Socialist South), and between armed groups (that is, between gangs in the North and those in the South) – there was a need not only for elections that legitimized the right of one party to govern, but also, as already noted, for national reconciliation.

The Italian Government was also working to facilitate national reconciliation, as advocated by Sant'Egidio, and was employing the resources and intelligence at its disposal to this end. Romano Prodi flew to Vlorë to meet with Nano, but also to Tirana to speak with Berisha. In other words, he not only met with Nano, which would have sat well with the way the Italian center-left envisioned the Albanian crisis, nor just with Berisha, as would have been logical in institutional terms given that Berisha was the legitimate President and Nano a recently released inmate. He met with both, thanks also to the efforts of Sant'Egidio, which acted as a liaison between the Italian Prime Minister's Office and the various Albanian political leaders.

Given the gravity of the crisis, it seemed to the international community that the ideal solution for turning the country around would be a strong national unity government in which Democrats and Socialists learned to live together despite their mutual dislike. The government of Bashkim Fino – an unknown mayor of Gjirokastër barely in his thirties, chosen precisely because he was an outsider – was definitely one of national unity, but was considered a temporary stopgap measure. In reality, neither the Democrats nor the Socialists wanted a "great coalition". As the elections of late June 1997 approached, Berisha and Nano openly declared that they had no intention of forming any national unity government after the polls. Both began claiming that their electoral victory was assured (privately, Berisha saw 35% of the vote going to his party and a relative majority of 45% to his coalition, whilst Nano more accurately reckoned on securing around 50% of the vote for the Socialists and even more for the left-wing coalition as a whole). The two leaders believed that, in the public's eyes, the prospect of a joint government was tantamount to an admission that their respective parties were weak, a perception that was to be avoided at all costs in the context of an election campaign.

With national political unity having been dropped from the agenda, the Community of Sant'Egidio began working in early June on a pact of assurances that would prevent the outbreak of unrest after the elections. It would primarily establish the necessary conditions for acceptance of the outcome of the elections by both sides. There were real risks that a failure to stabilize the situation would lead to armed conflict between the opposing forces. On one side was Berisha's well-armed presidential guard, supported by the gangs in the North. On the other side were the Socialists armed to the South, where they were backed by the people, driven by their loathing for Berisha whom they held responsible for the investment schemes that had sent the savings of almost every household up in smoke.

In the first week of June, Sant'Egidio submitted a draft of what would later become the Pact for the future of Albania to the Albanian political parties. Berisha and Nano considered the proposal acceptable and stated that they would be willing to sign it. Over the course of two weeks, Sant'Egidio acted as an intermediary, mainly between the Democrats and the Socialists but also the smaller parties[20], to facilitate agreement over the wording of the Pact. There was no rush to finalize the wording because it had been decided to make the agreement public only a few days before the elections, thereby ensuring it had the best possible impact on the political contest, cooling things down just when the situation might become more violent.

The polls were held on June 29, with a second round of voting on July 6, and were comfortably won by the Socialists. The successors to the old Workers' Party obtained an absolute majority of votes and more than two-thirds of the 155 seats in the Albanian Parliament. The Democratic Party retained thirty seats, after having held the overwhelming majority in the outgoing parliament. Of the minor parties making up the so-called "third pole", the Republican Party won 3 seats and Balli Kombëtar secured 1.

The elections took place in an orderly and dignified manner. Leaving aside the result, the Albanians, who flocked en masse to vote, had viewed the elections as a key step towards leading the country out of anarchy. The ballot had gone in favor of the opposition because the government was considered responsible for the investment scheme fiasco, but more importantly, the election had been seen as a way of turning the page on the crisis and returning to a civil existence.

With a new parliament formed and a new Socialist-led government installed, the victors were under an obligation to comply with the terms of the Pact signed in Rome. In the fall, six out of thirteen chairmanships of parliamentary committees were granted to members of the opposition. The office of Parliamentary Speaker went to the Social Democrat Skënder Gjinushi, a representative of the winning coalition, and the two Deputy Speaker positions went to a Democrat (Jozefina Topalli) and a Socialist (Namik Dokle). The important role of Chairman of the State Control Commission was assigned to a representative of Balli Kombëtar, Mustafa Kërçuku, whilst the Democrats were granted one of the two Deputy Chairman posts for the said Commission.

The fact that the position of Chairman of the State Control Commission was awarded to a minor opposition party and not the Democratic Party gave rise to resentment on the part of the latter. The Democrats argued that the role should have gone to themselves as they were the main opposition force. Yet the appointment of Kërçuku was not inconsistent with the wording of the agreement signed in Rome. Although Fatos Nano had stood by his undertakings in the Pact for the future of Albania, having granted the institutional positions specified in the agreement to the opposition, Berisha now dug in his heels in opposition to the Socialist majority, and developed a strategy to undermine the government outside the parliament. The political contest in Albania thus continued after the elections. Having at first accepted the result, Berisha later expressed doubts over the poll's validity, contrary to the verdict of the international community.

Nevertheless, the Pact helped reduce the risks posed to the stability of the country by this political confrontation than would otherwise have been the case. In short, it acted as a moderating and stabilizing influence. The Democrats and the other smaller right-wing parties relied on the Rome agreement, to the extent it suited them, in order to ensure they were not excluded from the corridors of power in Tirana. The election winners could not, at any rate, adopt a "winner takes all" approach. The agreement facilitated the Democrats' task of conducting a constructive opposition (whilst in contrast, opposing the government outside the institutional arena was not made easier for them). This explains the enduring gratitude for the Rome initiative of June 23, 1997 expressed by some Democratic Party officials of the time. For their part, even the Socialists were able to rely on the Rome agreement as proof of their democratic credentials, called into question by those who remembered their roots lay in Enver Hoxha's party.

Ultimately, both the Democrats and the Socialists gained from the agreement. More importantly, Albania gained in terms of democratic political debate, appeasement and stability. The restoration of the Albanian State – whose need to regain authoritativeness was highlighted in the speeches made by those involved in the proceedings of June 23 – was in part due to the Rome agreement, which eased tensions and put in place a framework of mutual guarantees. As the Pact for the future of Albania was being signed, Minister Andreatta observed: "Albania stands before a blank page to be written anew". The incipit to that page was the Rome agreement.

The Albania of the years that followed was politically quite different from that of the time of the severe crisis which gave rise to the Pact. At the time of the 1997 crisis, the Pact served a particular purpose, acting as a sort of firefighter, putting out or at least containing the flames. Whilst the cards of political power have been reshuffled on several occasions since then, the Pact still remains a vital reference point in debate between the Albanian parties and in the political forum of the Albanian media. It is frequently referred to in discussions regarding institutional counterbalances between the majority and opposition forces. An analogy can be drawn between the role played by the Pact and the Constitution in Albanian political debate. Just as the Constitution is invoked to justify one's own actions, or to accuse opponents of being unconstitutional, as the case may be, the Pact is cited either to praise or criticize certain political behavior. In a country that has a relatively recent democratic tradition, the Pact – like the Constitution – provides one of the few agreed benchmarks for judging the conduct of the parties. The Rome agreement of June 23, 1997 has, at any rate, become fixed in the memory of Albanians as proof that dialogue and agreement are possible, even in times of heightened political tensions.[21]

---

[1] The two rivals who dominated the Albanian political scene were Sali Berisha and Fatos Nano. Only the latter was in Rome, but Shehu, who until a few months previously had been the Deputy Prime Minister and was currently Chairman of Berisha's party, was at that time Berisha's most trusted man. As the then incumbent President of Albania, Berisha could not come to Rome to sign a political pact on behalf of his party and therefore delegated the task to Shehu.

[2] In respect of the Albanian crisis of 1996-1997, cf. *La crisi albanese del 1997*, A. de Guttry & F. Pagani (eds.), Milan, Franco Angeli, 1997; R. Morozzo della Rocca, *Albania. Le radici della crisi*, Milan, Guerini e Associati, 1997; and M. Vickers & J. Pettifer, *Albania: From Anarchy to a Balkan Identity*, London, Hurst & Company, 1997.

[3] The transition from the communist system to democracy took place in Albania following the protests of December 1990, and not in 1989 as happened in the countries of the former Soviet bloc. However, it was only after the second democratic elections in March 1992 that the ruling elite, molded during the days of Enver Hoxha, was replaced by leaders from Berisha's Democratic Party, who, due to their age, were also products of Enver's one-party culture.

[4] See the introductory speech given at the meeting with the leaders of the Albanian political parties on June 23, 1997, a copy of which is held (in the original Italian) in the Community of Sant'Egidio Archive (hereinafter referred to as "ACSE"), Albania collection.

[5] Original copies of the Pact (in Albanian and Italian) are held in the ACSE, Albania collection.

[6] Also in Rome to attend the signing of the Pact for the future of Albania were Sabri Godo and Hysen Selfo, the Chairmen of the Republican Party and Balli Kombëtar (the National Front) respectively, two very small right-wing political movements that wished to form a third electoral pole, in addition to the poles led by the Socialists and the Democrats. Godo and Selfo came as observers, although at a certain point they expressed an intention to sign the agreement. In reality, they had come to Rome for different reasons than the Pact for the future

of Albania. Since the beginning of June, Godo and Selfo had been seeking to have an electoral law reinstated which would ensure that 75% (or slightly less) of the seats decided on a proportional basis would be allocated to a coalition of smaller parties, which would be their two parties plus other formations with almost no electoral base. The two major parties, the Socialists and the Democrats, had had the law – previously supported by Franz Vranitzky, the former Austrian Chancellor who was the OSCE's special envoy to Albania during the elections – struck from the electoral rulebook. On the morning of June 23, at the monastery of Sant'Egidio, as the final details of the agreement were being discussed before signing, Godo stated that his signature would be subject to the reinstatement of the electoral law that guaranteed a fixed percentage of proportional seats to the smaller parties. Nano and Shehu would not bow to Godo's demands, nor could they in any formal sense, given that the final decision on the said law had been handed down by the Albanian Constitutional Court.

[7] After Albania's election, in "The Economist", July 5-11, 1997.

[8] T. Shehu, Sant'Egidio, Una parte di storia dell'Albania/Sant'Egidio, një pjesë e historisë shqipërisë in Albania e Comunità di Sant'Egidio: dieci anni di storia/ Shqipëria dhe Komuniteti Sant'Egidio: 10 vjet histori, Tirana 2003, pp. 29-33, 29.

[9] Cf. Albania e Comunità di Sant'Egidio, op. cit.

[10] Enver Hoxha's successor, who was head of the Albanian regime from 1985 to 1991.

[11] The last execution in Albania was carried out on March 15, 1995. In June of the same year, a moratorium was introduced on capital punishment, which was finally abolished in 1999.

[12] The documentation referred to is held in Tirana in the Albanian State Archives and in the archives of the Ministry of Foreign Affairs, which was consulted in circumstances that did not permit precise archival reference details to be ascertained, as the material was made available for viewing in a study room after having already been selectively vetted. Indeed, in some cases, direct access to the material was not granted, and a brief summary of the contents was provided instead.

[13] In Taranto, whilst greeting local Italo-Albanian communities, John Paul II took the opportunity to convey his "affection and blessing" for the "noble [Albanian] people, who throughout history have defended their cultural identity and religious faith, even at the cost of enduring many sacrifices and hardships". Andrea Riccardi had brought to the Pope's attention the ideal opportunity afforded by this visit to Apulia to address Albanians, as he had already done in Otranto in 1980 during a previous trip. Riccardi's suggestion was that John Paul II's speech could be "confined to expressing general admiration for the people and their culture and traditions, perhaps with a nod to the long suffering endured by Albanians in defending their national and cultural identity [...] Indeed, one has the impression that showing regard for the Albanian 'sense of pride' is essential in order to pave the way for renewed relations, of which Albania is greatly in need and which could result in an alleviation of the desperate situation of the Catholic Church and other religious communities in the country" (memo, n.d., held in the ACSE).

[14] Cf. the statements in this regard made to Paolo Rago by Bashkim Dino (on August 30, 2003) and Qazim Tepshi (on April 2, 2004): notes of the respective conversations are held in the ACSE, Albania collection.

[15] Cf. the statements in this regard made by Bashkim Dino to Paolo Rago (on August 30, 2003), ibid.

190

[16] Having only just been appointed Secretary of State, Sodano was not yet a Cardinal.

[17] In relation to the case of Troshani and religious persecution in Albania, see R. Morozzo della Rocca, *Nazione e religione in Albania*, Nardò 2002; and D. Rance, *Albanie. Ils ont voulu tuer Dieu*, Paris 1996.

[18] Two new articles amending the Albanian Constitution were drafted by Paglia together with Andrea Riccardi. Paglia submitted them for consideration by an Albanian government delegation visiting Rome on March 25, 1991. The wording proposed was accepted without reservation. "Very good" was the reaction of the Albanians, despite their concerns regarding the "delicacy" of the issue of religion in their country after many years of religious suppression. The Albanian delegation requested further clarification on two points, namely: how to go about structuring religious instruction in schools, and how to define the relationship between the provisions of the Constitution and any individual agreements between the State and religious communities. For further details, cf. the documents pertaining to this matter held in the ACSE. Due to government instability, reform of the Constitution was subsequently put on hold, to be reprised again years later under Sali Berisha's presidency.

[19] Paglia's efficacious interlocutor in this mediation process was the then Metropolitan of Chalcedon Bartholomew, who would soon, on November 2, 1991, become the Patriarch of Constantinople after the death of Dimitrios I.

[20] The representatives of the smaller right-wing parties were struggling for their political and parliamentary existence. From the outset, they sought to ensure that any pre-election agreements would guarantee seats and public positions for them. What's more, the parties were divided, and the so-called "third pole" – vis-à-vis that of the Socialists on the left and the Democrats on the right – was having difficulties getting off the ground. There were disagreements between the Republican Party, Balli Kombëtar, the Democratic Party of the Right and the Movement for Democracy, because each of these political formations intended running alone in the elections, even if only for the sake of testing the extent of their electoral support, despite knowing they would attract no more than 1-2% of the vote. One of Sant'Egidio's concerns at this stage was to encourage the smaller parties to join forces. Indeed, as the Democrats and Socialists had chosen not to form national unity governments but to take their place in power or in opposition depending on the verdict of the polls, the presence of smaller parties in a government coalition was considered desirable, regardless of whether the coalition was with the Democrats or the Socialists, so that neither of the two main contenders would govern alone and thereby exacerbate divisions within the country. However, the leaders of the smaller parties were undecided as to how to proceed, as they were worried about compromising their respective political platforms and their already small electoral base. They were also undecided as to what to do regarding the Pact proposed by Sant'Egidio.

[21] Tritan Shehu particularly stressed this point. Cf. T. Shehu, *Sant'Egidio, Una parte di storia dell'Albania in Albania e Comunità di Sant'Egidio*, op. cit., pp. 29-33.

Kosovo: The Milošević-Rugova Agreement

Kosovo

Area (in sq km)	10,887
Population (millions)	2.100
Population density (inhabitants per sq km)	175
Percentage of population <15 years	31
Annual change in population (%)	+1.3
Infant mortality per 1,000 live births (<1 year/<5 years)	35 (estimate)
Life expectancy at birth (male/female)	69 (estimate)
Fertility rate (average no. of children per woman)	2.5
Illiteracy rate (%)	5.8
Doctors (per 1,000 inhabitants)	0.9
Percentage of adult population living with HIV/AIDS (adult prevalence rate	-
Human Development Index (HDI), expressed on a scale from 0 to 1, to three decimal places	0.682
HDI, world ranking	-
GDP per capita (USD)	1,383
GDP per capita, world ranking	179
Personal computers (per 1,000 inhabitants)	10.0

Kosovo: The Milošević-Rugova Agreement

Roberto Morozzo della Rocca

Between 1993 and 1999, Sant'Egidio was involved in mediating the Kosovo conflict. Its efforts in this regard began with two meetings: one in Tirana with Ibrahim Rugova, and one in Belgrade with Slobodan Milošević.[1] The composition of the Community's diplomatic team dealing with events in the Balkans varied over time, but those who most frequently participated in the dozens of missions undertaken were Msgr. Vincenzo Paglia[2], Roberto Morozzo della Rocca, Paolo Rago and Mario Giro, supported by volunteers acting in the more strictly humanitarian capacity of providing aid to civilian populations. The Community of Sant'Egidio had been working in Albania since 1990 and had, from the vantage point of Tirana, gained an insight into the gravity of the situation in Kosovo. Since 1991, the Community had also been involved in helping to resolve the conflict in the former Yugoslavia by fostering diplomatic contacts and ecumenical initiatives between Catholic Croats and Orthodox Serbs – and part of this complex Yugoslav situation was Kosovo.

It was the Albanian President Sali Berisha who introduced Rugova to Msgr. Paglia, Andrea Riccardi and Roberto Morozzo, in Tirana on January 20, 1993, in a villa formerly owned by Mehmet Shehu[3] and now used by the Albanian government to receive guests. It was in Belgrade, however, that a Sant'Egidio delegation including Paglia and Morozzo met with Milošević for the first time, on July 9, 1993. The meeting was arranged by the Orthodox bishops, who were supporting the Community's efforts to bring an end to the conflict in the former Yugoslavia. At that time, this work mainly involved providing support for the peace plans of the international mediators Thorvald Stoltenberg and David Owen, as well as promoting dialogue between Serbian Orthodox bishops and Croatian Catholic bishops.

Initially, the two disputing parties in Kosovo refused any attempts at facilitation. Milošević categorically saw the issue of Kosovo as an internal matter. The Serbian leader tried to discourage the involvement of Sant'Egidio, warning that "for us, Bosnia is like Disneyland compared to Kosovo".[4] The Kosovar Albanians, however, maintained that Kosovo was not an internal Serb issue, but rather no longer had anything to do with Serbia. In an unofficial referendum held in 1991, they had voted for the independence of Kosovo and refused to discuss anything aside from that. They also firmly believed that a deus ex machina – in the shape of none other than American might – would secure them their independence.

The Albanians saw themselves as the victims of the situation, arguing that they accounted for 90% of the population of Kosovo, but were dominated by the other 10%, who were ethnic Serbs. In turn, the Serbians – who pointed to population statistics more favorable to their case – likewise felt that they were victims, describing themselves as a minority overwhelmed for decades by the great multitude of Albanians. On the basis of medieval history, they considered Kosovo to be inalienably sacred Serb land[5] – the very cradle of their nation.

For every aspect of public life in Kosovo there were two opposing versions of the truth – one Albanian and one Serb. Indeed, the first point to become evident in Sant'Egidio's mediation efforts was that Kosovo was considered by Serbs to be an exclusively internal political issue, and by Albanians as an entirely international political question.

In 1993, although Sant'Egidio was still some way off establishing formal talks on Kosovo, it nevertheless discussed possible negotiating scenarios with the Serbian government, the Kosovar Albanian leadership and various international political leaders. The initial approach – which was a sort of trial run – was to draw a parallel between the situation in Krajina, occupied by Serbs who were the majority population in that breakaway territory of Croatia, and the case of Kosovo, a breakaway region of Serbia. The proposal put forward was to grant an analogous degree of substantial autonomy to both Krajina and Kosovo within the sovereign States of Croatia and Serbia. This hypothesis was clearly repugnant to the Croatians, who were in full nation-building mode and would not even concede Krajina Serbs any cultural autonomy unless they first submitted to Zagreb's rule. For their part, Krajina Serbs dreamed at the time of attaining much more than autonomy, having already declared their – albeit would-be and internationally unrecognized – independence. In terms of the Serbians in general, in 1993 they felt they held the upper hand militarily and believed that autonomy for Kosovo was not even up for discussion. Kosovar Albanians, in turn, insisted on nothing less than independence. To them too, any talk of "autonomy" was offensive.

A second attempt by Sant'Egidio to sound out the parties considered the question of Kosovo with reference to the situation in Alto Adige/South Tyrol, where, as is well-known, an ethnic German majority had finally found a way of coexisting with the Italian minority within the framework of the Italian State. The question was: could the Alto Adige system – which essentially separates the two ethnic groups in public life but is at the same time based on mutual tolerance and respect – be adapted to the circumstances of Kosovo? Both the Serbs and Albanians studied the Alto Adige model, and both considered it feasible only in a "Western" context characterized by widespread prosperity. At the invitation of Sant'Egidio, Rugova visited Rome in March 1993, when his name was still unknown to the general public. He met with the Italian Prime Minister, Giuliano Amato, who, in agreement with Paglia, compellingly explained the Alto Adige cohabitation model. Rugova remained "skeptical".[6]

As Albanians by then on familiar terms with Paglia and Morozzo would be quick to observe, things were more uncouth, impoverished and brutal in the Balkans, and just as the Serbs were no Italians, neither were the Albanians Germans. Even the Serbians felt that the Alto Adige agreements were too complex and sophisticated for the character of the peoples fighting over Kosovo. In July 1993, Paglia discussed the matter with Milošević, "proposing the Alto Adige package for Krajina and Kosovo, and adding that if such autonomous regions were established, Andreatta [the Italian Foreign Minister] would work hard to have the embargo lifted".

The Serbian President stuck to what was Belgrade's standard response at that time: "Albanians in Kosovo are entitled to the same civil and human rights as everyone else and nothing more. They aren't a separate part of Serbia, but part of Serbia. There are eight thousand Albanians in Belgrade, and they are Belgradians like all the rest. Rugova should come here when he wants to talk; he has no business going anywhere else [...] There aren't going to be any compromises on Kosovo because there's no reason to consider making any".[7]

Paglia and Morozzo's numerous meetings during the course of 1993 with Milošević in Belgrade, with Rugova in Priština, but also with Berisha in Tirana, and their various visits to Kosovo, revealed a yawning gulf between the Serb and Albanian positions on Kosovo. A form of mutual apartheid prevailed within the region, with each side refusing to budge, and neither of the ethnic groups speaking to the other. In downtown Priština, they even walked on opposite sides of the street. Since the dissolution of Yugoslavia, the Albanians had fixed their sights on achieving independence and on treating Kosovar Serbs as outsiders, just as Belgrade became the capital of a foreign State for them. The Serbs, for their part, refused to give any political credence to the Kosovar Albanian separatist movement. After the repressive measures of 1989-1991, through which the Serbs secured political and military control of the region, the Albanians had developed a parallel society, with its own administration, schools, hospitals, health centers and economy.

In one sense, the Albanian decision to boycott all public institutions, viewed as Serb-dominated bastions they wanted nothing further to do with, facilitated the final stages of Serbian repression. This Albanian parallel society, set up as an alternative to the official Serb system, was also a striking demonstration of the steadfast desire for independence of Kosovo Albanians. As a side note, the Italian Minister for Foreign Affairs, Beniamino Andreatta, who had befriended Rugova during the latter's visits to Rome, particularly admired this parallel society for the spirit of unity and sacrifice it entailed on the part of all Albanians in Kosovo and of those who had emigrated and were financing it. A staunch liberal, Andreatta appeared to be fascinated by how a local community could set itself up as a self-governing entity outside the authority of the State. In the summer of 1998, Andreatta would be the first Western government minister to call for military intervention against Belgrade in support of Kosovo Albanians.

Dialogue becomes possible

Over the course of 1994 and 1995, Sant'Egidio's continued to meet with the two parties, without yielding any direct negotiations between them as yet. Both sides implacably persisted in reiterating their positions. In the meantime, however, further regular visits to Belgrade and Priština helped deepen relations with both the Serbs and the Albanians. Rugova visited Rome on several occasions, as a guest of the Community. With Milošević, there were talks aimed at facilitating some form of appeasement in Kosovo, as well as dealing with the question of a visit by John Paul II, who had asked Msgr. Paglia to help pave the way for a trip to the embattled Balkans which would take in Zagreb, Sarajevo and Belgrade. But beyond these talks with Rugova and Milošević, there was also dialogue with Serbian and Albanian civil society. Humanitarian aid was sent to both sides, especially medicines, which were scarce due to the embargo that affected all citizens of the new Yugoslavia, comprising Serbia (which included Kosovo) and Montenegro. In civilian hospitals, everything was in short supply, and patients were forced to seek out drugs on the black market. Mortality rates among the elderly and children were also on the rise.

In the summer of 1995, the Serbs appeared to be interested in engaging in talks with the Albanians to the extent that the latter would be willing to accept autonomy instead of independence. Milošević was under the illusion that Rugova was open to this option, mistaking his non-violence for political minimalism. He made the same error of judgment as many Western governments would go on to make. Rugova's pacifism stemmed from civil prudence and respect for others' lives. As far as independence was concerned, however, the Kosovo Albanian leader would not compromise: it was on a platform of pursuing this maximum program of independence that he had been elected with an overwhelming majority by his compatriots in 1992. In 1995, Rugova, who needed somehow to change the tone of his political discourse, made mention of the idea of an international protectorate, to be understood, however, solely as a stepping stone towards independence. His political adviser, the elderly and respected Fehmi Agani, went as far as intimating to Sant'Egidio that there might be a possibility of temporarily dropping demands for independence with a view to obtaining a legal status for Kosovo on par with that held by Serbia and Montenegro within the new federal Yugoslavia, which would thus gravitate around three quasi-sovereign but linked poles of power, namely: Belgrade, Podgorica and Priština. Meanwhile, Milošević urged Paglia to convince Rugova to meet with him. Rugova responded on various occasions that he did not rule out such a meeting, but only if Belgrade ceased the "occupation" of Kosovo.

Milošević's motivations were not purely nationalistic. He had exploited the Kosovo issue in order to paint himself as the Serbian people's best champion and thereby cement his position of power. He was not a strategist but a tactician. In 1995, he needed peace to be restored to Bosnia and Croatia, and for Serbia to resume its place in the international community. The country had been brought to its knees by sanctions, and its leadership was losing support. Public spirit was low among Serbs, the economy was debilitated, outward migration was high, and the nationalistic fervor with which Serbs had faced the wars of Yugoslav succession in 1991 was already a faded memory.

Milošević's fiercest opponents were now the very nationalists to whom he had given leeway in previous years, such as Vojislav Šešelj and Vuk Drašković. Pragmatist that he was, Milošević was now posing as a democrat, and indeed, it cannot be denied that his power had so far been based on elections and not coups. He spoke of a country that was not so much Serbo-Montenegrin as a reflection of the multi-ethnicity "of its people", recalling that in the new

Yugoslavia, there were large Albanian, Hungarian, Roma, Bulgarian, Croatian and yet other minorities, to say nothing of Montenegrin autonomist and separatist groups. Whilst it is true that these were just words and not deeds, to be fully accepted into the international community, Serbia – in addition to dragging itself out of the wars in Bosnia and Croatia – needed to ease the tensions in Kosovo somehow. However, even the Albanians seemed to have grown tired of the long-drawn-out abnormal situation. Their children no longer had access to regular schools, hospitals were makeshift health centers, and a million and a half people were at risk of *de facto* statelessness. It was not easy living within a State (with its attendant laws) and acting as if it did not exist. The Kosovar Albanian diaspora communities in Switzerland, Germany and Sweden propped up Kosovo's parallel society through remittances, which, though initially sent willingly, became like outright taxes that were increasingly unwelcome to the emigrants. Moreover, Albanian hopes of achieving the independence unilaterally declared in 1991, as Yugoslavia was disintegrating, were fading. Fearful of new conflicts in the Balkans, Western powers including the US insisted that the boundaries of the six former Yugoslav Republics, now transformed into five successor States, were settled. Rugova's strategy of passive resistance had brought the existence of the Albanian problem in Kosovo to international public attention, presenting the cause in a noble light, but it had not changed the situation within Kosovo itself.

After years of non-violent opposition to no avail, the number of Albanian extremists was increasing, especially among young people, who accused Rugova of being weak and ineffective. Within Kosovo Albanian migrant communities in Northern Europe, and underground in Kosovo, the Kosovo Liberation Army (Ushtria Çlirimtare e Kosovës) or KLA was taking its first fledgling steps, in defiance of Rugova's "passivity". The latter knew this, but in public denied the existence of Albanian fringe groups prepared to use violence, even though the KLA had already cut down its first Serbian victims. At any rate, Rugova needed to have some form of political initiative to show after years of no progress.

Paglia and Morozzo noted a certain level of interest on both sides towards dialogue. Italian diplomatic representatives also formed the same impression, and turned to Sant'Egidio, gently and amicably urging that it set up mediated talks.[8] In the meantime, American diplomatic officials advised the Albanians (naturally, without telling the Serbs) that they would support any mediation efforts by Sant'Egidio, whilst Warren Christopher, the then US Secretary of State, spoke publicly of a "new" or "enhanced status" for Kosovo, which would not amount to independence but would entail an unspecified yet very significant degree of autonomy within the confines of the new Yugoslavia.

The conditions were right for mediated talks. It was merely a question of deciding upon a schedule of work to be done in preparation for the talks, the people who would be involved, and a place where talks could get underway. The Rome-based Community was regarded by both the Serbs and the Albanians as an impartial organization, without any vested interests, and with the advantage of being well-known in diplomatic circles. The Serbs accepted Sant'Egidio as a "facilitator" after having rejected various proposals for international mediation on Kosovo. As far as the Serbs were concerned, Sant'Egidio could facilitate dialogue as a private, non-State humanitarian organization, which effectively it is.

The Albanians, in turn, accepted Sant'Egidio for the opposite reason: they saw it as an entity outside the Yugoslav State. Sant'Egidio's involvement would therefore internationalize the Kosovo question, which in effect was also the case. However, in the summer of 1995, the Albanians saw mediation by Sant'Egidio as only one of the possible options. They hoped that the United States would directly take on the issue of Kosovo, as their protectors. The Albanian lobby was extraordinarily influential in US political circles, and leading Democrats and Republicans were in favor of the Albanian cause. In Washington, Milošević was not yet equated with Hitler as he would be in 1999, but he was already being compared to Saddam.

There was a belief that a distinction could be drawn in the Balkans between the bad guys, namely, the Serbs, and the good guys, which included all the other players, including the Kosovo Albanians. But Belgrade would never have accepted US mediation on Kosovo. Sant'Egidio was aware of this. It also knew that it was the only actor whose good offices were acceptable to both Serbs and Albanians. Whilst the conditions for dialogue were in place, getting talks off the ground required patience. The first meeting between the representatives of Milošević and of Rugova was postponed several times, until the summer of 1996. During the summer/fall of 1995, both sides were at first engrossed in the final stages of the wars in Croatia (Krajina) and in Bosnia. Then came Dayton: the Albanians hoped that these talks under US stewardship would also include the issue of Kosovo.

Thus it was that they once again stalled the start of the talks with the Serbs proposed by Sant'Egidio, to which Milošević had in the meantime initially secretly appointed a well-known constitutional expert, Ratko Marković, who was immediately rejected by the Albanians in July 1995, and then a minister of the government in Belgrade, Slobodan Unković.[9] In Dayton, Kosovo was not discussed, as it would have been yet a further potential obstacle to the success of already arduous negotiations.

The Albanians were greatly disappointed. In Priština, the option of mediation by Sant'Egidio of direct talks with the Serbs was back on the table. However, at the end of 1995, in Belgrade's diplomatic circles word was spreading about the initiative, which, however, Milošević wanted to initiate in secret. The Serbian President thus put off the start of the talks, whilst government sources denied the existence of externally-mediated Serb-Albanian dialogue. In January, Unković was suddenly appointed Ambassador to China, a strategic country for Milošević. A new representative of the Serbian leader was therefore required, to which position Dojcilo Maslovarić – slated for a posting in Rome as Ambassador to the Holy See – was appointed. Maslovari was a close confidant of Milošević, who entrusted him even with his personal affairs.[10]

Paglia and Morozzo advised the Albanians that the Serbs were once again ready to engage in dialogue and suggested Rome as the setting for the start of the talks, a venue already accepted by the Serbs. Agani was all set to come to Italy. However, the Congress of Milošević's Serbian Socialist Party intervened in early March, absorbing the attentions of the

Belgrade political scene for a couple of weeks. This caused a further postponement of the talks, which again had to be prepared for by Paglia and Morozzo with visits to Belgrade and Priština. The Albanians wanted a demonstration of the intent of the Serbs to negotiate in good faith. Paglia asked Milošević – at the suggestion of the Albanian President Berisha – to restore the freedom of movement of people between Kosovo and Albania. Milošević agreed.

In April 1996, the Serbian government reopened several border crossings between Yugoslavia and Albania, abolished the exit-visa requirement for visits to Albania, and allowed the re-entry into Kosovo of Kosovar Albanians previously barred.[11] After years of difficulties, the movement of people within the greater Albanian community on both sides of the border was facilitated. The isolation of Kosovar Albanians was alleviated by this significant confidence-building measure. Rugova and his associates, who in public could only be seen to speak ill of the Serbs, privately acknowledged that some progress had been made with Belgrade.

A key breakthrough which paved the way for the commencement of dialogue was the temporary agreement of the Albanians not to hinge their negotiating position solely on their demand for independence. Instead of pursuing their maximum program, the Albanians agreed to negotiate with respect to narrower issues, on the proviso that this was without prejudice to their broader demand for independence. This was in keeping with Sant'Egidio's approach of conducting step-by-step negotiations, dealing with concrete issues such as education, health, employment, amnesties, culture, the media, the police, the judiciary, sports, and so on. Political and institutional matters and the status of Kosovo would come last. Naturally, the Serbs also had to be willing to accept this type of step-by-step dialogue, which implied that they would need to regard the Albanians as citizens of the new Yugoslav State with full rights.

The alternative to this approach would have been to negotiate immediately on the political status of Kosovo, taking into account the various options that were floated at the time (including independence, autonomy, a third federal Republic within the new Yugoslavia, "enhanced status", and so on). The decision to follow the step-by-step approach was dictated by its higher probability of success than negotiations over Kosovo's status, in relation to which the positions of the two parties were poles apart and both based on political maximalism. Furthermore, in 1995-1996, all international observers were of the view that it would be impossible to reach an agreement on Kosovo's status. Even Berisha and Gligorov, the Presidents of the two States bordering Kosovo, Albania and Macedonia, were skeptical regarding the prospects of any negotiations dealing with the issue of status, and advised Paglia and Morozzo to proceed using a step-by-step method.

The Agreement of September 1, 1996

Over the course of several meetings held in Rome between July and August 1996, the Albanians and Serbs[12] agreed on an agenda for their talks, and, in particular, addressed the issue of higher education, in relation to which the Albanians submitted a list of *desiderata*. On September 1, an agreement on schools and universities was signed, which for good reason would become well-known in the years that followed. Milošević and Rugova signed it without meeting each other, the former in Belgrade and the latter in Priština.

The document provided for the return to State-owned schools and to university of young Albanians who had not attended them for over five years (according to the Serbs, because the Albanians had boycotted them, and according to the Albanians, because they had been expelled). It also provided for the "normalization" of the education system in Kosovo, understood generally during the talks that had led to the signing of the Agreement as the return of young Albanians to the public school system, using Albanian as the classroom language. The implementation of the Agreement was to be overseen by a joint expert committee of both parties.

One singular feature of the Agreement lies in the fact that it was signed on an equal footing by the President of a State and an ordinary citizen who held no recognized office. With Rugova, light was made of the fact that, of the two signatures at the foot of the Agreement, the one that stood out was his

– the signature of a person who was legally-speaking an ordinary citizen. An English translation of the wording of the Agreement follows:

For several years now, the education system in Kosovo from elementary school to university level has not been functioning normally.

By mutual agreement, the undersigned, Mr. Slobodan Milošević, President of the Republic of Serbia, and Dr. Ibrahim Rugova, have agreed to proceed to the normalization of the education system for young Albanians in Kosovo at all levels.

This Agreement accordingly envisages the return of Albanian students and teachers to schools and faculties.

Given its social and humanitarian significance, this Agreement transcends any political debate. The deeply-held concern of both the undersigned for the future of young Albanians in Kosovo has led them to enter into this Agreement.

Both the undersigned express their gratitude to their mutual friends from the Community of Sant'Egidio for the generous commitment and the valuable help and support they have given to the dialogue process.

Both the undersigned are furthermore convinced of the commitment of all those entrusted with implementing this Agreement for the normalization of the education system. A mixed group (3+3) will be established to implement this Agreement.

When young people commit themselves with equanimity to their educational and cultural advancement to become responsible citizens, it is a victory for civilization itself, and not a triumph of one side over another.[13]

On the morrow of the signature of the document, the Albanians were gripped by internal disputes over whether or not entering the Agreement had been such a good idea. This political wrangling was due in part to the fact that only Rugova and his close entourage had been privy to the conduct of the negotiations, which perforce had been held behind closed doors to avoid the risk of their failure. It is also worth noting that President Berisha, in Tirana, initially applauded the Agreement but soon changed his tune, criticizing it as a Serbian ruse. However, unlike their leaders, the Albanian population greeted the Agreement with great enthusiasm, viewing in it a glimmer of hope for an easing of the difficulties they encountered in their daily lives. For Rugova, this was confirmation that signing the Agreement had been a good move.

Almost immediately, tensions flared up again between the parties, with controversy over the composition of the joint 3+3 Group. Milošević appointed the three Serb members of the committee, but the Albanians held back from doing so. Rugova was having to defend himself against attacks on the Agreement from several quarters, including Kosovar politicians (even from his own party), the Albanian President Berisha, and the media in Tirana. In keeping with his not-so-typically Balkan approach that had made him famous, Rugova did not react but waited for tensions to subside before making any decisions. In the end, however the Albanian appointees to the committee were chosen.

The first meeting of the 3+3 Group took place in late January 1997. The head of the Serbian delegation was Ratomir Vico, a government minister, whilst the Albanian delegation was led by Fehmi Agani.[14] The Albanians took a tough line, aimed at testing the seriousness of the Serbs' intentions. In particular, they maintained that their mandate only extended as far as dealing with the readmission of young people to high schools, higher education schools and university. This and nothing more, they insisted, was what "normalization" meant in the Agreement of September 1, 1996. The Serbs, on the other hand, argued that the return to schools and university should take place in conjunction with general discussions regarding the education system (dealing with curricula, diplomas, the responsible administrative authorities, and so on). They were, however, willing to assist with the readmission of Albanians to high schools and higher education schools to start with.

The Albanians responded that this was not enough, and that they wanted readmissions to university to take place immediately, at the same time as reentry to schools. In short, they argued that either everything happened at once or the September 1 Agreement fell over. The first meeting was a fiasco. Participation by Sant'Egidio representatives in 3+3 Group meetings was not envisaged by the Agreement, but after the collapse of the first meeting, Paglia asked

Milošević and Rugova to allow the Community to facilitate the dialogue. Both agreed that this would be beneficial. For Rugova, the move represented a further internationalization of the Kosovo issue, as well as a guarantee of the proper implementation of the Agreement. Milošević, for his part, wanted the 3+3 Group to get off the ground.

The Contact Group for the former Yugoslavia15 asked the Serbian leader to ensure that the Agreement was swiftly implemented, making the removal of "the outer wall of sanctions" imposed on the Federal Republic of Yugoslavia (which had remained in place after the lifting of the trade embargo in order to exert pressure on Belgrade to comply with all terms of the Dayton Peace Accords) also subject to progress on the issue of Kosovo. Faced with the need to bring international isolation to an end, the stalled 3+3 Group talks threatened to cost Milošević dearly. For this reason too, Milošević was not only convinced that it was necessary for Sant'Egidio representatives to participate in the 3+3 Group in order for it to function, but also wanted Msgr. Paglia to chair the Group, as a person who was acceptable to both himself and Rugova.

However, the second meeting saw the Serbs raise a number of objections to meeting the Albanians' demands. This time, it was they who appeared to be more rigid. They seemed to be bent on getting the better of the Albanians in the talks, rather than on ironing out any differences and moving forward in implementing the Agreement. In two meetings with Milošević during February, Paglia asked for an explanation of this behavior, pointing out that the university issue was a deal-breaker for the Albanians. In the meantime, Morozzo, Mario Giro and Paolo Rago travelled around Kosovo, conducting a further more thorough survey of the state of school and university facilities in the region, which were in many cases underutilized or unused by Serbs.

The Serbs' claims that university premises could not be made available, because the facilities were barely sufficient for the students already attending, were thus clearly driven by an unwillingness to make any concessions towards the Albanians. Perhaps there were fears of a strong backlash from Kosovo Serbs, a concern often voiced in Belgrade.

Whatever the reason, having been confronted by Paglia with the prospect of the breakdown of the September 1 Agreement, Milošević gave assurances that he would endeavor to have Albanians readmitted to university by exerting pressure on the various political and academic authorities in Priština.

Both Rugova and Milošević described the Agreement of 1 September as "humanitarian" rather than political, each for his own reasons. Milošević did so to avoid rousing any nationalist sentiments among Serbs and Kosovo Serbs in particular, and to stave off any accusation of having sold out to the Albanians on Kosovo. Rugova, for his part, did not wish to jeopardize his real political agenda – that of independence – through any agreements with the enemy that might be perceived as political in nature. Nevertheless, the events of the first six months after the signing of the Agreement demonstrated that it was understood by all as being entirely political.

The Albanians' very request for priority to be given to negotiating the university issue stemmed from a need to have a political trophy to hold up against internal opposition to Rugova's and his party's leadership. Similarly, the proposal to start with readmission to high schools and higher education schools, and not to university, was forced on Milošević by the political expediency of not ruffling too many feathers among the Serbian public. The 3+3 Group, which emanated from the September 1 Agreement, was the only forum for dialogue between Serbs and Albanians during that period. There were no other diplomatic or political platforms where Serbs and Albanians spoke to each other.

Since the breakdown of the talks opened in Geneva in 1993, the international community had not managed to bring the Serbs and Albanians to the negotiating table again – and, if truth be known, had not shown any great interest in doing so. The committee that was charged with overseeing the implementation of the Agreement thus came to represent a sort of clearinghouse for everything that happened in Kosovo, becoming an outlet for mutual polemics and political clashes that had nothing to do with the issue of education. At the same time, however, Group meetings provided an opportunity for Serbs and Albanians to exchange views, albeit in harsh tones, and for political debate to take place between them other than through abrasive statements traded from a distance between Belgrade and Priština.

At any rate, both parties had difficulty acting in keeping with the humanitarian significance ascribed to the Agreement, which was reflected in the 3+3 Group's meetings up until the summer. Also contributing to the impasse was the extremely serious crisis in Albania, which caused great concern in Kosovar Albanian circles and focused Sant'Egidio's attentions more towards Tirana than Priština.[16] Time after time, discussions on any point would run aground on political considerations. The interpretation of "normalization", as referred to in the Agreement, posed particular difficulties. The Serbs saw it as entailing some form of reintegration of Albanians into the national school system.

The Albanians, on the other hand, understood it simply as meaning that public school buildings would be handed over to them, without any correlation to the national education system that would have implied recognition of the Yugoslav State. It should be noted in this regard that, after 1991, the Albanians had continued to use the majority of primary schools (considering them to be outside the federal school system, whilst the Yugoslav authorities chose not to intervene in order to prevent any further strife).

The bone of contention thus centered around a few dozen high schools, higher education schools and the university. Indeed, approximately 300,000 Albanian children and youngsters regularly attended schools up till eighth grade, with classes and curricula both in the Albanian language. The young students who were not in the public system, and who made up the so-called parallel system of education, numbered around 60,000, of whom about 12,000 were university-level students. It was to these 60,000 that the Milošević-Rugova Agreement was meant to apply.

In order to implement the September 1 Agreement, Paglia and Morozzo, who took part in 3+3 Groups meetings, chose to give first priority to securing the readmission of Albanian students to school and university facilities. The Serbs would need to make the first concessions because those socially disadvantaged by the abnormal situation that had arisen were young Albanians. Discussions regarding diplomas, official stamps, curricula and administrative issues – that is, matters relating to reintegration, which the Albanians refused to entertain – would be postponed until after their return.

It was a question of making the Serbs accept this approach, but they seemed to be playing a double game. When speaking with Milošević, some glimmers of goodwill could be seen, but at the negotiating table, the three Serb delegates were inflexible, legalistic, and entrenched in their intransigence. Between August and December 1997, the negotiations were at a standstill. After the crisis in Albania during the first half of 1997, there was a political crisis in Serbia, with contested elections, non-stop public protests against Milošević, international missions to monitor observance of democratic process, and re-run elections, some of which failed due to insufficient voter turnout. Milošević was in the eye of the storm and was fighting to retain power. The talks could not be resumed before January 1998.

On the Serbian side, there was now a greater political willingness to implement the Agreement, if only because of Milošević's need to redeem himself internationally. With the Dayton talks, where his mediation proved decisive for peace, his fortunes had seemed to be taking a dramatic turn for the better; now, with the crisis in Serbia, where claims of electoral fraud had been substantiated (at least in respect of local elections in several major cities), his star was on the wane again.

The implementation of the Agreement

In the early months of 1998, Paglia, Morozzo, Giro and Rago shuttled back and forth between Belgrade and Priština, as the 3+3 Group began to meet frequently again. The mediators had their work cut out for them as neither of the parties showed any goodwill in committee proceedings. On the Serbian side, every step forward required Milošević to intervene personally, otherwise the three Serb members of the 3+3 Group seemed immovable, whilst on the Albanian side, American pressure was needed. Sant'Egidio had succeeded in actively engaging the US diplomatic machine in the negotiations. Bob Gelbard, who succeeded Richard Holbrooke as Washington's envoy to the region, worked in close collaboration with the mediation efforts, in direct consultation with US Secretary of State Madeleine Albright.

The latter, during a trip to Rome, visited the headquarters of Sant'Egidio in Trastevere on March 7, 1998 to discuss, among other matters, the issue of Kosovo. She made it clear that the US wanted to see someone other than Rugova lead the Kosovo Albanians. The question put was: "Do you think that Rugova is still the man to back?", to which the response was: "Yes, if we want there to be peace". In any case, at the time of this visit to Trastevere, Madeleine Albright believed that Sant'Egidio's mediation in Kosovo was effective and should be supported. It was in this context that she described the Community as a group of "wonderful people".[17]

In point of fact, within a few months Hashim Thaçi, head of the KLA, replaced Rugova as the Americans' preferred leader, so that later, during the Rambouillet talks18, Rugova – though reelected as President on March 22, 1998 – would have to settle for playing second fiddle, almost as if he were a minion of Thaçi, who was as yet unknown on the international stage. A clear distance would only be reestablished between Rugova and the guerrilla leader on the domestic political front during the elections held in Kosovo once the war of March-June 1999 was over, when it was no longer under Serbian administration.

However, returning for the moment to the events of March 1998, Albright's support of Sant'Egidio helped convince the Albanians to adopt a more cooperative approach in the 3+3 Group. If America approved of Sant'Egidio, then the Albanians could accept the latter's proposals. Even the major European countries and the Contact Group as a whole, including Russia, were behind Sant'Egidio's mediation efforts, though that was more helpful vis-à-vis the Serbs, as the Albanians only paid attention to the Americans.

Thus it was that on March 23, 1998, at the University of Priština library, in a ceremony not lacking in poignancy and solemnity, a timetable was signed for the implementation of the Agreement of September 1, 1996.[19] The Serbs viewed it as a phased "return" of young Albanians to the university and to high schools and higher education schools, whilst for the Albanians it meant the "restitution" of various university faculty premises and then high school and higher education school buildings. In reality, what took place was restitution rather than a return to schools, partly because Serb and Albanian students did not wish to share the same facilities. The Serbian government was essentially forced to accept the demands of the Albanians. The latter had conceded nothing, or rather, by accepting the "restitution" of the buildings, they had the made the political concession of furthering the implementation of the September 1 Agreement. At this point, the Albanians felt that they were in a strong position, internationally, knowing also that Serbia was, by contrast, in a weak position. On March 8, twenty Albanians had been killed – including women and children – from the Jashari family clan, the head of which had been an avowed supporter of the armed cause of the KLA, the anti-Serb guerrilla movement that had formed in the wake of disappointment over the Dayton process and as an alternative to Rugova's passive resistance. In the eyes of the international community, the massacre had put Serbia in the dock.

The Albanians were immediately granted possession of the Institute of Albanology at the University of Priština, a building of extremely symbolic importance as it was here that Kosovar Albanian nationalism had been forged in the 1970s. There was spontaneous applause from the thousands of Albanians gathered near the entrance of the Institute as one of Rugova's secretaries dangled the keys that had finally been reclaimed in the air (keys that the Serbian negotiators had not delivered to him directly but to Sant'Egidio's mediators, so that they could pass them on to the Albanians and avoid any misunderstandings, since neither party trusted the other and even to hand over some keys a mediator was needed who could guarantee, to one party, that they were delivered, and to the other, that they were the correct keys).

A few days later, the premises of the three technical faculties were turned over to the Albanians. In defiance, Serb students occupied them and the Serbian police had to forcibly remove them. This was a first: in Kosovo, Serbian police had never before been seen to use strong-arm tactics against fellow Serbs. Between April and June, there were discussions regarding which other university aculties were to be handed over to the Albanians. The Serbs made several proposals that the Albanians rejected because they wanted the buildings of the humanities faculties located on the university campus in the center of Priština. Moreover, the facilities offered by the Serbs, whilst ample, were of secondary importance on campus. These were highly-charged months: after the Jashari massacre in March, the KLA became a mass phenomenon, swelling in numbers from a few hundred members to 25,000 fighters equipped with weapons pouring in from Albania.

This paved the way for the open warfare of the summer of 1998, which would see Serbian forces prevail at the cost of 500 lives and tens of thousands of displaced persons, distributed proportionately amongst the two warring ethnic communities. The state of war prevented the continuation of the 3+3 committee talks. Everyone was focused on the outcome of the conflict, which would prove to be a Pyrrhic victory for the Serbs, who had momentarily been the victors on the ground but were also forced to admit that the Kosovo issue was now on the agenda of the major powers and would no longer be an internal matter. The internationalization of the conflict would lead, through a rather rapid succession of events, to the war of 1999, but that is another story.[20]

For present purposes, what is worth noting is that the escalation of the violence and the conflict contributed all the more to undermining the significance of the dialogue spawned by the Milošević-Rugova Agreement of 1996. Words had given way to weapons. Even the peaceful Rugova lost clout for a time, not among his own people but in the eyes of the international community. The Western powers looked with interest to the KLA, and the Americans preferred the guerrilla Thaçi to Rugova. The latter was forced by Holbrooke, who was temporarily back on the Balkan scene, to meet with Milošević for the first time.

After lengthy discussions that continued through the day and into the night, Rugova – recognizing that his cause needed the backing of a power like America – was persuaded to go to Belgrade, albeit against his will. The meeting on May 15, 1998 was, as he had feared, a humiliation for

Rugova, who gained nothing from it and was furthermore sarcastically derided in the KLA's propaganda as a friend of the Serbian dictator. This was also the last time that the Americans placed their faith in Rugova. Bob Gelbard, who in April 1998 had described the KLA's men as "terrorists", in June called them "insurgents", and neither the US nor NATO ever protested against the mobilization that took place in Albania from March 1998 onwards for the purpose of pouring KLA men, weapons and supplies into Kosovo in broad daylight. In Northern Albania, donkeys were nowhere to be seen anymore: they were all being used to transport war equipment over the mountains on the border with Yugoslavia. Sant'Egidio's efforts had always been backed by the Contact Group and, in particular, by the United States. Now, however, the situation had changed. Things were gearing up for NATO to wage war on Milošević.

Yet, in February 1999, in a reconvened 3+3 Group, the Serbs and Albanians unexpectedly agreed to full implementation of the 1996 Agreement as regards the university. All the faculties the Albanians wanted were handed over by the Serbs. But by this stage, it was too late. Rugova's doves of peace counted for nothing now – the game was being driven by KLA hawks with US and British backing. On March 23, the first NATO bombs fell on Serbia. The Serbs responded immediately by ejecting masses of Albanians from Kosovo. Within a few weeks, 800,000 of them – around half the Albanian population of the region – would become refugees in Macedonia or Albania. This would in turn enable NATO to maintain that ethnic cleansing was taking place and to justify a military campaign as humanitarian intervention, when instead, at least on the part of Washington (which had planned it) and the US General Wesley Clark (the then NATO commander who was heading it), the operation seemed to take on the character of an outright war on Serbia.

The media's juxtaposition of bombs with refugees from the outset of the conflict would firmly plant the idea in Western minds of a NATO humanitarian intervention in response to ethnic cleansing, when in reality the ethnic cleansing took place later as a consequence of Western military intervention, the reasons for which lay elsewhere. Without question, the contributing factors included not only the unwarranted and imperious political domination in Kosovo by the Serb minority of the overwhelming Albanian majority, but also the aversion of Western governments and public opinion towards Milošević, considered to be the person solely or principally responsible for a decade of conflicts in the former Yugoslavia.

In a last-ditch effort to facilitate a peaceful solution, ten days before the bombing, a Sant'Egidio delegation led by Paglia visited Belgrade. At this stage, Milošević was determined to hold out to the bitter end, perhaps hoping that internal divisions among the NATO countries might at any moment lead to the war being called off. Paglia asked the Serbian government not to take out on Kosovo Albanians its anger at the bombings, and to respect the human rights of the said population. Whilst in Belgrade, despite the wild and gruesome rumors circulating as to the fate that had befallen Rugova, Paglia unexpectedly managed to get in contact with the Kosovo Albanian leader, whose enemies had gone so far as to accuse him of collaborating secretly with Milošević. He was being held prisoner by the Serbian police in his own home in Priština. Sant'Egidio's efforts to secure the release of Rugova, in those early days of April and the ensuing four weeks, represented a hope for a negotiated peace settlement in the event that the Serbs insisted on not giving in to NATO's demands. By prior arrangement with Paglia, Cornelio Sommaruga, the President of the International Committee of the Red Cross, reiterated the request for Rugova's release during a meeting with Milošević.[21] The Albanian leader was finally set free and arrived in Rome on May 6 on a plane made available by the Italian government.

Would diplomacy have been better?

The war, which lasted from March 24 to June 10, 1999, marked a turning point in the history of Kosovo, which saw out the 20th century under Albanian rule. Over the course of that century, the Serbs had dominated for four periods and the Albanians for five.[22] On each occasion, the subjugated party had suffered. Resolving a dispute by resorting to arms, yet again in 1999, perpetuated ethnic enmities. The road of dialogue and diplomacy was the only one capable of fostering dignified coexistence between the two ethnic groups. The international community had steadfastly supported Sant'Egidio's mediation efforts from 1996 to 1998, almost as if to make up for the lack of international engagement with the Kosovo crisis from 1989 until the spring of 1998. When the KLA succeeded in precipitating the crisis, using clever strategy to provoke Serbian violence and hence bloodshed, the international community suddenly "realized" the gravity of the situation in Kosovo, which had now reached white heat. At that point, it seemed difficult to proceed by means of diplomacy. NATO had already geared up for war against Yugoslavia during the clashes in Kosovo in the summer of 1998, when the United States and the United Kingdom supported the KLA, first politically and then also logistically.

The mission of the two thousand OSCE observers deployed in Kosovo in the winter of 1998-1999 was undermined by the internal division between, on the one hand, members from the English-speaking countries, who in order to resolve the crisis set about looking for a *casus belli*, and on the other, those from Europe, who sought to remain neutral and work for peace. Washington and London were by now quite convinced that the problems of Kosovo (and of Bosnia and the Balkans in general) would essentially be resolved by eliminating Milošević and his regime.

The Racak massacre of January 16, 1999, the circumstances surrounding which and the responsibility for which have remained contentious, provoked a sufficient outcry for the Kosovo crisis – with KLA and Serb forces still shooting it out – to be dealt with once and for all at an international level. To prevent the immediate commencement of hostilities against the Serbs that Washington wanted, the Europeans called for last-chance talks. This led to the two summits held at Rambouillet, during which the Anglo-Saxon countries, with Madeleine Albright openly backing the Albanians, succeeded in pressing demands on Yugoslavia in the form of ultimatums (including insistence on free movement of NATO troops throughout Yugoslavian territory, tantamount to a military occupation) that were such as to make Belgrade's refusal, and hence war, inevitable.

It must be said, incidentally, that Sant'Egidio was not so much involved in the conduct of the Rambouillet talks as in the hasty preparations for them, due to the British Foreign Secretary Robin Cook asking Paglia, who was visiting London, to urge Milošević and Rugova to attend the Rambouillet negotiations in person. Paglia got on the phone and talked with both of them. In the event, Rugova went to Rambouillet, as did the number two in Belgrade, the President of the Serbian Federal Republic of Yugoslavia, Milan Milutinović, even though a lower-level delegation was initially expected. Cook also revealed to Paglia the demands that would be put to the Serbs, including the free movement of NATO troops throughout Yugoslav territory, which would later become an insurmountable obstacle in the negotiations. Paglia stated that the Serbs would not accept this, but the British were convinced that the Serbs would nevertheless submit to avoid being bombed and "obliterated".

If the implementation of the 1996 Agreement had not been delayed – and here the responsibility lies mainly with Milošević, an excellent tactician but a poor strategist, who for reasons of political expediency was reluctant to grant what he had promised to Rugova so as not to lose support within Serbia – events in Kosovo might perhaps have taken a different course, and both Albanians and Serbs would have suffered much less. Of course, that is assuming that a cohesive international community would have had the patience to maintain strong pressure on both the Albanians and Serbs to ensure the talks ran smoothly.

It must be pointed out, however, that even on the Albanian side there was much hesitation over whether to honor the Agreement signed. If they had known for certain that in 1999 NATO would attack Serbia, the Albanians would have held on (without signing anything) for Western bombers to secure their longed-for independence, as in some respects ended up happening – albeit after a wait of another nine years. It was the KLA's and not Rugova's strategy to involve Western powers in a war of liberation. Indeed, it was no coincidence that the KLA did everything within its power to thwart the Agreement of September 1, 1996. It saw war – not diplomacy – as the answer.

The Albanian members of the 3+3 Group received death threats from elements in the KLA the moment they were appointed, and this certainly impacted on their willingness to implement the Agreement, regardless of their instructions from Rugova. These threats were genuine. Between 1996 and 1998 the KLA killed dozens of Kosovar Albanians who were accused of collaborating with the Serbs because they had remained in public employment after 1989 or because they were members of parties represented in Belgrade. Then again, during the 1990s, on all sides of the Albanian political spectrum in Kosovo, there was one single recurring theme that fueled the political jostling between the various factions, including within Rugova's majority party, and that was intransigence towards the Serbs. In Priština, politicking consisted almost exclusively of accusing whoever one's current rival might be of being soft on the ethnic enemy.

The humanitarian spirit that marked Rugova as a cut above the rest of Kosovo's political class, had driven him to pursue the university and schools Agreement as a way of providing relief for Albanian civil society, which had been stretched to its limits. However, Milošević's delays in implementing the Agreement had undermined his efforts, providing fresh vindication for those – even within Rugova's own party – who maintained that it was futile to negotiate with the Serbs. It was better to remain victims of the Belgrade regime, until such time as the international community came to the rescue in some shape or form. This, as already noted, was the reasoning of the KLA, which sought to raise tensions, but was also that of the negotiating team appointed by Rugova to the 3+3 Group, which included Agani, a shrewd politician.

It was he who, one evening in a moment of confidence, explained to Morozzo and Rago, whom he had befriended, that in the end a solution of the school and university issue – and this was his own personal belief, which did not get in the way of his loyalty to Rugova – would deprive the Albanians of a formidable propaganda weapon. He felt it would reduce their status as victims and lessen international interest in Kosovo, which up till then had been high in part because international journalists who went there were taken to visit the Albanian parallel school system, with its classes of 20 students crammed into 15 square meters, in contrast with public schools where Serbs, in the absence of Albanians, had 15 square meters per pupil.

On other occasions, Agani would also go on to explain why Albanians preferred that Milošević stayed in power, since a more democratic government in Belgrade would have made the Serbs less unpopular with the international community. But this hesitation and resistance on the part of the Albanians does not diminish Serbian responsibility for delaying implementation of the Agreement. Even without the Agreement, and without Sant'Egidio, Milošević should still have normalized the situation in Kosovo, in order for his country to take its place in the international community and to avoid a further war. Sant'Egidio, with the only diplomatic initiative which presented itself in the decade-long Kosovo crisis that stood a chance of succeeding, offered him the opportunity to do so.

The Serbian leader was, however, only concerned with remaining in power, and therefore considered it more important to pander to the nationalistic sentiments of the majority of his voters, in the belief that making the slightest concession of civility to the Albanians would represent a step towards their independence. The opposition among Kosovo Serbs to any concessions being made to the Albanians should also be borne in mind. Members of Sant'Egidio in the disputed region frequently observed that orders of the Serbian government and of Milošević himself, issued from Belgrade to Priština, were not carried out and their authenticity was barely credited. Even individual police officers, teachers and janitors made it their duty not to obey them, considering any practical concession made to the Albanians as inconceivable.

In the case of Kosovo, Sant'Egidio worked to break down the logic of implacable confrontation, mutual intransigence, and ethnic hatred – the very logic that the resort to arms in 1998 and 1999 rekindled, eventually leading to the unilateral declaration of independence of Kosovo on February 17, 2008. In many respects, such independence is inevitable given the lack of willingness on the part of both Serbs and Albanians to live together civilly, and given that the Albanians overwhelmingly outnumber the Serbs. The Western contingent of the international community, as a matter of pragmatism, has rewarded the majority and sacrificed the minority.

The prospect of an entirely mono-ethnic Kosovo is now becoming increasingly more likely, just as it is gradually beginning to look like Kosovo's independence will become official and Serbs will leave or congregate to the north in an area around Mitrovica which has *de facto* separated from the rest of the region (an area of Mitrovica that has broken away from Kosovo, which in turn has broken away from Serbia). But will the reshuffling of territories and States in progress really bring this centuries-old dispute any closer to an end? Or will there be return offensives mounted by the ethnic group that is the current underdog? Would it not have been better to arrive at a compromise agreement instead of having to divide lands and peoples? The goal of Sant'Egidio's efforts in respect of Kosovo was to prevent oppression by Serbs of Albanians, as occurred during the course of the 1990s, and, in the event they in turn came to power, by Albanians of Serbs and other minorities.

[1] For some introductory readings on Rugova and Milošević, see: the conversations with Rugova himself in I. Rugova, *La Question du Kosovo*, Paris, Fayard, 1994; R. Morozzo della Rocca, *Rugova, una vita*, January 30, 2006, www.osservatoriobalcani.org; M. Nava, *Milošević, L'ultimo tiranno*, Rizzoli, Milan 2000; Id., *Imputato Milošević. Il processo ai vinti e l'etica della guerra*, Rome, Fazi, 2002; and J. Toschi Marazzani Visconti, *Milošević visto da vicino*, Supplement to "Limes", 1, 1999, pp. 27-34.
[2] In September 1993, John Paul II asked Msgr. Paglia to pave the way for a visit by the Pope to the former Yugoslavia, which would take in the three cities of Zagreb, Sarajevo and Belgrade. To this end, Paglia held talks with key political leaders in Croatia, Bosnia and Serbia.
[3] For 35 years, Shehu had been Enver Hoxha's right-hand man and the number two of the Albanian regime, before he died in unclear circumstances, apparently of suicide, perhaps prompted by Hoxha.
[4] Cf. *the report on the Visit to Serbia of Vincenzo Paglia and Roberto Morozzo della Rocca between July 8-11, 1993*: document held in the Community of Sant'Egidio Archive (hereinafter referred to as the "ACSE"), Kosovo collection.
[5] Given the relationship that exists between the Serbian national identity and the historical vicissitudes of Kosovo, the literature on this topic is vast. One example (in English translation) is the book *Art of Kosovo: The Sacred Land*, with text by Gojko Subotić, Monacelli Press, New York, 1999.

[6] Cf. *the report by R. Morozzo della Rocca on the Visit of Ibrahim Rugova to Rome between March 8-12, 1993*, ACSE, Kosovo collection.

[7] Cf. *the report on the Visit to Serbia of Vincenzo Paglia and Roberto Morozzo della Rocca between July 8-11, 1993*, ACSE, Kosovo collection.

[8] Cf. *the report on the Breakfast meeting of Vincenzo Paglia and Roberto Morozzo della Rocca with Stefano Sannino on July 1, 1995*, ACSE, Kosovo collection.

[9] The Deputy Prime Minister and Minister of Science and Technology in the Serbian Government.

[10] Dojcilo Maslovarić, Secretary for Foreign Affairs in Milošević's new Yugoslavia, was appointed Ambassador to the Vatican in 1996. He was a trusted confidante of Milošević and his wife Mira Marković. He lived in Dedinje, a Belgrade district that was the home of the ruling elite, near Milošević's villa, where he was a frequent guest. In Italy, he was tasked with handling various political and economic issues that Milošević had no intention of commending to his Ambassador to Italy, the Montenegrin Miodrag Lekić, whom he did not trust. During the stage of the talks in Rome held in the summer of 1996 which led to the signing of the Agreement between Milošević and Rugova, and later as a go-between for meetings with Milošević as and when necessary, Maslovarić played a significant role. After the death of his wife in 1999, however, Maslovarić fell out of favor with Milošević, who discharged him from his posting to the Vatican in February 2000.

[11] Cf. *Për herë të parë nga Jugosllavia pa viza*, "Gazeta Shqiptare", April 3, 1996.

[12] Represented by Fehmi Agani and Dojcilo Maslovarić respectively.

[13] A copy of the Agreement (in the original Serbian and Albanian) is held in the ACSE, Kosovo collection.

[14] Fehmi Agani, a notable of great prestige in Kosovo, can be considered Rugova's "political mentor". Until his death during the war in 1999, as he was evacuating to Macedonia with other refugees, Agani remained Rugova's principal political adviser.

[15] At that time, the Contact Group monitoring the situation in the Western Balkans comprised the US, Russia, Germany, France, Britain and Italy.

[16] See the chapter in this book entitled "Albania in transition", dealing with the Pact for the future of Albania.

[17] In M. Albright, *The Mighty and the Almighty: Reflections on America, God, and World Affairs*, New York, Harper Collins Publishers, 2006, pp. 76-77, Madeleine Albright refers to the "constructive role" played by the Community of Sant'Egidio in resolving various conflicts, including that of Kosovo.

[18] In relation to the two summits held at Rambouillet, near Paris, in February and March 1999, which led to NATO's war against Milošević's Yugoslavia, cf. *infra* in this chapter.

[19] The March 23, 1998 Agreement reads as follows:

1. The following measures have been temporarily adopted to enable the implementation of the Agreement on Education signed on September 1 by President Slobodan Milošević and Dr. Ibrahim Rugova.

2. The Institute for Albanology in Priština will be open to its previous users on March 31.

3. By March 31, the Community of Sant'Egidio will, taking into account the proposals submitted by the two sides in the 3+3 Group, determine the first three faculties of the University of Priština into which Albanian students and professors will be reintegrated by April 30, 1998.

In principle, reintegration is subject to the following condition: students currently normally conducting their studies at the University and Albanian students will use the University facilities and equipment alternately, through a system of double shifts which will change every semester.

222

During the first semester of the application of these measures, students currently normally studying in the University facilities will use them in the morning (until 2 p.m.), and Albanian students in the afternoon; in the second semester, the shifts will change and Albanian students will use the facilities and equipment in the morning and students now studying in the University facilities will use them in the afternoon, and this order will alternate in each following semester. Apart from using facilities for holding classes, Albanian students and professors will also have at their disposal the necessary space within each faculty for carrying out administrative functions and for teaching staff (where this is not possible, another solution will be found).

4. By April 30, 1998, the Community of Sant'Egidio will, taking into consideration proposals submitted by the two sides in the 3+3 Group, determine the next three faculties of the University of Priština into which Albanian students and professors will be reintegrated by May 31, 1998. The same conditions will apply as for the faculties in point 3.

5. Albanian students and professors of the remaining seven faculties will be able to re-enter the facilities of the University of Priština by June 30, 1998 according to the same conditions as apply to the faculties in points 3 and 4. By September 30, 1998, Albanian students and professors will be able to use University facilities (cafeterias, libraries, student dormitories, etc.) correspondingly. The Community of Sant'Egidio will, after hearing proposals from both sides, determine a solution for any problems which might arise. In any case, the school year must start as normal on October 1, 1998.

6. By June 30, 1998, Albanian students and professors will be able to use the facilities of seven schools of higher learning in Priština and other cities in Kosovo which specialize in business and technical subjects. Any such use of these schools will be regulated in keeping with the conditions for the renewed use of University facilities, as in point 3.

7. The 3+3 Group, with the support of Sant'Egidio, underlines the need to secure funds for the construction of new facilities as quickly as possible in order to make more space available for conducting courses, research and administrative functions, and which will be at the disposal of all. New University buildings, which can be built speedily, will enable all facilities of the University to be accommodated on an equal basis. This will form the subject of a special proposal, setting out the deadlines for financing and completing the project, in keeping with actual needs and available resources.

8. Similarly, by March 31, 1998, Albanian elementary and high school pupils will be able to return to elementary and high schools which are currently not in use, in keeping with a list to be prepared by the 3+3 Group. Sant'Egidio will determine a solution for any problems which might emerge. Albanian elementary and high school pupils will return to those elementary and high school buildings which are currently partially in use by April 30, 1998. Their use will be regulated in accordance with the conditions for the renewed use of University facilities specified in point 3, or as otherwise mutually agreed.

9. The 3+3 Group, assisted by Sant'Egidio, will meet by March 30 at the latest to guarantee the implementation of the transitional normalization measures. The 3+3 Group will immediately set up working groups for each faculty. The 3+3 Group will examine the remaining matters concerning the normalization of the education system (funding, administration, languages, curricula, diplomas, employee status issues).

[20] Cf. R. Morozzo della Rocca, *Kosovo. La guerra in Europa. Origini e realtà di un conflitto etnico*, Milan, Guerini e Associati, 1999.

[21] According to Sommaruga's account as related to the author (on November 17, 2008), the President of the ICRC was traveling by car from Zagreb to Belgrade when he received a phone call from Paglia, who asked him to convey to Milošević the simple message "Sant'Egidio is ready for Rugova". Sommaruga met with Milošević on April 24 and, after an hour of at times heated conversation, as he was taking his leave, repeated the agreed sentence, which was immediately greeted by an "I have understood" from Milošević, who was less surprised by the message than Sommaruga was by the Yugoslav President's lucid response. Ten days later, having just arrived in Rome, Rugova, in a press conference with the then Italian Prime Minister D'Alema, who had sent a plane to pick him up from Belgrade, thanked both Paglia and D'Alema for having secured his release. Cf. also J. Bischoff, *Jürg Bischoff im Gespräch mit Cornelio Sommaruga, Diplomatie im Dienste der Menschlichkeit*, Foreword by Kofi Annan, Zurich, NZZ Verlag, 2004.

[22] In relation to the twentieth-century history of Kosovo, cf. M. Dogo, *Kosovo. Albanesi e serbi: le radici del conflitto*, Lungro di Cosenza, C. Marco Editore, 1992; M. Roux, *Les albanais en Yougoslavie. Minorité nationale territoire et développement*, Paris, Maison des sciences de l'homme, 1992; M. Vickers, *Between Serb and Albanian: A History of Kosovo*, New York, Columbia Univ. Press, 1998; N. Malcolm, *Kosovo: A Short History*, New York, New York Univ. Press, 1998; and T. Judah, *Kosovo: War and Revenge*, New Haven, Yale Univ. Press, 2000.

The Peace Process in Liberia

Liberia

Area (in sq km)	111,369
Population (millions)	3.580
Population density (inhabitants per sq km)	32
Percentage of population <15 years	42.8
Annual change in population (%)	+2.7
Infant mortality per 1,000 live births (<1 year/<5 years)	157/235
Life expectancy at birth (male/female)	47/49
Fertility rate (average no. of children per woman)	6.2
Illiteracy rate (%)	41.1
Doctors (per 1,000 inhabitants)	0.3
Percentage of adult population living with HIV/AIDS (adult prevalence rate	5.9
Human Development Index (HDI), expressed on a scale from 0 to 1, to three decimal places	-
HDI, world ranking	-
GDP per capita (USD)	119
GDP per capita, world ranking	188
Personal computers (per 1,000 inhabitants)	-

The Peace Process in Liberia

Vittorio Scelzo

On August 18, 2003, the Comprehensive Peace Agreement on Liberia was signed in Accra, the capital of Ghana, putting an end to one of the most brutal wars in Africa which began in 1989. The talks that had opened on June 4 between rebels and the government had been difficult. Up to two weeks prior to the signing, the international press had written them off as a flop, just as previous attempts to bring peace to the small West African country had failed.[1] In the eyes of the world, the Liberian conflict had been a kind of postmodern war, whose causes and objectives were not understood and which was fought with ferocious violence by unknown "warlords" bereft of any ideology or political agenda.

The fighting had gone on for over ten years, with complicated reversals of alliances and betrayals between armed militia groups that had obscure origins. Images of rebels dressed in rags or in implausibly multicolored uniforms, and particularly of savage acts of violence perpetrated on civilians, were repeatedly beamed around the world.

In that August of 2003, perhaps also as a result of the sweltering summer, the hopes that had been revived with the start of new talks in June seemed to fade. International public opinion had long since grown weary of Liberia, seen as a lost cause – a victim of its own demons. The negotiations had stagnated and official mediation efforts were getting nowhere. The rebels, though also involved in the talks through their own delegation, continued to fight in the vicinity of the country's capital Monrovia, where Charles Taylor, the President and former rebel, was barricaded. Taylor was a sinister figure who bore responsibility for starting the conflict and stood accused of many crimes against humanity.[2]

Yet an unexpected event was to prove the pessimists wrong. On August 4, at the headquarters of the Community of Sant'Egidio in Rome, the leader of the rebels signed a declaration made public at a press conference. Sekou

Conneh, the leader of the Liberians United for Reconciliation and Democracy (or LURD, as the guerilla movement was known) was a former secondhand car dealer who had taken up armed struggle.[3] He had been fighting for years and had been a member of various factions. In 1999, he founded his own movement which brought together all the enemies of the President with the support of Guinea-Conakry, triggering in the process the final phase of Liberia's civil war. At a stage when the gridlock in the negotiations had reached its most critical point, Conneh visited Sant'Egidio in Rome.[4]

After a week of discussions, during which he was also joined by his delegation to the peace talks, he publicly declared that he had decided to go to Ghana, where the negotiations were being held, to sign the Peace Agreement. At the same time, he ordered his troops to observe a unilateral ceasefire and to withdraw from the outskirts of Monrovia. This was the turning point. From that moment on, everything happened quickly. In Accra, the delegations hammered out the final details of the Agreement. On August 11, Taylor – by then left isolated – abandoned the capital and went into exile in Calabar, Nigeria. Then, on August 18, the Peace Agreement was signed before the President of Ghana, John Kufuor.

The story of the Liberian Peace Agreement demonstrates that cooperation on conflict resolution between "institutional" and "non-institutional" actors – despite differences in their respective status and methods – is both desirable and productive. The Community of Sant'Egidio's peace initiative was conducted in collaboration with the official mediation efforts of ECOWAS[5] and of the government of Ghana. Beginning with the opening ceremony in June 2003, Mario Giro and Angelo Romano attended the negotiations on behalf of Sant'Egidio in Accra and Akosombo. They followed the proceedings initially as observers and later as facilitators, but their involvement was not confined to their mere presence.

The relationship established by Sant'Egidio with the LURD rebels was a widely-acknowledged fact, such that the Community's assistance was sought whenever the negotiations ran into difficulty.[6] By the end of July, Giro and Romano realized that a division had emerged between the LURD delegation at the negotiating table and military commanders on the ground, especially Conneh.[7] The discussions in Rome prevented a split within the rebel ranks and opened the way for the Peace Agreement of August 18.

Liberia, an atypical State

Liberia has an unusual history. Founded in 1847 by former American slaves returned to Africa through the efforts of the US antislavery movement, it did not undergo European colonization like all the other countries on the continent (apart from Ethiopia). The story of this nation is unique in African history.

The nation was formed at the initiative of private philanthropic societies, galvanized by the doctrine of "return". The idea was to send back to Africa the descendants of those who had been violently uprooted from the continent, as a way of making reparation for the injustice of the slave trade and of responding to the lack of civil rights for American blacks. Several organizations financed the creation of a "new land" of liberty, in the spirit of the return to the promised land. Foremost among these was the American Colonization Society (ACS), whose stated aim was to "to promote and execute a plan for colonizing [...] the Free People of Color residing in our Country, in Africa". Initial attempts in 1816 had proved disastrous: decimated by yellow fever, the new arrivals did not even manage to establish a settlement.

It was not until 1821 that the first "colony on Cape Mesurado" was founded. Subsequently, numerous similar societies sprang up in the United States with the aim of establishing further colonies in West Africa. Life was not easy for the new settlements, which broke up into separate administrative units. Nevertheless, in around 1845, a single united political entity emerged which declared its independence in 1847, receiving its first formal recognition in 1848 from the United Kingdom.

In the early years, political power was wielded by representatives of the aforementioned philanthropic societies, who only later relinquished it to the new settlers. Liberians were proud of this history and the relative prosperity they enjoyed for nearly 150 years. Today, however, the country is associated with harrowing images of a bloody civil war, child soldiers, and diamond trafficking. So how was it that the land of freedom – whose motto is "The love of liberty brought us here" – became emblematic of African wars and failed States?

In the scenario that prevailed before the fall of the Berlin Wall, the geopolitical positioning of African States hinged on the balance of power relations between the two superpowers. The continent was a favorable theatre for the enactment of the Cold War. Every African government had to take this into account and was forced to align itself with one or the other of the major blocs. In a sense, this never gave rise to a dilemma for Liberians, given their close ties with the United States. The country's real problem was – and continues to be – the power relations that exist between the descendants of the Afro-Americans and the natives, which have always been ambiguous and complex. It is precisely in this difficult relationship that the roots of the Liberian political crisis lie. Ironically, for a country established by freed slaves, in 1930 the League of Nations accused Liberia of practicing a system of forced labor that was "indistinguishable from slavery".[8] In Liberia, the natives had no right to vote until 1951. The Americo-Liberians had effectively replicated their socio-political system of origin.

During the early stages of independence, all power was in the hands of an elite group of new settlers.[9] With the emergence of a more educated generation, however, the balance gradually shifted in favor of the more numerous natives, until the military coup of 1980, which brought to power the first President of indigenous origin: Samuel Doe. Despite the hopes reposed in this change, Doe did not alter the political patronage system that had hitherto operated. Indeed, in order to stay in power, he chose to favor his own Krahn ethnic group, and a section of the Americo-Liberian elite, despite having previously been an opponent of the latter.

The other native ethnic groups were excluded and harassed. It was at this time that the first refugees began leaving the country seeking sanctuary in neighboring States. The country had descended into an era of turmoil and corruption, and was only able to survive thanks to generous aid from the Reagan administration.[10] Despite many concerns over the country's human rights situation, Doe was a frequent guest in Washington during those years. But when the flow of US funds came to a halt, the political crisis was compounded by economic woes. With the end of the Cold War, Liberia, having been a pawn in the United States' African geopolitics, lost its usefulness and ceased to be of interest to Washington. Without any more funds, the country progressively sank into a downward spiral that facilitated the outbreak of civil war.

Charles Taylor, the warlord

Charles Taylor, a former Minister in the government led by Samuel Doe and dismissed by the latter after a series of controversies, gave voice to the discontent of marginalized sections of the population, and succeeded – thanks in part to the training he had received in Libya – in establishing an armed movement known as the NPFL (National Patriotic Front of Liberia). On December 24, 1989, a group of around a hundred rebels crossed over from Ivory Coast to attack a border town in Nimba county, sparking a civil war that would steep the country in bloodshed for almost fifteen years. It also marked the emergence of the "warlord" phenomenon in West Africa. NPFL raids were brutal and targeted particularly at civilians, with the aim of engendering terror and forcing people to flee. Taylor made use of secret support from local and foreign political and business interest groups. To that end, he assiduously forged a complex web of international interests and alliances, but was always ready to change sponsors or allies depending on how events unfolded.

Yet despite the intricate interweaving of his relationships and the adeptness with which he cultivated or reshaped them, Taylor never bothered to furnish his movement with a real political – much less a revolutionary – agenda. The NPFL was the uncertain product of a new post-Cold War era. Its sole objective seemed to be to gain power, understood exclusively as meaning control over the nation's sources of wealth.[11] In this regard, the NPFL served as a model for all

231

future Liberian rebel factions – a model which was imitated subsequently by armed movements in correlated conflicts in Sierra Leone and on the border with Guinea, and spread within a few years to the entire area, spanning from Conakry to Abidjan.

The rebels advanced easily towards the capital Monrovia and were initially warmly received by the people, who were not enamored of President Doe's government. Within a few weeks, the NPFL's numbers were swelled by thousands of men with no military training, who soon bloodied their hands with atrocities against civilians – particularly against the Mandingo and Krahn ethnic groups from which the leaders in Monrovia hailed. In response to the attack by Taylor's men, Doe ordered the slaughter of those belonging to the rebel ethnic groups in Monrovia and in the ranks of the regular army, thereby undermining the strength of the latter.

In a few months, the Liberian war turned into a horrific series of ethnic massacres. Hundreds of thousands of terrified civilians fled. Under assault from the militias, the State crumbled, and the central government itself seemed indistinguishable from any of the other armed groups.[12] The NPFL also underwent splits, particularly when Taylor's deputy, Prince Johnson, decided to break away to form an independent group. The war had no real frontline as such. The fighting in Monrovia also involved other militia groups that opposed both Taylor and Doe, and which had likewise formed along ethnic lines. It was Johnson's militia that succeeded in killing Doe in September 1990.

The country no longer had a government and fell completely into the hands of ethnic militias. Americo-Liberians ceased to be represented in political institutions and in the military. The war continued even after the intervention of ECOWAS troops, which landed in Monrovia in August 1990 by decision of the neighboring African countries[13]. The Nigerian forces, which formed the core of the operation, failed to give a good account of themselves. Having arrived in a lawless country, rather than conducting peacekeeping activities (which, incidentally, was made very difficult by there being no specific arrangements to that end in place), they cornered the market in trade passing through the port of Monrovia (the offshore market), becoming central players in trafficking of all kinds.

In order to hold on to this lucrative position, and lacking any clear intervention guidelines, the ECOWAS troops became increasingly involved in the war, abandoning all neutrality. Taylor himself attacked them in Monrovia in the offensive of 1992 that was crushed just outside the city. The only response of the ECOWAS troops was to encourage the emergence of new armed groups, thus giving rise to an endless and unstable crisscrossing of alliances.[14]

Between 1990 and 1997, Europe and the United States took no interest in the war raging in the Liberian capital. By the end of 1996, after the failure of the thirteenth attempt at peace talks, which led to a spree of terror in Monrovia, Taylor was convinced that he would not be able to become President without at least securing Nigerian neutrality. He therefore agreed to disarm most of his men in exchange for the formation of a transitional government that would organize the first elections since Doe's coup in 1980.[15] The elections of 1997, arranged in haste and without any democratic safeguards in place, saw Taylor – the most powerful of the Liberian warlords – emerge as the victor. The international community accepted the verdict of the polls. Weary of war, the Liberians had voted en masse for the candidate who promised them peace, even at the cost of opting for as controversial and violent a man as Taylor. Indeed, his election campaign had been explicit in this regard, with its chilling slogan: "He killed my Pa, he killed my Ma, I'll vote for him!".

Having become the nation's leader, Taylor did not relinquish his role as a warlord. Power was concentrated in the hands of a few, along ethnic lines. The President also supported and armed the RUF fighters who laid waste to neighboring Sierra Leone with the same terror tactics used in Liberia.[16] It was in Sierra Leone that the use of child soldiers – only partly resorted to in the Liberian war – became a widespread practice. Taylor quickly became the *bête noire* of the West, particularly of Britain, which refused to look on as its former colony sank into chaos.[17] A media campaign was mounted against the Liberian leader. This was the time of the "blood diamond" trade[18], and Taylor was accused of financing armed rebellions and international terrorism with illegal diamonds.[19] The UN imposed an international travel ban on Liberian officials, who were no longer allowed to leave the country without special permission. From 2001, Taylor became an international pariah, though no less dangerous for it.

At this point, the second phase of Liberia's civil war broke out. Armed by Guinea-Conakry, which was ill-advisedly attacked by Taylor in 1999, a fresh group of rebels entered Liberia with the goal of expelling Taylor by force. The group was LURD, which brought together former followers of Doe, other disaffected elements, and Taylor supporters who had fallen from grace. By the end of 2002, LURD had managed to get close to the center of Monrovia, repeating the advance Taylor had accomplished in 1990. Later, on the Ivorian border, another movement known as MODEL (the Movement for Democracy in Liberia[21] appeared on the scene, making a push towards the port of Buchanan to the east. Taylor and his faithful took up a defensive position in Monrovia, which underwent three sieges, the last of which was staged between June and August 2003.

Sant'Egidio's first contacts

Sant'Egidio's first meetings with LURD date back to the summer of 2002, when Fabio Riccardi traveled to Conakry in July to establish contact with representatives of the movement.[21] In discussions with the group's then spokesman Hanson (William Nhinson), it was resolved that a delegation from the movement would visit Rome. This was followed in September by two visits to Rome of various members of LURD, including William Nhinson and Francis Nyepon. Together with Fabio Riccardi, Claudio Betti, Angelo Romano and Mario Giro, they made arrangements for a visit by a larger delegation which took place on December 1, 2002, when eight LURD officials were received at Sant'Egidio's Rome headquarters. They came from countries in the region (Guinea-Conakry and Ivory Coast), Europe and the United States. Their trip to Rome helped clarify many aspects regarding the nature of the movement, its agenda and its stance with respect to Taylor's government. It emerged that LURD had a fragmented structure, being made up of numerous factions.

What these disparate groups had in common was their hostility towards Taylor. In addition, the leadership position of Sekou Damate Conneh, who was younger than many other prominent LURD members, was based more on his links with the Guinean President Lansana Conté than on any personal charisma.[22] Finally, the political agenda of the movement seemed uncertain. Indeed, in those latter days of 2002, LURD had still not decided whether to persist with the military option or try pursuing the path of negotiation, as many were recommending it did.

Notwithstanding the repeated military offensives, Monrovia – though surrounded – had not yielded.[23] During the meetings in Rome, the prospects for a peaceful settlement of the conflict and possible ways of mediating between the parties were discussed. On January 15, 2003, on the sidelines of the opening ceremony in Paris for the Marcoussis talks on Ivory Coast[24], Mario Giro and Fabio Riccardi met the Liberian President Taylor, who had been invited for the occasion by the French government. Taylor, whilst claiming to be assured of military victory, showed a certain interest in opening up a private channel of communication with LURD officials through one of his close female aides.

In early 2003, contact between Sant'Egidio and LURD became more sporadic. This was due to internal divisions within the movement and to differences of opinion over which strategy to follow. The members of the delegation that had visited Rome were accused by the movement's leaders of pursuing their own independent agenda and of plotting a change in leadership.[25] Around the same time, due to a worsening of the humanitarian crisis, ECOWAS proposed that the parties meet to discuss a negotiated settlement of the conflict.

The original idea was for talks to take place in Mali in April and May of 2003. However, ECOWAS did not have the necessary contacts to set up the talks and the initiative failed to get off the ground.[26] Between January and April 2003, the situation within LURD was tense. There were rumors of disagreements and talk that Conneh might be ousted as leader. This prevented any talks being convened. Mali was also no longer willing to host the negotiations. As soon as the leadership dispute was settled in favor of Conneh, ECOWAS proposed that talks be newly convened for April 15 in Accra, the capital of Ghana.[27]

At first, LURD refused to take part in the talks, which were once again postponed. Conneh subsequently decided to make direct contact with Sant'Egidio with a view to seeking consultation. In order to coordinate any potential initiatives, a close liaison was established between ECOWAS and Sant'Egidio, particularly through the Ministry of Foreign Affairs in Ghana. Compelled to negotiate, the LURD leader nonetheless asked to come to Rome before the talks began. A report dated May 19, 2003 reveals as follows:

Telephone conversations with Sekou Damate Conneh, the leader of LURD. Through Hanson, we have talked with Conneh twice, and he has told us that he is willing to come to Rome. He would like to meet with us ahead of the talks in Accra, which he has yet to decide whether to participate in. He has sent us a list of eight proposed members of the delegation (they are all from LURD, none from MODEL). He is waiting for us to suggest a date. In an e-mail, Hanson states that Conneh is requesting that the Community be present at the talks, because it is seen as trustworthy given its complete neutrality.[28]

It also emerged from a visit to Sant'Egidio by a delegation from ECOWAS on May 10, led by the Ghanaian Foreign Minister Nana Akufo-Addo and composed of the Foreign Ministers of Ivory Coast and Guinea-Conakry together with the Deputy Foreign Minister of Nigeria[29], that the countries in the region, whilst convinced of the urgent need to address a humanitarian situation that was deteriorating by the day, had not established an effective channel of communication with the LURD leadership. Conneh did not trust ECOWAS and preferred to persist with a military solution. Taylor had concentrated his troops in the city center of Monrovia, but Conneh still held hopes of succeeding.[30] LURD's main political demand was for the expulsion of Taylor.

The rebels did not want any power-sharing arrangement with him, even if they agreed to his political party being involved in possible dialogue. Eventually, Conneh had to give in to the pressure he was under from all quarters, including from his backers in Conakry. Nevertheless, his agreement

236

to send a delegation to Accra for the talks – which in the meantime had been adjourned till June 4 – seemed little more than a polite gesture to the international community. The LURD leader's sights were still set on capturing Monrovia. Another factor would subsequently bear out the LURD leader's tough stand on Taylor: on June 4, 2003, the Special Court for Sierra Leone announced that it had issued an international arrest warrant against the Liberian President.[31]

The Accra talks opened in a surreal atmosphere. Taylor took part in the opening ceremony, but he was forced to leave Ghana hastily in order to avoid causing embarrassment to local authorities, who, pursuant to international law, were under an obligation to arrest him. The LURD delegation[32], after a burst of initial jubilation at his hurried departure, realized that the indictment of the Liberian President weakened the prospects of a negotiated settlement.[33] From a distance, Conneh was considering recalling his delegation, thinking that the game was almost up for Taylor. Others were worried that the President, who was now a hunted man, might be tempted to fight it out to the last man.

The negotiations in Accra were attended by representatives of countries in the region and envoys of the European Union and the United States. The mediation of the talks was entrusted to the former Nigerian President General Abubakar, assisted by officials of the Ghanaian Ministry of Foreign Affairs and ECOWAS. The immediate objective was to secure a ceasefire that would allow an easing of tensions in Monrovia, which had been under siege for months, as well as enable discussions regarding a possible transitional government to be conducted without any pressure.

The rebel leader Conneh in Rome

This complex situation provided the backdrop for Sekou Damate Conneh's arrival in Rome on June 6, 2003 to meet with the Community of Sant'Egidio. He was accompanied by Hanson, the spokesman who had previously come to Rome.[34] This represented an important step: until then, the rebel leader had refused to meet with representatives of the international community and had not wanted to go to Accra.

The talks were, however, very difficult. Conneh initially appeared to be certain of military victory and was not willing to make any concessions. He only seemed interested in the removal of Taylor. He divulged that the Americans were pressuring him to sign an immediate ceasefire, but he had no intention of agreeing to this. He also bitterly criticized the government of Ghana for the failure to arrest Taylor in Accra.[35]

Whilst Conneh was in Rome, there were news reports that LURD had got to within a few hundred meters of the Executive Mansion, Taylor's presidential palace. Conneh was thinking of returning to Liberia to enter Monrovia "at the head of his troops"[36], convinced that he had the right to assume leadership of the country:

June 8. Conneh explained that his issue with the position of the international community concerns the question of leadership during the transitional period once Taylor was gone. He believes that, having successfully led the struggle for freedom, he is entitled to be appointed leader of the transitional government. The international community has, however, made it clear that it prefers someone else be appointed – perhaps someone who has not been involved in the fighting. (From other sources, we have learnt that the persons considered – it being unclear whether a final decision has already been made or not – are Mrs. Sirleaf, the current head of the parliamentary opposition, and Tubman, a former minister in Samuel Doe's government and ex-President Tubman's nephew, now serving as a UN official). Conneh has no intention of stepping aside. As far as he is concerned, the conference in Accra has been organized with the aim of forcing the parties to accept a ceasefire as well as decisions that have been made elsewhere regarding the future of Liberia.[37]

Over the course of long and exacting discussions, the LURD leader's position gradually softened. As well as underlining the difficulties involved in securing a rapid military victory, Sant'Egidio focused Conneh's attention on two key issues: the delicate balance between the various factions within LURD and recognition by the international community. The LURD leader knew only too well that his movement was divided. Moreover, Conneh came to realize that neither governments in the region nor the countries that had a stake in the outcome of the Liberian crisis – first and foremost, the US – would accept the conflict ending in LURD's favor. That error had already been committed in 1997, by allowing Taylor to assume the presidency after elections of dubious fairness. International public opinion was opposed to leaving Liberia yet again in the hands of armed factions. Conneh would not find any allies willing to back him. The position of the international community on this was clear: Taylor certainly needed to be taken out of the picture, but LURD "must not be rewarded in any way; Liberia should have a new government", as Kofi Annan put it during a meeting in early July with Mario Giro in Maputo.[38] It was thus a question of insisting on a political approach that also raised prospects of a viable future for both LURD and Conneh.[39]

Eventually, Conneh was persuaded to ease the siege of the Liberian capital for humanitarian reasons, as conditions had since weeks become intolerable for the civilian population.[40] In addition to announcing a unilateral ceasefire, Conneh formally recognized the talks underway in Accra. The press statement issued in Rome stated: "LURD recognizes and supports the current Liberian peace process, and therefore orders all LURD soldiers to observe an immediate ceasefire and to stop the advance on Monrovia on humanitarian grounds".[41]

The meetings in Rome during June 2003 stopped the fighting around Monrovia for a few weeks and proved invaluable in enabling the negotiations to continue. Conneh began to take the political option seriously. Appreciating that it had no partisan interest whatsoever in the outcome of the crisis, he had come to see the Community of Sant'Egidio as a credible interlocutor. These initial talks in Rome laid the foundations for solutions that were to come. With the ceasefire, LURD's fighters retreated several kilometers from the city center.[42] At the negotiations[43], the LURD delegation agreed to sign a ceasefire in exchange for an assurance from the international community of a final negotiated political settlement being reached within thirty days. The task of mediating the conflict was thus able to proceed.

The conflict resumes

The tensions had not, however, disappeared. In mid-June, new major disagreements surfaced between the LURD delegation in Ghana and military leaders on the ground. Conneh returned to Conakry. The bone of contention related to who should hold the highest offices of State in any future transitional government. Due to pressure from the international community, the mediation team had decided to disqualify anyone who had taken part in the civil war. This entailed the removal from office of Taylor, but also meant that Conneh could not become the transitional leader of Liberia. It was proposed that there be a transitional government in which portfolios would be divided equally among LURD, MODEL and those loyal to Taylor, under the leadership of a prominent non-partisan figure from civil society. The LURD delegation was willing to discuss this proposal, whilst Conneh refused to consider it.

A few days after the renewal of the ceasefire on June 19, Conneh ordered the resumption of the siege of Monrovia, thereby disavowing the position of his representatives at the talks. A divide thus resoundingly reasserted itself between the negotiating team, who were engaged in the dynamics of dialogue, and a military leadership that was wary and distant. The mediation team nevertheless had to tread carefully: it was necessary to take Conneh's ambitions into account as it would not be easy to carry on without him. Thus, whilst in respect of Taylor there was already talk of exile, the question was what should be done about the leadership of LURD, which had Monrovia under siege.

Sant'Egidio advised the mediation group to do everything possible to get Conneh to Accra. Irritated, Conneh threatened to withdraw his delegation from the talks and once again demanded the top post in Liberia's transitional power structure as a mandatory condition of his personal participation in the negotiations. This was clearly an unacceptable condition for the mediation team, and an unwelcome prospect for the Liberian people, who wished to turn over a new leaf. Faced with inevitable rejection, the LURD leader returned to the ambivalent position he had previously adopted, maintaining a delegation at the negotiating table whilst at the same time persisting with the siege of Monrovia.

The confusion was further fueled by the fact that the LURD delegation on several occasions declared its willingness to renew the ceasefire, but was repeatedly contradicted by its leader. In the end, the delegation was forced to suspend its participation in the talks, whilst remaining on standby. For his part, Conneh cut himself off from all external contact, for fear of being subjected to pressure. The mediators began to believe that they could manage without the rebel leader and urged the LURD delegation to resume its participation in the negotiations. There were heated disputes, mistrust once again dominated and divisions within the movement seemed to increase. At one point, members of the LURD delegation in Accra went as far as challenging Conneh's very leadership, though the latter managed to hold on to his position of power within the movement's military wing. Gambling on a split between the leadership and the delegation seriously risked jeopardizing the entire peace process, and was a strategy that – as Sant'Egidio pointed out to the mediators – would lead nowhere.

An end to the crisis

Throughout that difficult juncture when it seemed that communications with Conneh had broken down, Sant'Egidio in fact maintained constant contact with him. Despite the pessimism that had begun to spread among observers and within the media, the Community's decision to do so proved to be providential. During the African Union Summit in Maputo, between July 4-12, 2003, a Sant'Egidio delegation composed of Mario Giro and Luca Riccardi met with the Presidents of the countries involved in the Liberian crisis in the presence of the mediator, General Abubakar.[44] The possibility of Taylor relinquishing the presidency in exchange for a golden exile in Nigeria was discussed[45], as was Conneh's future. It was necessary to clarify the future institutional framework of Liberia and the role that the guerrilla movements would play in the transitional government. There was all-round agreement on one point:

Conneh could only be asked to step aside if Taylor left the scene altogether.

Safely ensconced once again in Conakry, Conneh appeared to be almost *incommunicado*. In what were rare telephone conversations, he reiterated his total rejection of the solutions that were progressively being floated. His isolation had put him in a difficult situation. Moreover, the renewed attack on Monrovia did not seem to be yielding the desired results. The LURD leader began to realize that he had reached a dead end, even though he still cultivated hopes of a military victory. He was aware of the political weakness of his position, but could not bring himself to admit it. Sant'Egidio was his last remaining avenue.

In Rome, various options to overcome the impasse were thought through. It was felt that there was no alternative to the talks underway, notwithstanding the tensions they had been subjected to due to the internal dissension within LURD and the ill-advised ostracism of Conneh. After Maputo, it seemed clear that without Conneh's direct involvement, it would not be possible to achieve concrete results. In the meantime, Mustapha Kamara and Kabineh Ja'neh[46], on behalf of the LURD delegation in Accra, asked Sant'Egidio to facilitate a meeting with Conneh to clarify their respective positions. In late July, reassured that the meeting would not see him come under fire, Conneh agreed to return to Rome.

The frequent telephone conversations during the weeks that followed the resumption of the conflict contributed to his decision. Conneh was aware of Sant'Egidio's complete neutrality and knew that the members of his delegation would refrain from putting him under pressure or subjecting him to ultimatums. He understood, in other words, that any decisions he might make would not be unduly influenced or forced upon him. In this as in other cases, the apparent weakness of an organization like the Community of Sant'Egidio actually counted as one of its strengths as a mediator.

The members of the LURD delegation were preparing to leave Accra for Rome to meet with their leader. In Ghana, not everyone was convinced that this was a good idea. ECOWAS representatives, for instance, bemoaned the decision. It was feared that Sant'Egidio's initiative would undermine the negotiations in progress or would give rise to new talks. Some thought that the delegation would not return. There was disagreement among the mediation team and, at first, the delegates were prevented from boarding their plane for Rome. However, following a telephone conversation with Mario Giro, the mediator Abubakar gave his consent without qualms. For his part, the Ghanaian Foreign Minister, Nana Akufo-Addo, supported the initiative.

The attitude of mistrust exhibited by some members of the official mediation group towards the meeting in Rome revealed a lack of understanding of the dynamics of negotiation. Driving a wedge between the delegation and its leadership would eventually have scuppered the entire dialogue process; worse still, "detaining" the delegates in Accra risked putting the international community in an untenable position. The key actors in negotiations are the parties, and if those performing a mediation role begin to make "threats", without being able to follow through on them, then there is a serious danger of producing an adverse outcome.[47]

On July 27, 2003, LURD's representatives to the peace talks arrived in Rome from Accra. They formally requested, in writing, the good offices of Sant'Egidio to help resolve the crisis within the movement. The resentment towards Conneh was evident. Some wanted to see him removed as leader. In the end, the position which prevailed was that of Kabineh Ja'neh and Mustapha Kamara, who were in favor of postponing any showdown and were prepared to talk. A workable solution was needed to break the stalemate in the negotiations, as LURD feared that it would lose all credibility with the international community and would be unable to lay claim to any role in Liberia's future institutional set-up. The first two days of the LURD delegation's visit to Rome, prior to Conneh's arrival, were devoted to analyzing how things stood within the movement and the state of progress of the talks in Accra. Conneh arrived in Rome on July 29, aware that he was in a difficult position politically.

Nevertheless, he wanted to give the impression that he was in control of the situation on the strength of his ascendancy over the armed wing. At the first full meeting, he immediately claimed to have won the war and to be entitled to the post of the country's transitional leader. His thinking was shaped by fourteen years of civil war, and he assessed the state of play solely from a military viewpoint. He considered himself the mastermind of the victory and wanted to be recognized as the man who had freed Liberia from the tyranny of Taylor. Yet his analysis of the international situation was weak. He did not go into the merits of the issues his Ghana delegation raised with him, but felt the need to demonstrate that he was still in charge and had everything totally in hand.

It was only in separate conversations, with Fabio Riccardi, Giro and Vittorio Scelzo, that Conneh faced up to the facts more realistically. He seemed disturbed by what he read in the international press, which painted him as a bloodthirsty man and accused him of an unconscionable use of child soldiers.[48] Conneh understood that, in the eyes of international public opinion, he was one of the many leaders who had fought in Liberia, and not the new hope he would have liked to personify. He remarked bitterly that no one considered him politically trustworthy.

In such circumstances, how could he conceivably be accepted as the country's new leader? Somehow it began to dawn on Conneh that his own future prospects could likewise only benefit from a rapid peace settlement, and that the Liberians for whom he believed he was fighting did not see him as their liberator but as one among many warlords. He further realized that even within LURD his leadership was at risk, and that his prime objective must be to redeem his reputation, even at the cost of temporarily putting his ambitions on hold. After lengthy discussions, Conneh finally agreed to open up talks with his delegation regarding the terms of the Peace Agreement, particularly in relation to the chairmanship of the transitional government and the composition of the executive.

The rift that had developed between Conneh and his representatives, which had jeopardized the peace process, was thus healed.

In Accra, it had been proposed that the transitional leadership position of Chairman should go to a member of civil society, and the names of certain prominent figures not involved in the fourteen years of civil strife had already been floated. For their part, the LURD and MODEL delegations had suggested that there be three Vice-Chairmen appointed, and that these posts should be assigned, in accordance with the model applied in the Democratic Republic of Congo, to the three warring parties.

This proposal, at first considered reasonable, had fallen through precisely due to Conneh insisting on the leadership position and the resumption of the siege of Monrovia. Now the only option left was to propose that the Chairman be chosen with the agreement of the rebels. After days of talks in Rome, Conneh was won over and decisively embraced the path of negotiation. The relationship between him and the members of the delegation was fully restored. On August 4, 2003, from Sant'Egidio's headquarters, he announced his intention to proceed to the talks in Ghana with a platform put together in conjunction with his negotiating team:

LURD accepts the proposal of the ECOWAS Heads of State
"...that no Leader of the three Warring Parties should occupy the positions of President and Vice President in the Transitional Government of Liberia". (Paragraph 23, Final Communiqué, Extraordinary Summit of ECOWAS Heads of State and Government – Accra, July 31, 2003)
Regarding the transitional presidency, however, LURD proposes that the transitional President should be chosen from among political parties, civil society organizations and eminent Liberians, by consensus.[49]

LURD's demand for the removal of Taylor remained firm. In the same declaration, Conneh ordered a new ceasefire and the withdrawal of LURD troops from Monrovia:

We furthermore reaffirm that, concurrently with the arrival of ECOWAS troops, LURD forces will proceed to withdraw from Monrovia, and we hereby express our desire to make Monrovia an arms-free city for the immediate commencement of humanitarian services as well as to enhance security for all. We also appeal to the international community to extend humanitarian assistance and relief services to the whole country as soon as possible.[50]

At the request of Fabio Riccardi, the LURD leader gave an undertaking regarding the issue of child soldiers in keeping with human rights principles:

Similarly, we are aware of our responsibility to protect the rights of children in armed conflict, and we hereby reiterate our previous commitment to avoid any kind of involvement of children in armed conflict and call upon the international community to provide all the necessary resources to attend to this very serious problem.[51]

The political solution proposed by the Rome declaration lay in the mechanisms it outlined for choosing appointees to the new key offices of State during the transitional period. While LURD was permitted to resubmit its proposal for there to be three Vice-Chairmen, this time with Conneh's consent, it could not object to discussing other possible solutions. However, the declaration introduced a particular procedure for the designation of those who would hold the more politically sensitive roles, namely, the choice would require the "mutual agreement" of the representatives of the three warring parties. In this way, LURD retained a sort of power of veto, also as a means to ensuring it secured adequate representation in the new executive.

As agreed in Rome, Conneh immediately proceeded to Accra together with the entire delegation to take part directly in the negotiations. Reinvigorated by his presence, the talks resumed briskly. The international community was satisfied and honored its commitments: on August 11, Charles Taylor quit Liberia and went into exile in Calabar, Nigeria, thereby making it possible to usher in a transitional period.[52] Thus it was that a new institutional framework took shape in Liberia, in which the new Chairman was to be Gyude Bryant, a civil society representative accepted by all three parties, who would lead a national unity government in which members of the former Taylor government, LURD and MODEL would be equally represented. LURD was permitted to appoint George Dweh to the position of Parliamentary Speaker, which, in the Liberian political system, is the second highest office of State. Conneh also extracted a guarantee that no member of the transitional government would be permitted to participate in the presidential elections that were to be held in 2005, in which he, on the other hand, intended to run.[53]

It was on the basis of these arrangements that the Comprehensive Peace Agreement was signed in Accra on August 18, 2003, though by August 15, ECOMIL's first African troops[54] had already been air-transported by the Americans to Monrovia with the consent of the parties, as an interposition force between the combatants. Subsequently, the peace would be maintained by a massive United Nations mission, with 15,000 UNMIL blue helmets called in to monitor compliance with the Peace Agreement and disarm the many militias in the country. A new era came into being, marked by stability and the restoration of democratic normality. The transitional government had the task during its two-year term of steering the country towards the first free and peaceful elections in twenty years. As is common knowledge, those elections would see Ellen Johnson Sirleaf emerge victorious as the first female President of an African country.

Safeguarding the Peace Agreement

After the signing of the Peace Agreement, the formation of the transitional government and the appointment of Gyude Bryant as Chairman, relations between the three signatory factions, the transitional government and the UN went through varying stages, and at times were rather strained. Early in 2004, an ethnic rift appeared to be looming within LURD (between Krahns and Mandingos), a prospect that risked adding further difficulties to the delicate process of disarmament only just begun.[55] A call by one section of LURD for the Minister of Finance to be replaced threatened to bring the situation to a head. The demand, backed by accusations of corruption, was in reality a trial of strength between members of LURD and the transitional government. Internal frictions within LURD were endangering the entire peace process.

At this point, Sant'Egidio decided to call the three constituent members of the transitional government to Rome with a view to asking them to sign a Pact which reaffirmed the spirit and the letter of the Accra Peace Agreement. These discussions took place between May 25-28, 2004, and were attended by representatives of LURD and MODEL as well as by Taylor loyalists. The main difficulty encountered was in getting members of the different LURD factions to sit around the same table. By this stage, the long-delayed internal showdown seemed imminent.

The Parliamentary Speaker, George Dweh, now openly contested Conneh's leadership, aspiring to take his place. However, the Rome meeting was not aimed at resolving the internal problems of the former guerrilla movement, but rather at responding to the pressing issues facing the country during the difficult post-conflict reconstruction phase. The Pact communiqué which the parties signed at Sant'Egidio's headquarters on May 28, 2004 reflected this focus. Of significance in the document was not only the renewed commitment to abide by the terms of the Peace Agreement, but also the method it provided for resolving potential future crises, making it clear that any possible dispute would be settled by politic means.

Notwithstanding the difficulties that have marked the implementation of the Agreement, we, the parties – LURD, the former Government of Liberia, and MODEL – [...] hereby affirm and reaffirm that the CPA [Comprehensive Peace Agreement] remains the best negotiated means for ensuring a return to lasting peace in Liberia [...] We solemnly reaffirm: our joint and several adherence to the spirit and the letter of the Agreement signed in Accra on August 18, 2003; our gratitude to the mediators and to all those who have facilitated, supported and endorsed the Peace Agreement and its implementation; [...and] the need to proceed to implementation of the Peace Agreement without delay or reservation, in order to bring about the economic and social reconstruction of the country; in accordance with which, we, the parties gathered here at the headquarters of Sant'Egidio, call on the Community of Sant'Egidio to be available, as it has been in the past, to help resolve those issues that remain outstanding or which may later arise. [We affirm:] the determination to settle any possible disputes – which might arise in the discharge of the transitional government's functions – solely by political means, in the spirit of dialogue and cooperation that prevailed in the establishment of the said government; and our firm resolve not to take any action or make any statement that could damage or endanger the peaceful political process.[56]

The crisis in the spring of 2004 was perhaps the most serious in the two-year term of the transitional government. Six years on from the signing of the Peace Agreement in Accra, and after the holding of the first democratic elections in the history of the country, the challenges still facing Liberia are enormous. The wounds left by a conflict that affected all parts of the country and which also involved its neighboring States have yet to heal.

The younger generations have grown up knowing only war – whether as soldiers or victims. The country's already poor infrastructure was completely destroyed in the conflict. Nevertheless, peace seems to be establishing itself inasmuch as reconciliation between Liberians is also gradually gaining momentum, though this will take time and will require an unwavering commitment and vigilance on the part of the various national and international actors that helped steer the country out of its civil war.[57]

[1] Previous significant attempts included: the first ceasefire in 1990 (ECOWAS sent Ghanaian and Nigerian troops under the auspices of the ECOMOG (Economic Community of West African States Monitoring Group) mission; the Cotonou Agreement of 1993; the Akosombo Agreement of 1994; and the Abuja Agreement of 1995.

[2] He was indicted in June 2003, by the Special Court for Sierra Leone, on charges relating to the parallel war which ravaged that small neighboring country of Liberia. He is currently being held in custody in The Hague and must answer to charges of crimes against humanity in respect of that conflict.

[3] Sekou Conneh was born in 1960.

[4] LURD had for some time been in contact with the Community of Sant'Egidio, which was making efforts to gauge what leeway there might be to resolve the Liberian crisis.

[5] The Economic Community of West African States.

[6] On the very first day of the talks, the mediators asked Sant'Egidio to persuade the LURD delegation to return to the negotiating room after it had walked out in protest against the presence of Taylor, who was indicted on the same day.

[7] This is a common dynamic in peace talks: those actually at the negotiating table engage with the mechanisms of mediation, whilst those far away fail to grasp them. It is for this reason that ongoing liaison between negotiators and their leaders is always desirable.

[8] The accusation related in particular to the recruitment of workers for

shipment to the island of Fernando Póo (present-day Bioko), which took place in conditions similar to those of the slave trade in previous centuries.

[9] The Afro-American elite tended to treat the natives in the same way as white settlers did elsewhere.

[10] In respect of the history of Liberia during the years of Doe's presidency, cf. J.-P. Pham, *Liberia: Portrait of a Failed State*, New York 2004.

[11] Cf. W. Reno, *Warlord Politics and African States*, London 2008; and A. Sciortino, *L'Africa in guerra. I conflitti africani e la globalizzazione*, Milan 2008. The ongoing conflict and the effective anarchy that prevailed in the mining areas of the country ensured that the illegal trade in diamonds flourished, paving the way for a war economy. The support that Taylor's government offered the RUF rebels in neighboring Sierra Leone followed the same logic and favored control of the traffic in diamonds, which the Liberian dictator sought to take over.

[12] Cf. J.-P. Pham, *Liberia: Portrait of a Failed State*, cit.; and International Crisis Group, Africa Report No. 87, Tackling Liberia and Sierra Leone: Rebuilding Failed States, December 8, 2004.

[13] This was the ECOMOG operation.

[14] According to experts, the Liberian War produced at least eight main armed factions, each with its own foreign allies (some of whom were present within the country in the form of ECOMOG troops). All of these actors were also key parties in the various attempts to broker peace deals between 1990 and 1997. As a consequence, there were major conflicts of interest between the protagonists of the conflict. Liberia became a disputed territory between armed factions, business elites and military HQs in Abuja, Abidjan, Conakry, Ouagadougou and Freetown. Discernible in the background was the political influence of Libya, which backed Taylor from the outset, in opposition to Nigeria, which provided the bulk of the support for ECOWAS' military effort, as well as a range of French, Lebanese, Ukrainian and other interest groups.

[15] Nigeria was at that time under the military dictatorship of Abacha, and a deal with Taylor had become possible.

[16] In relation to the impact of the Liberian crisis on the region, see International Crisis Group, Africa Report No. 62, Tackling Liberia: The Eye of the Regional Storm, April 30, 2003.

[17] Eighteen thousand British soldiers and UN peacekeepers struggled to restore order to Sierra Leone between 1999 and 2001, defeating the RUF. From that point onwards, the British would do everything they could to bring about Taylor's downfall.

[18] See G. Campbell, *Blood Diamonds*, London 2002.

[19] Illegal diamonds are those sourced from unlicensed diamond mines controlled by traffickers, militias or smugglers. Cf. Kimberley Process aims to end conflict diamonds: the findings of the Kimberley Process review, Gale Reference Team in "African Review of Business and Technology", March 1, 2007, Vol. 43 Issue 2 p. 65.

[20] MODEL was supported by the government of Ivory Coast, out of gratitude for helping to fight the Ivorian insurgency in the west of that country.

[21] Report contained in the "Promemoria in preparazione della visita di una delegazione del LURD guidata dal presidente Damate Conneh", dated May 27, 2003: document held in the Community of Sant'Egidio Archive (hereinafter referred to as "ACSE").

[22] Sekou Conneh's wife, Aisha, was the personal soothsayer of the Guinean President. It was said that, thanks to her premonitions, Conté had evaded several plots against him.

[23] The city center, Mamba Point, remained inaccessible, as was the airport, though the port had fallen into LURD hands. Then again, not even Taylor had ever managed to take the city center by force, but only by political means.

[24] See the chapter in this book dealing with Ivory Coast.

[25] Hanson, the spokesman, was arrested and spent several months in Guinean prisons, cf. Tackling Liberia, cit., p. 5.

[26] Cf. the report on the ECOWAS visit to Sant'Egidio dated May 10, 2003, ACSE. It was during this period that, on the border with Ivory Coast, the second armed group, MODEL (the Movement for Democracy in Liberia), made its appearance. Its ethnic composition was predominantly Krahn, which was Doe's ethnic background.

[27] Ghana then held the rotating presidency of ECOWAS.

[28] Cf. "Promemoria in preparazione", cit.

[29] Cf. the report on the ECOWAS visit to Sant'Egidio, cit.

[30] The layout of the city of Monrovia is unusual: all government buildings are located on a peninsula (Mamba Point), making it easier to resist and to defend the city center.

[31] The indictment (as subsequently amended) can be found at: http://www.sc-sl. org/LinkClick.aspx?fileticket=lrn0bAAMvYM%3D&tabid=107

[32] Led by Kabineh Ja'neh, a lawyer and former human rights activist.

[33] Cf. the report regarding the Talks on Liberia dated June 12, 2003, ACSE.

[34] All the other LURD representatives who had attended previous meetings in Rome were now part of the negotiating delegation in Accra.

[35] Cf. the report on the Meetings in Rome with Sekou Damate Conneh Jr., Chairman of LURD dated June 12, 2003, ACSE.

[36] Ibid: "June 7 - afternoon. Conneh explained that he cannot order his troops to stop now because they are too close to achieving their goal. He has only requested that they hold off taking the presidential palace until he arrives in Monrovia, so that he can enter the city at the head of his troops".

[37] Ibid.

[38] Annan was a guest of the African Union Summit, which was also attended by a delegation from Sant'Egidio.

[39] Conneh had, however, indicated that LURD would not be transformed into a political party but would be disbanded after the war, as indeed it was.

[40] During an attack on the third bridge, the last obstacle in the push on Mamba Point, a group of children had remained cut off at a kindergarten facility. The "Corriere della Sera" correspondent Massimo Alberizzi, who was on the scene, telephoned Sant'Egidio, which secured a temporary ceasefire from Conneh to enable their evacuation.

[41] http://www.santegidio.org/news/attualita/2003/0608_liberia_EN.htm

[42] They withdrew from the third bridge to regroup at the first bridge, level with the port.

[43] The talks were temporarily moved from Accra to the nearby town of Akosombo, on Lake Volta.

[44] Cf. the Report on the Second Summit of the African Union dated July 16, 2003, ACSE.

[45] The Liberian President's escape route was guaranteed by the President of Nigeria Obasanjo himself, despite the disapproval voiced by human rights organizations.

[46] Cf. the letter to the Community of Sant'Egidio dated July 27, 2003, ACSE.

[47] A similar situation arose later during the Darfur Peace Talks, where forcing

some factions to sign but not others led to the agreement falling over and the resumption of the war.

[48] He was particularly shocked by what he read in an article in the newspaper "La Stampa", which described the LURD guerrillas' combat tactics. The paper focused on the goriest details and on the fighters' alleged practice of tearing out the hearts of their victims to carry them around their necks in a bag as a symbol of invulnerability. In reality, these were the sorts of stereotypes applied to all conflicts in West Africa, falling somewhere between factual reporting and myth.

[49] Declaration by the leader of LURD regarding the restoration of peace in Liberia, Rome, August 4, 2003, available in Italian at http://www.santegidio.org/IT/pace/news/20030804.htm

[50] Ibid.

[51] Ibid.

[52] In 2006, Taylor would be arrested and transferred to The Hague to be tried in respect of events in Sierra Leone. In a sense, the promise of immunity – in exchange for which he had left Monrovia in 2003 – was broken, under pressure from the US and Britain.

[53] Indeed, he would not accept any position in the transitional government precisely in order to be free to stand for election in 2005.

[54] The acronym for the ECOWAS Mission in Liberia, which comprised 1000 Nigerian troops, supported by 100 US marines.

[55] Cf. the report on the Visit to Liberia dated January 16, 2004, ACSE.

[56] The Sant'Egidio Pact, Rome, May 28, 2004, available in Italian at http://www.santegidio.org/it/pace/news/20040628_dichiarazione.htm

[57] In contrast with what happened in neighboring Sierra Leone, the Liberian government decided not to resort to the international justice system, and established its own Truth and Reconciliation Commission instead.

Civil War and Peace in Ivory Coast

Ivory Coast

Area (in sq km)	320,763
Population (millions)	19.097
Population density (inhabitants per sq km)	60
Percentage of population <15 years	41.0
Annual change in population (%)	+1.7
Infant mortality per 1,000 live births (<1 year/<5 years)	103.5/194
Life expectancy at birth (male/female)	49/53
Fertility rate (average no. of children per woman)	5.1
Illiteracy rate (%)	46.3
Doctors (per 1,000 inhabitants)	0.1
Percentage of adult population living with HIV/AIDS (adult prevalence rate	7.0
Human Development Index (HDI), expressed on a scale from 0 to 1, to three decimal places	0.420
HDI, world ranking	163
GDP per capita (USD)	850
GDP per capita, world ranking	134
Personal computers (per 1,000 inhabitants)	15.0

Civil War and Peace in Ivory Coast

Mario Giro

On March 4, 2007, the Ouagadougou Political Agreement was signed in the eponymous capital of Burkina Faso, putting an end to a war that had begun in September 2002. The ceremony was attended by the President of the Republic of Ivory Coast, Laurent Gbagbo, and the leader of the northern rebels, Guillaume Soro. Between them was the President of Burkina Faso, Blaise Compaoré, who had facilitated the negotiations. The Community of Sant'Egidio, in the person of Mario Giro, had been involved in the talks since their commencement on February 5 at the request of the Burkinabe authorities.

The Community was the only non-African actor present at the negotiations, which were conducted in a very different manner than the many previous such efforts. The two delegations – that of the Ivorian President led by Désiré Tagro[1], and that of Forces Nouvelles (or New Forces, the name under which the rebels from the three former armed movements united) headed by Soro – had worked together for a month, away from the glare of the media spotlight and without any third parties present, aside from the facilitation team assembled by President Compaoré.[2] The latter requested the involvement of Sant'Egidio due to its intimate understanding of the Ivorian crisis stretching back to its very beginnings, and because of the close relationship the Community had maintained over the years with the key parties to the conflict.[3]

The cooperative relationship between Compaoré and Sant'Egidio represented a rare occurrence in the context of crises in Africa, where peace mediation efforts are often conducted in a climate of intense rivalry and antagonism between the various regional, African and international actors called on to resolve such conflicts.

The Ouagadougou Agreement ushered in a new phase that is still ongoing, in which a national unity government led by Guillaume Soro as Prime Minister has been tasked with steering the country through a period of transition to culminate in the holding of new universally acceptable elections.[4] The new government's initiatives are aimed at bringing about the reunification of a country split between north and south since September 2002.

The public administration is in the process of being redeployed throughout the country and the demarcation line separating the two fighting forces has essentially been dismantled. The neutral (UN and French) forces interposed between the two rivals since 2002 have removed roadblocks and retreated to several predetermined locations. France is progressively starting to disengage. Transit between the north of the country (the rebel zone) and the south (the loyalist area) has been made easier, trade has resumed, and there is an increasing number of exchange visits between the two sides. A telling poster has appeared on walls in the capital Abidjan, as well as in the country's second city Bouaké (held by the rebels), with a photo showing the signing in Ouagadougou and a caption reading "Peace is here!" Since the signing of the Agreement in March, there have been no more reports of armed incidents or attacks of any kind.

And yet it had seemed no simple matter to unravel the Ivorian knot. Many had tried since the beginning of the conflict, including Togo, Senegal, France, Ghana, Nigeria, Gabon and South Africa. Then there were efforts of the UN, ECOWAS (a West African organization), the African Union, and the European Union. Some sections of the international community remained skeptical of the prospects for Burkina Faso's attempt. Would Ouagadougou succeed where other much better-equipped players had failed? Whilst the Ivorian crisis was an African one, it was also of particular significance in world political terms, both because of the nation's wealth of resources and traditional stability, as well as the role played by Ivory Coast as a sub-regional power. There were many (first and foremost France) who wished to resolve this conflict, which threatened the stability of the whole of West Africa, already undermined by long wars in Liberia and Sierra Leone and the situation of chronic insecurity in Guinea-Conakry.

Contradictions in the "land of brotherhood"

To understand the origins of the Ivorian civil war, it is necessary to look back to the final phase in the long reign of the country's founding President, Félix Houphouët-Boigny. Having come to power in 1960, the year the country gained its independence, he governed as an absolute ruler until his death in 1993. Houphouët-Boigny was characteristic of the group of African leaders aligned with the West and former colonial metropole France, having also been a Minister of the French Fourth Republic and a Member of the National Assembly in Paris. Unlike some of his African peers, who were more inclined towards the third-world dreams of non-aligned countries or to socialist and Marxist ideology, the Ivorian President wanted a Ivory Coast that was close to France – a "showcase" of Europe in Africa. He pursued this goal by heavily yoking his country's economy to that of France through the exploitation of and trade in agricultural commodities, and by becoming a privileged political interlocutor of France and the West in Africa.

Due to its unique agricultural features, Ivory Coast had been viewed by its colonizers as ideal for intensive exploitation through rural labor. Many natives of the Sahelian strip in other administrative regions of French West Africa were progressively transferred there to cultivate what was very fertile land. Paris went as far as shifting the administrative boundary between the colonized regions in order to facilitate this relocation of people. Thus, the border between the "productive" Ivory Coast, with its fertile and arable plains in the south, and the more arid and typically Sahelian area of the Upper Volta to the north, was frequently moved northwards, thereby changing (from an administrative standpoint) the place of origin of indigenous families.[5]

The landowners of the south demanded – and were supplied with – increasingly greater numbers of laborers for their cocoa and coffee plantations. Thus, on gaining independence, the country already had a diverse population, composed of Ivorians but also of families who originated from the Upper Volta (now Burkina Faso), Mali, Guinea, and Ghana. Ethnic identities became intermingled and blurred, transcending boundary lines that have now become international borders.

Houphouët-Boigny reprised the colonizers' approach, and indeed strengthened it by enshrining it in policy that would become emblematic of the country for decades and would make Ivory Coast rich in comparison to its neighbors. For the many immigrants from the other poorer young African nations on its borders, Ivory Coast became the "country of peace and hospitality" that its national anthem – the Abidjanaise – proclaims it is. In Ivory Coast, there was work, and it was easy for anyone to secure the right to settle on uncultivated land to turn it to good account.[6] By the end of the 1980s, it was estimated that one third of the population of 15 million people were either immigrants or foreign.[7] Over the years, the second and third generations of this influx were born in the country, seeing themselves as Ivorians to all intents and purposes. Indeed, they were treated as such, as was evident when it came to voting.

Although elections only involved one party, which – given that it had no rivals – had no need of any further votes than those cast by native Ivorians[8], nearly all residents obtained the right to vote regardless of their origin. Until the early 1990s, this peculiar situation presented no problem; on the contrary, in people's minds it was a point of national pride. Compared with the touchy nationalist sensibilities of other African countries, Ivory Coast seemed like a welcoming land of peaceful coexistence. This approach did not take long to bear fruit: the country drew much foreign investment and developed rapidly, becoming the world's leading cocoa-producing nation and the second-largest coffee producer. To Westerners, Abidjan was an advanced city with modern freeways and buildings, but above all, it offered an ideal environment for business. The coups and violent upheavals of so many other parts of the continent did not sully Ivory Coast, where stability was assured. From its rural beginnings, Ivory Coast became a major economic center complete with a stock exchange, and within a few years Abidjan replaced Dakar as the West African city most loved and frequented by the French and Europeans.

However, this led to the emergence of a grey area. During the tumultuous years of growth, the question of nationality had been put to one side. Many "non-natives" had two sets of identity papers, or none at all, even though their children were considered to be Ivorians. Title documents for buildings and land were of a poor standard and often consisted of what were commonly termed "petits papiers" – that is, unofficial records. The laws on citizenship, voting rights and land issues were numerous and contradictory. The Ivorian Constitution itself was not sufficiently clear on these matters. Added to this was a reluctance to register children at birth, a tendency which would increase over time. This did not create any major problems whilst the market thrived and exports grew, but towards the end of Houphouët-Boigny's long reign, the global economic situation took a turn for the worse.

In the early 1990s, new producers of agricultural commodities emerged, such as Malaysia, a forerunner to present-day India and China.[9] A free-trade philosophy prevailed and there was growing pressure on France to desist from its policy of maintaining preferential ties with francophone Africa – and with Ivory Coast in particular. In the name of free competition, the International Monetary Fund criticized the privileged trade agreements established. There was talk of devaluing the single currency of French-speaking Africa, the CFA franc, which was pegged to the French franc.

The economic crisis also began to be felt in Abidjan, especially when cocoa prices started to fall. Poverty, which had never disappeared from the country, became chronic in many areas, particularly in the shanty towns of Abidjan and in regions where there was no fertile land. Houphouët-Boigny, by then getting on in years, was unable to halt the downward slide and was persuaded by the Director-General of the IMF, Michel Camdessus, to take on Alassane Ouattara as Prime Minister[10] with a view to putting the now shaky public accounts back in order. It was not a habit of the aging leader to share power with others, but by this stage his back was against the wall.

Serious social problems ensued. Layoffs in the public sector and insolvencies of privately-owned businesses shattered the Ivorian dream of endless growth. The population began to complain and new opposition political movements – whose emergence was favored by the decision of French

President François Mitterrand to force multiparty systems on its African "protégés"[11] – tapped into this discontent. The fall of the Berlin Wall and the end of the Cold-War bipolar confrontation meant it was no longer possible to justify authoritarian regimes. As the French Cooperation Minister put it: "Le vent de l'est secoue les cocotiers".[12] It was during those months that the Ivorian Popular Front (FPI) emerged from the teachers' union. The FPI, at least to judge by attendances at public rallies, soon became the most widely-endorsed contender to President Houphouët-Boigny's Democratic Party of Ivory Coast (the PDCI). At the head of this new formation was a young teachers' union leader, Laurent Gbagbo. Scion of a clan and ethnic group that had long been political opponents of Houphouët-Boigny's regime, Gbagbo had been jailed several times and was also sent into exile in France. His vision for Ivory Coast clashed sharply with that of the PDCI worthies.[13]

As far as Gbagbo was concerned, Ivory Coast's economy was "artificially buoyed" by unequal trade with Europe, the handsome profits of which were only going to a small slice of the population and were not being distributed democratically. Gbagbo also criticized the ambivalent policy on citizenship and spoke of immigrants and non-natives as "electoral rabble" used by Houphouët-Boigny to secure his reelection. Thus, ironically, it was the country's democratic opening in 1990 that triggered the controversy over the presence of "foreigners" in the country – those millions of people who had hitherto enjoyed the right to vote. Whilst there was a one-party regime, it had not mattered whether they voted or not. Now things were changing. It was a major shock: for the first time, there were those who dared call into question the notion that this was the "land of hospitality".

Laurent Gbagbo had contacts in France. A history professor by profession, through his trade union he forged links with the European socialist movement, particularly the French Socialist Party (PS). During his exile, he had lived in Paris in the house of a senior official of that party and entertained close friendships with its leaders. He established an underground group and, as soon as he succeeded in having it legally registered[14], enrolled his formation, the FPI, with Socialist International.[15]

Ivory Coast is orphaned

As Gbagbo was breaking onto the public scene, Alassane Dramane Ouattara – a leading technocrat tasked with getting the country and its finances back into shape – was called in to take the post of Prime Minister. Ouattara held an Ivorian passport, but there were immediately rumors that his family was of Burkinabe origin. It was also whispered that old Houphouët-Boigny had chosen him precisely because, as a foreigner, he had nothing to fear from any political ambitions Ouattara might harbor. Indeed, pursuant to the Constitution, the President of Ivory Coast had to be Ivorian by birth and of Ivorian parentage. The question of Ouattara's nationality, together with Gbagbo's denunciation of the voting rights accorded to non-natives and immigrants, were the two initial ingredients of the looming Ivorian crisis, which culminated in the civil war that broke out in 2002.

The first measures taken by the new Prime Minister received widespread approval. Between 1990 and 1993, the State budget was brought back into balance, the economy picked up again, and the devaluation of the CFA franc was averted (mainly due to pressure brought to bear by President Houphouët-Boigny on the French[16]). Yet whilst the international market welcomed these initiatives, their impact on the population was not always negligible, with cuts to education, health and public services breeding discontent. Ouattara implemented classic free-market policies that, while managing to jumpstart the Ivorian economy, had negative social repercussions and provoked reactions of which Gbagbo's party, the FPI, took advantage. Ouattara was also responsible for organizing the first multi-party elections in the country: the presidential poll of October 1990 and the parliamentary elections of the following month. For the first time, Houphouët-Boigny was challenged by an alternative candidate, namely, Gbagbo, who managed to secure 18% of the vote.[17] But the democratic opening was still limited and the regime carried on in its authoritarian ways. 1992 saw the most serious public demonstrations ever witnessed in the country, all led by the Popular Front. The people protested against liberal economic reforms. Gbagbo himself was arrested once again, together with his wife Simone Ehivet and other close associates.

The new government initiative most fraught with dire consequences for the future was the introduction of residence permits for foreigners. No one seemed to be aware that a nefarious mechanism was being set in motion which would tear apart the fabric of the nation and which would paradoxically be the undoing of the Prime Minister himself. The measure was primarily adopted for financial reasons: to raise revenue in straitened times. However, it brought to the surface questions that had previously lain buried, such as: Who were the foreigners in Ivory Coast? Who was entitled to full citizenship? What was the status of second and third-generation children of immigrants born in Ivory Coast? And should the principle of *jus sanguinis* or *jus soli* apply? Ivorian law was ambiguous on this point.

Moreover, on some issues, the citizenship and electoral codes contradicted each other. As President Houphouët-Boigny lived out his last days, a time bomb was triggered. The most serious issue was that Ivorian citizens in the north of the country often belonged to the same ethnic group, and sometimes even the same clan, as immigrants from Burkina Faso, Mali and Guinea, thanks in part to the earlier northward shifting of the colonial boundaries and the displacement of people. Some very common surnames were identical on both sides of the various borders. A perverse association was thus formed in the collective imagination between immigrants and northern Ivorian citizens, which would soon spill over into ethnic mistrust and hatred.

In early December 1993, after last-ditch efforts in hospitals in Paris to save his life, Houphouët-Boigny was repatriated home by special flight, where – on the 7th – he died. Ivory Coast was in mourning. The President's grand funeral was conducted in the huge Basilica of Notre-Dame de la Paix (ordered by him to be modeled after St. Peter's) in his hometown of Yamoussoukro, which had become the official capital of the country.[18] The service was attended by 27 foreign heads of State and the representatives of 120 countries.

The Who's Who of France's most influential were in attendance, including the then President Mitterrand, his predecessor Giscard d'Estaing, former Prime Ministers, Ministers, and prominent figures from the worlds of business and culture. Overcome by a sudden sense of loss, Ivory Coast was in a daze. Nobody noticed the first sign of political instability: the contest that arose between Prime Minister Ouattara and the Speaker of the National Assembly, Henri Konan Bédié, who was designated to succeed Houphouët-Boigny pursuant to the dictates of the Constitution.[19] Ouattara, who had essentially carried out presidential duties over the past three years, wanted the presidency. However, he was faced with opposition from many PDCI notables, who were riled by the single-mindedness with which he had gone about rebalancing the State budget and removing many privileges. For several hours, tensions flared between the supporters of the two men. In the end, it was Mitterrand himself who came down in favor of Konan Bédié.[20]

The new President was little-known by the majority of Ivorians. He had been the Ambassador to Washington immediately following independence, a Minister at various times, and finally, Parliamentary Speaker. During his albeit long political career, he had granted interviews rarely and made few public appearances. He was described as being "as silent as the grave" and *effacé* (unassuming and reserved), even though he had always been on the shortlist of Houphouët-Boigny's possible heirs-apparent. As soon as he was installed in the presidential palace in the Plateau district, Konan Bédié revealed a peevish, brusque and insecure character, quite different from the apparently conciliatory though very authoritative founding father of the country. "I'm not your dad like Houphouët-Boigny was", Bédié would repeatedly insist.

The bout with Ouattara had left a gaping wound – a sense of deep mistrust of the State apparatus which, unlike the French, had not come sufficiently to his defense. Bédié believed he could only count on Paris and harbored resentment. In the lead-up to the expiry of his term in 1995, for fear of once more finding himself pitted against Ouattara, he unleashed a vigorous campaign focusing on the latter's supposed foreign origins and had him excluded from the ballot.

Meanwhile, Ouattara, having foreseen this cheap maneuver, had made contact with disaffected elements within the PDCI, a move which led to the establishment of the Rassemblement des Républicains (RDR).[21] This new formation was headed by Ouattara himself. Having emerged as a split from the PDCI, what differentiated the RDR was not so much its economic policy or ideology, but principally the origin of its members, who were almost all from the north of the country. The contagion of the citizenship question had by this stage also spread to the Ivorian political landscape, with the antagonism between Bédié's PDCI and Ouattara's RDR reflecting a conflict between the south and the north. The "northern" camp sympathized with the needs of non-natives, whilst the "southerners" refused to countenance them.

The ivoirité controversy

Soon, the dispute took on the bitter tones of ethnic division. This was fueled by Bédié's decision to launch a doctrine of Ivorian identity under the slogan of *ivoirité*.[22] To that end, the President established a research center[23] aimed at lending credence to this new concept with overt ethnic overtones. The notion of *ivoirité* soon became a veritable cultural scourge which spread rapidly from narrow political circles to wider society. Many within the PDCI believed they had found the decisive means by which to identify those who were truly Ivorian and those who were not. Bédié spoke of the "white cloak of *ivoirité*" that would restore "harmony between the people in power and the people of the land".[24] A xenophobic ethno-nationalism gained ground which had hitherto only been found in certain milieus and not amongst the general population.

The political manipulation of the principles of national identity and citizenship reached its peak in the years 1995-1999. Bédié believed he could strengthen his position by denouncing Ouattara as a non-Ivorian – and with him, all those who identified with the RDR. Besides, he argued maliciously, weren't they all "northerners"? The concepts of *ivoirité* and "doubtful nationality" were increasingly applied. Senior State officials suddenly saw their citizenship refuted, politicians used the new ideology to destroy the reputation of their opponents, and many were infected by the culture of suspicion. In Abidjan and in the major cities, the police began to tear up identity cards that were determined to be false on the spot, without any further checks being carried out.

There was no longer any guarantee that local authorities would accept the validity of any identity documents, and the judiciary allowed itself to be drawn into endless proceedings regarding the nationality of many citizens, the most symbolic of which involved Ouattara himself. Within a short space of time, conflicting decisions were handed down at each of the various court levels, in turns upholding then refuting the *ivoirité* of the RDR leader. Documents of dubious origin surfaced regarding Ouattara's relatives, written statements allegedly made by him were compared, evidence of his enrollment in foreign schools was produced, and so on.

The controversy over *ivoirité* swept through Ivorian society like a storm and transformed it forever. Mistrust and suspicion became rife. In rural areas, the crisis led to clashes between various groups. In November 1999, in the west of the country on the border with Liberia, Sant'Egidio intervened through its local communities to provide assistance to the thousands of internally displaced Burkinabes driven off the land they had worked for decades by native Ivorians. The economic crisis exacerbated the situation. Similar incidents also took place in other areas of the country.

They were almost like dress rehearsals for the conflict that would break out within a few years. The social fabric unraveled and many "natives" invoked "indigenous property rights" in order to get their hands on land and buildings held by "non-natives".[25] But the latter, especially when taken together with citizens of the north, comprised no small proportion of the country, representing half if not more of the population. The RDR flexed its political muscle, and its opponents feared that a large part of the Ivorian population would rally behind it.

President Konan Bédié was out on a limb. He had easily won the presidential elections of 1995, but only because Ouattara had been barred from them. Even Gbagbo, who initially had not gotten involved in the folly of *ivoirité*, chose to boycott the ballot out of solidarity.[26] The north of the country was in turmoil. In State institutions and in the army, northerners felt they were viewed with suspicion. The tension was palpable.

On the night of December 24, 1999, as Bédié was making his way to his native village for Christmas, a simple mutiny in an Abidjan barracks[27] turned into a coup d'état. The military took control without a shot being fired. Bédié was forced to take quick refuge in the French military base in the capital, from where he would be transferred to Lomé and then on to Paris. Nobody came to his defense – not even his party chiefs. People spilled out onto the streets to celebrate. In the excitement of those hours, in which supporters of Gbagbo and Ouattara merged with each other, and people from the north and south came together in one big crowd, no one seemed to realize that the old Ivory Coast – a country of peace and stability – had gone forever.

The coup and the election of Gbagbo

A military regime was established headed by General Robert Guéï.[28] The latter did not restore order, nor did he hand power back to civilians as he had originally promised. With all institutions swept aside, chaos prevailed. Unruly troops roamed at will through Ivorian cities, robbing and harassing the civilian population. The national unity government was not taken seriously by the army and did not get off the ground. In turn, the various parties walked away from it, accusing the military of bias. The political crisis damaged Ivory Coast's relations with its traditional African and Western partners. In the general upheaval, the economic system gradually fell into the hands of profiteers and criminals.

There was an endless succession of rumors of attacks and further coups. As the end of the presidential term loomed (2000), General Guéï, who had stated that he did not wish to stand for election, changed his mind and presented himself as a candidate. During his months in power, he had begun to think of himself as the new ruler of the nation, despite having no legitimacy as a leader.[29]

Meanwhile, the doctrine of *ivoirité* had not disappeared with the man who had devised it, but rather, also spread to the military – a sign that the damage wreaked was profound. A purge of officials from the north was followed by the exclusion of Ouattara from the elections once again on the grounds of "doubtful nationality". Even Guéï feared him and had a constitutional amendment passed that made the conditions for eligibility as a presidential candidate tougher.[30]

The elections took place in a climate of violence, but this time Gbagbo did not withdraw from the running. During the night, the vote count was suspended by the military when it became clear that Gbagbo had defeated the General. Crowds spontaneously took to the streets and the military retreated. This time it was Guéï's turn to flee, and Gbagbo was proclaimed President of the Republic on October 26, 2000. As he himself would later say on several occasions, he had been elected in "calamitous conditions".

The rise to power of the FPI leader seemed to bring a breath of fresh air to the country. Gbagbo had not been involved in the recent disastrous phase of Ivorian politics, nor had he taken an active part in the *ivoirité* controversy. General Guéï had underestimated him. The speeches of the new President expressed optimism. He promised stability, social justice, an end to ethnic divisions, and reconciliation. His platform envisaged sweeping social reforms which included social security and free welfare and healthcare services for all, echoing his socialist ideals.

In relation to *ivoirité*, Gbagbo stated that this was not a concept he had come up with, but nevertheless argued that there was a need to review the issue of citizenship. He was aware of the clout wielded by the RDR and feared the charisma of its leader Ouattara. Nevertheless, he did not wish the question of the latter's nationality to remain unresolved, promising to have it cleared up once and for all.

The first few months of the new Gbagbo government seemed to give reason for hope: new welfare laws were introduced, the country calmed down, trade resumed, and Ivory Coast was readmitted to international forums. In September 2001, the President participated in the inter-religious International Meeting of Prayer for Peace organized by Sant'Egidio, which took place in Barcelona. In addition to its leader's presence, Ivory Coast sent a large delegation of religious representatives. On that occasion Gbagbo took the floor several times, inspiring confidence and optimism. Upon his return to Abidjan, he convened a National Reconciliation Forum, which he also invited the Community of Sant'Egidio to attend.

The Forum's proceedings were conducted as public hearings in which everyone could have their say. For some months, a great national catharsis gripped the country: relayed by radio, the sessions of the Forum brought to light all the complaints, the suffering, the reproaches, and the hopes of Ivorians. Gbagbo even managed to have Bédié and Guéï, as well as Ouattara, return to their homeland, each of whom took it in turns to address the Forum. The four leaders were regularly seen together, in a sort of high committee of State which Gbagbo, however, only considered to be advisory in nature.

As regards the question of Ouattara's nationality, the President stated that it could not be framed in political terms, but would be resolved by the courts, before which Ouattara would be able to present all the evidence he wished. After years of heated debate over this issue, this represented a marked moderation in tone. It seemed that Ivory Coast had recovered its former composure. The President's political approach seemed geared towards strengthening democratic rights. Several laws which curtailed civil liberties were abolished, such as those that restricted freedom of the press.

Gbagbo brought a fresh slant to his role. He spent entire days meeting with delegations of citizens, ventured forth frequently from the palace, and traveled a great deal around the country. Unlike those who preceded him, he was straightforward and direct in his manner with the people. He spoke in various dialects, was informal, and joked and laughed with them. Even in the fields of foreign and trade policy, he sought to innovate. Without creating any rifts, he embarked on decisive efforts to extricate the country from its restrictive ties with France. He put the management of several State enterprises and Abidjan's freight port (the most important such facility in the region stretching from Senegal to Nigeria) out to international tender. He wanted to diversify investment in the cocoa industry and searched for new partners. He believed that the relationship with

Paris was economically stifling Ivory Coast, and meant that it missed out on valuable opportunities, but he did not want the large private French companies that had been investing in the country for some time to pull out. During his presidency, offshore oil was also discovered, and the tenders for exploitation of these deposits were open to all.[31]

A country divided in two

In a situation which – all things considered – was reassuring, the rebellion in the north on the night of September 19, 2002, came like a bolt out of the blue.[32] President Gbagbo was on an official visit to Rome. On September 20, he was scheduled to meet John Paul II. Early reports received from Abidjan were confused: it was not clear what was really happening, nor who was behind the rebels. What was certain is that several hundred armed persons had simultaneously risen up in revolt in Abidjan, Bouaké, Korhogo, and other smaller towns of the country. In the capital, they raided the house of the Interior Minister, a close supporter of the President, and killed him. Fortunately for the Prime Minister, he was away from the city.

The Minister of Defense managed to save himself and resurfaced many hours later. The rebels also tried to take over radio and television stations as well as other nerve centers, but army troops remained loyal to the government, as did the gendarmerie and the police. Even without orders, they struck back at the attackers. The battle raged for several hours, resulting in many deaths. Eventually the rebels retreated to the north. In Bouaké and Korhogo, however, they were successful: having rounded up the area authorities, they disposed of the local gendarmes – at times, brutally. Indeed, there was talk of massacres.

As Gbagbo – whose State visit was cut short – hurriedly returned to Abidjan, the authorities gradually regained control of the capital. During the night, General Guéï was also killed (though it was never understood by whom). A disturbing picture slowly began to emerge: even though they continued to conceal their identity, the insurgents declared themselves to be northern partisans.[33] Many were soldiers and noncommissioned officers who were disaffected or had been marginalized under Guéï's rule, precisely because they were northerners. Their leader was a military man who called himself "Dr. Koumba".

Only later would he be identified as Guillaume Soro, a former student leader once close to Gbagbo but who had long since passed over to Ouattara's camp, and who had now become a rebel chief. Soro was thirty years old and was of northern origin.[34] In the north of the country, the rebellion seemed impossible to contain. Once it became clear that northerners were responsible for the rebellion, it spread like wildfire without encountering any effective resistance. Units of soldiers in that region joined forces with the rebels, and there was no shortage of senior officers who did the same. In the west of the country, two new rebel groups emerged, claiming they were independent from – though acting in alliance with – Soro, whose movement called itself the MPCI (the Patriotic Movement of Ivory Coast).

Its initial demands were straightforward: rights for the excluded and marginalized north, renewed national unity, an end to discrimination, and the outlawing of *ivoirité*. People in the north demonstrated in support of the rebels, and the Charter of the Great North was recirculated.[35] The rebels seemed to be saying that what Ouattara had not succeeded in securing politically would be obtained by force.

Within the space of just a few weeks, the country was split in two: the rebel north versus the loyalist center-south.[36] Gbagbo's policy of reconciliation had not yielded the desired results.

Maybe it had come too late or been too circumspect and slow. Or perhaps the ethnic canker that had eaten away at Ivory Coast since 1993 was too far advanced. Gbagbo may have underestimated intelligence reports on former Ivorian soldiers who had taken refuge in Burkina Faso following Guéï's purges. Now President Compaoré was accused by loyalists of siding with the rebels and of having helped them. Burkina Faso categorically denied these claims, but the *ivoirité* policy, with its baleful consequences, certainly found no favor in Ouagadougou, where thousands of refugees had flooded in since 1999. The rebels were well-armed and everyone wondered who was funding them. In reality, entire barracks had gone over to the north and the army was virtually split in two.

The international response to the new Ivorian crisis was not long in coming. The country was too important for the area and the interests at stake were too high. It is at this point that the story of the quest for peace in Ivory Coast begins – a story which saw the Community of Sant'Egidio involved to the fullest. The first to react was France, which rapidly deployed its units as an interposition force between the two sides. Paris had important military bases in the country, that were a hangover of the Houphouët-Boigny era. Gbagbo unsuccessfully sought to trigger the operation of secret defense agreements which bound Ivory Coast and France, and which provided for French assistance in the event of external aggression. Despite the accusations leveled at Burkina Faso, there was no evidence of any such attacks. Moreover, France was going through one of its periods of governmental cohabitation between left and right (with Chirac as President and Jospin as Prime Minister), which did not make such decisions any easier.

The first visit to Bouaké – by now established as the rebel capital – by the Foreign Ministers of Senegal and Togo, the latter then holding the rotating presidency of ECOWAS, took place amidst a very tense situation. Within days, the delegation secured an initial ceasefire. The rebel leaders were invited to Lomé for talks in November 2002. The by then aging Togolese leader, Gnassingbé Eyadéma, wanted to act as a peacemaker. He also managed to persuade Gbagbo to send a delegation to Lomé to parley. However, Gbagbo did not have a high regard for the Togolese leader, whom he considered a military coup leader.[37] As would emerge later, the loyalist delegation had no real mandate to negotiate.

The Community of Sant'Egidio was invited by the Foreign Minister of Togo, Koffi Panou, to participate in the talks. Its delegation arrived in Lomé at a stage when the negotiations had stalled.[38] The loyalists, headed by a former supporter of Houphouët-Boigny with little authority[39], were employing delay tactics. Soro and his deputy Dacoury-Tabley[40] were peeved. President Eyadéma realized that Gbagbo did not want him as a mediator. He confided to the Sant'Egidio delegation that he felt a spontaneous affinity with the rebels, who reminded him of himself when he was young. Despite the patience shown by Koffi Panou, the impasse persisted. The Sant'Egidio delegation thus made direct contact with President Gbagbo and visited Abidjan. The atmosphere in the city was tense: there was a curfew in place and no one was out on the streets, not even in poorer neighborhoods, which was unusual for an African city. During those days, Gbagbo seemed to have taken heart again after his initial bemusement.

The loyalist army, at first caught off-guard, had regained control over parts of the territory and managed to stop the rebel advance, thanks also to the French interposition force. In addition, new weaponry, especially aircraft and helicopters, had been acquired. The real strength of the loyalists over the rebels lay in air power. Sant'Egidio tried to persuade the President to negotiate in earnest, at any venue of his choosing, and that when dealing with internal crises, a military solution is never desirable. Moreover, it was stressed that in this case the roots of the conflict ran too deep, extending beyond the protagonists themselves, for there to be any illusion of being able to resolve it militarily. However, Gbagbo was convinced at the time that the air force would guarantee him a decisive advantage and a quick victory. He announced to the Sant'Egidio delegation that within two weeks his armed forces would move into the offensive, which is precisely what happened, though without any significant results being achieved. The Togolese-mediated talks ground to a halt never to be resumed.

Meanwhile, the country slid into war mode. Both sides heavily armed themselves. Some African States offered assistance to Abidjan. Angolan tanks appeared in the streets of the capital. There was talk of Ukrainian or Eastern European mercenaries who had come to train the loyalists to use the helicopters. The new Russian-made fighter planes were flown by foreign pilots. War propaganda began to ravage the hearts and minds of civilians, particularly the "patriotic" campaign – as it was called in the south – of the official government. Gbagbo and his supporters saw themselves as under assault (calling the other side "the attackers").

The disappointment at not having been able to implement the social reform package developed over many years in opposition had turned to anger amongst all the senior ranks of the FPI. Ouattara was painted as the "grand old man" behind the rebels, who were northerners like him.[41] But Burkina Faso was also depicted as an enemy State. In rural areas and in the larger poor urban districts, the non-native population, Burkinabes in particular, became the targets of popular resentment. The situation, already serious due to the ethno-racist tenor of *ivoirité*, now turned intolerable. Young "patriots", who were generally ex-students and unemployed, banded together in violent groups that attacked suspected "foreigners".[42] They demanded weapons to go to the front, and put on shows of strength outside the French embassy and French military bases. Ivorians of northern origin were all regarded as tantamount to traitors to the national unity.

Many southerners who lived in the north, including State officials, teachers and doctors, fled to the south, abandoning their homes and belongings to the rebels. This contributed to increasing popular animosity. Ivorians in the south became embittered and spoke of nothing else but war. But the situation in the north was no better. Everything – including schools, offices and hospitals – had ceased to function. The rebels, in eccentric and chilling garb characteristic of African guerrillas, adopted frightening names, terrorized the civilian population and acted as a law unto themselves. Many people were killed for no apparent reason.

The war had its own violent logic that altered the soul of a nation. Just as the war propaganda corrupted the people's spirits, so too the frantic scrabble for weapons and resources with which to fight soon became a blight on Ivory Coast's society and economy. It seemed that there was no scope for anything other than the obsessive repetition of slogans and proclamations of hate. During this stage, Sant'Egidio's peace efforts were not confined to seeking out conditions conducive to dialogue and equitable negotiations. Its communities in Ivory Coast strove to maintain a sphere of peaceful coexistence and rationality, by remaining united, praying, and continuing their work with the poor, helping refugees from the north as well as non-native and foreign Ivorians stranded in the south. Special effort was put into countering the wave of xenophobia that had spread through Ivorian society, particularly amongst young people.

The Community's Schools of Peace – facilities which take in children who are poor and experiencing difficulty in order to assist them with their studies, enable them to reintegrate into formal schools or prevent them from falling behind – continued to operate[43]. Everything possible was done to preserve peace between neighbors, notwithstanding that they might be of different ethnic origin. Even Sant'Egidio's communities in the north, though reduced in size and isolated within the rebel area, carried on with their work, despite the many challenges faced.

Attempts at mediation and Sant'Egidio's efforts

Right from the start of the war, both President Gbagbo and his advisors as well as Guillaume Soro and the rebels clearly understood what Sant'Egidio's position was. Yet they never refused to liaise with the Community, even when their decisions were totally at odds with its requests. It very soon emerged that, thanks to the peacemaking efforts it had undertaken, the Community of Sant'Egidio was viewed as a respected byword for peace and goodwill by both sides. This was particularly the case in relation to its work with religious communities.

At the beginning of the crisis, attempts were made to exploit religious differences in order to escalate the hatred and hostilities. It was said that the "Muslim north" was waging a war on the "Christian south" and vice versa. This popular belief was fueled by certain religious extremists on both sides, despite the fact that the leaders of the government and of the rebellion were almost all Christians.[44] Sant'Egidio endeavored to oppose such manipulation, by gathering together Catholic bishops[45], the imam of Abidjan and other key Muslim figures, and leaders of Protestant faiths and of "independent" churches, such as the Harrists, on several occasions both in Ivory Coast and abroad. Out of these initiatives stemmed joint statements in support of peace and a commitment not to allow themselves to become involved in the war propaganda. Today it can be said that religion did not get caught up in the conflict, nor was it exploited for military ends.

After the meetings in Lomé, it was Paris' turn to host talks. The French were involved on the ground with their troops, which put them in a very awkward position. France needed to remain absolutely impartial in order to avoid becoming entangled. But this balancing act satisfied neither the loyalists nor the rebels, who sought by various devices, and by sparking ongoing controversy in the press, to bring the former colonial power round to their side. President Chirac thus decided to propose a political initiative, aimed at avoiding any dangerous standoff. Various options for peace talks were considered. Should only the warring parties be invited to participate, or should the political parties be involved as well? What about civil and traditional society? And should meetings be open or held behind closed doors?

The advice of the Community of Sant'Egidio was also sought by the French President's Advisor on Africa, the Elysée's so-called *Monsieur Afrique*.[46] In the end, a simple model was chosen: only the seven most representative parties, together with the three rebel movements, would come to France.[47] The government in Abidjan was not directly invited, but through a contrivance would be represented by Prime Minister Affi N'Guessan, who also happened to be the Secretary-General of the FPI. In this way, Gbagbo – who was averse to being put on the same footing as the rebels – would save face.

The talks took place behind closed doors at the French national rugby training center, in Linas-Marcoussis outside Paris, away from prying eyes. Chosen to chair the proceedings was a personal friend of Chirac, Pierre Mazeaud, a member of the Constitutional Council and a former Minister. The non-Ivorian invitees were: the EU, the International Committee of the Red Cross, the Community of Sant'Egidio[48], and La Francophonie. Pan-African institutions were represented by a former African President, whilst for the UN, Kofi Annan's Special Representative for West Africa was present.

Once the guests arrived in Marcoussis, on January 15, the doors were closed. No one would be allowed to leave until an agreement had been reached. It was like a form of communal seclusion, with no outside contact. Unexpectedly, during the opening session, Mazeaud announced that President Chirac had invited various heads of State for an international summit on Ivory Coast to be held in Paris on January 25, 2003. There were therefore nine days available in which to wrap up proceedings. The French sought by this means to put pressure on the Ivorians. However, they risked falling into a trap. Indeed, the Ivorians immediately realized that France had put itself into a position of having to produce a result to hold up to the international community. As a consequence, the negotiations would suffer.

In fact, the experience of various peace processes has demonstrated that when mediators impose very strict deadlines, they rob the proceedings of an invaluable asset: that of the parties being made responsible for the process. A mediator or facilitator chairs the meetings in order to ensure that the negotiations get off to a good start, but the real ownership of the process should be left to the parties. If the latter realize that the mediator has an interest (for instance, in obtaining a result at all costs or concluding by a certain date), they will more readily avoid taking responsibility and end up having greater misgivings over any eventual outcomes. This does not alter the fact that there are times when it is useful to apply pressure to indecisive parties or in order to overcome an impasse. It is better, however, for that pressure not to come from the mediators, who should never be under any constraints as regards the time frame and outcomes of talks, and should have all the time necessary at their disposal.

International negotiations often fail because rivalry between mediators is compounded by haste and an overriding need to succeed, unwittingly fueled by pressure from public opinion. Those who should be facilitating the dialogue become hostages to their own impatience for success and introduce an extraneous disruptive element into the proceedings which the parties involved will certainly not fail to exploit.

During those nine intensive days of work marked by meetings that went till late and extensive debate, many of the reasons for the Ivorian crisis were raised for discussion. At Marcoussis, all the unresolved issues such as citizenship and legal inconsistencies were revisited. The rebels were more sure of themselves and determined to get their own back on both Gbagbo's FPI and Ouattara's RDR. By inviting the rebels, the French had cleared the way for them to become major players. For the hawks in the government delegation, such as the Speaker of the National Assembly Mamadou Koulibaly, this was a humiliation at the hands of a former colonial master.[49]

Soro and his associates wholeheartedly embraced the "killjoy" role with which they had burst onto an Ivorian political scene they saw as both tired and stagnant. Nor did they hold Ouattara in any particular regard, accusing him of having become "bourgeoisified" and of engaging in political machination. By now, they saw themselves as the true representatives of the northern cause. Ouattara, who had arrived in Marcoussis very confident, believing that his opponent was Gbagbo, was surprised and concerned by the independence of thought of the young rebel leaders and their self-assurance.

Moreover, the RDR leader was not convinced that Gbagbo would accept any real negotiations. Bédié's PDCI was hamstrung by the grievances of its leader, who was also present at Marcoussis. Bitter and aloof, Bédié had not moved on from December 1999, and quietly blamed the French for not having supported him sufficiently. His delegation was made up of old PDCI worthies who were not up to the caliber of the others present. For its part, Gbagbo's FPI delegation, which came under fire from all quarters, was the one in the most difficult position and opted for a reticent and seemingly conciliatory attitude, except for Koulibaly, who challenged the conduct of his delegation and soon abandoned the proceedings in protest.[50] He would, however, be the only one to do so. The smaller parties, on the other hand, acted as useful buffers, especially when difficulties arose.

What was striking about the delegates present was the generational divide that separated the old Ivory Coast from the new. The rebels and the FPI representatives were younger, all coming from similar backgrounds of opposition to Houphouët-Boigny. The same could not be said for the PDCI or even the RDR. Soro had an elaborate vision for the country and his demands were not limited to the interests of his men. The rebels wanted a new more democratic and modern Ivory Coast. They maintained that Gbagbo had betrayed this dream and that power had corrupted him. Ouattara too was seen as being past his shelf life.

During those long days at Marcoussis, there were numerous opportunities for dialogue and exchange. Mazeaud frequently asked the Sant'Egidio delegation to talk to one or other of the Ivorian contingents, to sound out their mood or help moderate their tone. There were a multitude of issues, the most thorny of which were the conditions governing eligibility for the presidency, with the question of whether Ouattara himself might in the end be eligible still pending. The RDR leader was dogged in his defense, especially as regards the paragraph inimical to himself, which required that a candidate for presidential election "must not have availed himself of another nationality".

As it happened, certain official records apparently showed that Ouattara had in the past been appointed to a senior position at the West African Central Bank for Burkina Faso. It also seemed that he had occasionally made use of a Burkinabe passport. The situation was unclear and discussions regarding how the words "availed himself of" should be interpreted were heated.

The Community of Sant'Egidio delegation was entrusted with the drafting of a sensitive section of the Linas-Marcoussis Agreement: that dealing with human rights and violations thereof, including the summary executions carried out in the years preceding the conflict. There were many unexplained incidents, and almost all the Ivorian players involved in the roundtable had something to hide. This emerged clearly in conversations with the rebels, but there was also talk of "death squads" that ran amok at night in Abidjan at the bidding of the loyalists.

The discussion was tense. Many called for the involvement of the International Criminal Court, but only in respect of others' actions. In the end, a moderate position prevailed: with acts committed in the course of war covered by an amnesty, the national unity government would determine by consensus which serious crimes should be referred to the national and international justice systems. A human rights commission would be set up to establish and report on the facts of cases and make recommendations to the government. The decision on this point was therefore a political one, with the parties agreeing that it was not appropriate to use the international justice system as a weapon against their opponents, in part because there was a risk that this might backfire on them. In any peace negotiations, the issue of justice and the violation of human rights is a delicate one. There are legitimate expectations that justice should be done and that impunity must be curbed, especially as regards civilian victims. However, providing for a recourse to justice, whether at the national or international level, can derail negotiations if the parties feel that by signing any eventual agreement they will be sealing their own fate. This always presents a very complex dilemma, as achieving peace after a conflict requires that the horrors of war be reckoned with but also that they be permanently relegated to the past.

Another arduous phase of the talks involved discussions over the question of *ivoirité*, that is, regarding who could call themselves citizens of Ivory Coast. The delegations lashed out at Bédié, the erstwhile architect of the concept. Significantly, the FPI representatives remained silent. Towards the end, when substantial agreement seemed to have been reached, particularly on Article 35 of the Constitution establishing the conditions governing eligibility for presidential candidacy, the problem of transition was addressed. It was at this point that the negotiations were at their most animated.

The rebels wanted Gbagbo to go immediately, claiming his presidency was illegitimate. Obviously, the FPI would hear none of it. Ouattara sided with Soro but without much conviction. Indeed, he knew that the French could not come away from Marcoussis with an agreement that excluded Gbagbo. Hence, the elections could not be held within six months as the rebels wanted. However, the *quid pro quo* was that the key ministerial posts of Defense and the Interior would go to Soro and his men, whilst Gbagbo would stay on as President. As far as the rebels were concerned, this was merely a temporary reprieve, though it was already clear that the other side would contrive to stay in power till at least the natural expiry of its term in 2005. In reality, the FPI felt that power had been violently wrested from it. Indeed, the hasty departure of the Speaker of the National Assembly did not bode well: the laws of the national unity government still had to pass through parliament, as required by the Constitution. It was for this reason that Ouattara unsuccessfully requested that the Constitution be suspended.

The final document was signed at 1.30am on January 24. The next day, everyone was expected at a Foreign Ministry venue in Avenue Kléber, for a ceremony which would be attended by eleven heads of State[51], Kofi Annan, Romano Prodi as the then President of the EU Commission, and the Secretaries-General of La Francophonie, the African Union and ECOWAS. In the early morning of the 25th, last-minute changes were still being made to the ministerial line-up. Gbagbo, who had in the meantime arrived from Abidjan, rejected Henriette Diabaté, Secretary-General of the RDR, as Prime Minister, and accepted in her stead Seydou Diarra, a longstanding diplomat of northern origin who had previously held the prime ministership and had headed the Reconciliation Forum.

On January 25, the atmosphere around the large circular international conference table appeared serene. Chirac did the honors and spoke of a "new republican pact" for Ivory Coast. Beside him sat a seemingly relaxed Gbagbo, who stated: "You don't negotiate when you've won a war. But I haven't won the war, and we'll honor the Agreement that's been signed". In closing, he thanked everyone and added: "And I haven't forgotten my close friends from Sant'Egidio, who've always been there for us when there's been a crisis". Opposite him was Andrea Riccardi, the founder of Sant'Egidio, invited by the French to sit at the table with the leaders. One after the other, the authorities present proclaimed that the Agreement reached was a sound one and offered their endorsement.

However, certain warning signs foreshadowed that the implementation of the Marcoussis Agreement would not be trouble-free, nor would life for the fledgling reconciliation government be easy. To start with, it was President Chirac who publicly announced the name of the future Prime Minister during the session. This came across as a mark of disrespect towards a sovereign State. In addition, on reading the Agreement, the loyalist hawks who had remained in Abidjan began to protest. How could they accept rebels as Ministers for Defense and the Interior? In reality, this was intended as a form of insurance for Soro, but it did not meet with approval. On January 26, while the international conference was still in progress, the first reports came through that the French consulate and a French lycée in Ivory Coast had been set on fire by a mob of "patriots". Meanwhile, Gbagbo was already on a flight back to Abidjan.

Marcoussis not enough

The political period which followed Marcoussis was to be both protracted and confused. The new reconciliation government was only formed after further exhausting talks. The Defense and Interior ministerial posts remained vacant for months. On the plus side, at least the rebel candidates for government posts, including Soro himself, finally arrived in Abidjan. In order to support the implementation of the Marcoussis Agreement, which at least had the merit of setting down in black and white some of the thornier and more pressing issues facing Ivory Coast, many African States took turns in holding discussions with the parties. France's intensive efforts in this regard should also be noted.

In practice, the Marcoussis Agreement relied on the willingness of the parties to work together, as embodied in the reconciliation government led by Diarra. However, certain obstacles would not be surmounted until the Ouagadougou Agreement of 2007. In particular, there was the question of disarmament, which Gbagbo wanted (as he reiterated in every meeting) to take place before the administration was redeployed and preparations were made for the elections, which involved conducting a new census of the population.

The rebels resisted, knowing that this would deprive them of their only trump card. Soro needed to demonstrate that he could restore dignity to the north, which could only happen by immediately setting in train the delicate process of revising the electoral rolls. Months were spent in this to-ing and fro-ing, which at times almost reached breaking-point. Meanwhile, the government churned out the "Marcoussis laws" (the new electoral code, and new laws on citizenship, land tenure, and so on). These, however, regularly became hostage to a hostile parliament, where the Speaker Mamadou

Koulibaly, who had walked out in France, ruled the roost. What with amendments, delays and postponements, time passed and the standoff persisted.

It was the hour of the extremists, with mobs often called to the streets in violent demonstrations that increasingly targeted the French, their military base and their embassy. Gbagbo skillfully maneuvered between the hardliners in his party and the international community, which sought to convince him to implement the Agreement. But the situation was no better in the north, where it was more radical officials who held sway.

Many African leaders took it upon themselves to try and break the impasse. In Accra, Ghana, in March 2003, the issue of the Defense and Interior ministries was resolved, with the rebels dropping their demands for them in exchange for other posts. Prime Minister Diarra was delegated certain powers[52], though it was not until the Agreement of July 2004[53] that the extent of those powers was fleshed out. Meanwhile, the UN sent in peacekeepers to support the French interposition force. A representative of Kofi Annan was installed in Abidjan with hundreds of international officials to monitor implementation of the Marcoussis Agreement, which, despite the huge international effort, did not move forward. The parties were still at loggerheads.

Gbagbo insisted on disarmament and Soro demanded that the process of identifying the population commence. Several attempts at mediation on this key point by African heads of State failed.[54] Tensions mounted in the fall, with several incidents taking place in the buffer zone between the north and south, until early November 2004, when the loyalists unleashed a general offensive with an air raid on Bouaké. At first, the UN and French forces did not respond to the transit of loyalist troops, provoking a furious reaction from Soro and his men.

Two days after the launch of the offensive, a serious incident, the reasons for which were never ascertained, resulted in the death of nine French soldiers, stationed in the rebel capital, who were hit during an airstrike attributed to loyalist forces, provoking an angered response from Paris. Chirac ordered the shooting down and ground destruction of the entire Ivorian air force fleet. The loyalist offensive had failed. President Gbagbo called on the people to react to what he called a violation of national sovereignty. In Abidjan, "patriots" began hunting for Europeans. The French troops were ordered to spread out through the major roads of the capital and to occupy the country's airports. During those hours in Abidjan, mobs clashed with French tanks. Paris ordered the evacuation of its citizens, long present in the country in their thousands.[55]

The clock seemed to have been turned back to the beginning of the conflict. The country was a powder keg, with resentment on both sides running high.

In those hours of tension, the African Union called on Thabo Mbeki to lead a further attempt at mediation. The South African leader arrived in Abidjan a few days later. His forthright and resolute manner, without intermediaries or formalities, met with a certain receptiveness on both sides. The key players in the crisis were aware of having come close to disaster. Mbeki shuttled back and forth between Abidjan and Bouaké. In December, he proposed a road map for the resumption of dialogue. A summit was convened for April 2005 to be held in Pretoria. This time, the military leaders of the two sides were invited to meet directly and to formulate a plan for joint disarmament. After months of diplomatic efforts, the tension seemed to die down.

The international community took the opportunity to force President Gbagbo's hand, all the more so given the impending expiration of his term in October 2005. This was a mistake. Even Mbeki, who had done well in the early stages of the mediation, chose to adopt a top-down approach, to everyone's chagrin. The mediation team did not give itself enough time to win over the parties. In peace processes, patience is a crucial tool in the hands of mediators: any sudden surge in pace can have adverse effects. It is always necessary to allow time to tune in to the reasons for a crisis. Indeed, each party to a conflict believes it has good grounds for its position, which need to be patiently taken into consideration. However, the events of November 2004 had made the international community anxious to bring the Ivorian situation to a rapid close.

In December, Gbagbo's term was extended via UN Resolution 1721, in exchange for the appointment of a new

Prime Minister in place of the circumspect Diarra. France pushed for the appointment of a strong Prime Minister, capable of reining in Gbagbo and bringing the rebels into line. The memory of the events of November had left its mark and clouded judgments somewhat. These measures, which were backed by strong pressure, would produce the opposite effect. The new Prime Minister, the brilliant economist Charles Konan Banny[56], feeling himself supported by the international community and particularly by France, ended up underestimating the two sides with the result of pushing them closer together. Although a man of great ability, Konan Banny irritated Gbagbo by behaving as if he were the leader of the country. At the same time, he annoyed Soro and the other rebel leaders, who felt they were being treated like upstarts.

The fact of the matter was that Konan Banny was propped up by political parties such as the PDCI (of which he was a member) and the RDR. Meanwhile, the international community issued final warnings to the rebels, but particularly to the President. As usually happens in such cases, the real players in the crisis allowed Konan Banny to get on with his job, but at the same time secretly sabotaged everything he tried to accomplish. Simply spreading reports of his presidential ambitions was enough to put paid to even the best of intentions. It was obvious that without real ownership of the process by the parties to the dispute, any solution would prove ineffective. Humiliating them, or worse still, trying to exclude them, even if in the name of civil society and peace, was an act of naivety. The attempt at Marcoussis to foist rebel ministers in key posts on the loyalists had previously led to the impasse that followed. Now it was actually sought to disempower both the key protagonists to the conflict by externally accelerating the peace process but Gbagbo and Soro had it within their power to derail any solution that tried to bypass them.

The Konan Banny period was one in which the President's party and the rebels felt less involved in decisions, whilst, in contrast, the other parties hoped to gain some say. But it was an illusion: the dates fixed for the commencement of disarmament, the identification of the respective populations and the elections themselves passed one after the other with nothing done. Barely a year after his investiture, Konan

Banny, perceived by both the warring parties as an interloper, found himself stranded.

Not surprisingly, in December 2006, in the wake of the underhand opposition against the Prime Minister that had been forced upon him, President Gbagbo, proposed a so-called "Direct Dialogue" with the rebels, to the exclusion of third parties and, hence, of the entire international community. The idea put Soro in an awkward position. If he refused, he would have to bear responsibility for the ultimate failure of the peace process. Yet if he accepted, what guarantees would he have against being taken in by the shrewd President? Soro took his time and sought advice. At this point, Gbagbo made a second proposal, one that was too good to refuse: there would be a facilitator in the person of the leader of Burkina Faso, Blaise Compaoré – the very man who had been accused by the loyalists of supporting the guerrillas[57]. Gbagbo also suggested that the Direct Dialogue be held in the Burkinabe capital.[58]

How could such an offer be passed up? Embarking on the Direct Dialogue also represented a rejection of the international community, which had mapped out the various stages of the post-Marcoussis period. For Gbagbo and Soro, it had become preferable to negotiate directly with the enemy, than to carry on with exhausting rounds of meetings and with resolutions that would remain unimplemented.

Agreement in Ouagadougou

The Direct Dialogue brought the parties face-to-face, away from the other political parties. Although Ouattara and Bédié were mortified by this, they lacked the clout to do anything to prevent it. In addition, the Direct Dialogue had "facilitators" rather than "mediators". Compaoré himself attached great importance to the difference: it was the parties who had real ownership of these new talks, and they would be entirely responsible for their success or failure. Campaoré called on the Community of Sant'Egidio, which during the post-Marcoussis period had maintained contact with the various players in the Ivorian crisis, to participate in the Direct Dialogue also in the capacity of a facilitator.[59]

The Direct Dialogue was in line with Sant'Egidio's approach: small-scale meetings, involving solely the two parties to the conflict, with no third parties, time restrictions, or imposed dictates of any kind. It was necessary for the loyalists and rebels to take responsibility for the negotiations without seeking to play one mediator off against another, as had happened in 2004 and 2005. Even the press was kept at bay until the day of the signing. During the course of February 2007, the talks in Ouagadougou took place without intermediaries and without the agendas and ambitions of others getting in the way. Everything was put back on the table and realistic solutions to concrete problems were sought. On March 4, the Political Agreement aimed at reconciling and restoring peace to Ivory Coast was finally signed.

The success of Ouagadougou stemmed from the fact that the negotiations were entirely instigated and shaped by the two parties in dispute. All the time needed was taken and the date for signature was decided only after the talks had played out. In a rare occurrence for international meetings, nothing was leaked right up to the last day, despite discussions having been heated. Finally, solutions were sought that were not only mutually agreed but also practical and feasible.

In Ouagadougou, the more hotly-debated issues were not new: identification of the population, the elections, and the army. The first two were considered together, and an expedited identification procedure was adopted based on the old electoral roll dating back to 2000 (the one used when Gbagbo was elected and prepared during Houphouët-Boigny's time), which would not only serve as a common database for the issuance of voter registration cards but also of identity cards. Being listed on that roll was sufficient to give rise to an entitlement to the latter. The rebels had hitherto supported the international community's proposal of starting from scratch and conducting a new census of the entire population. However, the undertaking had proved impossible in practice, due to the state of the various registry offices.

The use of the 2000 electoral roll had previously been requested by Gbagbo, but the international community had always considered this roll to be incomplete and unusable. In actual fact, it contained the only documented records available and was thus the only realistic starting point. The innovation introduced by the Ouagadougou Agreement was that all those listed on the 2000 roll, who numbered more than 5 million people, would also automatically receive an identity card. Missing from the roll were another 3 or 4 million potentially eligible voters, including those who, in 2000, were considered foreigners or were not yet 18.

In exchange for agreeing to the use of the electoral roll requested by Gbagbo, the rebels obtained that all those not on the roll would be able to register at a later stage, by participating in mobile court hearings that could issue them with a substitute birth certificate. That document would enable them to register on the roll and thus also entitle them to an identity card. Gbagbo had always been opposed to the mobile courts, which were deemed unreliable by his advisors, even though the proper conduct of their hearings depended on special conditions being met (including reliance on credible witnesses, the presence of representatives of all the political parties, and appointment of mobile judges by mutual agreement of the parties to the proceedings).

At any rate, the rebels accepted the expedited identification process (based on the 2000 electoral roll) in exchange for the assurance that those not on the roll would be identified at a later date. Essentially, Gbagbo gave in on the identification of "non-natives", but was now able to call early elections, which he had strong chances of winning. Yet it was also a victory for the New Forces, the name under which the various rebel factions had now united. Indeed, the rebels could pride themselves on having resolved the matter of identification. Up till that point, the issue had been closely bound up with the electoral question (because of the Ouattara controversy).

After the Ouagadougou Agreement, this was no longer the case: identification and elections would be separate issues. As President Compaoré would later observe: "If Ivorians had to choose between having a valid identity card and a voter registration card, they would for the most part choose the former".[60]

The discussions regarding the army essentially revolved around one issue, namely: whether disarmament should take place before or after the identification process. Gbagbo wanted immediate disarmament, whilst the rebels absolutely refused. This is a classic question that comes up time and again in peace negotiations and goes to the heart of a key issue: disarmament deprives the rebel party of the only bargaining chip at its disposal. For these reasons, the problem was resolved by sidestepping the issue of disarmament and opting for merging or integrating the two armed forces. This approach reassured everybody.

The youngest fighters, those who enlisted after the start of the war, would instead join the Civic Service, a sort of guidance and job training service, so that they could be reintegrated into the education system or the workplace. There were around 20,000 such young people, between rebels and Gbagbo's militia fighters. Some of them, especially in the north, were underage. In order to begin merging the different forces, it was decided to form joint units with a single integrated command structure. Other minor contentious issues concerning the media, the financing of the peace process, and the dismantling of the buffer zone were resolved on the basis of various compromises.

During the course of the dialogue, away from outside influences, the two belligerents had the opportunity to build mutual trust. Herein lies the facilitator's role, which does merely consist of proposing fair solutions. At the beginning of the talks, there was a tense atmosphere, though this gradually eased as the parties came to realize that neither of them would be forced into decisions which they intended to take their time to think through. A case in point was the question of the transitional government that would be tasked with implementing the Agreement.

In a bold move, Gbagbo told Soro that he was willing to give him the post of Prime Minister, meaning that the two enemies would have to work together. Initially, Soro was wary. He was advised by the facilitators not to decide under pressure. The general Agreement could still be signed and Soro could take all the time he needed to think it over. A month after the signing, Soro accepted and Konan Banny was forced to resign. The deadlock was broken and Soro gained credibility by becoming the key interlocutor with

Gbagbo. It could be said that the Agreement was signed because the two belligerents took each other seriously and chose to take responsibility for putting an end to the crisis, without, however, totally excluding other parties (who were not invited to Ouagadougou) from playing a role.[61]

Despite the success of Ouagadougou, the road ahead still has its challenges. There are those who have not looked favorably on the end of the war, especially those that gained from it. The attack on June 29, 2007 on the plane carrying Prime Minister Soro, who escaped by a miracle, is proof of the fragile nature of the balances struck.[62] The assault was aimed at derailing the arms destruction ceremony scheduled to take place on July 1 in Bouaké, which was also to be attended by President Gbagbo. Yet despite the upheaval of those frantic moments and the flurry of speculations and suspicions regarding the incident, the ceremony was only postponed.

Thus, on July 30, 2007, President Gbagbo entered the rebel zone for the first time since the war had begun. A large festive crowd of northern Ivorians was there to welcome him. Also present at Bouaké Stadium, which was filled to overflowing, were several African Presidents and the leader of Burkina Faso, Blaise Compaoré. Soro did the honors and, together with Gbagbo, lit the great "flame of peace", to which many weapons were consigned for destruction. Soldiers from both sides stood shoulder-to-shoulder. Relegated to the role of extras, Ouattara and Bédié refused to participate, but the people were happy and saw an end in sight to the country's division.

The Community of Sant'Egidio has continued its efforts to stabilize the outcomes achieved with the signing of the Agreement.[63] It participates in the Evaluation and Monitoring Committee, whose meetings are held in Ouagadougou. During 2008, as the public administration was gradually redeployed, including in the rebel zone, several complementary agreements were signed by the parties, concerning military matters in particular. Towards the end of the year, the progress made in the process of identifying the population, though quite significant, was not such as to permit elections to be held by December as originally planned. It was therefore agreed that the new target date should be November 2009.

[1] A Special Advisor to the President on security matters, Tagro, later a Minister, was a trusted confidante of President Gbagbo.

[2] This was comprised of Burkina Faso's Security Minister, Djibril Bassolé, the Legal Advisor to the President of Burkina Faso, Vincent Zakané, and Mario Giro of the Community of Sant'Egidio.

[3] The work carried out jointly by Burkina Faso authorities and the Community of Sant'Egidio during the long period of instability in Togo had also fostered goodwill. Burkinabe authorities trusted Sant'Egidio and appreciated its discreet, patient and collaborative approach to peace negotiations.

[4] Which will probably be held in 2009.

[5] The internal borders between the colonies (particularly to the north of the southern plains) only became fixed in 1947, just thirteen years before independence. The division between Upper Volta and Ivory Coast is thus recent, and many problems that have emerged in the last few years stem from that not-too-distant period. Cf. J. Tokpa, *Côte d'Ivoire, l'immigration des Voltaïques*, Abidjan 2006.

[6] In 1963, Houphouët-Boigny proposed a law on "dual nationality" for citizens of member countries of the Council of the *Entente* (Ivory Coast, Dahomey – later known as Benin, Niger, and Upper Volta – now Burkina Faso). Houphouët-Boigny's plan was ambitious: "I would like to convey our warmest regards", said the President, "to all our brothers and sisters who are not natives of Ivory Coast: Ghanaians, Malians, Upper Voltans, Senegalese, Nigerians, and others (...) We confirm that they are welcome here and that, in the coming months, we will be engaging in talks with the leaders of their respective countries with a view to granting them dual nationality, which will enable them, in keeping with the African unity we are endeavoring to create and in recognition of their dignity and pride in the nation, to participate on the same footing as native Ivorians in the harmonious development of Ivory Coast, which embraces them with open arms". However, in 1966, the National Assembly conclusively rejected the proposal.

[7] In Ivorian political-speak, the term used is "allogènes" (or "non-natives").

[8] The President's PDCI-RDA party.

[9] This was the period in which Malaysia, along with Singapore, focused attention on the "Asian values" discourse.

[10] Ouattara was the Governor of the Central Bank of West African States. In relation to Ouattara's career, see C. I. Bacongo, *Alassane Dramane Ouattara, une vie singulière*, Abidjan 2007.

[11] Mitterrand used the France-Africa Summit in La Baule in June 1990 to call for an end to one-party regimes.

[12] "A wind from the East [namely, eastern Europe] is stirring the coconut palms".

[13] In respect of Laurent Gbagbo and his political views, see: L. Gbagbo, *Côte*

d'Ivoire, pour une alternative démocratique, Paris 1983; L. Gbagbo, *Agir pour les libertés*, Paris 1991; V. Gnakalé, *Laurent Gbagbo pour l'avenir de la Côte d'Ivoire*, Paris 2006; and E. Duhy, *Le pouvoir est un service, le cas de Laurent Gbagbo*, Paris 2006.

[14] The FPI was conferred legal status in April 1990. For the FPI's manifesto, cf. *Front Populaire Ivoirien, Gouverner autrement la Côte d'Ivoire*, Paris 2000.

[15] It was actually during a Socialist International meeting on the Algerian crisis, in Rome in 1995, that Gbagbo came into contact with members of the Community of Sant'Egidio.

[16] Who would in fact unilaterally devalue it shortly after his death and even before his funeral.

[17] In the parliamentary elections of November 1990, the FPI also succeeded in winning 9 seats in the National Assembly.

[18] Although neither public offices nor foreign embassies were ever transferred there.

[19] Article 21 of the Constitution provided for the Speaker of the Assembly to act as interim President.

[20] On the problems associated with the succession to Houphouët-Boigny's presidency, see A. Ellenbogen, *La succession d'Houphouët-Boigny, entre tribalisme et démocratie*, Paris 2002.

[21] The RDR formed as a split in the PDCI, fomented by those dissatisfied with Bédié's politics.

[22] Resurrecting an old idea from 1974, Bédié had the PDCI congress adopt the doctrine in August 1995.

[23] The CURDIPHE, or Cellule Universitaire de Recherche et de Diffusion des Idées et Actions Politiques du Président Henri Konan Bédié. In respect of the concept of *ivoirité*, see: R. L. Boa Thiémélé, *L'Ivoirité entre culture et politique*, Paris 2003; and *Côte d'Ivoire, la tentation ethnonationaliste* in "Politique Africaine", No. 78, pp. 5-156, June 2000.

[24] Cf. Henri Konan Bédié, *Les chemins de ma vie*, Paris 1999.

[25] Something similar happened recently in Kenya. In Africa, land is generally unsalable and non-transferable, considered the inalienable property of the indigenous ethnic group. This leads to all kinds of conflicts and manipulations.

[26] The FPI had, on that occasion, formed a joint ticket with the RDR, the so-called Front Republicain.

[27] The incident involved soldiers returning from a peacekeeping mission in the Central African Republic who wanted to be paid.

[28] A man from the west of the country who had been pensioned off early by Bédié and was called out of retirement by the coup officials.

[29] As regards this period, see M. Le Pape & C. Vidal (eds.), *Côte d'Ivoire, l'année terrible 1999-2000*, Paris 2002.

[30] Now, in order to become President, it was necessary to be Ivorian by birth and to have both a mother "and" father of Ivorian origin. This was the famous Article 35 of the Constitution, which was rejigged on several occasions.

[31] These days, Ivory Coast has an output exceeding 60,000 barrels a day and is on its way to becoming a medium-sized oil-producing country.

[32] In relation to the Ivorian crisis in general as well as the war, see: A. R. Anahoua, *La crise du systhème ivoirien*, Paris 2005; Le Toubabou, *Le Millefeuille ivoirien*, Paris 2005; T. Koffi, *Côte d'Ivoire, l'agonie du jardin*, Abidjan, 2006; K. G. Kouakou, *Le peuple n'aime pas le peuple, la Côte d'Ivoire dans la guerre civile*, Mayenne 2006; C. Bouquet, *Géopolitique de la Côte d'Ivoire*, Paris 2005;

P. Duval, *Fantômes d'ivoire*, Monaco 2003; and *La Côte Ivoire en guerre*, in "Politique Africaine", No. 89, March 2003, pp. 5-126.

[33] See A. Du Parge, *Parmi les rebelles*, Paris 2003.

[34] For background on his career, see G. Soro, *Pourquoi je suis devenu un rebelle*, Saint-Armand-Montrond 2005.

[35] This was a document calling for greater autonomy for northern Ivory Coast, distributed in 1995 by a group of intellectuals of northern origin.

[36] For a loyalist reading of the war, see G. G. Hilaire, *Le rempart, attaque terroriste contre la Côte Ivoire*, Abidjan, 2004; for a northern interpretation, see M. Bandaman, *Côte Ivoire, chronique d'une guerre annoncée*, Abidjan 2004.

[37] Eyadéma, a former noncommissioned officer in the French colonial army who served in the Indochina campaign, had been in power since 1967, following the military coup of 1963 against the elected President Olympio. The latter was unpopular with the French, who accepted the coup against him. Eyadéma ruled his small country with an iron fist.

[38] The delegation comprised Fabio Riccardi and Mario Giro.

[39] This was the President of the Economic and Social Council, Laurent Dona Fologo.

[40] Louis Dacoury-Tabley was from the south of the country and came from a distinguished family. He was the former right-hand man of Gbagbo, with whom he had fallen out several years before.

[41] Despite declaring he was not involved in the rebellion, Ouattara was targeted by the crowds and had to flee to Paris. His house was set on fire by patriots.

[42] See the account of one of the leaders of the "Patriots": C. Blé Goudé, *Crise ivoirienne, ma part de verité*, Abidjan 2006.

[43] Schools of Peace provide an after-school program for children in difficulty. They represent one of the most extensive services for the poor provided by Sant'Egidio communities around the world, involving tens of thousands of children in slums, shanty towns and working-class neighborhoods. In poorer countries, Schools of Peace often provide the only form of schooling received by children, who do not attend regular classes.

[44] Gbagbo, originally a Catholic, is now a practicing member of a Protestant church, as is his wife Simone. His closest entourage has included many Christians, as well as a few practicing Muslims, such as the Deputy Chief of Staff and Special Advisor Sarata Touré, responsible for handling US relations. Soro is a practicing Catholic, whilst Dacoury-Tabley is the brother of the Catholic Bishop of Grand-Bassam in the south.

[45] Cf. Bernard Cardinal Agré, *Témoin de son temps*, Abidjan 2006.

[46] This was the Ambassador Michel de Bonnecorse.

[47] Present at Marcoussis were delegations of the PDCI (headed by Konan Bédié), the RDR (led by Ouattara and Henriette Diabaté), the FPI (led by Affi N'Guessan and the Parliamentary Speaker, Mamadou Koulibaly), the UDPCI, the PIT, the UDCY and the MFA, together with delegations from the three guerrilla movements: the MPCI, the MJP, and the MPIGO. Each delegation consisted of two or three people.

[48] Sant'Egidio's delegation comprised Hilde Kieboom and Mario Giro.

[49] M. Koulibaly, *Les servitudes du pacte colonial*, Abidjan 2005.

50 Koulibaly wanted the role of parliament to be taken into account but he was not heeded. He left Marcoussis on January 20 and immediately returned to Abidjan. Back in Ivory Coast, he would go on to organize parliamentary resistance against the "Marcoussis laws", that is, the laws intended to enact the

terms of the Marcoussis Agreement as legislation, to the point of thwarting their provisions on several occasions.

[51] Attending in addition to Chirac were Toumani Touré for Mali, Kufuor for Ghana, Taylor for Liberia, Biya for Cameroon, Bongo for Gabon, Mbeki for South Africa, Wade for Senegal, Compaoré for Burkina Faso, Kérékou for Benin and Pires for Cape Verde.

[52] Ivory Coast is a presidential republic in which the head of State is also the head of the executive.

[53] An Agreement known as Accra III.

[54] In addition to attempts by Ghana's Kufuor, efforts were also made by the leaders of Nigeria (Obasanjo), Senegal (Wade) and other countries.

[55] Of the approximately 18,000 French people in the country, 10,000 were evacuated. In this regard, see *La crise franco-ivoirienne de 2004* in "Africa" No. 1, March 2006, pp. 66-93.

[56] Who up till then had been Governor of the Central Bank of West African States.

[57] In his capacity as then President of ECOWAS, even Compaoré was not in a position to refuse.

[58] Where, during this period, Soro often withdrew, to a house placed at his disposal by Compaoré himself.

[59] Compaoré was aware of the kind of personal relationship that Sant'Egidio had with every one of the key players. Indeed, all of them, including Ouattara and Bédié, maintained that it would be useful for the Community to be present at the Direct Dialogue. Each of them would later thank the Community, officially, personally, publicly or through their media outlets. Compaoré would in the end observe: "You have an ability to maintain even-handed personal relationships that help defuse stalemate situations, and which were of great assistance to us".

[60] It should be noted that 65% of Ivorians had no identity card, and many did not even have a birth certificate or proof of nationality.

[61] Indeed, these parties obtained positions within the government.

[62] There have already been three attempts to assassinate Soro. On June 20, at Bouaké airport, gunmen fired three rockets at a government plane which had just landed with Soro onboard. Several of his aides were killed, though he emerged miraculously unscathed. It has not been determined who was responsible for ordering and carrying out the attack.

[63] The key players in Ivory Coast's crisis appreciate Sant'Egidio's approach and method, and particularly its friendship. In his speech to the nation a few days after the signing, President Gbagbo publicly thanked the Community of Sant'Egidio, as he would again in a television appearance on August 7, the national holiday celebrating the country's independence.

Health Diplomacy in the Battle against AIDS

AIDS and DREAM

95% adherence to therapy: a figure very close to if not higher than that found in the West
88,000 patients assisted over the years (including 19,000 children)
1,000,000 people that have benefited from the program in the form of treatment, nutritional support, health education, social work, and prevention courses in the workplace
10,500 children born without HIV under the vertical transmission prevention program
52,000 people on antiretroviral therapy
3,600 doctors, nurses, biologists, lab technicians, center coordinators and IT experts trained via 14 courses held between 2002-2008
600 euro: the total annual cost per patient being treated with antiretroviral drugs
25,000,000 people living with HIV/AIDS in sub-Saharan Africa

Health Diplomacy in the Battle against AIDS

Leonardo Palombi

This is the story of a human, scientific and emotional venture involving Europe and Africa. It begins in the late 1990s with the fact that, in Africa, there was no treatment for HIV/AIDS, whilst close by, across the Mediterranean and the Atlantic Ocean, so-called "triple therapy" had by then alleviated much of the terror accompanying the epidemic and already offered dignified prospects for survival. A few hours away by plane from Europe, however, people were dying dehydrated, desperate and abandoned, from a disease whose containment was already in hand elsewhere.

Nor did the International Conference on AIDS held in Durban in 2000 offer any glimmers of hope for the treatment of Africans living with HIV/AIDS. Millions on the continent lost their lives, especially amongst the younger generations, decimating professional groups such as teachers, nurses, and even doctors – the very people who represented the future and prospects for development. The international community was slow to grasp the full extent of the tragedy. Official documents setting out guidelines for national health plans, and agreements proposed by large international agencies and by major donors, spoke only of "prevention" of the AIDS pandemic for Africa, as if there had ever been a real epidemic fought solely on the basis of prevention in modern times. Had there been a vaccine, this would have represented a viable option with greater chances of success, but there was no vaccine yet.

Hence, prevention consisted of raising awareness of the modes of HIV transmission and every now and again distributing condoms. It was at this point that a program called DREAM (Drug Resource Enhancement against AIDS and Malnutrition), focusing on treatment as well as prevention, was launched at the initiative of the Community of Sant'Egidio.

Over the years, Sant'Egidio had become a widespread presence in Africa as well, with thousands of members in sub-Saharan countries. Yet despite this growth, Sant'Egidio, which for good reason calls itself a "community", remained a group of people who saw each other as a family.

And in a family, the fate of one affects every other member, or to put it another way, when people see each other as brothers and sisters, it becomes unacceptable that the survival prospects of one or the other of them should depend merely on where they happen to live. DREAM was set up first and foremost as a response to experiences of the AIDS crisis as recounted and endured by African members of Sant'Egidio.

Before proceeding to discuss the DREAM program, however, it is worth stopping to consider some of the more salient aspects of the AIDS epidemic.

AIDS: the first epidemic of globalization

Africa is the global epicenter of what might be called the first epidemic of the globalization era. Indeed, AIDS has all the hallmarks of a "global" disease: it has spread, albeit by different modes and to varying degrees of intensity, to all corners of the planet, and its effects have not only translated into an annual toll in human lives but also into a powerful curb on development, through a cascade of consequences that impact on health, education and production mechanisms.[1] The scale of the disease, the therapeutic complexities it presents, and those whom it targets – mostly young adults of working age – pose a very tough challenge, especially in African countries, where the overwhelming majority of cases are found today. Since the early 1980s, AIDS has seen both a spatial and temporal spread that is unparalleled in the history of human diseases.

The tens of millions of victims of HIV from every country around the world are testament to the sheer momentum of acquired immunodeficiency syndrome. At the end of 2006, UNAIDS (the UN agency which coordinates the various initiatives to combat the disease) estimated that there were at least 40 million HIV-positive people across the globe, and that almost three million people died of AIDS in that same year, two million of whom in sub-Saharan Africa.[2] It is also estimated that since the beginning of the epidemic, no less than 30 million human beings have lost their lives to HIV, making AIDS one of the biggest challenges ever faced by health authorities worldwide. Today, however, that challenge is most keenly felt in Africa.

There are 25 million people living with HIV/AIDS in sub-Saharan Africa, representing almost two-thirds of the corresponding total for the world. Every year, throughout Africa, some three million adults and children are infected and another two million die. AIDS is the leading cause of death in Africa for people aged between 15 and 49 (whilst worldwide it is the fourth most common cause). In many sub-Saharan countries, AIDS has reversed the gains made over the last half a century in reducing infant mortality and increasing life expectancy. The average life expectancy in African countries most affected by the epidemic has fallen by a dozen years. In other words, populations that had achieved a life expectancy of around 50 years have seen it suddenly drop to below 40. AIDS has also reversed the trend of population growth in Africa, something which other – albeit quite widespread – diseases, such as malaria, have never done.

But why has Africa been hit so hard? Leaving aside the dynamics peculiar to the HIV virus and its African strains, the spread of the pandemic in Africa has been accelerated by many factors. These include formidable rates of urbanization, civil and ethnic wars, economic structural adjustment plans that have penalized health and education, the state of nutrition of the average African, and the overall fragility of welfare and healthcare systems. A person with full-blown AIDS in Africa dies earlier than someone with the same condition in the West, due to malnutrition and an immune system that is already weak to start with, poor drinking-water quality, and a greater exposure to infections.

Whilst the causes of the AIDS pandemic in Africa include poverty and underdevelopment, AIDS itself increases poverty. A vicious circle is thus created. If there is a lack of teachers, schools close, and as a result there is less health prevention taught. But if there is a shortage of doctors, who treats people? Just at the point when the cadres of society have been trained and enter the workplace, AIDS begins to strike them down.

As observed in the 2004 UN report The Impact of AIDS, society regresses and loses its stability. The epidemic mainly claims victims among the working-age population, thereby weakening society as a whole. Teachers, nurses, technicians, office workers and executives, but also laborers and farm workers – all die alike from the disease. Indeed, the harsh famine that hit Malawi in 2005 was in part due to a drastic reduction in the rural labor force, with much land no longer being cultivated due to a shortage of farmers.

In a great number of countries, the economic gains achieved through decades of efforts have vanished, and educational and social networks have collapsed. In many countries too, HIV tests are not followed up with any form of assistance, and AIDS continues to spread unimpeded. Paradoxically, efforts are made to deal with its consequences – namely, opportunistic infections – without seeking to stem its cause.

Women in Africa are significantly more severely affected by AIDS. In fact, they represent 60% of those who are HIV-positive on the continent. Despite their pivotal role in the family and the workplace, they are more malnourished and more poorly-educated than men, and more at risk of being socially marginalized. They are a vulnerable group, whose position is further weakened by the disease and the stigma attached to it. Yet we know that these susceptible individuals are the only ones capable of creating a future and supporting children in their growth. The death of mothers means a miserable fate awaits children. Indeed, the plight of many such children, who are very often orphaned as a result of AIDS and whose number is increasing and has now exceeded the 15-million mark, is tragic. Many of them are street children in African cities, living between sidewalks and landfills.

The international response

There were periods when the fear of AIDS as a global threat, though now tempered in large part by the development of drug treatment, was quite intense. Up until the early 1990s, when no form of specific therapy was yet available and the fatality rate of the disease was 100%, civil society, especially in the Anglo-Saxon countries, led a campaign to eliminate the stigma and calling for research into new treatments – efforts that have undoubtedly produced significant and positive results in the West. However, the fact that Africa was the epicenter of the epidemic was for a long time ignored. Data had been available since 1985 which showed an alarming incidence of HIV infection in cities such as Lusaka, Kinshasa and Kampala of between 3% and 15% of the population.

To give an idea of how worrying these figures already were back then, it is worth noting that, in the Western world, the incidence of the epidemic reached at most a few tenths of a percentage point. In any case, when the seriousness of the situation in Africa came to be appreciated, the response did not match the challenge faced. A solution was sought which could be described as minimalist when compared to the enormous problems posed by AIDS, and prevention was proposed as the sole response to the pandemic, with some diagnostic strategies developed on occasion. Then it was sought to apply these limited objectives to everyone within the shortest possible time. This in effect led to the creation – unwittingly – of a double standard, with full treatment and advanced diagnostics available in the West, and the use of condoms and public-awareness advertising campaigns advocated for the bulk of people in Africa. The extent to which AIDS required a developmental response and to which, due to its complexity, it did not permit procedural or methodological shortcuts to be taken, was not understood in time.

At the local level, African governments reacted to the spread of AIDS with great apprehension but also slowly, in part due to a lack of resources. For years, they refused to admit the significance and scale of the problem, going so far as to deny that there were people who were HIV-positive in their respective countries. Indeed, there was already a long-familiar and clear-cut cause to hand that could be used to provide an alternative explanation for the proliferation of certain types of clinical cases, namely: malnutrition.

Strangely enough (though not really), malnutrition effectively produces fairly similar damage to the immune system as that typically wreaked by HIV.

Even as late as the end of the 1990s, very little had been done to tackle the disease. In contrast with what happened in the West, where, in 1996, combination antiretroviral drugs (ARVs) became available, in Africa the introduction of such therapy for years met with the ideological skepticism of many in the aid community who believed that Africa was too backward for such complex medical treatments to be feasible. But this attitude was also accompanied by apathy on the part of African governments, who opposed the introduction of such treatment because their relevant national plans (be they those relating to the health sector in general or those specifically concerning the fight against AIDS) did not contemplate it.

African governments were rather concerned by the commitment that AIDS treatment programs would have demanded, both in terms of human resources and onerous costs, as indeed was the case in Western countries. It was deemed impossible to fund the treatment, and that the public health fears triggered would have resulted in unsustainable pressures on governments. Today, providing access to ARVs is a common objective of all African governments, thanks to the persistence of certain non-governmental pioneers, including Sant'Egidio, and to the now undeniable evidence of the effectiveness of this approach.

The Republic of South Africa, the most powerful and developed of the African States, experienced an early and widespread proliferation of the disease, such that recent figures indicate that 18.5% of South African adults are HIV-positive, 400,000 deaths a year are attributable to HIV, the country's mortality rate exceeds its birth rate, and its population is decreasing. Having assessed that it would not be possible to offer treatment to the great bulk those who were HIV-positive, South African policymakers spoke of AIDS as a Western invention. Others gave explanations for the phenomenon that had little grounding in science, with a belief that antiretroviral drugs were dangerous and that garlic was effective in fighting HIV infection gaining currency in the country.

The decisions of the government in Pretoria should not, however, be judged too quickly. Mass treatment for AIDS entails a huge financial outlay, to be borne for the duration of patients' lives. Fears of not being able to guarantee treatment in the long term played a key role. In South Africa, as elsewhere, AIDS was spoken of in hushed tones, to prevent unrest, to steer clear of having to explain why treatments known to be expensive were not being provided, and to avoid risking unpopularity and riots by declaring a problem without offering any solutions. Even well-intentioned African governments were afraid to lift the lid on the cauldron of AIDS and thereby unleash uncontrollable popular reactions.

Thus, the pandemic spread. When, however, African authorities were by force of circumstances compelled to make a political decision and resolved to tackle the disease solely through prevention without treatment, public-awareness advertising campaigns were launched, willingly funded by the West. These campaigns, devised outside Africa, assumed that the sole mode of HIV transmission was sexual intercourse and therefore focused on the use of condoms as the only way of fighting the pandemic.

But in Africa – where, as it happens, there is a reluctance to use condoms, which are not a part of everyday culture – many were also infected by other means, including via vertical transmission from mother to child, transfusions of infected blood, incorrect usage of medical instruments, and traditional medical practices. No attempt was made to delve into these causes. In addition, hinging AIDS campaigns solely on prevention meant that no assistance was given to those already infected. Indeed, the campaigns often increased social stigma, the fear of speaking out about being HIV-positive and the sense of living under sentence of death. Those infected, who were frightened of being identified as such through HIV testing, were only offered treatment, where possible, for opportunistic infections, that is, AIDS-related illnesses.

The resigned attitude of African governments in the fight against AIDS was matched by excessive caution on the part of the major global health agencies and international scientific bodies, which could have done much more than individual African States. This circumspect approach dictated that only prevention could somehow play a significant role in combating AIDS.

It is true that for around fifteen years, when AIDS first appeared, it was not possible to treat acquired immunodeficiency syndrome effectively, and that a heavy emphasis was placed on prevention. Sooner or later, people who were HIV-positive became ill and died. AIDS seemed like a death sentence with no reprieve. However, discoveries about the virus had, from 1996, finally led to the availability of effective drug treatments, namely, antiretroviral agents, as well as a combination therapy known as HAART (Highly-Active Antiretroviral Therapy).

This line of defense radically altered the evolution of the disease, at least in the West, where prevention and treatment began to go hand-in-hand. HIV mortality rates were cut down and AIDS was transformed into a chronic disease. Those patients who managed to begin the new treatment in time underwent what was hailed in 1996 as a "Lazarus syndrome", coming back to life. Since then, those with HIV in Europe and the United States no longer necessarily have a limited lifespan. They can lead a normal life and live well.

Today, it is estimated that people with AIDS in the West who receive proper treatment can go on living with a decent quality of life for at least thirty years. They need to have periodic checkups and, if the virus becomes resistant, undergo treatment with new drugs. But they can lead essentially normal lives, in good physical condition. The HIV virus is never entirely eliminated, but it can be rendered innocuous, dormant. AIDS is a chronic disease: like diabetes mellitus, high blood pressure and other such diseases, it can be controlled.

In Africa, however, even after 1996, specialist agencies confined themselves for years to recommending and funding only preventive intervention models, which were in any case rather poor, often based on advertising campaigns without any initiatives to provide basic health education or any training for healthcare workers. It was an exercise in partial prevention, which, more than anything, provoked fear. As AIDS was a disease without treatment in Africa, those infected were seen as a threat and shunned by society. As a consequence, nobody wanted to be identified as HIV-positive, and almost no one wished to take a test to determine if they were carrying the virus. This denial is understandable. In developed countries, the ability to access treatment and the social acceptance of those living with HIV/AIDS encouraged people to undergo voluntary testing.

In Africa, being HIV-positive was simply grounds for social exclusion, and being diagnosed with HIV worsened the person's situation due to the marginalization that ensued. It should have been obvious to doctors, epidemiologists as well as leaders of the international scientific community, that the unavailability of treatment drastically limited the effectiveness of prevention. Without treatment, there was no incentive to find out one's HIV status. Prevention needed to be combined with treatment.

There was no reason for choosing between prevention and treatment: both are necessary. Yet by the end of the century, there were not even any pilot projects for treatment in Africa. It was deemed impossible to sustain treatment in countries that were too lacking in facilities, too economically backward, and too technology-poor. This presumed impossibility allowed any ethical considerations to be laid to rest: in developed countries, AIDS could be treated, but not in Africa. Estimates of the financial, administrative and sociological costs involved were brandished in support of this view. A non-therapeutic approach to AIDS in Africa seemed easier to manage and infinitely less expensive. Moreover, this approach was in keeping with the minimalist efforts of African governments themselves, driven by the fears already described.

Without question, the timely introduction of anti-AIDS treatment in Africa would have come up against obstacles of an environmental, economic, professional, and cultural nature. But the fact remains that, by the end of the 1990s, there was a sort of dogma in place which held that treatment was unsustainable. In 2002, in Barcelona, at the 14th International Conference on AIDS, the President of the

305

International AIDS Society, Joep Lange, observed that: "If we can get Coca-Cola and cold beer to every remote corner of Africa, it should not be impossible to do the same with drugs".

Yet various justifications to the contrary were put forward. It was said that it would not be possible to set up treatment programs because the epidemic was already too widespread, and not localized. Finally, it was argued, that if the administration of treatment were to go ahead, the initiative would need to cover everyone at once, and not just a fortunate select few (even though in respect of malnutrition, tuberculosis and malaria, there are countless examples in Africa of programs that are limited in time and geographical coverage).

Treating AIDS in Africa: enter DREAM

The creation of the DREAM program stemmed from a refusal to accept that Africa should be left alone to cope with 30 million people living with HIV/AIDS and receiving no treatment. It was necessary to bring AIDS therapy to Africa, to the same level of quality and excellence that had enabled outstanding results to be achieved in the first world.

But was the problem too big? Did the scale of the undertaking make it out of the question? Were the costs insurmountable? And what about the extremely weak infrastructure, the cultural complexities, the lack of familiarity with complex therapies, the structural shortage of trained professionals that is part and parcel of Africa, as well as the environmental difficulties, ranging from the scarcity of clean water to mosquitoes complicating matters with malaria?

Sant'Egidio had several strengths in its favor to help it meet this challenge. Being well-established in Africa, it had a clear insight into the continent's structural weaknesses, as well as its significant human, social, and ultimately professional resources.

There was the Community's ability to wage difficult struggles with limited means, coming up with solutions that were out of the ordinary but achievable. There was its teamwork culture of men and women – with significant technical and scientific skills, gained in other fields of social endeavor and research, and with different areas of expertise – working together, without any professional rivalries. There was also its view of Africa not as some abstract concept, but as a community of people with an attachment to their land of origin and who were eager to find an antidote to the Afro-pessimism that drove many to seek to emigrate.

This was the backdrop to the creation of the DREAM program, designed and run by the Community of Sant'Egidio to fight AIDS in Africa.[3,4] The program aimed not only to make antiretroviral treatment possible and accessible, but also to bring into play a whole series of measures and factors that would make it effective, including health education for patients, nutritional support, advanced diagnostics, and on-the-job training for staff. At the same time, efforts would be made to combat other conditions and opportunistic infections, such as malaria, tuberculosis and, in particular, malnutrition.

Suddenly, an impetus emerged that made prevention itself more effective. There was no longer fear of taking an HIV test and finding out what previously had simply been an early death sentence. Knowing one's HIV-positive status became a means of protecting others and put people on track for surviving the condition. Women, already marginal in status and made outcasts by the illness, became the focal point of a new awareness. They embodied the possibility of fighting back and living, and the beginning of a fresh start in life – for them, and for their men, their villages, and their neighbors. After a while, children who were born healthy no longer joined the millions of orphans already in existence, doomed inevitably to live on the streets or in households made up of grandparents and children with no one left from the intervening generations.

It took two years of preparatory work to get DREAM off the ground, until, in 2002 in Mozambique, the first woman who came for a pregnancy test was also able to take the first HIV test and, immediately afterwards, a confirmatory test. On the same morning, she also received counseling, in the form of a talk with a doctor who explained what lay ahead of her, as well as telling her that there was a way of dealing with it: if she kept to the program, her child would be born healthy, without HIV, and she herself would have greater chances of surviving and living better, without the fatigue that worried her and would have otherwise inevitably gotten worse. Eight years on, DREAM operates in ten African countries, which, in addition to Mozambique, comprise Malawi, Tanzania, Kenya, the Republic of Guinea, Guinea-Bissau, Nigeria, the Democratic Republic of the Congo, Cameroon, and Angola.

Preventing mother-to-child transmission

Worthy of separate mention is the therapeutic approach of DREAM to what is strictly-speaking a prevention issue, though one of crucial importance, namely: maternal transmission of HIV to a child in utero, during childbirth or via breastfeeding.[5] In Africa, hundreds of thousands of children infected with HIV are born every year who are condemned to a very early death. Without treatment, around half of these babies die in their first year of life. The others are unlikely to reach 15 years of age. Prevention of this problem is possible: using a specific treatment, it is not particularly difficult to stop the virus being transmitted to the infant. DREAM centers administer antiretroviral drugs to pregnant women who are HIV-positive. This treatment, which begins during the third trimester of pregnancy, is able to significantly reduce the virus present in the mother's bloodstream, thereby preventing infection of the child. But it is not only the unborn child who benefits from the treatment. Indeed, admission of a pregnant woman to the program is the way to save not only the infant's life, but also the mother's.

It should be noted that there was a fundamental difference between DREAM's approach and other therapeutic practices aimed at preventing vertical transmission of AIDS that were widespread in Africa around 2002. Those practices involved administering a single dose to HIV-positive women about to give birth of only one antiretroviral drug, Nevirapine, during delivery, with a repeat dose administered to the newborn infant within 48-72 hours of birth.[6] This protocol reduces the risk of transmission of the virus only partially and in the short term. More importantly, however, it fails to treat the mother, who is abandoned to her own fate, that is, death, when her HIV develops into full-blown AIDS. The child, perhaps born healthy, becomes an orphan, assuming he/she survives without a mother, which is by no means a certainty in Africa.

In contrast, DREAM's view was that mothers should be given a complete course of antiretroviral treatment, which should likewise be continued after childbirth where the mother needs it, in order to save her life and ensure that she can take care of the newborn and her other children for many years to come. The response focuses on both the mother and child, and not just on one or the other. This was precisely the approach DREAM chose to adopt in Maputo in 2002, administering the same triple therapy to mothers that was already bringing so many sick people "back to life".

Nevirapine alone does nothing other than reduce the proportion of babies infected at birth from 35% to 12-15%, and only during the perinatal period.[7] Unfortunately, this procedure has no effect during breastfeeding, and consequently led to a further rise in the number of babies infected at one year of age.[8] Yet Nevirapine, due to its affordability and its ease of administration, for years provided African governments and health agencies in Africa with an easy option (though the use of dual and triple therapy is now prevalent). It epitomized the minimalist philosophy that for years created the double standard mentioned previously. Indeed, it would never have been administered in an Italian or US hospital, where triple therapy was the preferred option from the outset.

DREAM's approach also made breastfeeding safer, avoiding the dangerous alternative of administering powdered milk formula. As is well-known, in African populations that lack access to clean drinking water, powdered milk often leads to deadly infantile diarrhea.[9] In the eight years it has been operating, DREAM's mother-to-child HIV transmission prevention program has seen more than 10,000 children born healthy in various African countries.

DREAM as a model

Today, DREAM represents an AIDS-response model capable of being expanded further. In this regard, it is worth pointing out that the program could not have grown and successfully dealt with the significant organizational and therapeutic challenges faced if it had originated as an initiative of a single individual or an isolated group. The secret – indeed, the essential ingredient – of its success lies in a great many people working together, both from the global North and South, and including medical specialists and patients, lay people and religious brethren, volunteers and professionals, people on the ground and donors, and governments and nongovernmental organizations.

Everyone has their role to play, from home carers to biologists, and from doctors to those responsible for logistics in areas where there are hardly ever any maps, and where one would be lucky to find electricity or telephone lines. The ability to share any kind of problems that arise, as well as the solutions found to them, quickly obviates the need to start from scratch every time, whilst enabling people to grow together by taking on board others' experience, thereby making it transposable and reducing instinctive tensions in the face of difficulties. The ongoing relationship, based on the exchange of information and professional know-how, but also on friendship, between those who are temporarily based in the global North or South, together with the double-checking of epidemiological data, therapeutic difficulties encountered and options available, enables the high level of expertise amassed to be rapidly put to the best possible use and to be made permanently accessible, even when a new center is established with an almost entirely new complement of staff working alongside those with more experience. In the battle against HIV, no one is useless or marginal, and particularly not the patient, who is still a person with a right to privacy, notwithstanding the existence of extreme or complicated conditions.

One of the key contributing factors to the effectiveness of DREAM has been that it is a program with a core philosophy, rooted in spiritual and human values. It is this driving spirit that enables DREAM to create synergies that are not always obvious, and to serve as a replicable model, rather than being jealously guarded against use by others. Of course, there is a need to ensure adherence, wherever it is applied, to the same standards of quality that have permitted the program to be ranked amongst the most successful in countering AIDS in Africa. The following points illustrate the driving philosophy of DREAM:

1. The individual, whom we should reach out to as a neighbor, is key. In today's complex globalized scenario, our neighbor is also the person with HIV we come across on the streets or in homes without electricity in thousands of villages, in the outskirts of sub-Saharan metropolises, and along the byways of deep rural Africa. This individual invites the affluent world to "reach out": wise words, as this approach enables the creation from the ground up of what is at times more difficult to initiate "from the top down", due to bureaucratic difficulties and a failure of official thinking to keep pace with a rapidly-changing field. It is this emphasis on taking real men and women – rather than institutions – as the starting point that has led the DREAM program to adopt innovative organizational and operational practices.

2. There are no first- or second-class patients[10], in the sense that the availability of effective treatment for only 5% of the population infected with HIV is an unacceptable contradiction in terms when such access is denied to the remaining 95%. DREAM was established precisely to make it possible to administer therapy to those in the global South as well. It is a question of acknowledging the dignity of individuals in all its fullness, wherever they are born and whatever their affiliations and nationality. It was this that motivated DREAM to implement a system of excellence in treatment which, especially in the early years of the program, was in stark contrast with the approaches adopted by the international community, characterized as they were by minimalism.

Yet it seemed only natural to apply the same diagnostics and patient care procedures in Africa as were standard in the global North. As the years have passed, there has been a discernible shift closer to this approach by international agencies, due in part to the fact that minimalist strategies have not yielded the desired results, at times even worsening the situation. In addition, some services – such as systematic viral load assessment – that were considered "too expensive" (in Africa only, of course, and not in America or Europe), have significantly come down in cost over time, simply as a result of high-volume purchasing and consumption.

3. A strategy for life. Adopting a holistic approach to the individual as a starting point, it became clear that prevention needed to be combined with treatment. As has already been mentioned, DREAM took its first steps in a cultural climate that was decidedly hostile to the introduction of antiretroviral drugs in sub-Saharan Africa, and which was completely skewed towards prevention. It therefore seemed not only fair but also sensible to combine treatment with a range of measures aimed at staving off further infections. Treatment is a key element of prevention, as can be seen in the case of mother-to-child transmission, where the use of ARVs has not only proved its effectiveness in Africa as well, but has also become a proper treatment in its own right for mothers and a great help in ensuring their ongoing adherence.

4. A strategy of social justice and equity. Anyone can access the DREAM program, because all treatment, patient care and diagnostic procedures are completely free of charge. In a continent where hundreds of millions of people live below the absolute poverty threshold, this seemed to be the only realistic option. In addition to the indisputable inability of patients to pay, there is also the fact that the treatment needs to be taken for life and requires strict patient adherence.

As it is, the complexity of patient care procedures, which involve frequent appointments for check-ups, supplying drugs and carrying out tests, entails a cost to patients in any case. Indeed, many of them have to undertake long journeys on foot to reach the centers, all of which takes up several hours of their week. Social justice and equity entail not only enabling patients to obtain drugs but also to overcome chronic food insecurity. Nutritional support is thus provided in all cases where this is considered necessary.[11] The foodstuffs donated to patients for their own requirements, as well as for those of their entire family, also effectively help them regain both purpose and dignity, as they end up making a significant contribution towards meeting family household needs.

5. A strategy of development. Whilst on the one hand AIDS has been catastrophic for Africa, on the other, it has provided an impetus for renewed humanitarian efforts, with current investment levels having no significant historical precedent. DREAM's activities also include providing training and retraining for many health workers, who receive ongoing support through theory courses and hands-on internships.

DREAM regularly introduces new technologies and has helped retrain entire sections of the public and private health system in their use, thereby improving diagnostic skills across-the-board. The need to overcome the existing technological gap and the telecommunications infrastructure lag has led to the development of a satellite communications network and a fully-computerized management system as appropriate solutions for African conditions and the continent's isolation, and which are also of use in other contexts.

6. The individual restored to society. The inclusive approach adopted, the involvement of patients in their treatment and the provision of health education have proved an ideal way of making inroads into the health awareness of Africans and intervening effectively.[12,13] The key to this was actively involving patients in educational processes and in their own therapy.

There are now hundreds of so-called "activists" (or campaigners) who form part of the "I Dream" association, working together to welcome new patients, track down those who might be experiencing difficulties and carry out prevention initiatives. Their therapeutic pathway thus runs parallel with another trajectory – one which starts with them having the disease but also with being marginalized and socially isolated, unable to work or look after their family, and consequently plagued by guilt, but which sees them regain their health and undergo a social and cultural reintegration.

This process also leads to their reintegration into the workforce, as activists receive appropriate training and are regularly employed and paid. Many of the female patients, having found their strength again, become mothers to numerous children, not just their own, but also many of the other sick children who come through DREAM centers, most of whom have lost parents to AIDS and have been entrusted to grandparents or neighbors whose attentions are divided and who, while able to help them survive, cannot look after them. These women become like mothers, visiting the homes of these so-called "children of DREAM" several times a day, administering medicines, preparing meals and taking care of them, with a sense that these children are an integral part of their family. Thus, with few resources, these children are given a fresh chance to live and build a future. Some of these home help programs are also complemented by long-distance adoptions organized by the Community of Sant'Egidio.

This approach to AIDS forms the basis of the DREAM model – one that is replicable and, indeed, has already been embraced by many, especially those who have been engaged in Africa, including missionaries, volunteers and people of good will, with special personal care programs, health centers, and educational programs, but who were not equipped to deal with AIDS.

In fact, the rapid expansion of DREAM over the past eight years has been due not only to the widespread presence of the Community of Sant'Egidio in many African countries, but also to the decision of many religious congregations, NGOs, lay people, and health workers in various capacities, to share in this strategy for fighting AIDS. This joining of forces has enabled the number of HIV-positive Africans reached and treated to be increased every day.

It is possible to conquer AIDS through concerted and harmonious efforts that bring together many voices and resources. It is crucial for institutions, governments, local authorities, public and private health facilities, people who love Africa and international agencies to be able to work together. They need proven and effective knowhow and practices that permit the resources at their disposal to be put to good use, without rivalries and without any rigid insistence on their individual prerogatives. The very fight against AIDS itself could usher in a new positive phase in relations between faith-based and secular organizations, between the various major international agencies, and between governments and those who are implementing best practice in the field.

DREAM: a health diplomacy initiative

In July 2008, on the occasion of celebrations in Maputo, Mozambique, to mark the 40th anniversary of the founding of the Community of Sant'Egidio, Joaquim Chissano, a former President of the country, spoke as follows:

I would like to welcome Andrea Riccardi, founder of the Community of Sant'Egidio... I want to thank him for reminding us of times already long past but which, viewed in retrospect, seem like yesterday. As he said – and it saddens me to say it – between 1984 and 1990, we were all worried about what was happening in this country. There was a war on. And it was not so difficult to understand the problems of Mozambique. All that was needed was an appreciation of the country's history to gain an insight into the root of the problems. At that time, we saw that Sant'Egidio could help us solve our problems. We all wanted to resolve them, those in government and those fighting outside the government, against the government. We had to resolve them. Sant'Egidio then began to help us do so. We got to know Fr. Matteo Zuppi and others too, but Andrea Riccardi was always there in the background, with a vision but also an ability to interpret the various phases of the negotiations, and always ready with advice for the mediators and the delegations. And so, within two years, a peace agreement was signed. At that time, we knew Sant'Egidio as an organization that could help us make peace. Then we began to realize that Sant'Egidio was much more, and that it could help us maintain peace, through peace-building efforts. Keeping the peace means acting in the interests of the people. I remember at the time there was a great debate, almost tantamount to negotiations, over Sant'Egidio's proposal to embark on a program to combat AIDS in our country, which would involve introducing antiretroviral drugs in Mozambique. Our health system was in a state of panic, because it seemed that the conditions weren't in place to get such a program off the ground. I was of the same view as Sant'Egidio, and tried to convince our government that we needed to forge ahead. The right conditions would not be created all at once, but it was necessary to get the ball rolling. After a long time, we agreed to start, though still hesitantly. Today, Sant'Egidio has this program called DREAM, and we would like to thank the Community for its efforts in fighting AIDS, because when there's an illness like this, there can be no real peace – it remains incomplete.

The "great debate, almost tantamount to negotiations" that this former leader of Mozambique recalled stretches over a long period of time: it began three years before the actual launch of DREAM in 2002 and continues today in 2010. Indeed, DREAM has had to overcome an elaborate range of skeptical and unfavorable attitudes, and, right up to the present day, has found it necessary to come up with various strategies to this end.

In 1999, the reaction of Mozambican health leaders to a proposed AIDS treatment program was effectively one of firm opposition, because it really did seem that "the conditions weren't in place to get such a program off the ground". Other and much more concrete threats apparently required an immediate response, first and foremost, the recurrent epidemics of cholera that plagued the center and south of the country. Essentially, the Ministry of Health was drawing attention to what it considered to be the real emergency situations, and asking how a large (and expensive) treatment program for AIDS could be proposed at a time when it was not even possible to stem the seasonal crises that caused thousands of deaths from diarrhea.

The Community certainly did not intend to downplay the importance of the circumstances indicated. Indeed, it was also for this reason that, in conjunction with the Italian government's Development Cooperation office, it launched an initiative to combat cholera in March 2000, which led to the refurbishment of the main infirmary in Beira, the epicenter of the epidemic, as well as several health missions being undertaken to carry out studies and provide support in flooded areas.

In addition, the talks aimed at introducing AIDS treatment also came up against widespread skepticism from international agencies, which sometimes took the form of overt suspicion that there was an intention to use Mozambican patients as some sort of guinea pigs. Those most favorably disposed frequently urged Sant'Egidio to "go ahead and pave the way", and that others would follow. There was strong cultural and political pressure on the Community to desist from its proposal to treat AIDS patients with ARVs. Why – it was asked – introduce a disruptive element into existing five-year strategy plans that were heavily-focused on prevention? Why waste energy on initiatives that would not produce significant results in terms of large numbers? And why not focus on dealing with immediate emergencies and saving lives through acknowledged and affordable treatments?

However, the facts indicated that AIDS was spreading at an alarmingly fast rate, and that many young people in Sant'Egidio's African communities were dying of the disease. In 1998, it was already estimated that 1.3 million Mozambicans were infected and that they would all be dead within a few years. The country's long civil war had left a million people dead, and it was now clear that AIDS would do worse. Sant'Egidio was furthermore convinced that therapy could play a key role in prevention, as reducing the levels of the virus in circulation would also drastically decrease its capacity to spread. The Community would have the satisfaction of seeing this view authoritatively corroborated four years later, via a series of dedicated studies which confirmed the situation that was emerging worldwide, namely, that the number of new cases of infection in all countries around the world was inversely proportional to the level of antiretroviral therapy coverage.

A decisive breakthrough in the impasse of 1998-2000 came out of a meeting in Rome between the then Italian Prime Minister Giuliano Amato, Andrea Riccardi and President Chissano. It was then that the foundations were laid for a new political approach, even though there was still considerable resistance within the Mozambican Ministry of Health and within Italian Development Cooperation circles. Chissano was encouraged by Italian backing and by the suggestion of a new opportunity to tackle the disease. He came out of the meeting persuaded to take a bold step: that of devising a way to accommodate AIDS care and treatment within the health system. The arduous talks that followed finally culminated in 2001 in an agreement which provided, formally, for the setting up of molecular biology laboratories (necessary to perform HIV diagnostics and to monitor treatment) in the country's three main hospitals, and, somewhat less formally, for treatment to commence.

Two key characteristics may be noted from these first fledgling steps taken by DREAM: a notion of true partnership, based on shared decision-making and long-term commitments, and a vision of a project geared towards development and not crisis intervention. These are not as inescapably obvious as they might seem, considering that, even today, Mozambique's powerful neighbor, South Africa, has not yet developed an infrastructure network within its public health system for performing complete AIDS diagnostics. During DREAM's early years, South African officials and delegations were amazed and shocked to find antiretroviral drugs and well-equipped laboratories in poor Mozambican communities, when, in South Africa, such facilities were confined to a few private clinics in Johannesburg or Cape Town.

It should also be remembered that in 2000, even a simple red blood-cell count was not automated in Mozambique, but still carried out using optical microscopy! In this regard, DREAM has been one of the main drivers of the radical transformation that the country's entire public health system has undergone, in terms of both equipment and the training and deployment of human resources. Indeed, the benefits that accrued from the fight against AIDS very soon spread to many other crucial areas of the health sector.

Another hurdle that was encountered before long related to discrepancies between DREAM's treatment protocols and those outlined by international agencies. As mentioned previously, whilst the DREAM program envisaged pursuing the approach accepted in the Western world, the diagnostic and therapeutic solutions that were recommended for Africa were minimalist in character. It was also clear that some procedures widely adopted in the global North could not be applied in Africa, including, by way of example, the use of cesarean delivery and the substitution of breastfeeding with powdered formula. The prospect of subjecting hundreds of thousands of women to cesareans each year was simply inconceivable, as would providing them with powdered milk formula have been, due to the difficulties already noted.

It was therefore decided that, in order to provide it with a further resource to draw on, DREAM would also conduct operational research, which would involve scientific research into specific practical solutions. This approach lent itself well both to creating "niche" solutions that did not openly conflict with the guidelines of the various countries, and to exploring effective innovative solutions for the entire African continent. This development opened the doors of many countries and was truly useful in coming up with new responses, such that today, in Africa, for those being treated with the combination therapy offered by the program, it is possible to breastfeed and avoid having to resort to cesarean delivery.

Operational research also resulted in the entire project being equipped with a computerized patient management system, containing a complete record of each DREAM patient's clinical history. The privacy of such data was ensured by anonymous encryption (with only the responsible treatment center having access to it), whilst at the same time it was usable in epidemiological studies, or for specialist consultations, obtaining second opinions, and other similar purposes.

Hence, the program functions as a humanitarian intervention that, at the same time, provides a powerful scientific investigative tool capable of helping to find responses to the many questions concerning the control of HIV in Africa that remain unanswered.

Finally, DREAM has served – and continues to serve – as a meeting point for groups of people who, though quite diverse, are implicated in a broad sense in the dialogue between the global North and South. The major difficulties involved in redesigning and equipping African health systems to meet the challenge posed by AIDS call for intensive dialogue and very close collaboration. Yet, in contrast, there is a sense in recent years that non-bureaucratic and genuinely operational taskforces have become rarer and weaker. It is for this reason too that, every year, the program singles out certain issues for debate by a meeting of health ministers and senior officials from several African countries.

These informal and friendly discussions have identified certain agreed priorities, which have then formed the basis for joint international appeals, such as those set out in Appendices 1 and 2 to this chapter.

In its eight years of operation, DREAM has tackled various key issues that needed to be cast in new terms, such as: therapy for children, the provision of treatment free of charge, the need to adopt an inclusive and non-selective approach to people living with HIV, the involvement of patients in therapeutic processes, the need for nutritional support, and the need for a new international logistics. These are scenarios in respect of which debate is still very much open, with the positions taken by the program not being entirely shared by other actors in the fight against AIDS.

For current purposes, it is enough to highlight the effectiveness of a particular method – one involving open dialogue with all stakeholders, a commitment to providing all scientific corroboration required, collaboration with governments, institutions and ethics committees, and, without question, a great deal of advocacy. In relation to the latter aspect, it should be noted that "advocacy" on behalf of certain groups, and in respect of certain situations or rights, is now largely entrusted to the vast "I Dream" movement, whose thousands of members in many countries – all patients and all living with HIV – carry out this role with courage and determination. Indeed, the involvement of many African women and men in a campaign for life and hope certainly counts as the most remarkable outcome of this venture in health diplomacy.

DREAM's growth and results: key facts and figures

Since 2002, DREAM has undergone rapid expansion (see Fig. 1). From its beginnings in Mozambique, it has spread to Malawi, Tanzania, Kenya, Guinea-Conakry, Guinea-Bissau, Nigeria, Angola, the Democratic Republic of the Congo and Cameroon. DREAM now has 31 health centers operating, supported by 18 molecular biology laboratories.

It is estimated that, in total, the program has delivered a range of different benefits to a million people in Africa,

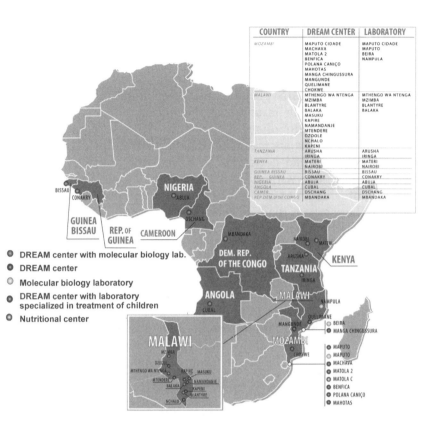

COUNTRY	DREAM CENTER	LABORATORY
MOZAMBI'	MAPUTO CIDADE	MAPUTO CIDADE
	MACHAVA	MAPUTO
	MATOLA 2	BEIRA
	BENFICA	NAMPULA
	POLANA CANIÇO	
	MAHOTAS	
	MANGA CHINGUSSURA	
	MANGUNDE	
	QUELIMANE	
	CHOKWE	
MALAWI	MTHENGO WA NTENGA	MTHENGO WA NTENGA
	MZIMBA	MZIMBA
	BLANTYRE	BLANTYRE
	BALAKA	BALAKA
	MASUKU	
	KAPIRE	
	NAMANDANJE	
	MTENDERE	
	DZOOLE	
	NCHALO	
	KAPENI	
TANZANIA	ARUSHA	ARUSHA
	IRINGA	IRINGA
KENYA	MATERI	MATERI
	NAIROBI	NAIROBI
GUINEA BISSAU	BISSAU	BISSAU
REP. GUINEA	CONAKRY	CONAKRY
NIGERIA	ABUJA	ABUJA
ANGOLA	CUBAL	CUBAL
CAMER.	DSCHANG	DSCHANG
REP. DEM. OF THE CONGO	MBANDAKA	MBANDAKA

DREAM center with molecular biology lab.
DREAM center
Molecular biology laboratory
DREAM center with laboratory specialized in treatment of children
Nutritional center

Fig. 1 – DREAM centers in Africa

some of whom, including approximately 90,000 HIV-positive people, have benefited directly in various ways from treatment, diagnostics and patient care services. Others, generally members of patients' families, have received significant food aid. To these must be added the people who have benefited from health education, and, finally, the thousands of children born healthy thanks to the preventive and therapeutic measures taken in respect of their mothers. Table 1 shows some of the overall figures for DREAM's activities.

321

A strategy for the future

Africa is an immense continent, whose area exceeds that of Europe, the United States, India and Argentina combined – a fact not always apparent from maps. The population density per square kilometer is amongst the lowest in the world, even though megalopolises do exist in Africa. Adequate, accessible and low-cost means of transport are a pipe dream, as are extensive road networks. In Africa, one out of every two babies is born without assistance of any kind, not just because of a lack of maternity centers, but also simply because there are no roads or means of transport.

Any health challenge in Africa must therefore be approached from a different perspective to what we might be accustomed to. In order to ensure the effectiveness of any mass health protection program in Africa, whether it involves carrying out vaccinations, basic medical checks, or measures in response to major epidemics, it is crucial to be not just reachable and accessible but to reach patients. DREAM has strived to achieve this goal, based on a simple albeit not easily achievable premise, namely: that of spreading across and "occupying" the territory in question, and avoiding the continued design of healthcare which hinges on services being immured within facilities that are difficult to access.

Major structural interventions in the health sector in sub-Saharan Africa have generally been based on models from economically-developed Western countries. It is for this reason that the notion of a "light and portable" health system that serves as a resource that genuinely covers the territory, is flexible, and is able to identify needs (even when these remain unvoiced or lack the momentum to translate into healthcare demand), has not gained ground in Africa. Very often, African health systems, in imitation of those in the global North, are made up of hospitals and other small or large health facilities, and the extent to which they function generally depends on the strength of public investment in human mobility and infrastructure that facilitates mobility. Such investment and infrastructure are almost always lacking or are, at any rate, out of the question as resource levels and income distribution currently stand.

This approach to healthcare, based on facilities that are isolated and hemmed in, has in many cases proved to be ineffective. It is common to see lines of patients and their families, with great numbers of children, outside health centers or other healthcare facilities, having arrived there after difficult journeys that put further strain on patients' health.

Yet Africa has an incredible wealth of human resources, which can be tapped into by providing appropriate training through basic health education programs aimed at quickly producing the professionals needed, even to a medium-qualification level. This decentralization of health is achievable at a reasonable cost to national governments and the myriad of international actors, and does not require lengthy timeframes or rigid procedures.

Based on these considerations, DREAM has promoted a mobility strategy in Africa that combines a vast range of diverse local initiatives with all the necessary technologies to underpin them. Through DREAM, a program of excellence has become accessible and taken root, even in rural locations which major programs aimed at preventing and combating the disease had previously shied away from.

Short of waiting for the entire continent to flock to unlivable megalopolises, this was a challenge that needed to be faced. Rural communities make up the lion's share of the continent's population, with their tiny villages of huts, dirt or mud tracks, subsistence economies, and existential and cultural isolation. Here, there are no telephones, newspapers, radios, or cars. Of course, the byproducts of the pollution and exploitation of the planet that accompany our overdevelopment are also lacking.

But in a situation of isolation that curtails lives when transport is not on hand, there was a need to develop an "outreach" strategy: a network of small health centers, unassuming and restrained in construction, and modest in size but dignified, which would serve as a point of reference for surrounding villages. These would be real havens of health and culture, where it would not only be possible to access treatment, but also to receive the kind of basic health education that has proved so fundamental. They would be run by medium-qualified personnel but also by patients themselves, integrated back into the system through the virtuous cycle that DREAM had devised to restore them not only to health, but also to the culture and dignity of employment.

This network seemingly differed to the kind that produce immediate, major results, being almost sprinkled, as it were, across the territory. But it was held together via appropriate monitoring and control technologies, communications and logistics. All patients were able to access the various service providers – from small health posts and medium-sized DREAM treatment centers, to the program's main centers and even major hospitals – as and when needed. It would no longer be necessary for the center with the highest concentration of therapeutic equipment to be made to carry the full medical caseload.

But it is the people working at the local community level who have truly provided the outreach capable of breaking through the isolation barrier, and who have been the key to finding flexible responses to health needs that are variable and complex by definition. They form part of a "care community", made up not just of healthcare professionals, but also patients, women and men as equals who have been restored to life but also to a job they are passionate about, through which they can save the lives of others. DREAM sees the breaking down of this isolation as the linchpin of its entire strategy to combating AIDS.

In our more developed world, loneliness is a condition that causes a rise in the incidence of all diseases, to the point that increased morbidity has become the key indicator of social isolation in many major cities. But loneliness and isolation also have a negative impact in other contexts and in rural African settings, acting as a socially disruptive factor. They have a multiplier effect on ignorance, unalleviated pain, and social exclusion, and although they might not seem to be health factors in the strict sense, they have serious health consequences everywhere. A recent study in the "Lancet" – only the latest to be published, but nevertheless providing very authoritative corroboration – showed that the risk of death, hospitalization, loss of self-sufficiency and even dementia among elderly people experiencing loneliness has more than doubled in the space of ten years. There is no doubt that social isolation can represent an even more acute factor of death and despair in a small village in the heart of rural Malawi or in the Democratic Republic of the Congo.

Teilhard de Chardin once wrote that "Only love can bring individual beings to their perfect completion... by uniting them one with another, because only love... unites them by what lies deepest within them... [W]hat more need we do than imagine our power to love growing and broadening, till it can embrace the totality of human beings and of the earth?" This is precisely what DREAM seeks to achieve. Humanitarian endeavor calls for this imaginative transformation of love into an ability to unite and bridge great distances, so as to begin the healing once thought beyond reach.

Appendix 1

Appeal for the fight against HIV/AIDS in Africa:
A Dream for Africa: Children without AIDS
Protocol of Rome - Sant'Egidio, May 27th, 2005

The HIV/AIDS pandemic continues to badly affect Africa and most of the rest of the world. Tackling and defeating HIV/AIDS is a global priority.

We want to express our particular concern for the large number of HIV-infected children in Africa today and those who are orphaned because of AIDS. This serious, worsening situation threatens the future of the continent itself.

The main strategy to stem the advance of the disease is to provide full ARV treatment to mothers to ensure both their survival and prevention of vertical transmission. The destiny of the African family and future generations lies with young women.

We believe that the fight against AIDS may and must be won in Africa, working together in a real partnership between the northern and southern hemispheres of the globe.

For this reason, we, as representatives of African countries, are gathered in Rome upon the invitation of the Community of Sant'Egidio, in the name of our peoples and our consciences, to make an appeal so that the fight against the HIV infection of millions of children and their mothers may become an immediate priority and true commitment.

We ask that research for the treatment of children be highly developed and oriented towards making more pediatric drugs available and affordable; this is a priority for Africa where nearly all the world's children afflicted by AIDS live.

The right to treatment is a new human right. For this reason, we ask the world's more developed countries and people who have decision-making power in this field, for their support, so that African countries may develop health services marked by the high standards of quality that this challenge requires.

We offer and ask every government, every company or agency, every man and every women of goodwill to join us in a new alliance to fight HIV/AIDS in Africa. For a future with a human face. For everybody.

Appendix 2

Appeal of the African Ministers of Health to the Pharmaceutical Companies that manufacture drugs, laboratory devices and reagents for treating HIV/AIDS

International efforts and the engagement of national governments against HIV/AIDS have made care and diagnostics accessible to many Africans in recent years. Though we are still far from providing adequate assistance to all those who are in need, we must also recognize the immense developments that have taken place. Africa now has not only the highest number of people infected by HIV/ AIDS, but also the largest amount of people who have access to antiretroviral therapy.

We are increasingly troubled, however, concerning the long term sustainability of this extraordinary result. Indeed, in face of a demand of drugs and diagnostic equipment which is still significantly on the rise, there is some concern regarding the limits of the supply of said products. In many of our countries there are frequent delays in the delivery, logistical problems, and regrettably long and tragic cases of stock breakage. These may all be accidents, but they may also be due to inadequate logistics, poor manufacturing and retail networks, or a major shortage of human resources involved in the sector.

While we sincerely appreciate the possibility for many of our fellow citizens to have access to an excellent and effective level of treatment, we feel we need to ask the international companies, corporations and UN agencies to establish the necessary infrastructures to guarantee a long term response for our continent.

Even in Africa drugs and equipment need to come with an adequate investment in terms of production and personnel required for maintenance and technical assistance.

We who are in charge of health in different African countries commit ourselves to support and facilitate the matching of demand and supply, in the framework of a long term and solid partnership. This collaboration between governmental programs, NGO initiatives, academic resources and enterprises is the tool that will allow us to further increase the amount of people cared for and treated. Only a complete and solid alliance will allow us to win the fight against HIV/AIDS.

Rome, 15/5/2008

[1] UNAIDS – WHO, AIDS Epidemic Update, Geneva 2006. See also Secretary-General Kofi A. Annan, *Address by Kofi Annan to the African Summit on HIV/ AIDS, Tuberculosis and Other Infectious Diseases*, Abuja (Nigeria) 2001.

[2] UNAIDS – WHO, AIDS Epidemic Update, Geneva 2007.

[3] M. C. Marazzi, G. Guidotti, G. Liotta & L. Palombi, *World Health Organization – Community of Sant'Egidio Perspectives and practice in antiretroviral treatment - DREAM an integrated faith-based initiative to treat HIV/AIDS in Mozambique* (case study), WHO, Geneva 2005.

[4] Community of Sant'Egidio, *DREAM Program, Viva l'Africa viva! Vincere l'AIDS e la malnutrizione*, Leonardo International, Milan 2008.

[5] L. Palombi, M. C. Marazzi, A. Voetberg, N. Abdul Magid & the DREAM Program Prevention of Mother-to-Child Transmission Team (E. Buonomo, A. Doro Altan, S. Mancinelli, G. Liotta, P. Scarcella, et al.), *Treatment acceleration program and the experience of the DREAM program in prevention of mother-to-child transmission of HIV*, in "AIDS" 2007 (21), S65-S71.

[6] E. M. Stringer, M. Sinkala, J. S. Stringer, E. Mzyece, I. Makuka, R. L. Goldenberg, et al., *Prevention of mother-to-child transmission of HIV in Africa: successes and challenges in scaling-up a nevirapine-based program in Lusaka, Zambia*, in "AIDS" 2003 (17), 1377–1382.

[7] S. Lockman, R. L. Shapiro, L. M. Smeaton, C. Wester, I. Thior, L. Stevens, et al., *Response to antiretroviral therapy after a single, peripartum dose of nevirapine*, in "N. Engl. J. Med." 2007 (356), 135–147.

[8] P. G. Miotti, T. E. T. Taha, N. I. Kumwenda, R. Broadhead, L. A. Mtimavalye, L. Van der Hoeven, et al., *HIV transmission from breastfeeding: a study in Malawi*, in "JAMA" 1999 (282), 744–749.

[9] M. Giuliano, G. Guidotti, M. Andreotti, M. F. Pirillo, P. Villani, G. Liotta, et al., *Triple antiretroviral prophylaxis administered during pregnancy and after delivery significantly reduces breast milk viral load* (a study within the Drug Resource Enhancement Against AIDS and Malnutrition Program), in "J. Acquir. Immune Defic. Syndr." 2007 (44), 286–291.

[10] L. Palombi, C. F. Perno & M. C. Marazzi, *HIV/AIDS in Africa: Treatment as a*

right and strategies for fair implementation. False assumptions on the basis of a minimalistic approach, in "AIDS" 19 (5), March 25, 2005, 536-7.

[11] P. Germano, E. Buonomo, G. Guidotti, G. Liotta, P. Scarcella, S. Mancinelli, L. Palombi, & M. C. Marazzi, *DREAM: an integrated public health programme to fight HIV/AIDS and malnutrition in limited-resource settings*, WFP – Community of Sant'Egidio, Rome 2007.

[12] M. C. Marazzi, M. Bartolo, P. Germano, G. Guidotti, G. Liotta, M. Magnano San Lio, M. A. Modolo, P. Narciso, C. F. Perno, P. Scarcella, G. Tintisona, & L. Palombi, *Improving adherence to HAART in Africa: the DREAM Programme in Mozambique*, in "Health Education Research" 2005 (9), June.

[13] M. C. Marazzi et al., *How is your Health?*, Leonardo International, Milan 2004. This book has been translated into English, French, Portuguese, Spanish and Albanian.

The Sant'Egidio Community's Humanitarian and Health Diplomacy

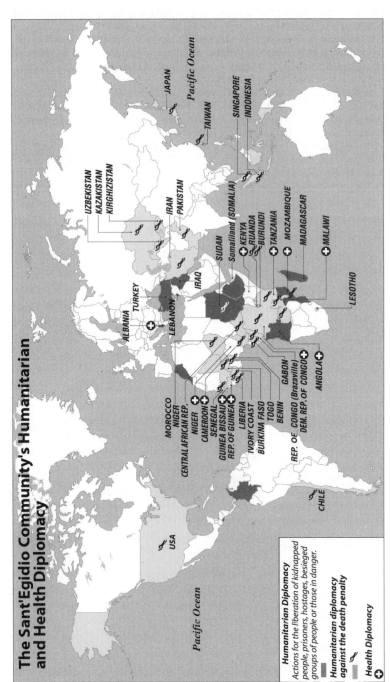

Pacific Ocean

Pacific Ocean

JAPAN

TAIWAN

SINGAPORE
INDONESIA

UZBEKISTAN
KAZAKISTAN
KIRGHIZISTAN

IRAN
PAKISTAN

SUDAN
Somaliland (SOMALIA)

KENYA
RUANDA
BURUNDI
TANZANIA

MOZAMBIQUE
MADAGASCAR

MALAWI

LESOTHO

ALBANIA
TURKEY
LEBANON
IRAQ

MOROCCO
NIGER
CENTRAL AFRICAN REP.
NIGER
CAMEROON
SENEGAL
GUINEA BISSAU
REP. OF GUINEA
LIBERIA
IVORY COAST
BURKINA FASO
TOGO
BENIN
REP. OF CONGO (Brazaville)
DEM. REP. OF CONGO
GABON
ANGOLA

USA

CHILE

Humanitarian Diplomacy
Actions for the liberation of kidnapped people, prisoners, hostages, besieged groups of people or those in danger.

Humanitarian diplomacy against the death penalty

Health Diplomacy

© Laura Canali

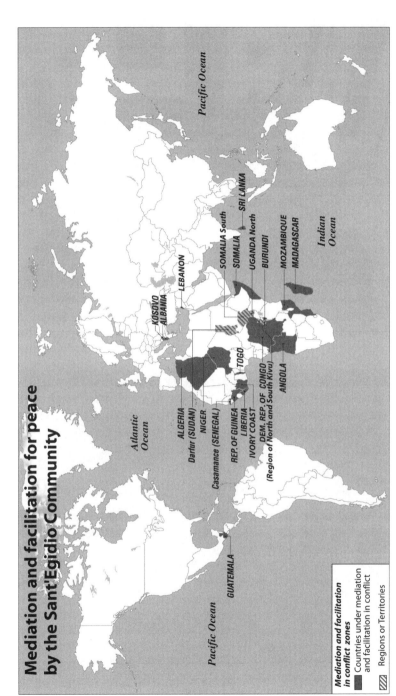

Mediation and facilitation for peace by the Sant'Egidio Community

Pacific Ocean

Atlantic Ocean

Pacific Ocean

Indian Ocean

GUATEMALA

ALGERIA
Darfur (SUDAN)
NIGER
Casamance (SENEGAL)
REP. OF GUINEA
LIBERIA
IVORY COAST
DEM. REP. OF CONGO
(Region of North and South Kivu)
TOGO
ANGOLA

KOSOVO
ALBANIA
LEBANON

SOMALIA South
SOMALIA
UGANDA North
BURUNDI
SRI LANKA
MOZAMBIQUE
MADAGASCAR

Mediation and facilitation in conflict zones
█ Countries under mediation and facilitation in conflict
▨ Regions or Territories

© Laura Canali

The peace negotiators in Mozambique: the negotiating room at the Sant'Egidio Community

The advanced stages of the negotiations. From left to right: Guebuza, Raffaelli, Domingos, Riccardi

Representatives of the Guatemalan government and the *comandancia* of the guerrillas meeting at the community of Sant'Egidio

After the signing of the Platform of Rome for Algeria

23 June, 1997. The signing of the Pact for the future of Albania

22 March, 1998. The signing of the implementation of the Agreement between Serbs and Albanians at Pristina

Negotiators for the Ivory Coast at Marcoussis

The negotiating table at Ouagadougou

A DREAM activity

Cities for Life: 30 November 2000 at the Colosseum

Humanitarian Diplomacy Efforts
against Capital Punishment

Facts and figures on the death penalty as at November 2010

144 countries in total no longer used the death penalty *de jure* or *de facto*
95 countries had abolished it completely
9 countries had abolished it for ordinary crimes (though it was still practiced in times of war and in special circumstances)
40 countries had not, in practice, used it for over 10 years
53 countries and territories had retained and continued to use the death penalty
192 countries were Member States of the UN General Assembly
106 Member States voted in favor of the 2008 UN Resolution for a Universal Moratorium on the Death Penalty (reaffirming the 2007 UN Moratorium Resolution)
46 Member States voted against
34 Member States abstained
6 Member States were absent when the vote was taken
72 countries had signed and ratified the UN's Second Optional Protocol (which commits party States to the abolition of the death penalty)
3 countries had signed but not ratified the Second Optional Protocol
4 countries still had the death penalty for children and minors: Iran, Saudi Arabia, Sudan and Yemen
714 people were known to have been executed in 2009 (in 18 countries)/ Around 5,000 people were estimated to have been executed around the world in 2009
72-87% percent of total executions in the world were carried out in China, whose per-capita execution rate was not, however, the highest among retentionist countries
5 countries with the highest number of reported executions in the world in 2009 were: China (precise figures not available), Iran (388), Iraq (120), Saudi Arabia (69), and the United States (52)
1,137 cities participated in the Community of Sant'Egidio's *Cities Against the Death Penalty Day* initiative in 2009

Humanitarian diplomacy efforts against capital punishment

Mario Marazziti

A day to remember

On December 18, 2007, the sixty-second session of the General Assembly of the United Nations in New York adopted a resolution calling for a "Moratorium on the use of the Death Penalty". The Resolution was carried by an overwhelming majority, with 104 votes in favor, 54 against and 29 abstentions.[1] There were also five absences when the vote was taken. It was a better result than that obtained during the previous crucial stage just a month earlier, namely, the approval by the Third Committee (dealing, inter alia, with human rights issues), also comprising representatives of all Member States. On that occasion, 99 countries had voted in favor.

Italy had played a decisive – as well as an effective and unobtrusive – role in this process, both through its diplomatic channels and by supporting the work carried out by the Portuguese-led European presidency and other sponsors of the draft Resolution, ranging from New Zealand to East Timor. Pivotal to achieving this outcome was the work of several organizations whose roots lay in Italy, including Hands Off Cain (Nessuno tocchi Caino) and the Community of Sant'Egidio, during the final weeks, over the previous year, and throughout the entire journey that from the initial setbacks of the late 1990s led to ultimate success. One of the keys to this success was the ability to forge partnerships with non-European governments and other humanitarian organizations, such as Amnesty International and the World Coalition Against the Death Penalty.

The Resolution endorsed a fundamental concept, namely: that the death penalty and aspirations to abolish it were no longer merely private matters or battles to be fought by abolitionist organizations. It established that the issue was a concern for the entire international community, and that henceforth it was the United Nations and the Secretary-General who would be called upon to monitor compliance or otherwise with the terms of the Resolution, "with a view to abolishing the death penalty". New standards were set for the respect of human life in the enforcement of justice – even in its most extreme form.

And whilst the Resolution was not binding, the death penalty became an issue for the international community and could no longer be treated as a question solely within the purview of national legal systems, though individual Member States clearly retained full sovereignty on matters pertaining to internal justice. Nevertheless, it was made clear that the desired goal of the international community was to put an end to capital punishment. So how was this result achieved? First and foremost, thanks to efforts undertaken at the UN headquarters in New York by Italy's Permanent Mission to the UN, and in particular by Ambassador Spadafora and First Counselor Gatti, in close liaison with the Italian government. But there was also extensive work carried out – both at the UN and in the vast global arena – by other actors, such as the Community of Sant'Egidio.

The Community became involved in the campaign against the death penalty starting with the case of the young Afro-American Dominique Green, who not long after turning 18 ended up in the Polunsky Unit in Huntsville on a conviction of having killed a black man during a robbery. The case was exemplary in the 'all-too-familiar' way it had played out: Dominique was with three accomplices at the time, one white and two Afro-Americans, of whom the former was released and not subjected to any prosecution. The other two were offered a plea bargain, on the condition that they identified Dominique as the sole perpetrator of the murder. Dominique was sentenced to death by a jury which had no Afro-Americans on it, with a judge who was eager to bring the case to a rapid close and a court-appointed defense team that did not object to testimony given by experts later criticized for explicit racism.

Over the course of his twelve years on death row, Dominique Green's story took on a symbolic significance internationally. His execution sparked an emotional response due, in part, to the unusual level of maturity and moral stature achieved by the condemned man, which was acknowledged both by those who knew him well and by his fellow inmates on death row. It was this very case that prompted Sant'Egidio to take up the struggle against capital punishment – a commitment which, as at 2008, had seen the Community involved to varying degrees in some 3,000 cases of people sentenced to death around the world.

The abolitionist stalemate

In 1994, a resolution sponsored by Italy was defeated by a mere 8 votes at the UN, though this was the culmination of an international struggle that had seen an abolitionist movement emerge only after the Second World War. Just twenty years before, when the Helsinki Conference was held between 1973 and 1975, there were only 23 abolitionist countries in the world.

From 1976 onwards, the movement gained greater momentum, though by the second half of the 1990s many countries still had not joined the abolitionist cause. By 1995, another 41 countries had abolished the death penalty for all crimes and 9 for ordinary crimes. Naturally, in certain cases there was a rite of passage from abolition for ordinary crimes to a complete rejection of capital punishment, including in the military justice system. The transition in France, led by Mitterrand and Badinter, which saw a move away from the use of the guillotine to a radical repudiation of the death penalty, was one that took place in another 14 European countries from 1996 onwards, including, in particular, the States of the former Yugoslavia, as well as Albania and the Baltic republics.

During the same period, spanning 1996-2008, 22 countries outside Europe abolished capital punishment for all crimes and 16 for ordinary crimes, culminating in Uzbekistan's abolition on January 1, 2008.[2]

As at 2010, 95 countries had abolished the death penalty for all crimes and 9 for ordinary crimes, whilst those considered abolitionists in practice – because they had not carried out executions for over ten years – numbered 40, making a total of 144 countries worldwide.

On December 15, 1989, the UN General Assembly adopted the Second Optional Protocol to the International Covenant on Civil and Political Rights, which encouraged Member States to abolish the death penalty and committed signatory countries to doing so. Progress on this important document has, however, been very slow, with a number of the party countries still not having given it the necessary parliamentary ratification. Indeed, as at 2007, 8 of the 72 signatory countries had not yet completed the ratification process.

Despite the growing number of abolitionist countries, after 2000 the international abolitionist movement seemed to lack unity in terms of its strategies and organization. From an operational point of view, there was a considerable divide between so-called strict abolitionists on the one hand, and organizations and countries in favor of a moratorium on executions on the other. Seen as an internal matter for each country, the abolitionist movement found it difficult to make any appreciable progress without having to go through the leadership channels of individual States.

Being generally highly critical of any initiative that supported a moratorium, the abolitionist movement appeared reluctant to come to terms with what – when all was said and done – seemed tantamount to an implicit acceptance of capital punishment, given its minimalist demand for a halt to executions through the adoption of appropriate legal measures.

The dearth of news in Europe regarding the situation in Asia was a further obstacle. The United States remained the major focus of attention, due to the availability of data and the ready flow of information. For better or for worse, the US monopolized both strategies and debate – including those of capital punishment opponents. After having made campaigning on this issue central to its mission since the 1970s, thanks to which the first international breakthrough in this area was made, Amnesty International had dropped it as a key plank of its agenda, though it continued to maintain a central office in London, highlight urgent cases promptly and issue an annual report on the use of capital punishment. There was, however, a certain degree of wariness within

344

Amnesty International towards the "moratorium" approach and the idea of getting such a proposal through the UN.

In the US in particular, whilst the abolitionist movement appeared to be widespread, it was heterogeneous and fragmented. Strategies varied between different States of the Union. The pan-American Convention against the death penalty, held in San Francisco in 1999 and organized by the National Coalition Against the Death Penalty and Death Penalty Focus California, which was attended by European representatives and co-sponsored by the Community of Sant'Egidio marked a watershed. The Community gave a final address at the Convention together with Sister Helen Prejean, who had become famous through the film "Dead Man Walking", which was inspired by her work in American prisons. It was the first sign of a breakdown in the isolation of the American movement, and the beginning of a rapprochement between the abolitionist front and those in favor of a moratorium.

At the end of the 1990s, the Community of Sant'Egidio identified at least three key problem areas. The first concerned the right to a fair trial of those sentenced to death, living conditions within prisons, and the limitation of human rights that went hand-in-hand with the wait on death row in certain legal systems. The second related to the strategic and operational rift between supporters of a moratorium and those advocating the abolition of capital punishment – the primary obstacle holding back grassroots and diplomatic action. Finally, there was a significant lack of national and international coordination of those most active in civil society, who were often isolated or in competition, with a consequent reduction in the effectiveness of their efforts both in individual cases and on abolitionist processes in the various countries.

The Appeal for a Universal Moratorium and the Cities for Life initiative

In 1998, Sant'Egidio launched the "Appeal for a Universal Moratorium". It was a cultural breakthrough which initiated the process of reconciling the two strategic approaches.

Amnesty International, under the leadership of Pierre Sané, assisted in the collection of signatures. Several Catholic-inspired movements in Italy and in other countries also helped gather signatures. In two years, Sant'Egidio had collected 3 million signatures in over 130 countries around the world, which brought together leading figures from different cultures and religions spanning the entire spectrum, with Rabbi David Rosen's signature to be found alongside that of the then Indonesian President Abdurrahman Wahid, a Muslim, and those of lay opinion leaders. On December 18, 2000, the three million signatures were delivered to UN Secretary-General Kofi Annan by Mario Marazziti, Sister Helen Prejean, and Paul Hoffman of the American arm of Amnesty International. "The New York Times" reported as follows:

Mario Marazziti, a 48-year-old Italian journalist, was bustling around Manhattan last weekend amid the throngs of shoppers and wide-eyed tourists. His goal, however, was not to find the perfect gift or to admire the Christmas tree in Rockefeller Center or to take in a performance of the "Messiah" or even to scout out projects for the official Italian television channel, of which he is a senior manager.

He was here to help put an end to the death penalty.

On Monday [December 18], Mr. Marazziti presented Kofi Annan, secretary general of the United Nations, a petition signed by 3.2 million people calling for a moratorium on executions. The signers, from 145 countries, included Elie Wiesel; the Dalai Lama; President Vaclav Havel of the Czech Republic; President Abdurrahman Wahid of Indonesia; the Most Rev. George Carey, the archbishop of Canterbury; and several high Vatican officials.

Some of those 3.2 million signatures were gathered by Amnesty International and some by Moratorium 2000, the campaign of Sister Helen Prejean, who wrote "Dead Man Walking" and also participated in the United Nations event.

But the bulk of the signatures – about 2.7 million – were gathered by the Sant'Egidio Community, an unusual movement of Roman Catholic lay people for which Mr. Marazziti is the spokesman. [...]

In accepting the petition, Mr. Annan seemed to agree. He acknowledged that "many still hold that the right to life can be forfeited by those who take life, just as their liberty can be

346

abridged". It was a position, he said, "strongly held by many persons of wisdom and integrity".

But "if I may be permitted a personal view", he added, "the forfeiture of life is too absolute, too irreversible, for one human being to inflict on another, even when backed by legal process. And I believe that future generations, throughout the world, will come to agree".[3]

On December 12, 1999, the Colosseum was illuminated using special lighting for the first time to celebrate the abolition of the death penalty in Albania. It was a symbolic and innovative initiative, devised by the Community of Sant'Egidio, Hands Off Cain, the Italian chapter of Amnesty International, and the City of Rome. Sant'Egidio, which had played a not insignificant role in the Balkan country since its fledgling steps towards democratic transition, helped guide the process that led Albania to join the rest of Europe in also abolishing capital punishment.

November 30, 2000 saw the beginning of the "World Day of Cities for Life – Cities Against the Death Penalty" movement, with the Colosseum at its symbolic heart and Rome as its driving force. The date settled on was the anniversary of the first abolition of the death penalty in law by a State, the Grand Duchy of Tuscany, which, under Grand Duke Peter Leopold I, outlawed torture and capital punishment in 1786. The event was aimed at mobilizing civil society. Cities were chosen as places of awareness and political initiative, in order to provide a vehicle for rallying support around the world that was further capable of generating interest in retentionist countries.

Sant'Egidio also furnished support during the various stages of the legislative process that led Chile to abandon the death penalty. President Lagos received numerous requests and suggestions on ways to facilitate the legislative process on an issue that was highly publicly sensitive. An important role was played by the Chilean Embassy in Rome and by Marcia Scantlebury, one of the journalists persecuted by the Pinochet regime to the point of being imprisoned and tortured, and who had been living in Italy for some time. The link between the campaign conducted within Chile and the international Cities for Life initiative was also to prove pivotal.

The decision to abolish the death penalty was made in April 2001, and the occasion was officially celebrated at the Colosseum in Rome in the presence of the Chilean Justice Minister José Antonio Gómez, together with the Chilean Ambassador to Italy. This "Chilean" event served as a sort of dress rehearsal for the first "World Day Against the Death Penalty", which would be held on November 30, 2002 and was preceded by the First World Congress Against the Death Penalty, held in Strasbourg at the initiative of the French organization Ensemble Contre la Peine de Morte (ECPM), with the support of the French government.

Strasbourg was chosen as the venue with good reason: the EU was exerting a considerable moral power of attraction which reached its peak, also in symbolic terms, when, with a view to paving the way for the commencement of talks over Turkey's accession to the EU, the Turkish parliament first halted the execution of Öcalan, leader of the armed Kurdish separatist movement the PKK, and then of others condemned to death. Within the EU, alongside Italy's capacity for initiative, that of Chirac's France was also growing. France still heavily reflected the moral influence of Robert Badinter, lawyer and Justice Minister during the first presidential term of Mitterrand (who, as previously mentioned, had spearheaded efforts to abolish the guillotine and State executions in a France still heavily divided on this issue). Twenty-six people, representing as many international organizations and institutions, signed the Final Declaration of the Congress of Strasbourg, which led to the establishment, shortly thereafter, of the World Coalition Against the Death Penalty (WCADP).

The wording of the Declaration was the fruit of intensive efforts, at times fraught with tension, to unite the "abolitionist" movement with those supporting a "universal moratorium". It echoed concerns over the continued use of capital punishment in Russia, Armenia and Turkey, some of Europe closest neighbors. It called into question the participation as observers in the Council of Europe of countries that had retained capital punishment, such as Japan and the United States. It pointed to the cessation of executions of minors and the mentally disabled as a goal requiring immediate action.

Most importantly, however, towards the end it stated in bold: "We, citizens of the world, call for an immediate halt to all executions of those sentenced to death and the universal abolition of the death penalty".[4] The marrying of these two objectives was, as we have seen, by no means an inevitable outcome. Indeed, the Community of Sant'Egidio, as it had on other occasions, mediated between Hands Off Cain and Amnesty International, in this case with strong support from the ECPM, the Fédération Internationale des ligues des Droits de l'Homme (FIDH), and the Ligue Interrégionale des Droits de l'Homme (LIDH), with the result that the two goals became part of a single strategy. Thus, the way was now paved, albeit yet to be tested.

Towards a common front: the World Coalition Against the Death Penalty

The Strasbourg Declaration made reference to the Community of Sant'Egidio's Appeal for a Universal Moratorium and the petitions of the FIDH, even though many during the Congress proceedings felt that these were modest in their demands, with a view to giving rise to a unified strategy, fostering the emergence of a coordinated international movement, and avoiding any definitive split between the two camps. It was the beginning of the journey that would lead, six years later, to the adoption by the UN General Assembly of the Resolution on a Universal Moratorium.

On May 13, 2002, at the headquarters of the Community of Sant'Egidio in Rome, the World Coalition Against the Death Penalty was founded. A Steering Committee made up of representatives of eleven associations and NGOs became its organizational hub and the forum where strategies would be developed. The ECPM was tasked with undertaking the work of the Coalition's Executive Secretariat. It was decided to hold the First World Day Against the Death Penalty on November 30, 2002, taking advantage of the international movement previously launched by Sant'Egidio with the Cities for Life initiative.

From 2003 onwards, the Steering Committee opted, not without some difficulty, to establish two worldwide rallying events: the World Day Against the Death Penalty, held on October 10 each year, and the International Day of Cities Against the Death Penalty, on November 30. October and November thus became months of global campaigning for the halting of all executions, to coincide with the opening of proceedings and debate at the UN General Assembly, during which draft resolutions are introduced each fall.

In the meantime, relations between Sant'Egidio and many US organizations that for years had been fighting to put an end to the death penalty grew stronger.[5] These contacts helped reduce a certain US tendency towards isolationism and bolstered European mobilization. Around this time, international public attention was becoming increasingly focused on the issue of "miscarriages of justice" due to the many glaring cases that had come to light, which within a few years led to the release of more than 120 people sentenced to death who were innocent or victims of blatant legal discrimination.

At the same time, there were increasing demands by families of victims of crime for justice without vengeance or expiation involving the death penalty. Efforts were also stepped up, on a case-by-case basis, to end executions in the US of the mentally retarded and those who were juveniles at the time of the crime in question. These battles were fought in the context of emblematic cases which took on great significance in the eyes of the public. Sant'Egidio got involved in the campaign to save John Paul Penry – a man suffering from mental retardation and accused of the rape and murder of a young Texan woman – from the death penalty. It was the only case in American judicial history where superior courts had intervened three times to overturn a death sentence and request a retrial. The case went on for 28 years, during which at one point the Supreme Court made a ruling that the execution of the mentally retarded was unconstitutional.

This, however, did not prevent the State of Texas from trying to have Penry condemned to death a fourth time, until a plea bargain was reached. Under its terms, the death penalty would not be sought but rather commuted, as agreed by the defendant's counsel, to life imprisonment. Since January 15, 2008, John Paul Penry has officially no longer been on death row. The Polk County District Court finally opted for a life sentence without any possibility of parole. Penry's death sentence was first overturned in 1989, and a second time in 2001. In 1999, on November 14, John Paul Penry was taken to the so-called "death house" in Huntsville and was given his last meal, after meeting his pen pal, the Roman physician and member of Sant'Egidio, Gianni Guidotti. In the evening, before six, following a major international and local campaign that had made it awkward even for the State of Texas to proceed in disregard of the many objections raised by the defense, a stay of execution was granted.

The campaign involving numerous associations for people with disabilities from around the world and coordinated by Sant'Egidio most likely contributed to this outcome, whilst humanitarian diplomacy efforts had, in the case of Penry, gradually taken the form of a public awareness-raising strategy, which succeeded in drawing attention to a standard of moral decency that was hard to ignore in a globalized world.

Safiya, Abok, Amina and others

Mobilization on this issue was not, however, confined to the United States. In the course of its humanitarian and legal efforts, Sant'Egidio – initially through written appeals and then by undertaking legal efforts in a diverse range of cases – came into contact with situations that went unheeded in Europe, particularly in Asia (ranging from Indonesia to Japan) and in Africa, until more than 3,000 individual cases of people sentenced to death were being monitored as part of the international campaign. Over the years, this has led to direct initiatives and urgent action in an attempt to halt executions in 80 cases worldwide.[6] Along the way, Sant'Egidio has gradually become a point of contact for abolitionist and humanitarian organizations in various parts of the world.

The widespread international presence of the Community, with local staff in several countries, ensures that first reports, the initial urgent appeal and early efforts at mobilization in individual cases are timely. This is precisely what happened in the case of a Nigerian woman sentenced to death, Safiya Hussaini, who would go on to become a *cause célèbre*. The particular type of strategy employed, which combined a focus on the needs of the individual concerned, a public awareness campaign, international mobilization, cooperation with other actors, and the involvement of parliamentary, institutional and international diplomatic channels, culminated in success.

Although the resort to publicity and public awareness campaigns is not a characteristic feature of Sant'Egidio's intervention strategy, it has tended to play an important role when silence and remoteness from the channels through which Western policies and public opinion are shaped threaten to make the violation of basic human rights (such as the right to a proper defense) and the death sentence inevitable.

On October 9, 2001, Safiya Hussaini Tungar Tudu had been sentenced to death by stoning on a charge of adultery by a court in Gwadabawa, in the Nigerian State of Sokoto, while she was still pregnant. Her acquittal came on March 25, 2002, after six months of international campaigning efforts. An urgent plea on her behalf, published on the Community's website, was the first to appear online reporting the incident, and was immediately picked up by the major international media outlets.

On November 27, 2001, twenty Italian senators took up the Community's appeal and urged the Foreign Minister in the first Berlusconi government, Renato Ruggiero, to intercede with the Nigerian government to save the woman's life. A letter to President Olusegun Obasanjo implored that the "inhuman sentence" not be carried out. On December 18, another 60 Italian MPs added their voices to the formal request made to the Nigerian government. Although the case involved a question of local justice, which apparently did not come within the purview of the central government due to Nigeria's federal structure, these were nevertheless important steps that contributed to the positive outcome of the case and the release of Safiya.

Abok Alfa Akok was another woman whose life would have been extinguished if her case had not been brought to world attention. A young Sudanese Christian who was unmarried and had fallen pregnant, she was sentenced to death on a charge of adultery by a local court in a remote area of Sudan. She was probably unaware of the diplomatic efforts being made to save her life, until February 9, 2002, when, after Sant'Egidio's repeated requests, the Sudanese government informed the Community that the death sentence by stoning imposed on the eighteen-year-old had been "reversed by the Supreme Court". She had been convicted by a court in Nyala, in South Darfur, without being given access to a defense lawyer during questioning or at the trial, which were both conducted in Arabic, a language she did not understand.

From the day reports of the case emerged, Sant'Egidio sought to collect what little evidence corroborating the story and information was available, and, from February 5 onwards, applied constant pressure on Sudanese authorities behind the scenes. On February 8, the Community made an appeal to the Sudanese President, Omar Hassan Al-Bashir, and all members of the government, to save the life of Abok Alfa Akok, and set about pursuing informal contacts until news that the sentence had been quashed was received. Similar in tone and strategy was the campaign undertaken in another case that became widely-known in Italy and which saw the Community of Sant'Egidio again engaged in efforts to halt an execution. It involved another woman in Nigeria: Amina Lawal.

Amina lived in Kurami, a small farming community in the Nigerian State of Katsina. Like Safiya, she was 35 years old when she was sentenced to death by stoning for adultery, following the birth of a daughter after she was divorced. Her sentence was handed down on March 22, 2002, by a court in Bakori, in the said State of Katsina, one of the twelve Muslim-majority States in northern Nigeria where, in early 2000, Shari'a law had been introduced. Amina Lawal was divorced between late 2000 and early 2001. Over the following eleven months, she had been seeing a man in her village, Yahaya Mohammed. Baby Wasila, the unwitting cause of the subsequent death sentence, was born in early

2002. Initially absolved, Amina was again brought before the courts by her fellow villagers and failed to prove that the child's father was the man she had been seeing and that he had promised to marry her.

The Islamic judge presiding, Nasiru Lawal Bello Dayi, acquitted the man Yahaya Mohammed (no DNA testing was performed in this northern Nigerian province) and sentenced Amina to death. The sentence was upheld on August 19, 2002, and the execution was scheduled to take place in January 2004. Statements made by Sant'Egidio's spokesperson on August 20, 2002 stressed that Amina's sentence stemmed from an intolerant application of Shari'a law, against the backdrop of tensions between President Obasanjo, who wished Nigeria to embrace the model of the world's leading democracies, and certain regions in the country who were opposed to this, emphasizing religious differences. It was suggested that the symbolic case of a woman sentenced to death for adultery and the international outcry that followed could "help Islam forge its own connections with democracy" and reveal a more tolerant face of Islam, which did exist.[7]

On September 25, 2003 Amina was finally acquitted of the charge of adultery and released. In order to succeed in having the sentence overturned, legal inquiries and research into Islamic law proved necessary, efforts which were sponsored by Sant'Egidio. Hauwa Ibrahim, Amina's lawyer, and the Indian attorney Sona Kahn, working in an international pool of experts assembled especially for the occasion, opened the way for a reconsideration of the local Islamic court's decision and the quashing of Amina's death sentence, as finally ruled by the Supreme Court, on the basis of the invalidity of evidence obtained at first instance without access to legal representation.

Further humanitarian efforts by the Community resulted in the death sentence of two Lebanese men, Sami Yassine and Khalil Ghodban, set aside in the Democratic Republic of the Congo. Laurent Kabila, the then President of the country, accepted Sant'Egidio's plea for clemency. In Morocco, the same happened in the case of the Algerian Merzoug Hamel, who was sentenced to death for a massacre he never went ahead with because, at the last minute, he could not bring himself to harm Jewish children who were present.

Direct inquiries carried out at the request of Sant'Egidio led to a review of his death sentence.[8] A similar outcome was achieved in Cameroon in respect of two young inmates awaiting execution in Tcholliré prison who had turned to the Community for assistance, and whose sentences were commuted after Sant'Egidio instituted legal efforts and interceded with State authorities. Thanks to other interventions in Cameroon, between 2003 and 2004, the death sentences of Mathias Mandoline, David Bonabé, Hyacinte Yedem Djemb, Roger Paul Mbah, Simon Owona and Raphael Mbarga were also commuted. During 2004, Modeste Laritia, Yaya Bouba, Albert Oudini, Martin Oudate, John Wanda, Daniel Kombo, Germain Belibi, Philippe Balkai Mokoyom and Joseph Anguissa, all of whom were detained in Tcholliré prison and had been sentenced to death, were also finally set free.

The situation across Asia

In Central Asia, the Community of Sant'Egidio's strategy initially involved supporting and empowering local actors, and then developed into fostering direct institutional and diplomatic contacts, culminating in the abolition of capital punishment in Uzbekistan and Kyrgyzstan and a *de jure* moratorium in Kazakhstan.

In Uzbekistan, execution was accompanied by secrecy regarding the place of burial, making it practically impossible to verify whether the death penalty had been further compounded by physical torture. This was the starting point for the Community of Sant'Egidio's efforts, supporting the work of a courageous woman, Tamara Chikunova, and the Mothers Against the Death Penalty and Torture association. Up until January 1, 2008, when the death penalty was abolished in Uzbekistan, the executions of 19 people were averted, whilst ten other detainees were acquitted of murder on a retrial or acknowledged as innocent before the death sentence was carried out and thus immediately released. This required both legal efforts as well as an active presence within the country, which necessitated an international support network involving the embassies of Italy, Germany and France in Tashkent.

This external safety net and a series of logistical support measures proved crucial to maintaining ongoing efforts against capital punishment and to discouraging any actions that might jeopardize them. The journey towards abolition took around seven years, culminating in the undertakings given in 2006 that were fulfilled with the final abolition of capital punishment for all crimes at the beginning of 2008.

In March 2007, the Community of Sant'Egidio organized a mission to Kazakhstan aimed at discussing with local authorities the possibility of the country supporting the Resolution for a moratorium on the death penalty that would be put to the vote at the UN the following fall. Indeed, Kazakhstan was one of the Member States which voted in favor of the UN Resolution in December 2007. The mission was preceded by talks with Laura Mirachian, Director-General for the Countries of Europe at the Italian Ministry of Foreign Affairs, and was organized in collaboration with the Italian Ambassador to Kazakhstan, Bruno Antonio Pasquino. This was a case where institutional cooperation paid off. During the visit, discussions were held with numerous civil and religious authorities and figures in the country, including Kasymzhomart K. Tokayev, the President of the Senate who, in October 2007, participated in the inter-religious Meeting of Prayer for Peace in Naples sponsored by the Community.

The talks touched on various religious and political issues, focusing in particular on an international moratorium on the death penalty and interfaith dialogue. Sant'Egidio made an official request for a moratorium on executions to be enshrined in law and offered to assist in facilitating the associated legislative process. An initial response by Kazakhstan to the Community's request, formulated in agreement with the Italian Embassy, was to sign the Declaration of Association on May 12, 2007 that was a prelude to the UN initiative launched by the Italian Foreign Minister. At the end of 2007, the Kazakh parliament formally put in place a permanent legal moratorium on executions, replacing the previous 2003 moratorium which had been subject to renewal on an annual basis.

Progress towards the abolition of capital punishment met with less resistance in Kyrgyzstan than in Uzbekistan. Indeed, the efforts of the Community along with Mothers Against the Death Penalty and Torture, in conjunction with Amnesty

International, were rewarded there with success before they were in Uzbekistan. The capital Bishkek was the first city in Central Asia to join the Cities for Life movement. On April 26, 2007, a law was passed that introduced "amendments and further provisions to the Criminal Code and the Code of Criminal Procedure". From the following July, the death penalty was replaced by life imprisonment. The new law also provided for a review of the trials of those who had been sentenced to death.

It is also worth noting here the initiatives carried out over the last decade aimed at encouraging a reconsideration of the use of capital punishment in many other Asian States. In this regard, Indonesia merits a special mention. At the end of the 1990s, the then President Abdurrahman Wahid, head of the most populous Muslim nation in the world, was the most prominent figure in the Islamic world to have signed the Appeal for a Universal Moratorium on the Death Penalty. That signature was followed by a process of discussion and reflection, which Sant'Egidio continued to nurture through direct contact with Indonesian authorities, including when "crises" arose over the use of capital punishment, such as preceded the execution of Fabianus Tibo, Domingus da Silva and Marinus Riwu.

As is well-known, these three Catholic Indonesians were charged with inciting clashes between Christians and Muslims in Poso, on the island of Sulawesi, which had led to the deaths of many people in 2000. Their conviction had seemed unfounded from the outset and gave rise to an extensive international campaign calling for a halt to their executions and a reopening of the case against them. The international initiative of the Catholic Church and the various Indonesian social groups that took up their cause did not prevent their execution from going ahead in 2006, but contributed to increasing parliamentary support for a moratorium law.[9] A similar public campaign directed at the Indonesian authorities was launched in September 2007 to save the life of young Amrozi bin Nurhasym, accused of being one of the perpetrators of the 2002 Bali bombings and accordingly sentenced to death.

In Pakistan, whilst debate raged between the Minister of Justice and the Supreme Court over the commutation of 7,000 death sentences, on October 30, 2006 and August 8, 2008 the Community of Sant'Egidio successfully negotiated with victims' families to grant their forgiveness to three prisoners sentenced to death, thereby averting their execution.

Joining forces: the World Congress Against the Death Penalty in Paris

From 2003 onwards, the Cities for Life Day and the World Day Against the Death Penalty became the two main international events for mobilizing support against capital punishment. 2006-2007 ushered in the beginning of the European Union's recognition and backing for the efforts of the WCADP and the Community of Sant'Egidio to create an international network in support of civil society organizations working to bring an end to the death penalty in retentionist countries in certain geographical areas, ranging from the Great Lakes and Central Asia to the Caribbean. Sant'Egidio's view was that stepping up direct contacts with and pressure on governments and leaders of retentionist countries would enable a more rapid transition towards abolition to be achieved.

Special attention was devoted to sub-Saharan Africa, where, in the space of a few years, the number of abolitionist countries increased from only 4 to 15. In 2005 and 2007, in addition to numerous direct meetings with government representatives of retentionist African countries, and partly due to the fact that by its very nature the Community of Sant'Egidio is present in all of these countries with local staff and not European aid-workers or agencies, two international conferences were organized in Rome which saw thirty Ministers of Justice (in total over the two events) participate in public forums and workshops held behind closed doors.

2007 marked a turning point in progress towards a goal that initially only a few saw as attainable, namely: the adoption by the UN General Assembly of the proposed Resolution for a Universal Moratorium. The change in climate seemed to stem from negative reactions – mainly of international public opinion and Arab countries in the Mediterranean – to the execution of Saddam Hussein. Well- and broadly-targeted public appeals by a wide range of actors, including Sant'Egidio, did not succeed in halting the execution, which was broadcast around the world despite official efforts to prevent this.

A political window of opportunity did, however, open up. It seemed clear that Italy would put forward an international initiative, and its first litmus test was to be the Third World Congress Against the Death Penalty in Paris, held on February 1-3, 2007. The Congress was organized by the ECPM with the assistance of the WCADP. Some participants sought to gain the support of the Congress to present the draft Resolution in the "current" session of the General Assembly, which had opened in the fall of 2006. However, as no efforts at garnering international consensus in favor of the Resolution had yet been made, the initiative would probably have failed.

This proposal therefore received little backing. Sant'Egidio, on the other hand, endeavored to have the draft Resolution submitted at the following session, which would open in September 2007, so as to allow time for Italy and other European governments to gather the necessary support for what needed to be more than just a European initiative; otherwise, there was a risk that the defeat of a decade before would be repeated. Prior to approving the final document, extensive private discussions took place between the leaders of Amnesty International, the Community of Sant'Egidio, Hands Off Cain, the FIDH, and the American Civil Liberties Union (ACLU).

Eric Prokosch, who had been working on drafting the Final Declaration of the Congress, introduced a paragraph concerning the commitment of all sections of the worldwide movement to the adoption by the United Nations of a moratorium. However, the paragraph did not meet with approval and was on the verge of being left out of the final wording. Sant'Egidio's view was that this seriously risked undermining the potential of the process being embarked upon to become the most significant international initiative against the death penalty, and would mark a divide between international institutional dynamics and the efforts of key civil society actors on the world stage. Given the need to reach an agreed position, a small working group was established.

While the ECPM had always been unreceptive to the idea of a moratorium, Amnesty International, as a matter of prudence in the face of the complex workings of international institutions, had for years preferred a strategy of seeking to increase the number of countries that had ratified the "Second Optional Protocol", leaving resort to the General Assembly to serve as a final confirmation of an international change that had already taken place. The offices of Amnesty International in New York and London were consulted, and eventually a compromise was found which hinged on the addition of the qualifying adjective "successful".

The point of contention was not whether to go to the United Nations with the proposed Resolution, but rather "when" and with what backing. In short, Amnesty International came to the Congress in Paris with its established position, which would have led to a wait of three, five or even more years – the time needed to produce an overwhelming increase in the number of countries that had ratified the "Second Optional Protocol". For its part, Hands Off Cain wanted to introduce the Resolution immediately, whilst Sant'Egidio preferred to go to the next session, at the end of year.

The revised wording of the Congress' Final Declaration inserted the adjective "successful" before the word "resolution". Essentially, the entire international abolitionist movement called on the Member States of the UN General Assembly to take all necessary steps to ensure the adoption by the General Assembly of a "successful resolution", in recognition of the great impact that this would have on "the abolition of the death penalty worldwide".

Broadening the consensus: the "Africa for Life" Conferences

The compromise reached in Paris represented an important step forward. Indeed, it paved the way for the diplomatic efforts, in the lead-up to the UN vote, of Italy and non-governmental actors such as Hands Off Cain, Amnesty International and Sant'Egidio, working towards the common goal of broadening consensus on the issue of a moratorium.

In the spring of 2007, the Italian government prepared a "Declaration of Association" outlining the underlying strategy and substance of the initiative, and sought support for the initiative that was to be taken in the second half of the year. By March, the Declaration prepared by Italy had received unanimous support from the 27 EU countries and had been signed by 89 countries around the world, including Russia. The goal had been to reach 97, the minimum required to ensure the adoption of the future Resolution at the UN, but this number was not achieved. On April 23, the EU Foreign Ministers agreed on the initiative and it was placed on the agenda for the upcoming EU presidency of Portugal, which would become responsible for its coordination from June. At the beginning of August, at the Ministry of Foreign Affairs in Lisbon, representatives of Hands Off Cain, Amnesty International and Sant'Egidio agreed the terms of the international initiative with the Portuguese Foreign Ministry, and hence with the EU presidency.

Sant'Egidio stressed the need for a cross-regional initiative involving at least two key countries from each geographic area as co-authors of the draft Resolution, and pressed for the participation of Russia and South Africa in the preparatory stages. There was substantial agreement on these matters and the next meetings were scheduled to take place directly in New York in September. Nevertheless, there were still strong fears that a majority might not be reached during the vote in the Third Committee. The wording of the Resolution also still needed to be checked with the other co-authors.

The Community of Sant'Egidio had already been working towards widening consensus against the death penalty. In November 2005, it had organized the first international "Africa for Life" Conference, with the participation of twelve African Ministers of Justice, along with jurists and constitutional experts, aimed at prompting a re-examination of the use of the death penalty, especially in Africa, where there seemed to be more of an inclination towards a change. On June 18, 2007, the second "Africa for Life" Conference held at the Capitol in Rome gathered together an even higher number of political leaders and parliamentarians from abolitionist and retentionist African countries. This led to a significant "pooling of experiences", enabling difficulties and opportunities on the road towards abolition, as well as solutions and proposals, to be shared.

The initiative had its roots in Sant'Egidio's widespread presence in Africa and in diplomatic efforts involving visits and talks with institutions in African capitals and in Rome. As has already been noted, the interfaith Meeting of Prayer for Peace in Naples in October provided a further such opportunity for countries like Kazakhstan. In response to the Community's direct solicitation, Burundi and Burkina Faso changed their position to support the Resolution during the final vote at the UN on December 18, 2007. Guinea-Conakry, Cameroon, Tanzania and the Central African Republic also shifted from their previous opposition to the proposal and abstained.

The President of Burkina Faso, Blaise Compaoré, went as far as giving an undertaking to Sant'Egidio's delegation that a law abolishing capital punishment would be introduced in Burkina Faso after the adoption of the Resolution by the UN, though in the months that followed the proposal ran into difficulties. On the day of the final vote, Ivory Coast also officially joined the list of co-sponsors.

It was the representative for Gabon who introduced the draft Resolution into the Third Committee at the UN headquarters and who responded in the General Assembly when strong objections were raised by those seeking to label it a neo-colonialist initiative. Gabon was one of the countries that had worked hardest to translate the outcomes of the second "Africa for Life" Conference, held in Rome, into concrete action. The undertakings made on that occasion by Justice Minister Martin Mabala were enshrined in legislation and abolition received parliamentary approval earlier than expected, thanks also to the efforts of the country's head of State, Omar Bongo Ondimba.

But Sant'Egidio's diplomatic initiatives have been even more far-reaching, and have included the involvement of African civil society through public events in support of the abolitionist campaign. Worth recalling are the meetings held with Lesotho's Minister of Justice M. Mahase in Maseru, aimed at obtaining at least an abstention at the UN. Similar efforts were undertaken in Niger, at first with a view to securing an abstention at the UN, and later to help usher in legislative moves to adopt the new international "trend" towards abolition. A public conference under the banner of *Lutte pour l'abolition de la peine de mort au Niger* was held in the capital Niamey in January 2008.

Meanwhile, talks were also conducted at the General Assembly with opposition leader and former Foreign Minister Mohamed Bazoum. These initiatives have made an impact in the national media, helping to pave the way for the legislative processes to be undertaken. Sant'Egidio's support in the move towards abolition of the death penalty in Rwanda had its roots in the Community's efforts to put an end to ethnic conflict and promote civil coexistence after the genocide, just as it did in Burundi and throughout the Great Lakes area, where the Community has for years been working to bring about an end to armed conflict.

Mention should be made here of the meetings held in 2007 and 2008 with representatives of the Rwandan university sector in Butare and Kigali, and then with leaders of the country and, in particular, with Justice Minister Tharcisse Karugarama. In the case of Somaliland, during a visit to Rome by President Dahir Rayale Kahin, the Community secured the commutation of the death sentences imposed on the murderers of the Italian aid worker Annalena Tonelli, following a request made in conjunction with the victim's family.

Of particular note have been Sant'Egidio's efforts in Malawi, where it has deployed an extensive AIDS prevention and treatment program across the country. Here, it has sought to involve wide sections of the public, including village chiefs, churches and NGOs, in creating a common front. These initiatives have seen the participation of Christian church leaders, the Apostolic Nuncio Nicola Girasoli, and the Vice President of the Conference of Imams, but also prison governors and opinion makers in the country, culminating in five national public conferences held in Zomba, Lilongwe, Balaka, Mangochi and Blantyre, and involvement in events held by the three major public universities: Chancellor College in Zomba, Blantyre Polytechnic and Bunda College in Lilongwe.

In early 2007, the Commission tasked with review and amendment of the Constitution recommended the reduction of the range of cases in which the death penalty could be imposed and launched the second stage of the campaign to abolish capital punishment with a new petition signed by 98 members of the preceding Commission, including the President of the Episcopal Conference, Tarcisius Ziaye, and the former Attorney General, Ralph Kasambala. Malawi ended up abstaining in the UN vote, thanks to media and public awareness campaigns, combined institutional and legal efforts, and contact with leaders.

In recent years, similar processes have taken place in Ivory Coast, Cameroon, Rwanda, Guinea and Mozambique, with a focus on also bolstering public support after abolition. In contrast, abolitionist efforts in Liberia – in the wake of support given to ensure a nonviolent transition in Monrovia, which saw Sant'Egidio directly involved in facilitating the handover of power from the dictator Taylor to a democratic government – ran into difficulties in 2008. Like the WCADP, the Community is currently working to secure a review of the Liberian leadership's decision reintroducing the death penalty.

2007: the culmination of a 200-year journey

The history of capital punishment goes back a long way – probably as far back as that of humanity. Popular in almost all cultures, it met with the approval of major thinkers in the Western world for centuries. The reasons for this support varied considerably, ranging from the view that capital punishment provided a way of healing society by severing its "offending limb", as represented by the grave criminal, or by a man that could be equated to a ferocious beast or a disease capable of corrupting the social body, to the idea that a criminal, by his or her very crime, already placed him or herself outside society and the fellowship of man.

The death penalty was accordingly seen as merely a confirmation that he or she had ceased to be "human". In modern times, arguments based on retributive justice or utilitarianism have prevailed over others as justifications for capital punishment, with a focus on deterrence. This view holds that the fear of death is in itself a deterrent to potential criminals. Yet it is also on the basis of utilitarianism that opposition to capital punishment has, in the modern age, slowly gained ground. Today, in major democracies like the

US, the deterrence argument is often raised in debate and is increasingly countered by a utilitarian critique that points to the excessive costs inherent in a justice system based on capital punishment.

The first ever recorded abolition of the death penalty by a State was effected by the so-called "Leopoldine Code" of November 30, 1786 promulgated by Peter Leopold, Grand Duke of Tuscany, which also abolished torture. Beccaria's writings had a direct bearing on this reform, and for a while, even Catherine the Great's Russia drew on their influence. But the resolve of this school of thought still seemed to falter in the face of civil unrest, such that even Peter Leopold himself temporarily reintroduced the death penalty for those responsible for popular uprisings (in 1790). Under his successor Ferdinand III, there was a renewed resort to capital punishment in the Grand Duchy of Tuscany in 1795 and again in 1816.

In other parts of Italy, the death penalty gradually ceased to be a given, with capital punishment abolished in the short-lived 19th-century Roman Republic, and then in unified Italy under the Zanardelli Penal Code (1890). However, this did not signal its definitive abolition, as it was reintroduced under the fascist laws of 1926 "for the defense of the State", and again under the Rocco Code (the basis for Italy's current penal code, which has, however, undergone substantial amendment over the years).

The Italian Constitution of 1948 contained a prohibition on capital punishment, which was subsequently also extended to apply in times of war.

From the 1970s onwards, the fight against capital punishment became part of Amnesty International's worldwide campaigning efforts and the number of abolitionist countries began to grow, though there were only just over twenty by about 1975. In the US, there was a halt in executions. They later resumed and, in 1982, the lethal injection technique was introduced, coming under fire in 2007 and 2008. Since this resumption in the US, Texas alone has gradually come to account for half the executions carried out in the entire Union, whilst California has the highest number of people on death row in the US, with over 600 prisoners awaiting their deaths.

Elsewhere in the world, the death penalty has had a potted history. Although the last execution in San Marino was carried out in 1468 (complete abolition came in 1865), Venezuela and Portugal hold the distinction of having already abolished capital punishment in 1863 and 1867 respectively. In the United States, Michigan abrogated the death penalty on March 1, 1847. Since then, another 12 States and the District of Columbia have followed suit, whilst it remains in force – albeit used to varying degrees – in the remainder of the country.

China has the highest absolute number of executions in modern times, despite the fact that, during the Tang Dynasty, Emperor Xuanzong (who reigned between 712-756) had completely abolished the death penalty. Britain joined the ranks of abolitionist countries in 1971, Canada in 1976, and France in 1981. Australia, in turn, abolished it in 1985.

As can be seen, the move towards the abolition of capital punishment is a recent one. It largely coincides with the post-World War II period, in which European democracies have increasingly made it an identifying attribute of the European Union. In short, Europe is the first "death penalty-free" continent. On an international level, 1976 saw the entry into force of the International Covenant on Civil and Political Rights. As noted previously, the Second Optional Protocol to the Covenant is the international instrument that most clearly rejects the use of the death penalty, even though it does permit a reservation allowing for the application of capital punishment in times of war.

Thirty years on, as at 2008, 72 countries had signed and ratified this Protocol. Gradually, the sentiment once expressed by Albert Camus with reference to his personal experiences in French Algeria has gained acceptance: "The death penalty is not a simple sentence. An execution is not simply death. It is just as different from the privation of life as a concentration camp is from prison. It adds to death a rule, a public premeditation known to the future victim [...]".

The reasons for the success

As already mentioned, an earlier resolution for a universal

moratorium that had been presented to the UN General Assembly in 1994 by Italy, with the active support of Hands Off Cain, was narrowly defeated by only 8 votes. A second attempt led by Europe in 1998, which marked a major setback, was faced with opposition principally from Egypt and other Arab nations, Singapore and other Asian countries, and the Caribbean group of countries. Theirs was a blanket resistance to what was seen as a unilateral imposition on the rest of the world of a "European" – and not a universally-accepted – conception of human rights. The EU, which was divided in its strategies, decided to withdraw the draft resolution before it was put to the vote.

It was from this point that a long-term strategy was set in train which would culminate in the success of nine years later. The international efforts of the Community of Sant'Egidio contributed to this outcome, also thanks to the Appeal for a Universal Moratorium, which saw the collection of five million signatures in 153 countries around the world. These were delivered by a delegation of the Community and the WCADP to the President of the sixty-second session of the UN General Assembly, Srgjan Kerim, on November 2, 2007.

Also crucial was the establishment in Rome of the WCADP itself, at the initiative of the major world abolitionist and humanitarian organizations, including the ECPM, Penal Reform International, Amnesty International, the FIDH, the International Federation of Action by Christians for the Abolition of Torture (FIACAT), Sant'Egidio, Death Penalty Focus, Murder Victims' Families for Human Rights (MVFHR), the Texas Coalition, the National Association of Criminal Defense Lawyers (NACDL) and the Paris Bar Association, together with the principal Asian organizations (which, since 2006, have joined forces under the regional umbrella network ADPAN).

Within the space of a few years, the WCADP had brought together 76 local, national and regional organizations. Finally, mention should also be made of other initiatives that contributed to success at the UN, namely, the World Day Against the Death Penalty, observed on October 10 each year, and last but not least, the World Cities Against the Death Penalty Day, which sees "Cities for Life" linked up in a global network every November 30.

When, in early 2007, the world was still perturbed by the execution of Saddam Hussein, and the international grassroots movement was still uncertain as to whether to step up efforts for a moratorium as part of its abolitionist strategy, there was growing public and institutional support in Italy for the view that the time was ripe for a successful initiative at the UN. The Prodi government and Foreign Minister D'Alema worked on forging a common European position. Meanwhile, Hands Off Cain urged the Italian public and the country's political forces to proceed immediately to debate the issue at the sixty-first session of the UN General Assembly, as mentioned above. It was a risky strategy, but this pressure helped to get the ball rolling and fuel Italian diplomatic action.

Efforts were made to establish a common international front of governments and NGOs in support of the draft Resolution to be presented at the sixty-second session in the fall. In Brussels, in June, at a meeting of the WCADP's Steering Committee, Sant'Egidio and Amnesty International prompted a radical shake-up of the agenda, refocusing attention on ensuring the success of the UN initiative, at a time when mobilization was still entirely geared towards the objectives identified before the Third World Congress Against the Death Penalty held in Paris (in February 2007). From the summer onwards, cooperation between all actors within and outside the WCADP, Italy's strong initiative, and the work of France, Portugal and the group of co-drafters at the UN headquarters, all contributed to a growing consensus for the final wording of the draft Resolution, which, by the day of the final vote, had attracted 87 co-sponsors.

The draft Resolution was presented on the last possible date: November 1. In the Third Committee, there was heated debate over proposed amendments, some of which were aimed at undermining the Resolution. However, these were all rejected by a majority. Once again at the forefront of the opposition were Egypt and certain Arab States, Singapore, the Caribbean countries and Nigeria. It was Gabon that introduced the draft Resolution, which no longer represented a solely European initiative. The exhaustion induced by the debate gave way to loud applause when the vote approving the Resolution was taken in the Committee.

The following month served to heal relations and agree on the procedures for the final vote. There would be a limited number of statements given by those voting against and a single statement for those in favor. Italy would refrain from doing so separately. There would also be no applause, in order to reinstill a spirit of collaboration within the UN. But the result of what would normally have seemed a bureaucratic formality was that an even greater vote was obtained in favor of the Resolution at the highest level of the United Nations. On the day after the vote, the story received no coverage in the American media. On December 20, however, two days after the vote, "The New York Times" unexpectedly ran an editorial on capital punishment entitled A Pause from Death. The "Gray Lady's" opinion piece observed as follows:

The United States, as usual, lined up on the other side, with Iran, China, Pakistan, Sudan and Iraq. Together this blood brotherhood accounts for more than 90 percent of the world's executions, according to Amnesty International. These countries' devotion to their sovereignty is rigid, as is their perverse faith in execution as a criminal deterrent and an instrument of civilized justice. But out beyond Texas, Ohio, Virginia, Myanmar, Singapore, Saudi Arabia and Zimbabwe, there are growing numbers who expect better of humanity.

Many are not nations or states but groups of regular people, organizations like the Community of Sant'Egidio, a lay Catholic movement begun in Italy whose advocacy did much to bring about this week's successful vote in the General Assembly.

APPENDIX 1

Resolution 62/149 of the General Assembly of the United Nations, Sixty-Second Session, Promotion and protection of human rights, on a Universal Moratorium on Capital Punishment, December 18, 2007

Moratorium on the use of the death penalty

The General Assembly,

Guided by the purposes and principles contained in the Charter of the United Nations,

Recalling the Universal Declaration of Human Rights, the International Covenant on Civil and Political Rights and the Convention on the Rights of the Child,

Recalling also the resolutions on the question of the death penalty adopted over the past decade by the Commission on Human Rights in all consecutive sessions, the last being resolution 2005/59 of 20 April 2005, in which the Commission called upon States that still maintain the death penalty to abolish it completely and, in the meantime, to establish a moratorium on executions,

Recalling further the important results accomplished by the former Commission on Human Rights on the question of the death penalty, and envisaging that the Human Rights Council could continue to work on this issue,

Considering that the use of the death penalty undermines human dignity, and convinced that a moratorium on the use of the death penalty contributes to the enhancement and progressive development of human rights, that there is no conclusive evidence of the deterrent value of the death penalty and that any miscarriage or failure of justice in the implementation of the death penalty is irreversible and irreparable,

Welcoming the decisions taken by an increasing number of States to apply a moratorium on executions, followed in many cases by the abolition of the death penalty,

1. Expresses its deep concern about the continued application of the death penalty;

2. Calls upon all States that still maintain the death penalty:

(a) To respect international standards that provide safeguards guaranteeing protection of the rights of those facing the death penalty, in particular the minimum standards, as set out in the annex to Economic and Social Council resolution 1984/50 of 25 May 1984;

(b) To provide the Secretary-General with information relating to the use of capital punishment and the observance of the safeguards guaranteeing protection of the rights of those facing the death penalty;

(c) To progressively restrict the use of the death penalty and reduce the number of offences for which it may be imposed;

(d) To establish a moratorium on executions with a view to abolishing the death penalty;

3. Calls upon States which have abolished the death penalty not to reintroduce it;

4. Requests the Secretary-General to report to the General Assembly at its sixty-third session on the implementation of the present resolution;

5. Decides to continue consideration of the matter at its sixty-third session under the item entitled "Promotion and protection of human rights".

APPENDIX 2

Strasbourg Declaration

We, citizens and abolitionist campaigners gathered in Strasbourg from 21 to 23 June 2001 for the First World Congress Against the Death Penalty, organized by Ensemble contre la peine de mort/Together against the death penalty, declare:

The death penalty means the triumph of vengeance over justice and violates the first right of any human being, the right to life. Capital punishment has never prevented crime. It is an act of torture and the ultimate cruel, inhuman and degrading treatment. A society that imposes the death penalty symbolically encourages violence. Every single society that respects the dignity of its people must strive to abolish capital punishment.

We are pleased to note that many Speakers of Parliament have decided to launch on 22 June a "Solemn appeal for a world-wide moratorium on executions of those sentenced to death as a step towards universal abolition" at the European Parliament.

We demand the universal abolition of the death penalty. In this respect, we call on citizens, states and international organizations to act so that:

- *states ratify all abolitionist treaties and conventions on an international and regional level;*
- *countries which have stopped executing people sentenced to death remove the death penalty from their statute books;*
- *states which sentence to death persons who were juveniles at the time of the crime end this blatant violation of international law;*
- *mentally disabled people may not be sentenced to death;*
- *no states having abolished or suspended executions may extradite anyone to third countries still applying the death penalty, irrespective of guarantees that it will not be imposed;*

- *states regularly and openly publish information on death sentences, detention conditions and executions.*

We support the investigation of the Council of Europe into the compatibility of the observer status of the United States and Japan with their adherence to the death penalty.

We call on the Council of Europe and the European Union to insist that Turkey, Russia and Armenia permanently abolish the death penalty for ALL crimes and commute all death sentences.

We call on the European Union to continue its efforts to achieve the abolition of the death penalty in the ordinary course of its international relations.

In addition to these general recommendations, we will issue specific recommendations, on a country-by-country basis, to support abolitionist campaigners.

We commit ourselves to creating a world-wide co-ordination of associations and abolitionist campaigners, whose first goal will be to launch a world-wide day for the universal abolition of the death penalty.

We call on the judicial and medical professions to confirm the utter incompatibility of their values with the death penalty and to intensify, on a country-by-country basis, their activities against the death penalty.

We associate ourselves with the petitions collected by Amnesty International, the Community of Sant'Egidio, Ensemble contre la peine de mort, the International Federation of Human Rights Leagues, Hands Off Cain and any other organizations, and call on all abolitionist campaigners to sign the following international petition:

"We, citizens of the world, call for an immediate halt to all executions of those sentenced to death and the universal abolition of the death penalty".

Lastly, we call upon every state to take all possible steps towards the adoption by the United Nations of a world-wide moratorium on executions, pending universal abolition.

[1] The text of the Resolution can be found in Appendix 1 to this chapter.

[2] Following is a list of States that abolished the death penalty to varying degrees between 1976 and 2008: Portugal (1976), Denmark (1978), Luxembourg (1979), Nicaragua (1979), Norway (1979), Brazil (1979), Fiji (1979), Peru (1979), France (1981), Cape Verde (1981), the Netherlands (1982), Cyprus (1983), El Salvador (1983), Argentina (1984), Australia (1985), Haiti (1987), Liechtenstein (1987), the German Democratic Republic (1987), Cambodia (1989), New Zealand (1989), Romania (1989), Slovenia (1989), Andorra (1990), Croatia (1990), the Czech and Slovak Federal Republic (1990), Hungary (1990), Ireland (1990), Mozambique (1990), Namibia (1990), São Tomé and Príncipe (1990), Angola (1992), Paraguay (1992), Switzerland (1992), Guinea-Bissau (1993), Hong Kong (1993), the Seychelles (1993), Italy (1994), Djibouti (1995), Mauritius (1995), Moldova (1995), Spain (1995), Belgium (1996), Georgia (1997), Nepal (1997), Poland (1997), South Africa (1997), Bolivia (1997), Azerbaijan (1998), Bulgaria (1998), Canada (1998), Estonia (1998), Lithuania (1998), the United Kingdom (1998), East Timor (1999), Turkmenistan (1999), Ukraine (1999), Latvia (1999), Ivory Coast (2000), Malta (2000), Albania (2000), Bosnia-Herzegovina (2001), Chile (2001), the Federal Republic of Serbia and Montenegro (2002), Armenia (2003), Bhutan (2004), Greece (2004), Samoa (2004), Senegal (2004), Turkey (2004), Liberia (2005), Mexico (2005), the Philippines (2006), the Cook Islands (2007), Rwanda (2007), Kyrgyzstan (2007), Kazakhstan (2007), and Uzbekistan (2008). Source: Amnesty International.

[3] Cf. P. Steinfels, Beliefs; *A community of lay Catholics, working mostly in small groups, seeks to end the death penalty*, "The New York Times", December 23, 2000.

[4] The text of the Strasbourg Declaration is set out in Appendix 2 to this chapter.

[5] The organizations were: Journey of Hope, Murder Victims' Families for Reconciliation (hereinafter referred to as "Murder Victims' Families for Human Rights"), the National Coalition Against the Death Penalty, Death Penalty Focus, the Texas Coalition Against the Death Penalty, and the National Association of Criminal Defense Lawyers (NACDL).

[6] As at September 30, 2008, urgent appeals were on foot in respect of Seijiro Yamano (Japan), Anwar Kenneth Masih (Pakistan), thirty detainees in the Democratic Republic of the Congo, Alakor Madina Lual Deng (Sudan), Chong De Shu (Taiwan), Percy Walton (USA, whose execution was set to take place on June 10, 2009), Charles Dean Hood (USA, whose execution was scheduled to be carried out on June 17, 2009), Guy Tobias LeGrande (USA), Tony Egbuna Ford (USA), Pablo Melendez (USA), Mark Lankford (USA), Tommy Zeigler (USA), Hector Torres Garcia (USA), Gregory Van Alstyne (USA), Elkie Taylor (USA), and Rickey Lynn Lewis (USA).
In addition, death sentences were set aside following appeals made in respect of Afsaneh Nouroozi (Iran), Nazanin (Iran), Jibrin Babaji (Nigeria), Yunusa Rafin Chiyawa (Nigeria), Ahmadu Ibrahim (Nigeria), Sarimu Mohammed Allam (Nigeria), Fatima Usman (Nigeria), Zafran Bibi (Pakistan), Jerome Campbell (USA), Kenneth Foster (USA), Scott Panetti (USA), Thomas Miller-El (USA), Efrain Perez (USA), Charles Andy Williams (USA), Evgeny Gugnin (Uzbekistan), Sadik Kadirov (Uzbekistan), Iskandar Khudayberganov (Uzbekistan), Ikram Mukhtarov (Uzbekistan), and Peter Cassam Kundai (Zambia).
The following people were put to death despite appeals to save their lives: Iwuchuku Amara Tochi (Singapore), Okele Nelson Malachy (Singapore),

Nguyen Tuong Van (Singapore), Bobby Swisher (USA), Bryan Eric Wolfe (USA), Clarence Hill (USA), Donald Jay Beardslee (USA), Henry Dunn (USA), Edward Hartman (USA), Elijah Page (USA), Granville Riddle (USA), Greg Summers (USA), Scott Allen Hain (USA), Henry Lee Hunt (USA), Bruce Jacobs (USA), James Allridge (USA), Joseph Nichols (USA), Justin Fuller (USA), Keith Clay (USA), Kevin Kincy (USA), Mark Bailey (USA), Javier Suarez Medina (USA), Michael Thompson (USA), Lorenzo Morris (USA), Patrick Knight (USA), James Powell (USA), Robert Morrow (USA), Robert Shields (USA), Vincent Gutierrez (USA), Willie Shannon (USA), Willie Jones (USA), Azizbek Karimov (Uzbekistan), Akhrorkhuzha Tolipkhuzhaev (Uzbekistan), Azamat Uteev (Uzbekistan), and Yusuf Zhumayev (Uzbekistan).

[7] Cf. "L'Unità", August 20, 2002.

[8] Cf. M. Giro, *Gli occhi di un bambino ebreo. Storia di Merzoug terrorista pentito*, Milan 2005.

[9] The death sentence was carried out on September 21, 2006, despite repeated calls for mercy from the international community, Pope Benedict XVI, and the former Indonesian President Abdurrahman Wahid.

Index of Names